Relationship Enhancement Therapy

Relationship Enhancement Therapy

Healing Through Deep Empathy and Intimate Dialogue

Robert F. Scuka

Routledge
Taylor & Francis Group
NEW YORK AND HOVE

The Relationship Enhancement skill guidelines that appear in chapters 7, 8, and 10–14 come from Guerney, B.G., Jr. & Scuka, R.F. (2005). *Relationship Enhancement Client Manual* (4th ed.) Silver Spring, MD: Relationship Press. With permission of IDEALS, Inc.

Relationship Enhancement is a registered trademark of IDEALS, Inc.

Published in 2005 by
Routledge
Taylor & Francis Group
270 Madison Avenue
New York, NY 10016

Published in Great Britain by
Routledge
Taylor & Francis Group
27 Church Road
Hove, East Sussex BN3 2FA

© 2005 by Taylor & Francis Group, LLC
Routledge is an imprint of Taylor & Francis Group
Formerly a Brunner-Routledge title.

Printed in the United States of America on acid-free paper
10 9 8 7 6 5 4 3 2 1

International Standard Book Number-10: 0-415-95014-7 (Hardcover)
International Standard Book Number-13: 978-0-415-95014-5 (Hardcover)
Library of Congress Card Number 2004027505

Library of Congress Cataloging-in-Publication Data

Scuka, Robert F.
   Relationship enhancement therapy : healing through deep empathy and intimate dialogue / Robert F. Scuka.
      p. cm.
   Includes bibliographical references and index.
   ISBN 0-415-95014-7 (hardbound : alk. paper)
   1. Marital psychotherapy. 2. Interpersonal relations. 3. Man-woman relationships. I. Title.

RC488.5.S387 2005
616.89'1562--dc22   2004027505

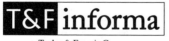

Taylor & Francis Group
is the Academic Division of T&F Informa plc.

Visit the Taylor & Francis Web site at
http://www.taylorandfrancis.com

and the Routledge Web site at
http://www.routledgementalhealth.com

To

Bernard Guerney, Jr.
Mentor, Colleague, and Friend
For everything you have helped me to become professionally

and

Mary Scuka
Wife, Partner, and Friend
For everything you have helped me to become personally

The ability to imagine another's pain is essential to our humanity.

Jacob Bronowski, *The Ascent of Man*

Contents

Foreword

Relationship Enhancement® Couples Therapy (RECT) is part of a Relationship Enhancement (RE) family of family therapies (Guerney, 1977; Ginsberg, 1997). Other types of RE therapy are designed for parents and their young children, parents and adolescents, and whole-family groupings. All of them rest on the same values: openness, honesty, and compassion. In this book, Dr. Scuka conveys and demonstrates a deep understanding of the importance of these values.

Similarly, he elucidates the kind of interpersonal framework the RE therapist creates. That framework is crucial to bringing couples to a deeper knowledge about themselves, their partners, and their interactions, which in turn permits them to make the difficult decisions to change dysfunctional attitudes and behaviors. This framework is vitally important in helping them build richly satisfying and fulfilling relationships. Dr. Scuka does this in such a way that makes it very likely that therapist-readers will want to learn to do likewise with their own clients. Deep empathy is a key part of that interpersonal framework, and I believe that chapter 3, "Deep Empathy as the Foundation of RE Therapy," is an important theoretical contribution to the understanding of empathy.

After they understand the values underlying RE, I think therapist-readers would next want to know how effective RECT is, and especially how it compares in effectiveness to other methods of couples therapy. Dr. Scuka delivers this information with a summary of research on RECT that is accurate and wide in scope, yet condensed and easily understood. In my view, readers are very likely to find in these research findings strong motivation to include RECT within their own therapeutic armamentaria.

But can one really learn a therapeutic method through reading alone? For therapist-readers who answer "no," the fact that consultation/supervision is readily available might be reassuring.[1] My supposition is that for a large majority of readers learning RECT through reading will be possible. And, if ever a book made it easy to learn to conduct a therapeutic method, this book does so. Dr. Scuka draws upon his many years of experience as an RE therapist to provide what I believe to be one of the clearest, most carefully detailed guides for conducting a particular therapeutic method in the realm of therapeutic literature.

Dr. Scuka understands why many therapists who feel fully at ease with individual clients hate working with couples. It is because they so often encounter contentious and even out-of-control interactions during the session. Dr. Scuka shows exactly how RECT virtually eliminates that problem.

He also explains how RE handles the issue of confidentiality between each spouse and the therapist vis-à-vis the other spouse. He explains how RECT not only eliminates problems but also elicits and achieves a couple's positive goals. He shows the importance of showing empathy equally to both partners. He covers with precision and thoroughness the use of RE techniques such as Laundering and Becoming and the necessity of making explicit the underlying positive factors that exist beneath conflicts and problems. He explains the readiness and motivation to change one's behavior that occurs when RECT brings about the "magical confluence"—that magical confluence being the ability to experience the love of one's partner while simultaneously identifying with the pain one's own behavior is causing the partner. He shows how to use the Relationship Questionnaire in RECT, and everything else one needs to know to be an effective RE therapist.

The therapeutic treatment of affairs is one of the most difficult issues a therapist must face in working with couples. After having studied the literature in that field, Dr. Scuka provides his own integrated, theoretical statement about how to understand and treat affairs. He also provides clinical vignettes that demonstrate the special power of RECT in helping couples deal effectively with the trauma of infidelity, thereby permitting healing in the relationship. He makes crystal clear not just what the therapist does, but the therapist's *thinking*—so the reader can fully grasp not only the how, but the when and the why of what is being done.

So, it is with the greatest of confidence that I recommend Dr. Scuka's *Relationship Enhancement Therapy: Healing Through Deep Empathy and Intimate Dialogue* to all individual therapists who wish to learn precisely how to work with couples. And, of course, I heartily recommend it as well to all couples therapists who wish to expand their present therapeutic repertoire. In fact, even therapists already very experienced in RECT will find this clearly written, thorough, systematic, and insightful book highly interesting and extremely valuable.

Bernard G. Guerney, Jr., Ph.D.

Notes

1. Consultation/supervision is available nationwide from certified supervisors through the National Institute of Relationship Enhancement (NIRE), which is approved by various national professional organizations to provide Continuing Education Units (CEUs). For further information, call 1-800-THE NIRE (1-800-843-6473) or visit www.nire.org.

Preface

My professional passion lies both in conducting couples therapy in order to alleviate marital distress and in leading psychoeducational couples workshops in order to enhance relationship satisfaction. I was blessed in the early stages of my clinical training to have been introduced to Bernard Guerney, Jr., and his Relationship Enhancement (RE) model for working with couples, both clinically and educationally. I have been even more blessed to have been mentored by him in this method for the past 11 years and to have co-led numerous professional training workshops with him. As a result, my passion for working with couples has become my passion for the RE model, a method that has provided the foundation for my work with both couples and families.

My goal in writing this book is to provide a comprehensive and systematic guide to conducting RE therapy with couples. RE therapy was developed, studied, and refined over a 40-year period by Guerney and numerous colleagues who have conducted research on the RE model with a wide variety of client populations. Its original theoretical statement was the book *Relationship Enhancement: Skill-Training Programs for Therapy, Problem Prevention, and Enrichment* (1977), which reflected 15 years of collaborative research and development. Prominent contributions to the development of the RE model have been made by Maryhelen Snyder (1994a, 1995, 1996, 2000; Snyder & Guerney, 1993, 1999), William Nordling (Nordling 1993; Nordling & Guerney, 1992), Barry Ginsberg (1997), John Griffin (Griffin & Guerney, 2001), and Mary Ortwein (in press-a, in press-b). The present author took the lead in writing the *Couples' Relationship Enhancement Program: Leader's Manual* (Scuka, Nordling, & Guerney, 2004), and in producing two videotape sets and home study programs based on live workshops involving Guerney and several colleagues: *How to*

Conduct a Couples Relationship Enhancement Program (Guerney, Scuka, & Scuka, 1999) and *How to Conduct a Relationship Enhancement Therapy with Couples and Families* (Guerney, Nordling, & Scuka, 2000). Despite all this activity, an up-to-date, comprehensive theoretical statement and application of RE therapy to clinical work with couples has been lacking. It is this void I seek to fill.

I have had the enormous benefit of working closely with Bernard Guerney since the early 1990s. During that time I have been able to observe and internalize Guerney's way of thinking and working. I owe much of what I have learned and much of the talent I may have developed as a clinician and as a trainer to his modeling and his mentoring. On the other hand, I bring my own distinct gifts to the enterprise and, in particular, I always strive to conceptualize with clarity what is at the heart of the matter with regard to theoretical considerations and applications of technique. At times, this leads me to formulate things in a way that is different from how Guerney might formulate them or to apply the RE therapy process in ways that vary from his way of doing things. In the former instance I believe that my formulations are true to the essence of the RE model itself, while in the latter instance I believe that the differences can be understood either as variations due to personal style or as allowable (and inevitable) variations in the application of the method. What I am striving to offer in this book is simultaneously a faithful representation of Guerney's RE therapy and a reconceptualization and relanguaging of elements of the model in a manner that brings added clarity and depth. At the same time, this book seeks to offer a comprehensive guide to conducting highly effective, and deeply rewarding, RE therapy with couples. I hope you enjoy the journey.

If you would like to engage me in dialogue about RE therapy or give me feedback on this book, you may contact me at robscuka@earthlink.net.

Rob Scuka, Ph.D.
National Institute of Relationship Enhancement

Acknowledgments

Two people in particular deserve special appreciation and thanks for reviewing the manuscript for this book. I owe William Nordling an undying debt of gratitude for having agreed to have me come to the National Institute of Relationship Enhancement (NIRE) in the final year of my M.S.W. program at the University of Maryland at Baltimore for a clinical internship. Second only to Bernard Guerney, Bill has been my other principal mentor in the Relationship Enhancement method. Indeed, his modeling, encouragement, and faith in me were instrumental in helping me grow into the roles of clinician, RE educator, and trainer in RE methods. Bill and I have continued to be colleagues at NIRE ever since, and his support, encouragement, and positive feedback during the writing of this book have been deeply appreciated. Few people have as deep an understanding of RE therapy as Bill, and his keen eye in reviewing the manuscript consistently yielded helpful observations as well as welcome validation that I was on the right track.

My professional relationship with Mary Ortwein, now executive director of IDEALS, is of more recent vintage, though her acquaintance with Bernard Guerney and the RE method are about as long as Bill's. Mary was particularly helpful as a sounding board for me to express and explore my emerging ideas about the structure of the book and various thematic topics along the way. She, too, was very supportive and encouraging of this project, and provided exceedingly valuable editorial feedback on the manuscript in terms of both stylistic and substantive considerations. She also was a model of selfless facilitation of my thinking and writing process in that she always kept her eye on what would be helpful to me even when she might, ever so occasionally, have a different way of thinking about something. And when we might have differed on something, our conversations were always respectful and, in the end, often informative to me as well. I could not have hoped for two better reviewers of the manuscript than Bill and Mary, and their feedback was often marvelously complementary and always helped me strengthen the book.

I have benefited from and been inspired over the years by Maryhelen Snyder's cogently written presentations of RE therapy in a variety of journal articles. I appreciate the helpful feedback she provided me on an article draft that was the predecessor to much of what is now chapter 3 of this book.

I would also like to express appreciation to Robert Brown, professor emeritus of psychology at the University of Maryland, College Park, for his helpful feedback on the section in chapter 2 on how the RE model relates to the research of John Gottman. He confirmed my approach and provided several useful pointers that helped strengthen the presentation.

Joanne Kempher, a long-time assistant to Dr. Guerney, deserves my appreciation for having provided computer backup of all my chapter files while I was writing and editing this book, for archival assistance in tracking down historical data relating to the evolution of RE, and for providing me with copies of research articles and other archived resources.

I am grateful to George Zimmar, publishing director of Routledge, for inviting me to write this book. It was an honor to receive the invitation. I also appreciate the able staff and editorial support provided by Dana Bliss, Patricia Connolly, Lori Frederickson, and Allison Taub.

I also owe a debt of gratitude to Eliot Applestein, who first made me aware of Bernard Guerney and RE therapy. Had it not been for an accidental crossing of our paths in the summer of 1993, I perhaps would never have met and come to work with Bernie, in which case this book would never have been written. Life is full of events of grace that alter one's life forever. This was one such event in my life.

In Memorium

Little did I know in the spring of 1975 that the graduate course I was taking in Buddhist religion and philosophy would gradually come to have a profound impact on my understanding of the human condition. I would like to acknowledge Frederick J. Streng, the teacher of that course, for his quiet wisdom, his stellar teaching, and his deep empathic commitment to bridging the gaps between peoples and cultures. In addition to being an exemplary model of those qualities, his book, *Emptiness: A Study in Religious Meaning* (1967), laid the conceptual and experiential foundation for my later ability to understand and practice the art of deep empathy. I hope that this book, in its own way, honors the spirit of this compassionate soul and his life's work.

Introduction

Origins of Relationship Enhancement Therapy

Relationship Enhancement (RE) therapy was created by Bernard Guerney, Jr., beginning in 1962. At the time, he and his wife Louise had been working collaboratively in the area of child-centered play therapy, under the influence of Virginia Axline's book *Play Therapy* (1947), which itself was grounded in Carl Rogers's client-centered theory. During the 1950s and early 1960s the Guerneys worked to extend the framework and principles of Axline's child-centered play therapy model in a new direction, which they called Filial Family therapy.

The Guerneys' guiding principle in creating Filial Family therapy was the conviction that it would be better in the long run for therapeutic healing to be mediated by another family member than by a mental health professional (Guerney, 1969; Guerney, Guerney, & Andronico, 1966). After all, they reasoned, children's relationships with therapists are temporary, while children's relationships with their parents are permanent. This led to the idea that it would be better for the therapist to teach parents to conduct therapeutic play sessions with their own children than for the therapist to conduct them. The Guerneys then set about the task of developing a teaching methodology to train parents in the basic principles and techniques of child-centered play therapy so that they could become the primary agents through which the child's, and by extension the family's, healing would take place.

RE therapy developed as a direct outgrowth and extension of Filial therapy. As the Guerneys were training parents under the Filial therapy model, Bernard Guerney began to ask himself how it would be possible to take the underlying Rogerian principles that informed Filial therapy and apply them to the relationship between the parents for the purpose of enhancing the primary couple/marital relationship. This led Guerney to develop RE therapy and its nonclinical psychoeducational sibling, the RE Program.

From the beginning, RE therapy was conceived by Guerney on the basis of an educational model as opposed to the then dominant medical model (Guerney, 1985; Guerney, Guerney, & Stollak, 1971–1972; Guerney, Stollak, & Guerney, 1971). This meant that couples were not to be viewed primarily through the lens of pathology, which carries with it the dual implication that the clinician engages in diagnosis to identify the source of the problem and then aims to fix it as a healer would do. This is not to say that a clinician using the RE model does not engage in diagnosis as appropriate for the purpose of making needed referrals, but it is to say that a diagnostically oriented frame of reference is deemphasized. More to the point, it means that couples are primarily viewed in the RE model as lacking certain essential life skills and as needing to be trained in how to improve their interpersonal interactions so they can enhance the quality of their primary intimate relationship. This can be done either clinically in order to repair relationships that are in trouble, or nonclinically in order to enrich fundamentally sound relationships. In either case, the same basic skills-training model would be used to help couples learn new and more positive patterns of interaction by giving them the tools necessary to solve problems on their own and to improve their overall relationship satisfaction (Cavedo & Guerney, 1999, p. 75).

This also meant that the RE model, whether in its clinical or nonclinical form, was from the beginning conceived with the idea of *prevention* in mind. This was a necessity, from Guerney's point of view, because even in the case of the clinical application of the RE model to the solving of current problems and the repair of troubled relationships, the goal should not be simply to resolve current issues; instead, the goal should also be to equip couples with relationship skills that enable them to solve future issues successfully on their own. This implies that the therapist's role is inadequately framed, as it is in the medical model, in terms of the therapist being the agent who solves the couple's current problems. Instead, the RE model defines the therapist's role as primarily that of an educator who teaches couples interpersonal skills that enable them to solve current *and* future problems as well as to work at enriching the quality of their relationships by proactively addressing relationship enhancement issues.

Evolution of the RE Model

Over its 40-plus years, the RE model has evolved and been refined in the light of research, clinical experience, and lessons learned from conducting the RE Program in nonclinical settings. In its initial formulation, the RE model included only three skills: Empathic, Expressive, and Discussion/Negotiation. (These three skills are referred to in this book as the core RE skills because they permit the initiation of a couple's intimate dialogues, which is where the heart of the work is done in RE therapy.) Guerney gradually added new skills in three stages: first he added Facilitation; then Problem/Conflict Resolution, Generalization and Maintenance; and finally Self-Change and Helping-Others Change. In each case, the new skill was added in response to the realization that (1) there are additional facets of how people relate to one another that need to be addressed if couples are to maximally benefit from a psychoeducational skills-training approach designed to improve their patterns of interaction; or (2) the effectiveness of client learning would be enhanced by incorporating additional techniques designed to reinforce maintenance of gains. One of the marks of Guerney's acumen is that he was open to learning anew from his clinical, educational, and research efforts in order to expand and refine the RE model so that it could become increasingly comprehensive and effective in meeting couples' needs.

In a similar spirit, and with Guerney's collaboration and blessing, the RE model is being formally expanded by the addition of a new, tenth skill: Conflict Management. Guerney himself has taught couples (under the rubric of "restraint") some of what is being included under this new skill, but in adding Conflict Management as a new skill, I have sought to extend and formalize other elements of what the RE model itself represents and implies. Moreover, formally designating Conflict Management as a new skill allows for the dual advantage of drawing people's attention more explicitly to what the concept represents and, even more importantly, increasing the likelihood that people will benefit from what this skill has to offer in terms of a set of preventative strategies for dealing more effectively with intense conflict situations.

In writing this book, I also undertook to revise the formal RE skill guidelines for each of the nine established skills. The guidelines have been rewritten for increased clarity and conciseness. In some cases, new guidelines have been added to amplify certain points or to make explicit elements of the model that previously were implicit. These revisions have been reviewed and accepted by Guerney following a collaborative process whereby he provided feedback to help ensure that the revisions faithfully represent the RE model. These revised guidelines have been incorporated in new editions of the *Relationship Enhancement Couple/Marital/Family Therapist's Manual* (Guerney, 2005) and its accompanying *Relationship Enhancement Client Manual* (Guerney & Scuka, 2005), as well as in the *Couples' Relationship Enhancement Program: Leader's Manual* (Scuka, Nordling, & Guerney, 2004) and its accompanying *Relationship Enhancement Program: Participants' Manual* (Guerney & Scuka, 2004a) and *Relationship Enhancement Program: Auxiliary Manual* (Guerney & Scuka, 2004b). The explanatory comments accompanying each RE skill guideline in this book are by the present author.

Several other developments should be mentioned. Maryhelen Snyder (personal communication, 2004) and I independently came upon the idea of having couples use the "Identification Mode" of empathy while conducting their intimate dialogues instead of the conventional "You Mode" of empathy (see chapters 3 and 6). The Identification Mode of empathy had originally been developed by Guerney for the purpose of demonstrating empathy and having couples practice it before they would revert to the You Mode of empathy in their dialogues (see chapter 6). Snyder and I both have experimented by having couples use the Identification Mode while conducting their intimate dialogues and we both have found it to have a very positive effect on the couples' dialogues and the course of therapy. Snyder and I both now advocate that couples use the Identification Mode of empathy as their standard mode of empathizing during dialogues. This represents an extension and expansion of the use of the Identification Mode in a way that represents a shift in therapeutic practice. It is, of course, entirely legitimate for couples to elect to use the You Mode of empathy during a dialogue, but there are distinct advantages to couples using the Identification Mode of empathy in their intimate dialogues, and I encourage clinicians to consider recommending its use to the couples with whom they work.

I have also introduced a change in terminology that involves distinguishing between "Laundering" and "Doublebecoming." The term *Laundering* has had, in effect, two meanings. The first, metaphorical, meaning refers to the therapist "cleaning up" one partner's inflammatory language and negative personal attacks on the other (most typically during the clinical intake). The therapist "launders" by not repeating those negatives as part of his or her empathic response. The second meaning refers to the therapist alternately representing each partner to the other by using the Identification Mode of empathy, typically for the purpose of bridging an emotional gap between the couple. I reserve the term *Laundering* for the former, metaphorical, usage of the term. I am introducing the new term *Doublebecoming* to designate the process by which the therapist uses the

Identification Mode of empathy to alternately represent each partner to the other. The reason it is important to disentangle these two distinct meanings is that the therapist may engage in Doublebecoming as a process because of an impasse in the therapeutic process that has nothing to do with either party being verbally unskillful per se. Conversely, the therapist may engage in Laundering independent of the use of Doublebecoming. Indeed, the therapist should always launder one partner's personal attacks on the other, regardless of whether the therapist chooses to use the distinct process of "becoming" in order to represent each partner in turn to the other.

Doublebecoming may be used in several different contexts. Its most frequent use will be in the clinical intake when the couple is facing a crisis or remains emotionally disconnected and their future commitment to the therapy is in question (see chapter 4). It may also be used in the experiential format because of either time constraints or the difficulty of the issue. Doublebecoming may be used in the Time-Designated format when the couple is unable at that moment to conduct a skilled dialogue due to strong emotion or defensiveness. Doublebecoming may also be used for several noncrisis reasons. It may be used at the end of a session to summarize and pull together what has been communicated by each partner in order to consolidate their gains. Doublebecoming may also be used at the beginning of a session to summarize what had been communicated during the previous session in order to help the couple resume their dialogue. In each of these instances, the use of Doublebecoming is not necessarily motivated by the couple being verbally unskillful. Instead, the therapist may choose to use Doublebecoming in order to facilitate and advance the therapy process.

Design of the Book

I have written this book with a view to enabling any therapist to follow the presentation and to then implement the RE therapy process effectively and with confidence. The book is divided into five parts. Part I, "Theory, Methods, and Research," begins (in chapter 1) with the theoretical foundations of RE therapy, the principal formats for conducting RE therapy, the skills and dialogue process that make up the RE model, basic therapist methods and procedures, the special RE therapy technique of Troubleshooting, and the values embodied in the RE model. Chapter 2 continues with a summary of the empirical research validating the effectiveness of RE therapy, the application of RE to various populations, limitations in the use of RE therapy, the use of RE therapy in the assessment and treatment of domestic violence, and the ways in which the research of John Gottman lends indirect support to RE therapy and helps explain its effectiveness. Chapter 3 examines deep empathy as the foundation of RE therapy and describes the two distinct modes of empathy and the special RE therapy technique of Becoming.

Parts II to IV are devoted to a step-by-step explanation of the entire RE therapy process. Part II, "Beginning the RE Therapy Process," provides a detailed description of how to conduct a clinical intake with couples when using the RE model (chapter 4). Part III, "Teaching the Core RE Skills and Launching a Couple's First Dialogue," continues with how to introduce the RE model and how to teach effective Conflict Management strategies (chapter 5); how to use the Time-Designated format to introduce the three core RE skills and launch a couple's first dialogue (chapters 6 and 7); how to accomplish the same thing by using the Experiential format (chapter 8); and an extended look at the dialogue process in action, including coaching tips on how to manage the couple's dialogue process effectively, and two clinical vignettes that bring to life the richness of the couple's process of intimate dialogue that is at the heart of RE therapy (chapter 9). Part IV, "Integrating the Other RE Skills into the Couple's Dialogue Process," explains how each of the remaining six RE skills can be gradually folded into the couple's ongoing dialogue work (chapters 10–14). Chapter 12 includes a clinical vignette that models how a therapist can incorporate one of the later skills into a couple's unfolding dialogue process. A distinctive feature of each of the skills-oriented chapters in Parts III and IV is the inclusion of revised RE skill guidelines with explanatory comments. These guidelines and explanatory comments can be used either verbatim with couples or as a framework for elaborating the therapist's own explanation of each of the skills as they are introduced into the therapy. Another distinctive feature is the inclusion of a section devoted to home assignments in the chapter on the clinical intake and in each of the skills-oriented chapters. This is designed to reinforce the centrality of home assignments in RE therapy and to make that part of the therapy process as concrete as possible.

Finally, Part V, "The Application of RE Therapy to the Treatment of Affairs," concludes the book with a consideration of the key thematic considerations in the treatment of infidelity and why RE therapy constitutes an ideal therapeutic framework for treating affairs (chapter 15), and three clinical vignettes that illustrate the power of RE therapy and various aspects of its use in the treatment of affairs, one of the most challenging issues in couples therapy (chapter 16).

Use of Sources in This Book

The primary written sources for understanding the RE model include Guerney's book *Relationship Enhancement* (1977), his *Relationship*

Enhancement Couple/Marital/Family Therapist's Manual (2005), its accompanying *Relationship Enhancement Client Manual* (Guerney & Scuka, 2005) and the *Couples' Relationship Enhancement Program Leader's Manual* (Nordling, Scuka, & Guerney, 1998). In addition, Nordling's *To Love and to Cherish* (1993) has influenced how I have come to think about the RE skills. However, much of what I have written in this book is based on my collegial work with Guerney and on my own distillation and assimilation of the RE model on the strength of my own clinical work and my training of other RE therapists and RE program educators. As a consequence, I will not notate every possible reference to ideas and concepts by providing specific citations in the literature. I will provide such citations when they are particularly important or when I am referencing specific written sources by Guerney or other authors. In the end, I want this book to stand on its own merits, both as a faithful representation of RE therapy and as a personal synthesis and integration of the RE method as seen through my eyes.

Two Terminological Clarifications

First, readers will note that this book variously refers to the RE model, RE therapy, and the RE Program. The RE model encompasses both RE therapy and the RE Program in that the skill content and dialogue process is identical in both, and this is what is referred to as the RE model (and sometimes as the RE method). Alternatively stated, the RE model (or method) is what RE therapy and the RE Program share in common. On the other hand, RE therapy and the RE Program may be distinguished from each other in that RE therapy represents the reparative, clinical application of the RE model, while the RE Program represents the RE model's nonclinical, psychoeducational application, generally for enrichment and problem prevention (as in premarital education or marital and couples enrichment). In addition, RE therapy and the RE Program each have distinctive elements. In the case of RE therapy, it is the special RE therapy techniques that are designed to deepen the therapy process and move it forward as rapidly as possible (see chapters 1, 3, and 4). In the case of the RE Program, it is the distinctive ways in which the RE model is presented in a psychoeducational group setting for prevention and enrichment purposes (see Scuka, Nordling, & Guerney, 2004). While occasional reference will be made to the RE Program and psychoeducational applications of the RE model, this book is principally focused on RE therapy and its application to clinical work with couples.

Second, there is the distinction between RE couples therapy and RE family therapy. They obviously are not identical, even though they share much in common, that is, the RE model (and method). Guerney himself has always conceptualized RE therapy as applying equally to couples and families. Nonetheless, they are distinct, and this book is written from the vantage point that couples therapy is a distinct branch of therapy with its own unique dynamics, issues, and demands. For an analysis of varied uses of RE therapy with families, see Ginsberg (1997).

My Philosophy in Working with Couples

One of the things that was established in the late 20th-century philosophy of the social sciences is that there is no such thing as a value-free position. The implication is that it is incumbent upon any theorist or practitioner to be aware of and to make explicit his or her assumptions and values so that they can be openly acknowledged and discussed. I therefore want to lay out my assumptions, values, and commitments in conducting couples therapy.

First is my assumption that most (admittedly not all) couples who seek couples therapy do so because no matter how deep the anger, the pain, the sense of alienation or estrangement, they nonetheless are holding onto some (perhaps quite thin) thread of hope that things can be turned around and the relationship saved. With the occasional exception aside, couples do not come to therapists to conduct funerals; they come because their relationship is on life support and they are seeking expert help to resuscitate the relationship so that it can breathe again and thrive. I therefore operate with the assumption, and take at face value, that a given couple is coming to me for therapy because they genuinely want help with their relationship, and I remain committed to operating with that assumption until they prove to me otherwise. I am willing to be proven otherwise, but I cannot be of maximal service to my couple clients if I give up on them before they have given up on themselves.

Second is my assumption that whenever I work with a couple I have three clients in my presence: one individual, a second individual, and the relationship between the two of them. I assume further that it is the relationship between the two members of the couple that is my primary client. That does not mean that I am not interested in or concerned about the individuals as individuals, but it does mean that my working assumption is that the couple has come to me as a couple *for the purpose of working on and improving the relationship between them*. Hence, I regard the proper object and primary target of clinical intervention to be the couple as a couple.

These two assumptions lead me directly to the most important value to which I am committed in conducting couples therapy: I am committed to doing everything within my power (ethically speaking) to make it possible for two people to discover reasons as to why they want to remain together and preserve their relationship. However, in saying this I must hasten to add that I in no way presume that it is up to me to decide whether or not two people choose to stay together. In fact, I regard it as bordering on the unethical for me make such a presumption. The choice as to whether or not to remain together is entirely up to the couple, following yet another value to which I am committed, namely, the principle of client self-determination. My job, as I see it, is to provide both an environment and a structure conducive to emotional safety and a set of skills and a process that permit the couple to engage their issues as deeply and as constructively as possible with a view to determining whether or not they are capable of resolving their issues sufficiently well that it makes sense to them to remain in their relationship.

There is a process corollary to the value just articulated: In conducting couples therapy, I assume that it sometimes is part of my job to hold people accountable for the decisions they make by questioning their thinking process in a manner that lessens the likelihood of decisions being made on the basis of self-deception or an all-too-easy abdication of responsibilities. (This represents an instance of "Therapist Troubleshooting"; see chapter 1.) In practice, this can cut either way: I may challenge the rationalizations and hidden motivations of one person who is contemplating leaving a relationship without really facing him- or herself or the relationship. Or I may challenge the rationalizations or self-deceptions of another person who is choosing to stay in an emotionally unsatisfying or even abusive relationship. In either case, I conduct the therapy process in such a manner that encourages people to face themselves honestly and without self-deception. I often explain to clients that my intent in challenging them is not to prevent them from making a "bad" choice (from some presumed moral point of view) but to help them avoid making a decision badly. This kind of therapeutic accountability process can help clients gain clarity and deeper self-understanding as well as a better understanding of their partners and the possibilities for their relationship so that each person can make more informed and responsible choices. This stance also reflects, to my mind, the impossibility of conducting value-free therapy, and two of the values to which I am committed are self-honesty and accountability in one's decision-making process, regardless of the actual decision made. In the end, however, it also is important to recognize that the decisions always properly remain with the clients themselves. Moreover, I believe that respecting the couple's right to make their own decisions about their relationship not only preserves genuine client autonomy and the principle of self-determination—an important value to be upheld in its own right—but also constitutes a necessary precondition for a genuinely collaborative approach to therapeutic work.

All these considerations point, I believe, to an inescapable implication, namely, that therapy is intrinsically and unavoidably a moral enterprise. As Goldner (1999, p. 333) observes, our "psychological culture" has in effect thrust "a kind of moral authority" on the therapist in that "what we say has direct social consequences" on the choices people make. As a consequence, Goldner argues, we as therapists "ought to think about ways of enhancing our sense of responsibility about that authority by cultivating a stance of self-conscious moral engagement in our work" and, by implication, in our clients. I couldn't agree more. Yalom's existential psychotherapy (1980) presents a complementary view of the therapeutic enterprise as intrinsically involving clients' engagement in four "ultimate [i.e., existential] concerns of human life," one of which he terms "freedom." As Yalom's analysis reveals, freedom has an irreducibly moral dimension in that it involves the exercise, or abdication, of responsibility by virtue of the choices made and the actions undertaken by each person. So, in the end, there is no avoiding the question of responsibility and choice, whether in personal or professional terms.

A final implication follows from the preceding considerations: The preferred outcome of couples therapy, globally speaking, is that the partners are given every possible advantage and opportunity to come to a decision to stay together. But the mark of success in couples therapy in any given instance is not whether a couple actually chooses to stay together. The final mark of success, I submit, is whether the therapy has enabled each member of a couple to come to a judicious—that is, well-informed—decision as to whether to remain together on the basis of having seriously engaged the core issues of their relationship in a manner that gives each person confidence that he or she is making the right decision for the right reason(s). This is facilitated in RE therapy by the therapist teaching the couple skills that enable them to operate at their best so that they can have confidence in the decision that they make. If that happens, then, regardless of the actual decision or outcome, I believe I have done my job as a couples therapist.

PART I
Theory, Methods, and Research

CHAPTER **1**
Introduction to Relationship Enhancement Therapy with Couples

Theoretical Foundations of Relationship Enhancement Therapy

From its inception, Relationship Enhancement (RE) therapy was conceived by Bernard Guerney, Jr., as an integrative therapy that systematically incorporates and harmonizes concepts and methods from four different theoretical orientations/models (Accordino & Guerney, 2002; Guerney, 1990, 2005). These include the client-centered theory of Carl Rogers, the learning and behavior modification theories of Albert Bandura and B. F. Skinner, the interpersonal theory of Henry Stack Sullivan, and the psychodynamic theory of Sigmund Freud. Guerney regards each theoretical orientation to be of equal importance to the conceptualization and implementation of RE therapy.

However, from my point of view, the heart and soul of the RE method, both theoretically and in terms of its clinical application, is the client-centered theory of Carl Rogers (1951), in two respects in particular. First, there is Rogers's focus on the importance of human emotion, both intrinsically and as an essential ingredient in personal healing. Second, there is Rogers's use of empathy as the primary therapeutic tool both to access (often out-of-awareness) feelings and to effect client healing and client change. This Rogerian influence will be observed throughout this book in two ways: First, in the centrality of emotion to human experience, to interpersonal difficulties, and in the successful healing of significant relationships; and, second, in that empathy constitutes the foundation of so much of what the therapist does in conducting RE therapy and what couples are taught to do in order to deepen mutual understanding and intimacy.

But if Rogerian empathy provides the foundation and the cornerstone of the RE method, then it is the combination of learning and behavior modification theories that constitute its superstructure and its guiding methodology; together, they provide what may be referred to as the RE model's teaching technology. This points to the second distinctive feature of RE therapy, namely, that it is psychoeducational at its core in that it emphasizes and implements skills training as a fundamental component of the therapeutic process with couples. This is rooted in Guerney's guiding conviction that the best way to facilitate client healing and change in the long run is to teach couples interpersonal skills and to coach them intensively in the use of those skills so as to empower them to be able eventually to solve even their most difficult issues on their own. In this sense, the RE model has always been committed to promoting authentic client empowerment and to minimizing even an indirect fostering of client dependency on the therapist or the therapy—an all-too-common feature of intervention strategies based on a medical model.

For many years this emphasis on skills training has led RE therapy to be viewed as a "soft" therapy because it was "simply" an educational approach focused on communication training and therefore could not possibly be very sophisticated, either in its formulation or in its execution. Such judgments, in my opinion, represent a bias fostered by a medical model paradigm. RE therapy is a very demanding therapy in that it requires the therapist to be very active throughout the therapeutic process. In fact, RE therapy calls upon therapeutic skills that many other models seldom require. The most central of these skills, though by no means the only one, is the therapist's skill at teaching, demonstrating, and coaching clients in the use of practical relationship skills that can help them reconstruct their most fundamental patterns of interaction and thereby transform the very fabric of their relationship. But RE therapy involves much more than simply teaching communication and other relationship skills to clients. RE therapy also involves both an elaborate teaching technology designed to achieve a maximally effective transfer of those skills to clients and a set of sophisticated therapeutic techniques. The latter techniques are designed to deepen the therapy process and to manage the inevitable difficulties that emerge in the context of conducting therapy with sometimes highly conflicted or emotionally distraught couples.

With regard to the teaching technology that is at the core of RE therapy, three key elements derive from learning theory (see Bandura & Walters, 1963). As synthesized by Guerney (1977), any effective teaching strategy must encompass three components, like three legs to a stool: didactic teaching, demonstration and modeling, and supervised client practice. To this Guerney further added the behaviorally derived insight that reinforcement is absolutely essential to ensuring high-level client performance of desired new behaviors. Reinforcement operates on two levels: First, there is the classic level whereby the therapist provides positive reinforcement to clients as early and as often as possible in order to validate even moderately successful performance, thus reducing performance anxiety and encouraging further skilled performance. Second, the therapist models additional expressive statements or empathic responses, thus coaching clients as to how they can perform even better. This modeling helps couples go even deeper into one another's experience and the content of the issue being addressed.

With regard to RE therapy's arsenal of sophisticated therapeutic techniques, Guerney has developed a set of interventions that collectively enable the therapist to deepen a couple's therapeutic process quickly and efficiently, thereby enabling the partners to make more rapid progress than would be the case if they were simply to dialogue on their own using the RE skills and dialogue process. These special RE therapy techniques include Troubleshooting, Becoming, Doublebecoming, and Laundering (see below). But these techniques also include ways in which the RE therapy intake process is structured in order to quickly gain client trust, and increase therapist leverage. In addition, it is intended to move very highly fractured couples from a place of disengagement or hostility to a place of at least being willing to buy into the therapeutic process for its potential to help them overcome their conflicted dynamics and mutual alienation. So while RE therapy is indeed a psychoeducational model, it is so much more than that.

The third theoretical orientation that contributed to the development of RE therapy is Sullivan's interpersonal theory (1953), and most especially his theory of human personality. Sullivan suggested that human personality is not best understood as a self-contained substance that manifests itself in a variety of ways, including how a person relates to other people; rather, human personality is better understood as the sum total or byproduct of a person's patterns of interpersonal behavior. The implication of this theory is that if a person were to change patterns of interpersonal behavior, then that person in effect would change his or her personality. This carries a powerfully optimistic implication, namely, that human personality can be changed for the better by helping a person change typical patterns of relating to other human beings. Further, this provides a rationale for turning to the insights of learning and behavior theories to develop and apply a teaching technology. This technology would indeed help people modify their interpersonal behavior in a manner consistent with developing more positive and more satisfying interpersonal relationships. In other words, Sullivan's theory provides the rationale for believing that helping people learn how to relate to others more effectively—that is, in a manner that others would experience as more positive and more satisfying—helps them to become better people.

The fourth theoretical orientation that contributed to the development of RE therapy is Freud's psychodynamic theory, though principally limited to two key ideas: the notion that the human psyche includes both conscious and unconscious psychological processes (not a reified unconscious) and the idea of abreaction or catharsis. The significance of the notion of unconscious psychological processes is that there are elements of human experience that remain outside of awareness. Some of those unconscious elements can develop into or constitute blocks that interfere with optimum human flexibility and the spontaneous exercise of human freedom. This is the meaning of the psychodynamically derived concept of defense mechanisms, which connotes both the distorting of reality and the compromising of a person's ability to negotiate both the interpersonal environment and relationships. The implication is that a means needs to be found to unblock the blocks in a manner that permits the development of self-awareness and thereby facilitates the liberation of human freedom and flexibility, most especially with respect to interpersonal relationships.

This is where the idea of abreaction or catharsis comes in. Abreaction represents, in Guerney's appropriation (2005), a means by which an unconscious process in the form of an emotional blockage is worked through by bringing someone to the point of simultaneously releasing the emotion and achieving a level of self-awareness that is transformative in the dual sense of being liberating and empowering. This is in contrast to a model of catharsis as purging in that, for Guerney, genuine catharsis involves not just the releasing of emotion but also the eliciting of self-awareness and cognitive understanding in a manner that enables the individual to see him- or herself in a new light. However, Guerney argues that it is the classic Rogerian conditions of empathy, congruence, and unconditional positive regard in the form of nonjudgmental acceptance—rather than the psychodynamic techniques of probing, questioning, and interpretation—that best create the conditions for both insight and positive therapeutic change.[1]

Given the varied and interactive influences that have contributed to the development of its theoretical foundations, RE therapy does not represent simply an arbitrary pulling together of pieces from different theoretical models or an eclectic collection of techniques that can be used in any happenstance manner. To the contrary, RE therapy was envisioned and consciously constructed as an integrative theoretical model in its own right that carefully selected the best elements from several distinct theoretical orientations and combined them synergistically into a unified theory and model for conducting couples (and family) therapy in a highly systematized and structured manner. This, to my mind, is one element of the creativity that Guerney has brought to the field, and one of the reasons that explains the effectiveness of RE therapy.

The Role of Emotion in RE Therapy

The role of emotion deserves special attention because the processing and transformation of human emotion, and thereby interpersonal relationships, are at the very heart of RE therapy. RE shares this focus on the importance of emotion in intimate relationships with Emotionally Focused Therapy (EFT), originally developed by Leslie Greenberg and Susan Johnson (1986, 1988). In developing EFT, they, and especially Johnson (1996; Johnson & Denton, 2002), have performed a singular service for the field of couples therapy by highlighting the profound theoretical and clinical significance of John Bowlby's attachment theory for understanding adult love relationships and the importance of fostering attachment bonding (or rebonding) experiences between the couple as part of the therapy process. RE therapy shares with EFT the goal of fostering an increased sense of emotional connection and bonding between partners through the therapeutic process. Both RE and EFT involve an exploration, unpacking, and transformation of human emotion in service of this goal.

At the personal level, emotion represents an experiential and motivational system that seeks out elements that are experienced as pleasurable, rewarding, and satisfying and that avoids elements experienced as unpleasant, unrewarding, and dissatisfying. At the interpersonal level, emotion is the stream that carries the flow of energy in a relationship, both positive and negative. When emotion flows freely and smoothly between two people, then that relationship is likely to be experienced as vibrant and satisfying. When the flow of emotion between two people is blocked, then that relationship is likely to be experienced as lifeless and unsatisfying. Alternatively, when the flow of emotion between two people is volcanic, then that relationship is likely to be experienced as turbulent and perhaps even as threatening.

In relationships where emotion is blocked, energy tends to flow in fits and spurts in mild to moderate cases and not at all in the most severe cases. The result is an emotionally distant, disengaged, or perhaps even lifeless relationship. The goal with such couples is to free up the blocked flow of positive energy by helping the couple learn how to reengage one another at the level of their submerged but nonetheless present positive emotion. In relationships where emotion is volcanic, energy tends to flow in sudden outbursts of negativity. The result is a stormy relationship that may swing back and forth between intense negative engagement and either a peaceful truce or emotional disengagement. The goal with such couples is to tame the frenzied outbursts so that the partners are enabled to reengage their positive emotions in a safer environment. In both cases, the goal is to help distressed couples come closer to the more freely and smoothly flowing energy characteristic of happy, engaged, nondistressed couples.

When there is a free and smooth flow of energy in a relationship, then both partners are able to be more open and honest about their feelings because they feel that it is safe to share them. Moreover, as Guerney observes, the emotional well-being of a relationship is dependent upon a couple being able to express feelings both at "the *most intense* level" and "the *deepest* levels" possible (1994a, p. 129; emphasis in original). The former means expressing negative emotion, such as anger, at its most intense level, rather than at a more superficial level, such as annoyance. The latter means accessing the deepest underlying positive emotion that a person feels, such as love, despite the fact that feelings such as anger are also present. In addition, accessing and expressing negative emotion, and feeling understood around that in the form of receiving empathy, often is a necessary step on the way toward accessing, unblocking, and liberating the underlying positive emotion(s). These emotions may have become buried, either because the flow of energy in the relationship has become blocked or because the flow of energy is too volcanic and threatening. It then becomes the task of the therapy, and the job of the therapist, to facilitate the *safe and constructive* accessing of negative emotion in order to also liberate positive emotion in the relationship. All the elements of the RE therapy process, including the skills and the structured dialogues, as well as the special RE therapy interventions, are designed to accomplish this dual goal.

One implication is that the RE therapist does not shy away from emotion when it presents itself in therapy: quite the contrary. When emotion arises, most especially emotions that are outside the immediate awareness of either partner, the goal is to process it and take it to the deepest levels possible. The key, of course, is to do so within the context of the safety created by the RE therapy process. But within that context, "the RE therapist pursues emotional truth fearlessly" and follows it wherever it may lead (Guerney, 1994a, p. 145). From this point of view, RE therapy embraces the biblical dictum, "The truth will make you free," to which we could add, the truth will also liberate your relationship.

One final observation is relevant here. As Guerney observes, "our current perceptions, emotions, feelings and behaviors" often are colored by past experience (1994a, p. 130). Often, the normal course of therapy is sufficient to help a person see through the manner in which current experience is being shaped by his or her past experience. Sometimes, however, the magnitude of past experience may be such that it causes distortions in one's current experience. This may happen, for example, because of the traumatization resulting from childhood sexual abuse, sustained physical abuse as a child or an adult, or even emotional abuse. An additional point, however, is that the reasons for the coloration or the distortion of current experience do not necessarily lie in earlier relationships (e.g., from childhood). Sometimes, as Guerney observes (1994a, p. 131), "the traumatic event(s) may have taken place with the partner." The importance of this insight therapeutically, relative to some alternative contemporary models of couples therapy, is that it is not always necessary to go back to a person's childhood in order to understand the nature of his or her experience and difficulty in the present. Sometimes the focus of the therapeutic work is simply on the dynamics of the present relationship. That said, RE therapy is always prepared to follow a couple into exploring earlier relationships when the need clearly presents itself. However, this is an important instance where RE therapy follows the Rogerian dictum, "The client leads, the therapist follows." The implication is that the therapist does not presume the need to deal with past relationships as a matter of theoretical conviction. On this count, RE therapy agrees with both Ackerman (1966) and Gottman (1999).

RE Therapy and Systems Theory

Systems theory provides a common frame of reference for much of couples (and family) therapy. It thus would be appropriate to address the manner in which RE therapy is correctly regarded as a systems theory.

There are several key assumptions of systems theory that are relevant to a discussion of RE therapy. First, systems theory posits that the system as a whole is greater than the sum of its parts (see Watzlawick, Beavin, & Jackson, 1967). A second tenet of systems theory is that it is the pattern of interactions and relationships that defines a system, and a system's patterns of interaction and relationships involve reciprocal influence and circular causality. A third tenet is that when a system (i.e., its pattern of interactions and relationships) is flexible and adaptable, it evolves naturally over time in a manner that both reflects and encourages freedom and flexibility of response on the part of its constituent members. Conversely, when a system is inflexible and rigid, then the system has difficulty adapting over time because the patterns of interaction become (metaphorically speaking) sedimented in stone. Of course, these constitute two poles of a continuum from flexible and adaptable to inflexible and rigid, with various gradations in between. A fourth assumption of systems theory is that a system can be changed by changing one element (i.e., one pattern or relationship) within the system.

Applied to couples, these assumptions of systems theory have the following implications. The first implication is that the couple's relationship transcends either individual and thus represents the primary client in couples therapy. Second, how a couple interacts will impact and define the nature of that couple's relationship. Furthermore, because a couple's pattern of interaction involves reciprocal influence and circular causality, no one is the (sole) cause of (or to blame for) a particular pattern, and yet both parties are responsible for creating and sustaining the pattern that defines the relationship. Each person's behavior in effect elicits, reinforces, and sustains the other person's behavior. Third, when a couple's pattern of interaction is flexible and adaptable, then that couple's relationship likely will flow more smoothly and be experienced as nurturing and sustaining. Conversely, when a couple's pattern of interaction is inflexible and rigid, then the couple's relationship likely will encounter significant problems and be experienced as stultifying and disempowering. This happens when the reciprocal influence that each person has on the other becomes sedimented into self-perpetuating negative patterns and repetitive cycles of interaction that become virtually predictable in terms of how a given interaction plays out. When a couple seeks professional assistance to ameliorate the problem, then the focal point of a systems-based assessment is to identify the couple's negative interactional pattern(s), while the generic goal of a systemic intervention is to alter the couple's repetitive negative cycles of interaction in the direction of more positive, and therefore more satisfying, cycles of interaction. Finally, such an intervention can be undertaken either with the system as a whole (i.e., with the couple), or with one of the partners, on the principle that intervening in one part of the system can effect change in the patterns of the entire system.

When measured against this framework, RE therapy clearly qualifies as a systems intervention. RE therapy not only accepts as a premise, but actively promotes as a value, that the couple's relationship transcends either individual. As a natural consequence, RE therapy advocates that it is the relationship between the couple that constitutes the appropriate focal point of intervention in couples therapy. This is true whether working with a couple or with a single partner, because it is possible to intervene and foster change in the system by working either with the couple or one partner. RE therapy also posits that it is a couple's pattern(s) of interaction that define the quality of the couple's relationship and that each person's patterns of interpersonal responses influence and shape the partner's responses. (These patterns take the form of "interpersonal reflexes" that operate unconsciously and reciprocally influence or prompt similar responses in others; see Guerney, 2005, citing Leary, 1957.) Given this element, RE therapy defines its principal task as one of helping couples change the quality of their relationship by helping them change how they interact with each other, including their mutually reinforcing negative cycles of interaction. This includes helping people "gain conscious control" over their own behavior and in this way transform their interpersonal relationships in more positive directions (see Guerney, 2005, p. 6). What is distinctive about RE therapy is that the facilitation of change in a couple's patterns of interaction is to be accomplished by teaching couples practical relationship skills. In the case of enrichment, these skills will help a basically good relationship function even better by increasing the couple's flexibility of response. In the case of couples requiring clinical intervention, these skills will enable a poorly functioning relationship to begin to function in more flexible and adaptive ways. This change is achieved by breaking negative and mutually reinforcing cycles of interaction and replacing them with more positive patterns of interaction that enable the couple to experience healing, a renewed sense of connection, and deepened intimacy. RE therapy thus constitutes at its very core a systems intervention that aims to restructure a couple's patterns of interpersonal responses and cycles of interaction in more positive directions.

Guerney (1990, p. 117) addresses this issue explicitly when he states, "I would define a systemic family therapy as one that deliberately seeks and directly instigates change in the rules, patterns of organization, and the nature of the interpersonal interactions existing in a family." He goes on to say that within this framework, the goal of RE therapy is "to create a therapeutic family system" (p. 126), by which he means a system in which its members are able to serve as mutual psychotherapeutic agents in support of one another's positive growth and constructive change. The potent implication of this approach for systems change is that the process of change does not begin and end with the intervention of the therapist; instead, the process of change is designed to continue after the therapy is concluded. In this way, over time the couple or family in effect becomes a self-generative (and flexible) system of continued positive change with regard to its core interactional patterns. The wedding of Rogerian client-centered theory, interpersonal theory, behavior modification, and psychoeducational skills training is designed to bring about just such fundamental and self-generative change in a couple or family. This combination thus represents both a powerful and unique approach to systems change in its own right and the distinctive contribution of RE therapy to systems theory.

Formats for Conducting RE Therapy

There are three principal formats for conducting RE therapy. These include the Time-Designated, Experiential, and Crisis Intervention formats. The number of sessions available to work with a couple may affect the therapist's choice of format because more reliance must be placed on the therapist managing and directing the process when fewer sessions are available. Conventionally, the Time-Designated format involves somewhere between 10 and 20 sessions (or longer in more involved cases), the Experiential format involves somewhere between 5 and 10 sessions, and the Crisis Intervention format typically fewer than 5 sessions. However, these figures are simply benchmarks, and are fluid. More important are the substantive differences among the three formats, which may be delineated as follows.

Time-Designated Format

The Time-Designated format is the most structured of the three. It involves the therapist systematically teaching and demonstrating the RE skills, with the couple first doing practice exercises with the Empathic skill and then moving into a structured dialogue under the facilitation of the therapist. This format also usually involves a gradual progression from relationship neutral issues (while practicing the Empathic skill) to relationship enhancement issues (during a couple's first dialogue) to minor issues or conflicts and finally to the major issues or problems in the relationship. This gradual progression is designed to facilitate the learning of RE skills (while minimizing negative emotions and defensiveness) and to increase the couple's confidence in the RE dialogue process and in the partners' own ability to use it well before moving into the couple's core issues. It also fosters an increasingly positive atmosphere between the partners as they experience success in dealing with initially easier but nonetheless real relationship issues.

Experiential Format

The Experiential format involves the therapist teaching just enough of the core RE skills (Empathic, Expressive, and Discussion/Negotiation) to allow a couple to initiate a substantive dialogue as quickly as possible, often on one of the partner's most serious issues. The therapist would continue to teach additional points or skills as appropriate. This format might be chosen for any number of reasons: the number of sessions available is limited, the couple responds impatiently to the Time-Designated format, the couple has a sense of urgency to get to their core issue(s) as quickly as possible, or therapist preference. However, a therapist's ability to utilize this format well is dependent upon having first mastered the Time-Designated format and all the special RE therapy techniques. This is because the Experiential format involves a more concentrated and fast-paced application of the RE process, and its successful employment requires that the therapist know how to tailor an intervention to what is needed at any given moment.

Crisis Intervention Format

The Crisis Intervention format is used when the therapist is confronted with a situation, such as the recent revelation of an affair, in which he or she must take more direct and immediate control of the therapy process in order to prevent premature termination of the therapy or the couple's relationship. This typically involves the therapist's use of the special RE therapy technique of Doublebecoming, whereby the therapist alternately represents each member of the couple to the partner for the purpose of eliciting each person's deeper positive feelings and motivations in order to help bridge the emotional gap between them. This application of Doublebecoming might be limited to the initial intake session, could be continued for several sessions in the case of a highly conflicted couple, or might be resorted to at any point in the therapy when the process has broken down and the couple is unable to conduct a skilled dialogue.

Other Formats

There are two additional formats for conducting RE therapy with couples: front-loaded and marathon. In the front-loaded format, a couple learns some or all of the RE skills in concentrated 2- to 3-hour blocks, perhaps several times a week over a 2- to 3-week period, at the beginning of therapy, after which the couple moves into a more traditional weekly therapy format. Another variation on the front-loaded format, used frequently at the National Institute of Relationship Enhancement, is to have couples attend a Couples Relationship Enhancement Weekend where all the skills making up the RE Program are taught as a complete package. The advantage of this approach is that by learning all the RE skills near the beginning of or prior to entering therapy, time need not be taken during therapy sessions to teach the skills, and the couple is ready to begin to tackle their major issues immediately with the facilitation of the RE therapist.

In the marathon format, the therapist would work with a couple in 3- to 4- or even 6- to 8-hour time blocks, either in a concentrated period of time (such as a weekend) or over a more extended period of time. This is usually done when there is a crisis that needs immediate attention, there is a looming deadline for a major decision, or the partners' travel demands make normal scheduling difficult. Working in a marathon format might typically involve a combination of elements of the Crisis Intervention and Experiential formats, but could also incorporate elements of the more structured Time-Designated format, transitioning from one format to another quite fluidly. Indeed, the therapist's ability to choose from and even go back and forth among the three principal formats gives the RE therapist a high level of flexibility to match RE as an intervention to the unique characteristics and needs of each couple. Jacobson and Addis (1993, p. 89) indicate that this kind of flexibility is an important element of effective clinical practice. RE therapy meets the clinician's need for flexibility in approach while nonetheless providing a systematic framework for conducting the therapy process.

Brief Overview of the RE Skills and Dialogue Process

The 10 skills that make up the RE model will be described in greater detail in Parts III and IV as part of a step-by-step explanation of how to conduct RE therapy. However, I would like to introduce each of the RE skills here by providing a brief description of its purpose. Conflict Management skill is listed first (and taught first as relevant) because it represents a kind of metaskill that makes possible the effective use of the other RE skills. Nonetheless, the Empathic skill remains the foundational skill of the RE model.

Conflict Management skill enables couples to better regulate their emotions and to manage difficult conflict situations more effectively and in a manner that preserves emotional safety and respect for the relationship.

Empathic skill enables couples to listen to and empathize with one another in a manner that leaves the partner feeling understood, deepens his or her self-understanding, and encourages further self-exploration and self-disclosure; it also enables the Empathizer to connect more deeply with the partner's experience in a manner that increases receptivity to and acceptance of the partner's point of view; finally, it fosters a deepened sense of intimacy, compassion, and emotional bonding in the relationship.

Expressive skill enables couples to promote a spirit of cooperation and to express themselves openly, honestly, and clearly, but in a manner designed to minimize defensiveness on the part of the Empathizer. This, in turn, maximizes receptivity to hearing the Expresser's point of view and to constructive resolution of an issue.

Discussion/Negotiation skill enables couples to dialogue with one another in a manner that fosters emotional safety, promotes deepened understanding and acceptance of one another's point of view, and helps build a commitment to finding an appropriate solution to a problem when that is called for.

Facilitation skill enables couples to keep their dialogues on track when either partner fails to be skillful, and to do so in a manner that minimizes the risk of disrupting the dialogue.

Problem/Conflict Resolution skill enables couples to devise creative solutions that genuinely address the concerns and meet the desires of both partners and that are sufficiently detailed to help ensure implementation.

Self-Change skill enables the person who is agreeing to make a change in behavior to do so more quickly and reliably.

Helping-Others Change skill enables the person who has requested and is hoping for a change in a partner's behavior to be patient and constructively supportive of that person's change efforts.

Generalization skill enables couples to consolidate and integrate their use of the RE skills into their daily lives and to use these skills unilaterally to improve communication in virtually any relationship.

Maintenance skill increases the likelihood that couples will continue to use the RE skills and dialogue process on a long-term basis.

Equally important to the 10 skills is the RE dialogue process because the real work of RE therapy takes place when couples engage directly in intimate dialogue. It is the structured nature of the dialogue process that creates the requisite emotional safety that opens up a space for couples to be able to engage the difficult issues in their relationship and to explore them more deeply than would otherwise be the case. Empathy plays a central role in grounding the dialogue process and could metaphorically be described as the engine that drives couples' dialogues. But it is the back-and-forth dialoguing that is the vehicle that promotes a deepened sense of emotional engagement, mutual understanding, and acceptance of the other person. This, in turn, fosters a deepened sense of intimacy, compassion, and emotional bonding in the relationship, all of which contribute to genuine healing in the relationship as well. This also allows us to say that while from one point of view the purpose of a particular dialogue is to overcome misunderstanding and (when relevant) create a solution to a specific problem, from another point of view the purpose of dialoguing at a global level is to change how a couple interacts in ways that transform the relationship at its very core. We could even say that a couple's specific issues are simply an entry point for engaging their relationship at a deeper level. From this vantage point, couples' dialogues are the heart of the matter in terms of the RE therapy process, and couples' dialogues are what enable couples to get to the heart of the matter in their relationships.

Given the dual importance of the RE skills on the one hand and the RE dialogue process on the other, the RE model can be viewed as operating on multiple levels. On one level, there are the 10 RE skills that are taught to couples for the purpose of helping each partner alter his or her fundamental patterns of interaction for the better. On another level, there is the RE process of intimate dialogue that makes possible both the engagement and resolution of particular issues in the relationship. It also creates an alteration in the dynamic between the partners that leads to a deeper transformation of the very fabric and texture of the relationship. This, in turn, leads the couple to have a different experience and understanding of their relationship. The final point to be made, in this context, is that the process of intimate dialogue takes on an added significance within RE therapy because it is the cauldron within which the couple engages its most difficult issues. At this level, a couple's intimate dialogues are the path not just to a deepened connection, compassion, and acceptance, but to genuine healing as well.

Basic Methods and Procedures in RE Therapy

There are nine basic methods and procedures used by the therapist in the process of conducting RE therapy. These methods and procedures have their primary application in the Time-Designated and Experiential formats and represent the RE therapist's common repertoire of interventions to facilitate the couple's assimilation and mastery of the RE skills and the dialogue process. The effectiveness of the RE therapy process is in no small part a function of how well the therapist masters these basic methods and procedures.

Administering for the RE therapy process involves what the therapist does to structure the RE therapy process or move it forward. This includes structuring the clinical intake for success, deciding which RE therapy format to use, proposing and negotiating topics for a couple's intimate dialogue, suggesting who might begin a dialogue, negotiating home assignments, and deciding when to resort to any of the special RE therapy techniques.

Instructing involves the therapist explaining the goals, rationale, and guidelines for each of the RE skills and the dialogue process. It also involves responding to questions the couple may have for purposes of clarification.

Demonstrating involves the therapist showing the couple how an RE skill or the dialogue process is used, often by means of a role-play exercise, a videotape, or an audiotape. Following the principles of learning theory, it is important to first demonstrate the use of the initial RE skills before expecting the couple to practice or use them.

Reinforcing involves the therapist saying things like "Good," "Great," or "Well done," or giving a thumbs-up signal or a nod of the head in order to let the client know that he or she is performing as desired at that moment. Reinforcement is important, not simply to encourage continued performance of the newly acquired skill, but also to help alleviate the performance anxiety that many clients experience when first attempting to perform a new skill. For the same reasons, it is important to provide reinforcement at whatever level is possible before modeling for the client what else he or she might add to what has already been said. Reinforcing is most relevant early in the therapy, but it is always appropriate to reinforce a client for an especially clear and skillful expressive statement, an especially good empathic response, or a self-correction. Reinforcing can also take the form of the therapist providing the partners with feedback about the progress they have made or the hard work they have accomplished in a particular session in the face of disappointment or a sense of weariness with the therapeutic process.

Modeling involves the therapist taking what the Expresser or Empathizer has said and showing how it can be rephrased so that it becomes more skillful. Or the therapist can encourage the person to take it a step further by suggesting additional ideas or feelings that would further amplify the Expresser's meaning or deepen the Empathizer's empathy. The therapist can achieve the same end in terms of content either by modeling for the Expresser ways in which to express him- or herself more clearly and more fully, or by modeling for the Empathizer how to empathize more deeply. The choice may be a function of whether in that moment the therapist wants to help the Expresser own his or her experience more fully or whether the therapist wants to help the Empathizer learn how to read between the lines more deeply.

Preemptive modeling involves the therapist anticipating that the Expresser might say something unskillfully or might omit an underlying positive at the beginning of an expressive statement, or that the Empathizer might not be able to empathize well or might omit something important from the empathy. In either case, the therapist would model in advance what he or she would like the Expresser or the Empathizer to say. Preemptive modeling is preferable to having to provide corrective feedback, following the principle of minimizing the potential for felt failures and maximizing the potential for experienced success.

Prompting involves the therapist making suggestions regarding a way of beginning, continuing, or correcting an expressive statement or an empathic response. This might involve, for example, saying to the Empathizer, "And how do you imagine that leaves her feeling?" Or the therapist might say to the Expresser, "Please say that more subjectively instead of stating it as a fact." In either case, a prompt is used only if the therapist has a high level of confidence that the person would be able to respond successfully, again following the principle of minimizing felt failure and maximizing the client's experience of success. In the absence of that confidence, the therapist would instead resort to modeling preemptively the specific expressive statement or empathic response he or she would like the client to provide. Early in the therapy, preemptive modeling predominates over prompting; as the couple becomes more skilled, prompting tends to replace preemptive modeling.

Coaching involves the therapist monitoring and facilitating better performance on the part of the couple. This most typically takes the form of helping the partners express themselves more clearly and more fully and helping them empathize more deeply. In practice this usually is accomplished by modeling, preemptive modeling, or prompting, but the therapist can also coach a couple at the level of helping them manage the direction of their intimate dialogue. This could take the form of identifying that their dialogue appears to have reached an impasse or of reframing to deepen the focus of the couple's dialogue.

Supervising home assignments is vital. All home assignments should be negotiated with the couple. Examples might include completing the Relationship Questionnaire (to be discussed in chapter 4), reading chapters in the *RE Client Manual* (Guerney & Scuka, 2005), listening to an RE demonstration audiotape or viewing an RE demonstration videotape, implementing an agreed-to plan or a change in behavior, initiating relationship enhancement activities at home, conducting home dialogues, or assigning Generalization skill applications at home or at work. The key principle in supervising home assignments is that the therapist must follow up on any home assignment that has been negotiated in order to reinforce for the couple the importance of completing the home assignments.

Special Techniques in RE Therapy

There are four special RE therapy techniques: Troubleshooting, Becoming, Doublebecoming, and Laundering. Becoming will be addressed in chapter 3 as a special application of the Identification Mode of empathy. Laundering and Doublebecoming will be addressed in chapter 4 in the context of their use in the clinical intake. Troubleshooting is addressed below. There are two forms of Troubleshooting: Client Troubleshooting and Therapist Troubleshooting. When the word *Troubleshooting* alone appears, it refers to Client Troubleshooting.

Client Troubleshooting

Client Troubleshooting often is the first special RE therapy technique that a therapist will resort to. There are two principal occasions for its use: in response to either partner having an objection to something about the therapy process (e.g., having difficulty with the skills or an objection to their use), or in response to either partner becoming too emotional to be able to participate in the process at that moment (e.g., becoming upset when hearing what the partner has to say). Either occasion should be treated as an obstacle to progress in the therapy and requires the therapist's intervention. Troubleshooting involves two components: first, the use of empathy to acknowledge whatever the client is experiencing that is getting in the way and second (when appropriate) the therapist communicating his or her own perspective on what the client is experiencing. In applying the technique, the therapist continues to empathize as long as necessary until the person feels sufficiently well understood that he or she is able to listen nondefensively to what the therapist might have to say or is able to reenter the therapy process. A few empathic responses may be sufficient; but sometimes the therapist may have to empathize for 10 minutes or more. The psychological point is that it is important to give that person the space to either have their concern acknowledged and resolved or to discharge whatever emotion has been blocking that person's participation in the therapy process. The reason is that this person will be unable to move forward freely and constructively until he or she feels understood or has processed things sufficiently to be able to move past the emotional obstacle. It is the therapist's job to facilitate that internal process, and it is the sustained use of empathy that constitutes the primary tool of Client

Troubleshooting (for a videotaped illustration of the therapist's varied and extended use of Troubleshooting, see Guerney, Jungkuntz, & Scuka, 1999).

Therapist Troubleshooting

In Client Troubleshooting, the therapist responds to a difficulty experienced by a client. In Therapist Troubleshooting, the therapist departs from the primary role of teacher, coach, and facilitator and takes the initiative to communicate his or her own feelings or concerns to one or both members of the couple in order to address an issue of perceived relevance to the therapy. This could involve addressing a pattern of missed appointments or uncompleted home assignments. At a deeper level, it could involve expressing concern about the couple's choices or actions because of potential negative consequences, either on the couple or a third party (such as their children). Or the therapist might be concerned about the nature of a solution the couple is considering while negotiating a relationship agreement, again because of potential negative consequences that the therapist believes the couple is not recognizing.

Therapist Troubleshooting can also take the form of the therapist introducing relevant informational resources to prompt the partners to broaden their perspective about the issue(s) with which they are confronted (see clinical vignette 5, chapter 16, for an example). Finally, in a more positive vein, it could take the form of the therapist disclosing how he or she has been deeply moved by a couple's poignant dialogue. When providing feedback, it is imperative that the therapist expresses him- or herself skillfully in order to reduce potential defensiveness.[2] This also creates an isomorphic modeling effect that reinforces the couple's learning. It would also be wise to begin by providing direct or preemptive empathy to what the therapist imagines the client's perspective to be. In order to increase the likelihood that the person(s) being addressed genuinely hears what is being said, the therapist may request that the client(s) enter into a minidialogue for the purpose of having the client(s) verbally empathize with what the therapist has to say. This can also help lower client defensiveness and maximize client internalization of the therapist's perspective.

It is worth noting that Therapist Troubleshooting, from one point of view, is less a technique in the strict sense of the word than it is a framework that allows the therapist to intervene in the RE therapy process whenever the therapist believes that such an intervention is called for in order to facilitate and increase the efficacy of the couple's therapy (see Accordino & Guerney, 2002, p. 413). As such, the framework of Therapist Troubleshooting permits a wide range of potential interventions to be brought to bear by the therapist, including using therapeutic techniques that fall outside the scope of RE therapy techniques per se but that the therapist judges may nonetheless facilitate the couple's therapy process. For example, in response to a client feeling emotionally overwhelmed and stuck during a dialogue, the therapist could engage that person in a quasi-hypnotic induction involving the use of guided imagery to help access more deeply buried aspects of the person that otherwise may not be easily accessed.

To illustrate, a wife with whom I was working in couples therapy, in the context of a terminated affair that had recently been revealed by her husband, was feeling emotionally paralyzed and torn among too many different responsibilities in her life. She metaphorically expressed how she felt "tied down" and a "heavy weight" pressing down on her chest. In response to her being unable to express herself any further at that moment, I elected to temporarily break out of the couple's dialogue and suggested that we use guided imagery to help her better access her dilemmas. After a 20-minute quasi-hypnotic induction in which I used guided imagery to help her get in touch more deeply with the feelings of being tied down and having a weight on her chest, the wife was able both to regain a sense of her own power and get greater clarity about what her most important priorities were. Having accomplished that, we brought the induction to a close and the couple resumed dialoging. But whereas earlier the wife had felt emotionally stuck and overwhelmed, now she felt liberated and empowered by virtue of the guided imagery through which she had been taken.

This minivignette illustrates how an external therapeutic technique can be brought to bear in the service of the couple's dialogues. The flexibility that this provides points to yet another respect in which RE therapy is an exceedingly flexible model for conducting couples therapy. On the other hand, it is important to be cautious and judicious both in choosing to intervene in the therapy process in this way and in the choice of any specific intervention, because the couple's dialogues are the heart of the RE therapy process and the most important context within which the partners will experience their most valuable therapeutic gains. The criterion for evaluating both the decision to intervene under the rubric of Therapist Troubleshooting and the specific choice of intervention is the extent to which the decision and the choice of intervention serve the purpose of advancing the couple's dialogue.

Values Embodied in the RE Model

There are six principal values embodied in and promoted by the RE model. The first is the transcendence of the relationship relative to the individuals who make up the relationship; the second is respect for the other person and the relationship; the third is nonjudgmental acceptance of the other person; the fourth is openness and honesty in communication; the fifth is caring and compassion toward the other person; and the sixth is equity. Guerney explicitly discusses the last three values (see Cavedo & Guerney, 1999). The first three values have been added on the basis of my reflections on the meaning and implications of the RE model.

As to the question of how to introduce these values to couples over the course of therapy, my approach is to gradually introduce each of these values at a point in the teaching of the RE skills and the conducting of the RE therapy process where that value has particular relevance. For example, the notion of the relationship as an entity that transcends either individual is naturally introduced during the clinical intake. This value also operates as an underlying principle of the Problem/Conflict Resolution skill in that it promotes a spirit of mutual accommodation, a necessary ingredient of any committed relationship that is to be more than a matter of simply ensuring the satisfaction of one's own desires. The value of respect also is introduced in the clinical intake, but is even more overtly invoked and promoted in the course of teaching the Conflict Management skill. Respect also plays a significant role in both the Empathic and Expressive skills. The value of nonjudgmental acceptance represents one of the key goals of the RE dialogue process. It also plays an important role in the Empathic skill as a precondition for being able to empathize; conversely, increasing a couple's ability to become empathic fosters an increased capacity to become nonjudgmentally accepting of one another. The two sets of values of openness and honesty, and caring and compassion, are most naturally introduced either during the introduction of the RE model or in the teaching of the Expressive skill, though the values of caring and compassion also are relevant to teaching the Empathic skill. The value of equity operates more at an implicit level in that the RE dialogue process creates a level playing field between two intimates by virtue of (1) creating a process that encourages equity in both expressive sharing and in empathic receiving and acknowledging, and (2) requiring both partners to abide by the same rules and guidelines in order for the dialogue process to work. I also look for opportunities throughout the therapy process to refer to and to promote these values as a way of strengthening the couple's awareness of the importance of their commitment to the relationship as an entity that transcends them as individuals.

As stated in the introduction, it is impossible for therapy to be value-neutral. The responsible approach, then, is for the therapist to be open about the values to which he or she is committed. In the process, the couple benefits from hearing a perspective about what it means to be in a relationship or marriage, a perspective that our culture has done a poor job of explaining and promoting. As a couples therapist, I see it as part of my job to share and promote a vision of relationship and marriage that provides an opportunity for deepened self-reflection on the part of the couple. What the couple chooses to do with what I share is up to them, so the principle of self-determination is preserved.

Notes

1. More recent developments within psychodynamic theory, such as Kohut's self psychology (1977, 1984), Stolorow's intersubjectivity theory (Stolorow, Brandchaft, & Atwood, 1987), and Mitchell's relational theory (1988), in many respects parallel lines of thinking developed earlier by Rogers, especially in terms of the importance of empathy and the manner of the therapist's relating to the client being central to the therapeutic process and client healing.

2. Kiesler (1996) observes that how therapist feedback is delivered to a client is extremely important and must always be given respectfully and supportively in order to preserve client self-esteem and reduce client reactivity and defensiveness. Kiesler identifies a number of additional conditions necessary for effective therapist feedback, including (among others) that it be focused on "specific and concrete events" or "observable behaviors" (p. 294) and that the feedback is "consensually validated" with the client both out of respect and in order to preserve a collaborative approach to the therapeutic work (p. 296).

CHAPTER 2

The Empirical Validation, Application, and Effectiveness of Relationship Enhancement Therapy

Summary of Research Validating the Effectiveness of RE Therapy

The RE model has a strong empirical research base that encompasses both RE therapy and the RE Program. This research covers the period since the mid-1970s, and the accumulated total of empirical studies and case reports is a sound indicator of the effectiveness of RE therapy. The most comprehensive summary of RE research in terms of outcome is provided by Accordino and Guerney (2002). This summary includes 25 independent studies, each of which demonstrates the effectiveness of RE in terms of one or more outcome measures. Five of these studies involved a direct comparison of RE with another model, and in each study RE was shown to be at least as effective as the comparison model on specific outcome measures and was shown to be clearly superior on a majority of the outcome measures. This superior comparative effectiveness of RE was independently confirmed by an award-winning meta-analytic study (Giblin, Sprenkle, & Sheehan, 1985) that demonstrated the clear comparative superiority of RE to any of the other 13 models for which data were available and with which it was compared (see below).

This chapter provides an overview of the research that is most relevant to RE therapy in its application to couples, though reference will also be made to studies that do not directly involve couples but that nonetheless reinforce various aspects of the effectiveness of the RE model. Reference will also be made to research involving the RE Program. The reason is that the lines between therapy, prevention, and enrichment are not necessarily as clear-cut or as absolute as our binary thought processes might lead us to believe. This is especially true for the RE model where the skills taught, the teaching technology employed, and the intensive coached skills practice and coached dialogues are quite similar whether one is leading an RE Program for prevention or enrichment purposes or conducting RE therapy for reparative purposes. The difference between the two, as already explained, is that RE therapy involves both a more sustained and intensive application of the RE model's generic process and the application of a number of specialized RE therapy techniques. This permits the therapist to intervene in the therapy process and the couple's dialogues in a way that deepens the couple's work and fosters forward movement toward resolution. Nonetheless, as Cavedo and Guerney observe (1999, p. 75): "From the RE perspective, therapy, prevention and enrichment are seen primarily as different points on the same continuum." In other words, they represent different applications of the same model, the common goal of which is "helping people change in positive directions." From this vantage point, a case can be made for the inclusion of validation research involving the RE Program in the context of a book devoted to RE therapy.

Two technical observations further support this approach. First, "the average level of relationship distress or adjustment" of participants in RE Programs "generally fell half-way between clinic samples and the general population" (Accordino & Guerney, 2002, p. 419). When this is linked to the positive correlation that Giblin et al. (1985) found between the initial level of couples' distress and the degree of couples' improvement from participation in an intervention, the implication is that the positive effects experienced by participants in the RE Program would be matched or even exceeded by participants in RE therapy. (This point will be revisited below in the Brock and Joanning study.) Second, in their evaluation of a decade of research in the marital and family enrichment field, Guerney and Maxson recommend (1990, p. 1129), on the basis of the methods successfully employed by the Giblin meta-analysis, that "certain kinds of therapy studies [be treated] as also being studies of enrichment, ...or at least [be treated] as analogs of enrichment" when the therapy methods and the enrichment methods are "identical" or "very similar." Conversely, they argue, "it would be appropriate to do likewise in the reverse direction when findings of studies using methods that are common in enrichment programs seem applicable also to therapy."

Let us now take a look at the most relevant research on the RE model. In one of the earliest studies comparing RE therapy to both a wait condition and another therapy model, in this case Reciprocal Reinforcement

(RR) therapy based on Stuart's operant-interpersonal therapy (Wieman, 1973), participants in the wait group (not unexpectedly) showed virtually no change, while participants in both therapy interventions registered significant and comparable gains in adjustment, communication, integration, and cooperation between the spouses. Moreover, the gains were shown to have been maintained at 10 weeks follow-up. Subjectively, participants in RE therapy rated their experience in therapy and their therapists more favorably than participants in RR therapy. (Potential therapist influence on the results was controlled for by having three pairs of therapists each lead two groups, one following each therapy model.)

In a study of married couples in an intensive 2-month RE Program (Rappaport, 1971, 1976), couples made significant gains compared to a similar wait period in the following areas: expressiveness and empathy while discussing emotionally significant topics, marital adjustment, general quality of the relationship, trust and intimacy, marital satisfaction, and their perceived ability to resolve problems satisfactorily. Brock (1974) conducted a follow-up study with the following mixed results. Marital adjustment and marital communication fell from posttreatment and did not differ significantly from pretest levels. Empathic skill fell significantly from posttreatment, but Expressive skill did not; yet, both remained significantly improved over pretest levels, a not insignificant result. As Guerney and Maxson observe (1990, pp. 1128–1129), negative findings on one measure do not invalidate positive findings on another measure. An intervention may not succeed on one dimension yet succeed on another dimension. Each dimension needs to be evaluated on its own terms. Nonetheless, it is worth observing that the mixed results of the follow-up study did point to the need to improve maintenance of gains on a longer term basis. This indirectly contributed to the expansion of the RE model to include the Generalization and Maintenance skills in order to address this very point.

In one of the more significant comparative studies evaluating the effectiveness of the RE Program in comparison with a no-treatment condition and the Couples Communication (CC) program (Brock & Joanning, 1983, p. 419), "the results … demonstrated rather convincingly that RE was a more effective intervention strategy than CC." This was true at both posttest and follow-up. Posttest results showed that RE was more effective than CC at increasing marital communication (including the expression of affection) and marital satisfaction. At 3-month follow-up, RE couples' outcomes were superior to CC couples' outcomes on all outcome variables. A significant aspect of this study that makes it particularly relevant to the clinical application of RE is that "the mean total score [of participants at pretest] on the Dyadic Adjustment Scale (DAS) (Spanier, 1976) was 105.1" (p. 414). This is compared to a mean average of 114.8 of married couples who participated in the original validation research for the DAS. The pretest scores of this study's participants mean that 67% of the sample couples were in the distressed range, experiencing low marital satisfaction. An analysis of a subsample with DAS scores of 109 or below revealed that "low marital satisfaction RE spouses scored significantly higher than CC spouses on nearly all dependent variable measures" (p. 418), meaning that RE was more effective than CC with more severely distressed couples. Moreover, at 3-month follow-up, the low satisfaction RE couples maintained their gains relative to posttest. The implication of these results is that the RE model would be an appropriate and effective intervention with typical clinical populations experiencing low levels of marital satisfaction.

Another study involving the RE Program showed positive maintenance of gains at 1-year follow-up (Griffin & Apostal, 1983). Couples participated in an RE group for 2.5 hours per week over a 6-week period after waiting for 6 weeks in order to create a control condition. The study was designed to evaluate the capacity of RE to increase the general quality of the marital relationship, functional differentiation, and differentiation of self—the latter a concept deriving from Bowenian therapy (Bowen, 1978). At posttest, couples experienced significant increases in their functional differentiation and the equality of their marital relationships. At 1-year follow-up, these gains were maintained. A further interesting result is that gains in differentiation of self were found at 1-year follow-up that had not been present at posttest. This suggests that RE intervention results in long-term positive change in couples that may not be found significant at posttest. This is an important finding in support of the long-term effectiveness of the RE model.

In a study comparing Jessee's therapy-based Gestalt Relationship Facilitation groups and RE groups (Jessee & Guerney, 1981), the sample of distressed and nondistressed couples in both groups made comparable significant gains on the following variables: marital adjustment, trust and harmony, and the rate of positive change in the relationship. However, RE group participants showed greater gains on communication, relationship satisfaction, and the ability to handle problems. The RE couples thus experienced greater overall gains.

In a study of RE therapy involving the random assignment of couples (Ross, Baker, & Guerney, 1985), the outcome effects of RE therapy were compared with those of the therapists' own preferred treatment, including client-centered, interpersonal, behavior modification, and psychodynamic methods. One important feature of this study (designed to control for potential therapist influence) is that both treatments were administered by the same five therapists. These therapists had an average of 6 years' experience with their own preferred approach, but no previous experience with RE. All five therapists received a standardized 3-day training in RE therapy, and then were randomly instructed to use either their own preferred treatment or the RE methodology with each couple, but to not mix the two. (Therapist compliance with this protocol was verified by review of session tapes.) At 10-weeks' posttesting, couples receiving RE therapy showed significantly greater improvement on all measures: quality of communication, general quality of relationship, and marital adjustment.

In a study comparing the use of Strategic marital therapies (ST) and RE therapy with highly distressed couples (Steinweg, 1990), all four hypotheses positing the superiority of ST were disconfirmed, whereas the hypothesis concerning the superiority of RE relative to the quality of couples' communication was confirmed. RE was thus shown not only to be at least the equal of ST in the areas of marital happiness; cohesion-adaptability; male, female, and couple real–ideal discrepancy scores; and family goal attainment, but it also was shown to be superior at improving communication.

In a more recent study of the efficacy of RE therapy in a southern rural outpatient setting with distressed couples (Brooks, 1997), participants completing a 12-week time-limited course of RE Couples Group Therapy showed significantly more improvement during the treatment period than those who were initially assigned to a 12-week wait period. This was true for all variables studies: quality of marital communication, trust-intimacy, dyadic adjustment, and problem solving. Moreover, a 12-week follow-up test demonstrated maintenance of gains.

One study involved mother and daughter pairs assigned to a no-treatment group, an RE therapy treatment group, or a Traditional Treatment (TT) group involving unstructured open communication about roles, feelings, and desired behaviors (Guerney, Coufal, & Vogelsong, 1981). Participants in the no-treatment group showed virtually no improvement while the TT group participants showed improvement only in the general quality of their relationships. By contrast, participants in the structured RE therapy group showed significant gains in all areas measured: empathy, Expressive skill, general communication patterns, and the general quality of their relationships. This study lends some indirect support to the supposition that the structured nature of the RE skills-training model is one factor contributing to its outcome effectiveness.

Maintenance of gains from the previous study was demonstrated in a follow-up study (Guerney, Vogelsong, & Coufal, 1983) designed to evaluate the comparative effectiveness of a booster program in reinforcing the gains from the original interventions. Fifty percent of the original participants in both the RE group and the TT group took part in a booster program at 6-months' follow-up. Both booster and nonbooster RE treatment groups gained more than their TT group counterparts on measures of empathy, expressiveness, and general relationship quality, again reinforcing the superiority of the RE intervention. Not surprisingly, RE booster group participants gained more than RE nonbooster participants, thus validating the hypothesis that booster sessions would help maintain gains. But the most interesting result was that posttesting of nonbooster RE participants showed *gains* on all measures rather than the expected decrease that typically follows posttesting. This result demonstrates not only that RE can foster a longer-term maintenance of gains even in the absence of a booster intervention, but that the positive effects of RE treatment may continue to build long past the termination of treatment. This parallels the finding of the Griffin and Apostal study (1983) discussed above.

Brief mention may be made of five studies of dating or engaged couples (see Accordino & Guerney, 2002, pp. 428–429 for citations) that consistently demonstrated the superiority of RE on a variety of measures when compared to a variety of relationship lecture-discussion, relationship discussion, or problem-solving groups. Mention should also be made of a single study (Sams, 1983) that demonstrated the superiority of premarital RE programs compared to Engaged Encounter programs on behaviorally measured variables of empathy, expressive skills, and the ability to solve problems effectively. Two additional research studies on RE in the treatment of domestic violence (Waldo, 1986, 1988) will be reviewed below.

While doubt may always be cast on a single study, the collective weight of this body of research on the RE model, especially given the superior results of its head-to-head comparisons with other interventions, provides significant empirical validation of RE therapy and the RE Program. Perhaps most significantly, several of these studies (Griffin & Apostal, 1983; Guerney, Vogelsong, & Coufal, 1983) not only substantiate maintenance of gains over time but also document that RE therapy can have a continuing positive influence resulting in an actual *increase* in gains at follow-up compared to posttest as couples' relationships continue to benefit from the self-reinforcing gains derived from skill learning and the resulting transformation of their patterns of interaction.

The Munich Group Study—An Analysis

Gottman (1999, pp. 10–11) cites the comparative outcome study conducted by the Munich group (Hahlweg, Schindler, Revenstorf, & Brengelmann, 1984) to support his contention that an "active listening" model which "followed Guerney's method precisely" is ineffective in comparison to a "behavior exchange plus problem-solving" model and therefore, by implication, "isn't an effective intervention for distressed marriages." However, a careful reading of the Hahlweg et al. (1984) study reveals that Gottman cites only certain (one-sided) results from the study. He also overlooks several important considerations that call into question his implied dismissal of the RE model as a legitimate therapeutic intervention for distressed couples.

First, Gottman is incorrect when he states that the active listening model employed ("communication training" was the language used in the Hahlweg study) "followed Guerney's method precisely." The Hahlweg study is very clear that while the general "procedures" were derived from Guerney's book *Relationship Enhancement* (1977), couples were instead given a textbook that was "a rewritten version" of a German language book on communication skills. Therefore, whatever results the Hahlweg study may yield are not legitimately generalized to the RE model per se. This is further reinforced by two important considerations. The Hahlweg study used the common "active listening" technique of "paraphrasing" instead of the more distinctive and more powerful RE technique of deep empathizing (see chapter 3 for a discussion of the difference). As a consequence, the results of Hahlweg et al. (1984) may be relevant to approaches other than RE, but not to the RE model itself. In addition, the "behavioral marital therapy" (BMT) intervention with which the ad hoc communication training (CT) was compared included "specific problem-solving skills … [that] were not included in the [CT] treatment" (p. 7). While it is historically true that Guerney's 1977 book did not include specific problem-solving skill guidelines, this was no longer true of the RE model by the time the Hahlweg study was conducted and published in 1984. By that time a formal Problem/Conflict Resolution skill and guidelines had been added to the RE model, so any comparisons in the Hahlweg study between their ad hoc CT model and their behavioral intervention model would have no direct relevance to the RE model. Indeed, the RE model in its fullest form is not all that different from the behavioral intervention model described in the Hahlweg study in that the RE model, properly implemented, also includes elements of "establishing positive reciprocity" and "crisis management," including an emphasis on "generalization" (pp. 7–8).

But even allowing, for the sake of discussion, that there is some legitimacy in using the results of the Hahlweg study as a basis for evaluating the comparative effectiveness of the RE model, the data and the results are far more mixed and less unfavorable to that study's ad hoc CT model than

Gottman's selective citations would lead one to believe. First, there were four conditions tested in the study, not just two: conjoint BMT, conjoint group BMT, conjoint CT, and conjoint group CT. While the data on conjoint group CT were not favorable, Hahlweg et al. (1984, p. 14) report, "Couples who received BMT, irrespective of modality, or conjoint communication training showed significant improvement when compared to the waiting-list control group on six out of seven variables." Second, while the BMT interventions did show superiority to CT interventions at posttest relative to the percentage of nondistressed couples in each condition, the percentages remained virtually unchanged for the CT couples at follow-up (FU) 1 and 2, whereas there was a significant drop in the percentage of BMT couples who remained nondistressed. The net effect, as Hahlweg et al. explicitly state, was that "The differences between BMT and CT were not significant at FU 1 and 2" (p. 16). Third, there is reason to believe that the Hahlweg study's failure to include "specific problem-solving skills" in their ad hoc CT model skewed the results against the conjoint group CT condition. Hahlweg et al. indirectly support this supposition when they hypothesize that the poor results for the conjoint group CT condition might be attributable to "a 'negative modeling effect' with each couple observing other couples in the group not improving," the point being that this most likely happened precisely because "specific problem-solving skills and measures to increase positive interactions were not taught" (p. 20). Indeed. But the RE model in its fullest form explicitly does both of those things. Finally, in one of their concluding statements, Hahlweg et al. make the rather modest claim that, "When comparing treatment formats, BMT seems to be moderately superior to CT" (p. 20). All told, the results of the Hahlweg study do not support the use to which Gottman attempts to put it in terms of a critique of the effectiveness of the RE model.

A Meta-Analytic Study

The meta-analytic study published by Giblin et al. (1985) represents a landmark accomplishment. It was the first comprehensive "study-of-studies" that included all the then available experimental or quasi-experimental studies in the areas of premarital, marital, or family enrichment. Eighty-five studies were included, involving 3,886 couples and families, with both clinical and nonclinical populations. Studies of clinical populations of couples and families were included when two additional criteria were met: the goal of the method employed was "greater than symptom removal" and the intervention also employed "processes of enrichment." An important finding was that more distressed couples and families, that is, those more typically found in therapy, showed greater change than the less distressed.

(The effect size for distressed was .51 compared to .27 for nondistressed participants.) One important implication of this finding is that the most distressed couples and families potentially have the most to gain from such enrichment-type interventions, and that such interventions can themselves constitute core components of an "enrichment-like therapy," as is the case with RE therapy (Guerney & Maxson, 1990, p. 1130). Indeed, Giblin et al. (1985, p. 263) lend direct support to this interpretation when they conclude, "These findings appear to challenge the belief that enrichment 'works' with only normal, healthy nondistressed populations."

The outcome comparisons from Giblin et al. (1985) yielded the following results. Effect sizes (ES) were obtained for 14 specific interventions plus additional categories of "other" and "placebo." These were also divided into two categories of marital and family interventions. The "combined effect sizes averages" were .419 for marital interventions and .545 for family interventions. Two interventions, rational-emotive (ES = .041) and behavior exchange (ES = .212), scored lower than discussion-attention placebo (ES = .219). Marriage Encounter (ES = .416), Couples Communication (ES = .437), and "combined communication-behavior exchange" (ES = .445) matched the average effect size. A group of minor programs in the "other" marital category (ES = .583) and Communications in the family category (ES = .633) were the only interventions other than RE to significantly exceed the average. The RE model's effect size score in both its marital version (ES = .963) and its family version (ES = .961) far exceeded that of any other intervention included in the meta-analysis.[1] These scores also exceed the reported average for psychotherapy research of .85, with effect size typically ranging from -1 to +1 (as reported by Giblin et al.). The RE model was thus shown to be a powerful intervention and superior to any of the other intervention models with which it was compared in this groundbreaking meta-analysis. In addition, the RE model exceeded the reported average for psychotherapy research in general, and thus receives indirect but explicit validation as an effective therapeutic intervention in its own right.

Two additional observations from this meta-analysis are of particular relevance for the RE model. The first is that Giblin et al. (1985, p. 262) found that there was a modest positive correlation between highly structured programs and their success (i.e., their effect size).[2] This suggests that the highly structured nature of the RE model is one of the reasons for its effectiveness compared to less structured interventions. It also is worth noting that when considering the relative effectiveness of program components and characteristics, Giblin et al. (1985, p. 262) concluded that better outcomes occurred with models that emphasized skills and behavioral practice as opposed to discussion. Because the teaching of specific relationship skills and coached skills practice (together with continued coached dialogues) are two of the distinguishing characteristics of RE therapy, it is reasonable to infer that these are among the key elements that explain the effectiveness of RE therapy.

Appropriate Populations for the Use of RE Therapy

In addition to the controlled experimental studies that have validated the effectiveness of RE therapy for premarital couples, couples seeking enrichment, and couples and families in distress, there are numerous case studies that report the effectiveness of RE with a wide variety of clinical and other special populations. These include:

Premarital couples (Ginsburg & Vogelsong, 1977)
Couples dealing with alcoholism (Matter, McAllister, & Guerney, 1984; Waldo & Guerney, 1983)
Drug addicts in rehabilitation settings (Cadigan, 1980)
Spouse batterers (Guerney, Waldo, & Firestone, 1987; Waldo, 1986, 1988)
Couples with depression or bipolar disorder (extensive experience by the present author)
Couples recovering from the trauma of infidelity (see chapters 15 and 16 below)
Couples with sexual issues (Harman, Waldo, & Johnson, 1994)
Eating disordered clients (Santhouse, 2003)
Borderline clients (Waldo & Harmon, 1993)
Narcissistic clients (Snyder, 1994a)
Couples suffering from schizophrenia (Zahniser & Falk, 1993)
Psychiatric inpatients and their families (Vogelsong, Guerney, & Guerney, 1983)
People recovering from severe mental illness in community residential rehabilitation centers (Accordino & Guerney, 1993; Accordino & Herbert, 1997)
Prisoners and their wives (Accordino & Guerney, 1998)

In addition, RE has been found to be effective in several special areas of application: It has been judged to be outstanding with respect to gender sensitivity (Snyder, 1992a); it has been used effectively as a basis for cross-cultural couples counseling (Ibrahim & Schroeder, 1990); it has been found to be an effective and culturally sensitive approach for African-American couples (Moore & Fletcher, unpublished); and it has been used successfully to facilitate the postdivorce adjustment for both women and men (Avery & Thiessen, 1982; Thiessen, Avery, & Joanning, 1980).

Limitations

Active psychosis and active substance abuse would constitute two of the most serious limitations to the application and effectiveness of RE therapy with couples. The reason is that in each case the necessary preconditions for conscious and meaningful participation in the couples therapy process are not present. Another limiting condition, as Accordino and Guerney observe (2002, p. 418), is systematic lying (as in sociopathy), because persistent dishonesty subverts the integrity of both the therapeutic process and the possibility for authenticity in a relationship. On the other hand, the RE therapy process creates conditions that are conducive to the development of increased openness and honesty when both partners embrace the process—or at least give it a chance. A third limiting condition would be either partner's systematic inability or refusal to empathize (as in antisocial personality or narcissistic disorders). Since empathy constitutes the foundation of the RE dialogue process, its utter absence would sabotage the very possibility of constructive dialogue. Once again, however, the RE therapy process creates conditions that for most couples are conducive to the development of empathy and increased mutual acceptance. A fourth possible limitation would be either partner's inability or unwillingness to acknowledge ownership for his or her part of a problem (e.g., one partner's decision to have an affair), since this tends to leave the other partner in an emotionally untenable position. However, one purpose of the RE dialogue process is to help each partner feel safe enough from being attacked by the other that it then becomes possible to own responsibility where it is appropriate to do so. Another possible limitation for the use of RE therapy with couples would be the presence of domestic violence. However, the issues here are so complex, and the issue is of such intrinsic importance, that this topic deserves independent examination.

RE Therapy and the Assessment and Treatment of Domestic Violence

The field of domestic violence has at times been characterized by deep ideological divisions and competing paradigms (see Goldner, 1999; Greene & Bogo, 2002). This has included competing theories of domestic violence rooted in feminist theory versus systems theory on the one hand, and legal/moral perspectives versus psychological/therapeutic perspectives on the other. However, since the mid-1990s there have been hopeful signs that the field is entering a new period of synthesis and integration.

These new developments offer the prospect for a more balanced approach that takes into account the multiple complexities and variations of domestic violence. Perhaps the best summary of research and reflection in the field of domestic violence currently is Holtzworth-Munroe, Meehan, Rehman, and Marshall (2002). The account here relies heavily on their comprehensive presentation, though additional citations will be added as appropriate.

Estimates are that "one out of eight husbands engages in physical aggression against his wife" each year, with a lifetime prevalence of 30% (Holtzworth-Munroe et al., 2002, p. 442). One-third of men engage in physical aggression toward their fiancées in the year prior to marriage. Among community and young dating couples, women actually engage in slightly more physical aggression than men. The presence of physical aggression prior to marriage tends to carry over into marriage, for both men and women. It is estimated that over 50% of couples seeking marital therapy experienced physical aggression on the part of the husband during the preceding year. A survey of marital therapists and family psychologists (Whisman, Dixon, & Johnson, 1997) identified physical abuse as the most damaging problem to relationships. Collectively, these data point to the importance of identifying the presence of physical aggression or violence during a couple's clinical intake process.

One of the most important shifts in the past decade has been the growing recognition that there is no single unitary portrait of domestic violence. There is now an emerging consensus that couple aggression can and should be divided into two distinct subtypes: (1) "severe physical aggression" or "patriarchal terrorism" and (2) "mild physical aggression" or "common couple violence" (Holtzworth-Munroe et al., 2002, p. 441). Severe physical aggression is what most people think of when they hear the words *battering* or *domestic violence*. It is usually characterized by severe male violence, female self-defensive violence, high levels of female injury, male psychological intimidation and control, and female fear of male violence. However, it is becoming increasingly clear that there is a second form of couple aggression with a significantly different profile. Common couple violence tends to be bidirectional, is of mild to moderate severity, less frequent, not typically motivated by a desire for control, and does not typically result in female fear of male violence. Common couple violence tends to be found more often than severe physical aggression in couples voluntarily seeking marital therapy, whereas severe physical aggression is found more often in court-ordered and women's shelter populations. Unfortunately, most of the research in the field of domestic violence has not distinguished between these two subtypes of couple aggression, and most models of domestic violence have historically operated with a unitary model fitting the severe physical aggression subtype. This has probably indirectly contributed to and perpetuated some of the controversies in the field (see Greene & Bogo, 2002, p. 455). The good news is that this is beginning to change with the recognition that there are two distinct subtypes of couple aggression. As a result, it also is increasingly accepted that each subtype deserves both to be understood on its own terms and to have appropriate treatment protocols developed to address its unique realities and needs.

This also points to the importance of a clinician being able to identify not only the presence of couple aggression during the assessment phase of therapy, but which of the two subtypes characterizes any given couple as well. Because of the prevalence of couple aggression in couples requesting marital therapy, it is generally recommended to use a combination of a structured instrument plus joint and individual interviews to assess for the presence and degree of couple violence (Holtzworth-Munroe et al., 2002, pp. 450–451), though some practitioners in the field simply advocate an initial joint interview followed by separate interviews (see Bograd & Mederos, 1999). The immediate goal is to rule out severe physical aggression and, through the individual interviews, to provide safety to an abuse victim while screening for domestic violence (see Almeida & Durkin, 1999, p. 318). Ruling out severe violence may be done by assessing the severity and frequency of the couple's violence, resulting injuries, involvement of the police or the courts, and potential danger to children. In cases involving severe or frequent physical aggression, "the potential lethality of the situation should be assessed immediately" (Holtzworth-Munroe et al., 2002, p. 451). Practitioners interested in a detailed screening protocol of questions to ask while conducting an evaluation of the potential for domestic violence are referred to Bograd and Mederos (1999, pp. 298–303) for their comprehensive screening protocol. At the same time, the clinician should also assess factors that may be relevant to the possibility of conjoint treatment. This may be done by assessing the level of the woman's fear for her safety, each partner's acknowledgment that the physical aggression is a problem and willingness to take responsibility for his or her own actions, and each partner's motivation to enter couples therapy and to remain in the relationship. Bograd and Mederos (1999, p. 295) add to the important factors the woman's willingness to discuss the man's violent behavior in his presence, while Greene and Bogo (2002, pp. 460–461) point to a person's sense of shame over his or her violent behavior. Stith, Rosen, & McCollum (2003, p. 420) also include each partner's willingness to take responsibility "for contributing to the quality of the relationship" independent of the violence issue.

The general consensus among practitioners who specialize in the treatment of domestic violence is that conjoint treatment should not be conducted whenever severe physical aggression is present (Holtzworth-Munroe et al., 2002, p. 453). Indeed, many states prohibit couples treatment for cases involving severe domestic violence, so practitioners should always know and follow their state legal code in this matter. The principal consideration, in any case, is the preservation of safety for the female in cases of severe physical aggression, and Bograd and Mederos (1999, p. 300) add that couples therapy should not begin until the children's safety is assured. In cases of severe physical aggression, the general practice is to refer the perpetrator of severe violence to a domestic violence treatment group and the victim to an appropriate battered women's support group or advocacy service. However, it is becoming increasingly common and accepted to follow the successful completion of a domestic violence treatment program with conjoint treatment when the woman no longer feels threatened or unsafe and when both partners wish to remain together and want to improve their relationship skills (see Almeida & Durkin, 1999; Bograd & Mederos, 1999; Goldner, 1999). From the perspective of RE therapy, it would even be argued that this should become a standard part of the treatment of domestic violence, assuming that the appropriate conditions are met, because the changes in the dynamics of the relationship that can be expected from RE skills training not only should result in positive change in the couple's relationship but also should serve as a kind of relapse-prevention strategy designed to further decrease the likelihood of future episodes of interpersonal violence. Stith et al. (2003) give indirect support to this position when they observe that "failure to address marital problems at some point in the treatment" and "failing to provide services to both parties in an ongoing relationship may inadvertently disadvantage the female partner" (p. 411).

It has become increasingly common since the mid-1990s to pursue couples therapy in cases of mild physical aggression. This is because of the significant shift that has taken place in light of the recognition that the dynamics and risks associated with mild physical aggression are different from those of severe physical aggression. Alternatively, couples therapy is used as the avenue for addressing the problem of couple aggression in its milder forms (Holtzworth-Munroe et al., 2002, p. 455). One reason for this shift is the recognition that "if reciprocal violence is taking place in relationships, treating men without treating women is not likely to stop the violence" (Stith et al., 2003, p. 411). Another reason is that teaching the standard time-out procedure to couples together is likely to increase its effectiveness as a violence prevention technique (see Rosen, Matheson,

Stith, McCollum, & Locke, 2003). The reason is that this helps females overcome their frequent misgivings about the use (or abuse) of time-outs by helping them understand their purpose and by involving them as active participants in the negotiation and implementation of their use in the relationship.

When undertaking couples therapy in cases of mild physical aggression or common couple violence, three general recommendations are made. First, it is recommended that an educational approach is taken to inform the couple of the risks for increased violence if the current aggression in the relationship is not addressed and eliminated (Holtzworth-Munroe et al., 2002, p. 455). Second, it is recommended that a "no-violence" contract be made between the couple and with the therapist, and that the therapist regularly follow up on compliance. Finally, it is recommended that the therapy take a two-pronged approach of anger recognition and management followed by communication and problem-solving skills training (p. 456).

The first "prong" involves a focus on techniques for the recognition of angry feelings and the management of anger-related behaviors (pp. 456–458). The anger recognition component includes each person identifying typical physiological reactions and "hot thoughts," and then keeping logs of their experiences between sessions. The principal behavioral management strategy involves self-initiated time-outs when either partner experiences an intensification of angry feelings. That person is to give the partner a time frame for when he or she intends to return to readdress the issue. In the meantime, that person is also to engage in active self-calming strategies during the time-out period. This anger recognition and management phase of treatment is then followed by a communication and problem-solving skills training phase (pp. 458–460). This involves establishing common ground rules for skillful communication, including techniques for "nonverbal listening;" listening and paraphrasing; skillful expression of feelings; and strategies for effective problem solving, including distinguishing a problem definition phase from a problem solution phase. Recent research appears to indicate that following such a dual intervention strategy for the treatment of mild physical aggression in the context of couples therapy is an equally viable approach relative to the more traditional approach of treating each person in a gender specific treatment group (p. 461). The latter, of course, remains the treatment of choice in cases of severe physical aggression.

In light of these recent developments in the field of domestic violence, and given the recommendations for a two-pronged approach to couples treatment when dealing with common couple violence, RE therapy would appear to be an appropriate and perhaps even an ideal treatment intervention for cases of mild physical aggression. RE therapy's Conflict Management skill (see chapter 5) provides a systematic framework for addressing the very points identified by Holtzworth-Munroe et al. (2002) regarding the identification of angry feelings and the management of anger-related behaviors, including a systematic and contractually negotiated procedure for the execution of time-outs. If anything, RE's Conflict Management skill includes elements that go beyond what Holtzworth-Munroe et al. identify to be important (especially the unilateral use of empathy as a partner-calming intervention in response to a partner's angry feelings), and may therefore represent an even stronger intervention on this score. With regard to the communication and problem-solving component of a couple's aggression intervention, RE's Empathic, Expressive, Discussion/Negotiation, and Problem/Conflict Resolution skills not only match but exceed in content and scope everything that Holtzworth-Munroe et al. identify as important in these two areas. Moreover, RE therapy's emphasis on the importance of deep empathy as opposed to paraphrasing (see chapter 3) and its inclusion of explicit strategies to facilitate positive behavior change (see Self-Change and Helping-Others Change skills in chapter 12) further strengthen the case for the RE therapy model as an exceptionally strong intervention for the treatment of mild physical aggression in the context of conjoint treatment.

There is an additional consideration lending support to the utility of RE therapy as a treatment model for cases of mild physical aggression. Greene and Bogo (2002, pp. 461–463) observe that one of the reasons it is important to develop alternative treatment approaches for the unique experiences and needs of couples experiencing mild (as opposed to severe) physical aggression is that there is evidence that the primary reason why many couples drop out of various forms of treatment for domestic violence is because they do not identify with the classic batterer–victim portrait. Another reason such couples drop out is that the content of the treatment is not meeting their relationship needs, which encompass but go far beyond the mild physical aggression in the relationship. From the vantage point of these two considerations, the distinct strengths and characteristics of RE therapy may make it an ideal approach for a couples treatment model in cases of mild physical aggression because it includes an explicit focus on Conflict Management skills (that can be flexibly applied), while also devoting most of its attention to practical relationship skills and an accompanying dialogue process that allow couples to explore a wide range of issues that pertain to each couple's unique needs.

Finally, there is empirical evidence confirming the effectiveness of RE therapy in the treatment of wife abusers alone and a case study confirming its potential effectiveness in a couples format. Waldo (1986) conducted a relatively small, nonrandomized, group-based intervention for military personnel who battered their wives. The intervention involved teaching abusers unilateral applications of RE communication and problem-solving skills as well as anger management techniques. Pre- and posttest measures indicate that there were significant gains in the men's communication skills and that there was a significant reduction in the incidence of violence at the 12-week posttest and a sustaining of those lower levels at the 3-month follow-up. Waldo (1988) reported on a larger pilot study that evaluated pretrial diversion treatment of civilian abusers by comparing their recidivism rates with those of untreated batterers. Of 154 men arrested for assault or battery of their wives or female cohabitants, 46 accepted referral to a treatment program as an alternative to legal proceedings, 49 declined the treatment option, and 59 were not offered the alternative treatment option because of lack of familiarity with the program on the part of some of the state attorney's office staff. Thirty men from each condition were randomly selected for comparison. Following completion of a unilateral RE group program for abusive men that included both communication and problem-solving skills as well as anger management training, outcomes were assessed by checking court records 1 year after each individual's arrest. The two untreated groups each had a 20% recidivism rate, whereas the RE treatment group had a 0% recidivism rate. Finally, a case study report involving an RE couples group therapy format (Guerney, Waldo, & Firestone, 1987) for abusers and their wives or female cohabitants in a suburban Washington, DC, crisis center showed promise for a couples-based group intervention to treat physical abuse. Three of four couples completing the program experienced a cessation of violence and a reduction of female fear at posttest; the fourth couple decided to proceed with a divorce that had already been initiated. The 8-week follow-up revealed no incidents of violence and no recurrence of fears of violent behaviors for the female partners in the three remaining couples.

To summarize, the most recent research and clinical practice in the field of domestic violence suggests that in cases of severe physical violence separate treatment for abusers and victims remains the (initial) treatment of choice. In cases of mild physical aggression, however, conjoint treatment involving a dual focus on anger recognition and management training and communication and problem-solving skills training is increasingly regarded as a legitimate treatment option. Even in cases of severe physical violence, however, conjoint treatment may legitimately be considered (depending on state regulations or codes) (1) following successful treatment of a domestic violence treatment program by the abuser, (2) with the consent of both partners, and (3) when the female does not fear for her safety. Alternatively, a case could be made for teaching unilateral applications of RE to separate gender-based groups in cases of severe physical violence so that both batterers and victims receive the benefits of the RE model. In addition, RE therapy meets or exceeds all the stipulated criteria and content for an effective couples therapy intervention in cases of mild physical aggression, and preliminary research suggests that RE therapy can be effective either in a unilateral group format for abusers alone or in a couples group therapy format. It appears reasonable to conclude that RE therapy would likely be effective in a solo couples therapy format in cases involving the treatment of mild physical aggression.

How the RE Model Relates to the Research of John Gottman

John Gottman's research since the mid-1970s represents one of the important contributions to the field of couples and marital therapy. The research derived from his now famous "Love Lab" has shed light on both the negative and positive dynamics in couples' relationships, enabling him to construct a theory of what works and what doesn't work as well as a framework for understanding why marriages succeed or fail (Gottman, 1994). He has since developed his own therapy model for treating relationships that are in trouble in *The Marriage Clinic* (1999). Both are valuable contributions, though it should be noted that the research stands independent of his own treatment model in that the latter is grounded in but is not identical to the former.

The significance of this last point is that Gottman's research, as research, may lend indirect support to other treatment models to the extent that their assumptions and intervention strategies are consonant with the results of his research. It is my belief that this is exactly what Gottman's research does relative to the RE therapy model: It lends indirect support to the RE model and helps explain some of the elements of its empirical validation and clinical effectiveness. Given the exemplary depth and reach of Gottman's research, an entire chapter could be written on this topic alone. However, I will limit myself to highlighting some of the ways in which his research helps explain why RE therapy is effective.

One of Gottman's most famous notions, stemming from his empirical research on "negative affect reciprocity," is his metaphor of "The Four Horsemen of the Apocalypse" (1999, pp. 41–48). This metaphor refers to the four "most corrosive" negative behaviors in an intimate relationship: criticism, defensiveness, contempt, and stonewalling. Criticism refers to what I would summarily call "global character assassinations." Gottman defines defensiveness as "any attempt to defend oneself from a perceived attack," typically manifesting as "countercomplaining or counterattacking," and designed to deflect the perceived attack. Contempt refers to any behavior or statement that implies one's superiority relative to the other person, which may take the form of mockery or condescension. Gottman's research also indicates that contempt turns out to be the "single best predictor of divorce" (p. 47). Stonewalling involves "the listener's withdrawal from the interaction." The paradoxical nature of stonewalling is that it represents a form of physiological "self-soothing" for the person who withdraws (usually the male) but a physiologically arousing, "aversive" experience for the other partner (usually the female). As Gottman notes, criticism starts off a negative sequence that in the worst cases results in the cascading of the other three negative behaviors, culminating in stonewalling. The goal, according to Gottman, is to facilitate "repair attempts" when the negative sequence occurs.

From the very inception of the RE model, the Expressive skill was designed to help couples eliminate from their behavioral repertoire precisely the kinds of negative behaviors that characterize the Four Horsemen. Not that there is any illusion that a given couple will never again indulge in such negative behavior, but one of the primary goals of the Expressive skill is to teach couples how to address important issues in their relationship without causing the other person to needlessly feel defensive as a result of unskillful attacks on the other person's character. Indeed, from this vantage point, the RE model's Expressive skill functions as a *preventative tool* designed to reduce the need for repair attempts by helping couples learn how to avoid up front the initiation of the negative sequence that Gottman has so effectively described. This involves teaching couples alternative, skillful ways of communicating their feelings, concerns, and desires fully and honestly, but in a manner that simultaneously avoids eliciting defensiveness and conveys caring and compassion for the other person.

Another of the valuable insights that Gottman derives from his research is the importance of the initiator of a complaint using a "softened start-up" (Gottman, 1999, pp. 224–227). By this he means that the partner wishing to initiate a conversation about a potentially difficult topic is well advised to do so in a manner that makes it easier for the other partner to hear. This also has been one of the distinguishing features of the RE model's Expressive skill. At a general level, every Expressive skill guideline is oriented toward promoting "softened start-up" (see chapter 7). It is interesting to note, in this context, that Gottman's "Rules for Softened Start-Up" are in many respects similar to the RE Expressive skill guidelines. More specifically, however, the Expressive skill guidelines' encouragement of the use of "underlying positives," has been one of the most important and distinguishing features of the RE model. This is because it both helps create a positive, cooperative atmosphere at the beginning of a dialogue and helps sustain a positive atmosphere throughout a dialogue by its continued use.

Even though prevention is at least as important a goal, Gottman's concept of repair attempts referred to above is a useful idea in its own right (1999, pp. 48–51). This refers to either partner's attempt to respond to an escalation of negative emotion, or emotional flooding, in a manner designed to deescalate it. Gottman's research indicates that the success of a marriage is in no small part tied to the success of repair attempts, which can take many forms in response to an escalation of negative emotion. One of the most important of these is what Gottman refers to as "soothing," which can take the form of self-soothing or soothing one's partner. Gottman mostly discusses various strategies of self-soothing, such as deep breathing and time-outs, with some attention given to the importance of interpersonal soothing in the form of a woman's ability to use humor to help defuse the man's heightened negative emotion (p. 85).

RE therapy actively promotes self-soothing under the Conflict Management skill (see chapter 5 and below). But one of the hallmarks of RE therapy is that it devotes a considerable amount of time and attention to teaching couples how to facilitate interpersonal soothing. The most important strategy that the RE model teaches couples for the purpose of interpersonal soothing in the face of heightened emotion or flooding is the use of empathy (see chapter 5, Conflict Management scenario 2). It is interesting to observe, in this context, that Gottman (1999, p. 275) makes reference to "empathy [being] central to soothing one's partner," yet he devotes no time to actually teaching or encouraging the use of empathy as a distinct intervention for couples to use for the purpose of soothing the partner's heightened negative emotions. From the perspective of RE therapy, the use of deep empathy is one of the most powerful tools available for one partner to use to soothe the emotions of the other. Teaching couples how to employ empathy in this way is one of the most important things that any intervention model can accomplish. Moreover, when couples use empathy in this way it adds to their "emotional bank account" in that one partner is "turning toward" rather than "turning away" from the other when empathizing in the face of the other person's strong emotion. This turning toward the other can also contribute to an increase in "positive sentiment override." In both these ways, RE therapy thus fosters building layers of what Gottman refers to as a couple's "sound marital house" (p. 105).

Another finding from Gottman's research concerns the importance of the male accepting influence from his wife (1999, pp. 51–56). The failure to accept influence, according to Gottman, is a reliable predictor of the likelihood of divorce. Accepting influence involves being responsive to a partner's complaints and working toward finding common ground. The RE model agrees with Gottman about the importance of accepting influence in marriage. From the perspective of the RE model, however, the accepting of influence ideally is mutual in that accepting influence is a sign of respect in an intimate relationship and is a concrete way of embodying the value of the relationship as an entity that transcends either individual. More to the point, however, the RE model recognizes that the ability to be influenced by another person phenomenologically presupposes the ability to be empathic with that person's feelings, concerns, and desires. This points to yet another reason for the importance of the RE model's focus on actively teaching and coaching intimate partners how to be empathic experientially and how to give good verbal empathy. It also demonstrates how the practice of RE therapy is consonant with the results of Gottman's research.

Two additional aspects of Gottman's research are worth mentioning briefly with respect to the RE model. The first is the importance of positive affect in a marriage; the second is the importance of being able to reduce negative affect during conflicts. Both of these represent important elements that contribute to Gottman's "sound marital house" (1999, p. 105). With respect to positive affect, the RE model fosters its development by encouraging a number of couple's activities that also add to a couple's emotional bank account: daily partner appreciations; daily connection time; fun time at least weekly; and less frequent but regularly scheduled special couple's activities, like weekend getaways and vacations (see chapter 14). With respect to reducing negative affect, RE's Conflict Management skill teaches four distinct Conflict Management interventions to deal with the effective regulation of both emotion and behavior, including: requesting a dialogue when emotions first flare, spontaneously empathizing with an upset partner, initiating a time-out from an unskilled argument, and self-initiating a time-out when a person recognizes that his or her own emotions are flaring (see chapter 5).

Finally, Gottman advocates couples' dialogues as essential to the maintenance of sound marital relationships, especially with reference to "perpetual problems" (1999, p. 186). Intimate dialogues are at the absolute center of the RE therapy process and are designed to foster deepened understanding, intimacy, and acceptance, just as Gottman advocates. One key difference, however, is that the RE model systematically teaches couples *how* to dialogue in a skillful way. This is one of the distinct advantages of RE as a psychoeducational treatment model, because it empowers couples to have a better relationship by teaching them how to achieve it.

Also, with regard to relationship problems, the RE model advocates that couples revisit and evaluate solutions via dialogue until a permanent satisfactory resolution is found and fully integrated into the relationship. In the case of perpetual problems, this means initiating dialogues on a regular basis to help ensure that couples are trying to make such problems livable.

There are many more comparisons that could be made between Gottman's research and the practice of RE therapy, including how RE fosters other elements of a couple's "sound marital house." But this should be sufficient to make the basic point that the RE therapy model is consonant with the results and the implications of Gottman's empirical research.

Notes

1. It also is worth observing in this context that another meta-analytic study (Hahlweg & Markman, 1998) confirmed the superiority of a premarital RE program (ES = 1.14) to both Couple Communication (ES = .71) and PREP (ES = .61) premarital programs.

2. Giblin et al. (1985, p. 262) venture that the correlation is "significant but probably meaningless." However, as Guerney and Maxson (1990, p. 1131) observe in their evaluation of the Giblin meta-analysis, "The relationship was weak (r = −.10), but since all programs were at least moderately structured, variability and, therefore, the size of the correlation might be artificially low." In other words, the highly structured nature of an intervention may be a more significant variable than the data was able to reveal.

CHAPTER 3

Deep Empathy as the Foundation
of RE Therapy

Empathy is central to RE therapy in two ways. First, it is the foundation of much of what the therapist does in the practice of RE therapy. Second, it is the foundational skill of the couple's dialogue process and one of the keys to fostering understanding, acceptance, and intimacy in a couple's relationship. In what follows, I offer an interpretation of empathy that is rooted in Rogers and Guerney, but goes beyond either in its conceptual elaboration.

The Opportunity and Challenge of Empathy

Empathy simultaneously represents a compelling opportunity and a difficult challenge. The opportunity is that our shared humanity makes empathy possible and calls us to make an empathic connection out of respect, compassion, and love. Conversely, the realization of empathy is a validation of our shared humanity. But empathy also represents a challenge: every one of us as human beings is unique—as individuals; as male or female; and as a member of ethnic, cultural, racial, religious, and other subgroups. This uniqueness represents the irreducible otherness that we encounter in each other. As Cavedo and Guerney observe (1999), certain stances toward the other perpetuate and reinforce the sense of the other person's "separateness and differentness," and by implication, are intrinsically nonempathic. The stance of genuine empathy, on the other hand, involves an attempt at "a total *identification* with the speaker" in the form of "an erasure of a sense of differentness and separateness" (pp. 78–79; emphasis in original).

I completely agree with Guerney about the goal of empathy in the moment of its enactment, which is to bridge and, to the extent possible, overcome the chasm of otherness that separates us by identifying totally with the experience of the other on the other person's terms. I believe that it is also important to hold in tandem, and perhaps even in tension, with this essential goal of empathy the recognition that your experience is irreducibly unique to you and to who you are, and that it is different from my experience and who I am. To acknowledge our differentness in the midst of recovering and reclaiming our shared humanity is also, I believe, a sign of respect on the part of one human being toward another. It is also about recognizing that it is not an either–or, but a both–and situation. It is not about our differentness versus our shared humanity; it is about our differentness within our shared humanity, or our shared humanity within our differentness. When both our shared humanity and our differentness are embraced, and the embracing is mutual, then, I believe, genuine acceptance becomes possible. Were this mutual embracing of our shared humanity and our differentness to be practiced on a global level, then we would have a meaningful chance of achieving what the Vietnamese Buddhist monk Thich Nhat Hanh (2003) calls "true peace." That is the deepest opportunity that empathy offers.

Understanding Deep Empathy

Empathy often is misunderstood, both conceptually and in terms of application and technique. Empathy is comprised of two distinct components. On the one hand, there is the experiential process or act of becoming empathic with another person by means of imaginatively identifying with that person's experience at both the cognitive and emotional levels. On the other hand, there is the giving of good verbal empathy. Clearly, a person cannot give good verbal empathy unless that person has first made a genuine empathic connection with the other person. Yet, many theorists and practitioners in effect talk only about the verbal side of empathy and essentially ignore the more foundational and experiential process of *becoming* empathic with the internal experience of another human being.

This combined overemphasis on the verbal side of empathy, together with a neglect of its imaginative–experiential side, is reflected in some of the ways that empathy is typically described. One of the most common metaphors for empathy is that of "mirroring." This is a most unfortunate metaphor because, if taken literally (as it sometimes is), it involves simply repeating or reflecting back to the Expresser whatever has been said. Rogers himself (1962, p. 161) explicitly rejected the description of empathy as one person "reflect[ing] back what the [other person] has just said." As a consequence, the concept of "reflective listening" also is a poor way of representing what empathy involves. Nor is empathy well represented by the notion of paraphrasing what has been expressed, as advocated in many models of "active listening." While paraphrasing may be regarded as one step better than just repeating back to the Expresser what has been said, paraphrasing still fails to capture the deeper dimension of empathy.

Part of what is problematic about each of these of ways of describing empathy is that they place too much emphasis on expressing verbal empathy while overlooking the phenomenological essence of the experience and the act of *becoming* empathic, which is to imagine oneself into another person's experience in a deep way. This overemphasis on the verbal aspect of expressing empathy engenders a second problem, namely, a tendency to place too much emphasis on memorizing and simply repeating back (at its worst, in a rote way) the cognitive content of a person's self-expression, to the neglect of the vitally important and deeper emotional dimensions of that person's experience. Taken together, these two problems weaken not just our understanding of empathy, but its clinical and psychoeducational applications as well. When little or no attention is given to what it means to empathize deeply at the experiential level with another person and how to accomplish that, then the result is likely to be a focus on "techniques" that will almost certainly result in a diminution of genuine empathy into mere paraphrasing or, even worse, mirroring. The difficulty is that empathy is not a technique; it is first and foremost an experiential process of identifying with the experience of another person.

What the experiential process or act of becoming empathic with another person involves, phenomenologically, is to experience things from the other person's point of view; to see things as the other person sees them; to feel what the other person feels, including grasping the nuances of those feelings; to identify with the other person's inner conflicts and ambivalence as experienced by that person; to connect with the other person's deepest concerns and desires; and through them to connect with a person's core values and goals in life. This is what is meant by *deep empathy*: connecting with the other person's experience, feelings, concerns, and desires in all their breadth and depth, on the other person's terms.[1]

This deep empathic connection is best facilitated by the self surrendering itself in the moment (and act) of empathizing in order to enter experientially into the life-world of the other person on that person's terms. The etymology of the word *empathy* is enlightening in this regard: The German word for empathy, *einfühlung*, literally signifies "in-feeling," that is, "feeling one's way into," or entering into, the experience of the other. The old saying about "walking in another person's moccasins" also is revealing. The point of that saying is that one person cannot understand another person's experience unless he or she first steps into the other person's shoes, and then walks around in that person's world, imaginatively being that person, having that person's experience. This is in contrast to someone, in the role of Listener/Empathizer, imagining him- or herself in the other person's circumstances, but still being oneself. Empathy is *not* about what I might feel or do were I in your circumstances. This is a mistaken notion of empathy, and runs the dual risk of perpetuating the Listener/ Empathizer in the stance of an external observer looking at the other person from the outside in or the Listener/Empathizer projecting him- or herself onto the other person. Instead, in genuine empathy, the Empathizer so enters into and identifies with the other person's experience from the inside out that it is as though the Empathizer has become that person and is having his or her experience. This is accomplished by the Empathizer not evaluating or judging the other person from his or her own point of view, but instead surrendering (or emptying) the self in a manner that enables the Empathizer to be selflessly present to the experience of the other person, without the Empathizer's own experience, judgments, or self-preoccupations getting in the way. All too often, however, the listener's feelings, preferences, opinions, concerns, desires, goals, and values—all those things with which the ego-self tends to be preoccupied—do get in the way and at the extreme reinforce egocentricity. This, in turn, can make it almost impossible for the listener to experience things from the other person's point of view. (It is no accident, in this context, that one of the key characteristics of narcissistic personality disorder is the inability to empathize with another person's experience.)

It is also important to observe, in this context, that empathy makes no presumption about the Empathizer having had an experience similar to that of the other person. Indeed, empathy presupposes the ability to empathize with another person *without* having had a similar experience. Moreover, it is arguable that having had a similar experience can be counterproductive in that it becomes an impediment to deeply empathizing with the other person's experience *from that person's point of view*. The reason is that empathy is not about the experienced event per se, but about the *meaning* a person attaches to an event. So, if I believe that I have had an experience similar to yours as I am listening to you share your experience (such as the death of a loved one), I could fall into the trap of imagining that the *meaning* that I attach to my experience is similar to the *meaning* that you attach to your experience. As a consequence, the risk that I project my subjective experience onto you, and thereby totally miss the unique meaning of your experience from your point of view, is greatly increased.

This can be helpfully elucidated from the perspective of Buddhist psychology, where the self's preoccupation with itself is regarded as a false attachment to a mental construct that distorts the fundamental truth that *there is no distance between me and you,* that there is only the space and the relationship between us which, when surrendered to in a moment of enlightened nonattachment—that is, in a moment of relational selflessness—reveals that there is no separate "me" or "you" but only the connection between us. The resulting state of nondualistic "emptiness" permits the making of an empathic connection with another person's experience in such a way that the Empathizer is able, in the moment of surrendering preoccupation with the self, to enter into the other person's experience so completely that the Empathizer metaphorically "becomes" the other person and experiences his or her experience as though the Empathizer *were* the other person.[2] The experiential quality of the act of empathizing thus involves the Empathizer surrendering preoccupation with the self and entering into the other person's life-world and experience in such a manner that the self fades away and the Empathizer selflessly "becomes" the other person by identifying with the immediacy of that person's experience. Then, having become empathic—that is, having metaphorically become the other person, having that person's experience—the Empathizer is able to give voice to that experience from the inside out.

A clarification is in order. Despite the language of selflessly surrendering the self in such a manner that the Empathizer metaphorically becomes the other person while empathizing, it is important to recognize that this is a temporary state of affairs. In effect, the Empathizer chooses to become selfless in the moment for the sake of connecting with and understanding the other person's experience, and in this way helps the other person feel understood and perhaps even deepens his or her self-understanding. As Rogers puts it (1962), the act of empathizing carries an "as if" quality to it: *as though* I become you. This means that in the moment of empathizing, in my becoming selflessly present to and establishing an experiential connection with your experience, the distance between the two of us temporarily disappears; but at the conclusion of the *act* of empathizing, I surrender my selflessness and return to being myself. This helps ensure that the act of empathizing does not involve an unconscious blurring of ego boundaries between me (the Empathizer) and you (the other person), because at the end of empathizing you remain you and I return to being me. What we hope has transpired in the meantime is that both of us have gained deeper insight into your experience and the emotional distance between us has been diminished because you feel understood by me, and you no longer seem so "foreign" to me. In this sense, the act of empathizing results in an enlargement of my life-world by virtue of my having made contact with your experience. In other words, by my entering empathically into your experience I am in turn touched by and transformed by your experience. Indeed, at its furthest reaches, our respective empathic connection with one another's experience enriches and transforms each of us. This may be understood simultaneously to be one of the goals and one of the benefits of deep empathy.

Now we can turn to the second part of empathy, which involves giving good verbal empathy to the person being empathized with, and doing so from the inside out, as though one were that person. In practice, this involves going beyond what the other person actually says about his or her experience and reading between the lines in such a way that the Empathizer is able to identify deeper dimensions of the other person's experience as well as the meaning or significance it holds for that person. From a different angle, in reading between the lines, the Empathizer is seeking to identify the unstated but implied meaning of the other person's experience.[3] In contrast to mirroring, with its implied literal reflecting back of what the Expresser has shared, deep empathy involves reading between the lines of another person's self-disclosure in a manner that permits one to fill in the blank spaces imaginatively or add additional content by way of giving back to the Expresser an enhanced or deepened version of his or her experience. When the Empathizer is able to imagine him- or herself into the other person's experience and successfully read between the lines, the reading between the lines will immediately be recognized as valid and be accepted by the Expresser as though he had verbalized it himself.

This imaginative reading between the lines can take a variety of forms, such as surfacing the Expresser's unstated feelings; identifying inner conflicts or ambivalence the Expresser may be experiencing; making explicit the Expresser's concerns, goals, or desires; or explicitly identifying the Expresser's intended course of action (see Empathic skill guideline 4, chapter 6). Snyder also suggests tuning in to that person's emerging "meanings that are [in the process of] being formulated" as well as "the growing edge of the individual's struggle to develop a stronger adaptation to the world" (1992b, p. 321). This nicely captures a not easily apprehended aspect of the texture of human experience: A person's experience often is in the process of unfolding in ways that are not yet fully settled and remains open to future influence and changes in direction while it is unfolding. But this simply opens the door to another valuable way of reading between the lines, because in representing the Expresser as being in process and as not yet having reached resolution, the Empathizer may help that person gain clarity about the direction he or she might wish to take.

A deep empathic representation that successfully reads between the lines accomplishes three important things for the Expresser: First, it leaves the Expresser feeling deeply understood and accepted by the Empathizer; second, it enhances the Expresser's self-understanding because the Expresser will have been presented with a deeper, richer version of his or her experience; third, it encourages the Expresser to go deeper in exploring and sharing his or her experience. By having identified with and given voice to the Expresser's experience, well-executed empathy also accomplishes something vitally important for the Empathizer: It helps the Empathizer better understand the Expresser's feelings, concerns, and desires, and thereby dissipates negative feelings and increases receptivity to the Expresser's point of view. We can hypothesize a neuropsychological and neurolinguistic basis for this impact of empathy on the Empathizer; the overt verbalization of empathy creates a change in the Empathizer's neural pathways that reconfigures that person's understanding of the Expresser and his or her experience, and the issue at hand. This increased receptivity is concretely reflected in structured dialogues in that the Empathizer (following a formal role change that permits that person to become the newly designated Expresser) often ends up expressing something quite different to the previous Expresser than would have been the case in the absence of empathizing. This indirectly points to another benefit of empathy for the Empathizer, namely, that it fosters compassion for the other person and his or her experience because the Empathizer is now better able to see things from the other person's point of view. When engaged in by both parties, the compassion that is generated by the process of mutual empathizing tends to foster a deepened sense of connection, emotional bonding, and, when relevant, healing in the relationship.

There is one additional benefit of the process of empathizing that is worth observing: The dialogical requirement that the Empathizer first empathize with what the designated Expresser has expressed before expressing his or her own point of view inhibits the otherwise prevalent tendency on the part of the listener to respond reactively to what the designated Expresser has said. This structural obligation to first empathize before expressing oneself also helps slow down the entire dialogue process and creates a calmer and safer atmosphere for both parties. This makes it easier for both parties to become empathic and give good verbal empathy, because ego defensiveness is less likely to have become activated. This, in turn, makes it easier for the partners to address their issues constructively and resolve them more expeditiously.

A Reply to Gottman's Challenge to Teaching Empathy in Marital Therapy

In his book *The Marriage Clinic* (1999) and in a now famous essay written with several colleagues (Gottman, Coan, Carrere, & Swanson, 1998), Gottman argues that teaching couples how to give verbal empathy to one another in the midst of a conflict (he actually refers to paraphrasing and empathic validation), is beside the point when it comes to improving distressed couples' relationships, and therefore should be abandoned in the practice of marital therapy. The basis for this argument, according to Gottman, is that research on the interactional patterns of newlywed couples (in the context of a longitudinal study of factors contributing to marital stability and instability) revealed that while the couples were dealing with a conflict issue (under observation), few of them paraphrased what the spouse said or validated the spouse's feelings.

This is a striking argument, and has generated serious discussion in the field (see Gottman, Coan, Carrere, & Swanson, 2000; Stanley, Bradbury, & Markman, 2000). Without reviewing that discussion per se, I would like to address several problems with Gottman's argument because of its direct relevance to the theory and practice of RE therapy. First, however, a preliminary observation. It is clear from Gottman's presentation (Gottman et al., 1998, pp. 7–8; Gottman, 1999, pp. 8–11) that he does not differentiate between the use of paraphrasing in an active listening model as practiced by PREP (and others) and a deep empathy model as used in RE therapy. RE is in agreement with Gottman that "active listening skills such as paraphrasing" (Stanley, Blumberg, & Markman, 1999, p. 284) are not very helpful clinically. Yet, Gottman lumps the RE approach to deep empathy together with the active listening model's use of paraphrasing under a generalized rubric of "empathizing." That issue aside, there are several serious problems with Gottman's argument challenging the relevance of teaching empathy to distressed couples in marital therapy.

First, Gottman commits a serious error in logic when he claims that it is irrelevant to teach distressed couples how to empathize in order to help them improve their relationships *because* couples do not "naturally" empathize with one another when faced with a serious conflict or negative emotion. This argument represents a version of the naturalistic fallacy, that is, making the mistake of assuming that because something is not observed in a "natural" state of affairs it therefore is not important. Gottman's argument is analogous to saying that because two preschool-aged children have been observed successfully dividing four apples equally between them, they have no need to learn long division. Gottman's observational research of "natural" couples therefore is irrelevant to the question of whether couples in distress would benefit from learning empathy skills.

Second, Gottman's argument about empathy is limited to the second part of empathy previously identified, namely, the giving of verbal empathy to the Expresser. In the process, he overlooks the primary and in the long run much more important part of empathy, namely, the experiential process or act of one person tuning in empathically to another person's experience. Moreover, when Gottman argues that one predictor of marital happiness and stability is that the husband be open to being influenced by his wife, that argument logically presupposes the husband's ability to be empathic with his wife in the primary experiential sense of empathy. The reason is that it is far more difficult to be open to being influenced by another's desire unless that person has first, at least implicitly, empathically understood the other person's desire.

Third is an equally important methodological point that Gottman overlooks. Being empathically attuned to one's spouse, which presumably would be one of the characteristics of "happy, stable couples," also precludes the necessity of having to *verbally* empathize with each other's concerns or complaints because a natural empathic responsiveness that leads one to accept influence is already operative. So it is no wonder that Gottman and his colleagues' study of newlywed couples' interactional patterns failed to reveal the active use of *verbal* empathy on the part of happy, stable couples.

Fourth, Gottman is in conflict with himself. He argues, on the one hand, that a husband's willingness to be influenced by his wife is one predictor of a happy, stable marriage. Yet, he argues that there is no point to the use of empathy training in marital therapy for distressed relationships, where, presumably, one's unwillingness to be influenced by one's spouse is a major factor contributing to the distress. But this unwillingness to be influenced by one's spouse likely is rooted in large part in an inability to empathize with the spouse's experience. Thus, Gottman in effect is advocating that marital therapists deprive themselves of the one tool, the teaching of empathy, that stands the best chance of helping that spouse *actually learn how to become empathic and therefore become receptive* to being influenced by his or her spouse, as opposed to an empty admonition to "just be more receptive to listening to and being influenced by your spouse."

A fifth observation: Gottman implies that it is unrealistic and even unnatural to expect couples to empathize directly with one another in the face of a conflict because it involves "a form of emotional gymnastics" (1999, p. 10). The further implication of Gottman's argument is that couples are incapable of learning how to empathize with one another, either experientially or verbally. That implication is quite a stretch. Like any skill, empathy is capable of being learned, regardless of whether couples do it "naturally." Some of the outcome research on the RE model cited in chapter 2 validates that. What matters, in practice, is the motivation and commitment to learn, together with the requisite effort. Effective modeling and intensive coached skills practice, as is done in RE therapy, increase the odds of a successful outcome.

In conclusion, despite the creativity and usefulness of much of the empirical research conducted by Gottman, his interpretation of the results of that research and its meaning with regard to empathy is seriously flawed. More to the point, Gottman's inference and claim, that marital therapy should "abandon" teaching distressed couples how to empathize for the purpose of improving their relationship, is in no way legitimated by the research itself. It also is contradicted by some of Gottman's own assumptions, as well as the results of his own research.

The Two Modes of Empathy

Virtually all couples therapies and psychoeducational programs that teach empathy or active listening techniques involve teaching what can be referred to as the conventional You Mode of empathy. This involves the Listener/ Empathizer using the pronoun *you* to represent the experience of the Speaker/Expresser. So if Sally were to say to her husband, "I'm really torn up about our son having separated himself from us in the aftermath of your affair and his being so depressed that he's unable to make use of his great talents or do anything constructive with his life," then an empathic response by her husband Larry might be something like the following: "You're really sad about Dave and where he is in his life because he has so much to offer and he's not making use of his many gifts. You're also heartbroken about his not talking to us and you're angry at me because my affair played such a large part in his disenchantment with us. But what you're really wanting is for him to open the door to us so that he can be a part of our lives again." This way of verbally empathizing by using the pronoun *you* is the conventional form of empathy, and it generally serves its basic purpose.

There is, however, an alternative form of empathy that Guerney has termed the "Identification Method" or "I Mode" of empathy (Guerney, 1999b; Guerney, Nordling, & Scuka, 2000; Snyder & Guerney, 1999). In the Identification Method, the Listener/Empathizer uses the pronoun *I* to represent the experience of the Speaker/Expresser as though the Empathizer *were* the Expresser. In other words, the Empathizer temporarily assumes the identity of the Expresser and gives voice to the Expresser's experience from the inside out by speaking as though the Empathizer were the

Expresser. So, for example, Larry might empathize with his wife by temporarily assuming her identity and giving voice to her experience in the following way: "As Sally, I'm incredibly distressed about our son and really worried about Dave's emotional well-being. He had so much going for him; it saddens me that he's not doing anything with his life because he's so depressed. And it really breaks my heart that Dave won't have anything to do with us. And it's all because of your affair. I may be able to get over the affair, but I'm not certain he'll ever get over it. If only we could find a way of reaching out to him. Then, maybe, he'd open the door to us so that we can be a whole family again." Notice that this latter empathic representation feels less mechanical and more alive than the previous example of empathizing, which utilizes the conventional You Mode. This is because the Identification Mode of empathy tends to foster a deeper sense of identification with the experience of the Expresser in the form of a vivid image in the mind of the Empathizer. This in turn permits the Empathizer to present a richer empathic representation of that experience back to the Expresser.

This Identification Mode of empathy originally was developed as a time-limited teaching tool to facilitate couples (and families) learning the Empathic skill in either RE therapy or RE psychoeducational programs (Snyder & Guerney, 1993). The rationale for having people experiment with using the Identification Mode of empathy while learning the Empathic skill is that it more clearly reveals that empathy is fundamentally an experiential process of identifying with the other person's experience by imagining one's self being the other person, having the other person's experience. As a result, using the Identification Mode of empathy as part of the skills training usually facilitates a deeper, quicker, and more intuitive empathic connection with the other person than is typical with the conventional You Mode of empathy. (For an example of a demonstration of empathy using the Identification Mode, see chapter 6.)

The principal reason the Identification Mode takes people deeper experientially into a genuine empathic connection with another person is that it overcomes the implicit distance between the Empathizer and the Expresser that the conventional You Mode of empathy still implies. Every time "I" empathize with "your" experience using the conventional You Mode of empathy, it indirectly reinforces my self as the (external) point of reference between the two of us. This subtly reinforces the tendency for me to regard your experience as different from mine, and further encourages me to keep your experience psychologically at a distance. In practice, this paradoxically makes my genuinely connecting with your experience potentially more difficult. This also runs counter to the very intent of empathy which, as previously noted, is to experience things from the other person's point of view, as the other person experiences them, that is, with the meaning the other person attaches to the experience. The Identification Mode of empathy, whereby the Empathizer temporarily assumes the other person's identity and reenacts that person's experience as though the Empathizer were the Expresser, thus better captures the experiential core of empathy.

From this perspective, the Identification Mode of empathy could be said to represent an experiential exercise in relational selflessness that fosters the making of a deeper empathic connection. The reason is that the Identification Mode of empathy overcomes the implicit dualism of the conventional You Mode by virtue of its embodying more fully a stance of selfless identification with the experience of the other person in the moment of becoming empathic. In effect, I enter your experience in such a way that both you and I are in your experience, and so the distance between us has momentarily evaporated because we are both walking around in your moccasins, having your experience—you literally, and I vicariously. By contrast, the conventional You Mode of empathy can indirectly perpetuate a psychological distance between the Empathizer and the other person's experience in that the very form of the empathy itself reinforces that there is an "I" in contrast to the "*you*" with whom "I" am trying to identify. The nondualistic nature of the Identification Mode of empathy—whereby "I" vicariously become "you" in the moment of empathic identification so that there is no separate "I" or "you" because we are both occupying the space of your experience—thus facilitates the making of a deeper empathic connection and in this sense constitutes a deeper mode of empathizing. The Identification Mode of empathy thus phenomenologically and experientially grounds the conventional You Mode of empathy. Stated conversely, the You Mode of empathy, though more conventional in usage, represents a derivative mode of empathy in that it is phenomenologically dependent upon what the Identification Mode of empathy represents and embodies in its very essence.

As a result of fostering a deeper empathic connection and sense of identification with the experience of the Expresser, the Identification Mode of empathy also tends to foster a richer empathic representation of the Expresser's experience on the part of the Empathizer. A significant part of the reason for this has to do with the Empathizer temporarily assuming the identity of the Expresser and speaking out of the Expresser's experience as though the Empathizer were the Expresser. This helps the Empathizer *feel* the Expresser's experience more directly, from the inside out. This has the effect of liberating the Empathizer to experience and give voice to spontaneous realizations about the Expresser's experience that emerge out of the very act of "becoming" the other person and living in his or her world as though one were that person, having that person's experience. And it is, in part, the spontaneous quality of these new realizations about the experience of the Expresser, and how they are creatively given voice, that gives the empathic representation such power. This power can be enhanced by modulating one's tone of voice and the use of inflections; using vivid metaphors; and either intensifying one's emotional expressivity or, in some cases, providing a more dispassionate presentation that lessens the intensity of felt emotion. At its deepest level of impact, the spontaneity and power conveyed by means of an I-Mode empathic representation can engender a quasi-hypnotic or trancelike state which reinforces the healing impact of the empathic representation for the person whose experience is being represented. I believe this also helps explain how it is that an I-Mode empathic representation can become "the channel for the flow of [interpersonal] empathy" that Barrett-Lennard (1993, p. 8) suggests is the true "active ingredient" of empathy.

Indeed, being the recipient of an empathic representation in which the Identification Mode of empathy is creatively employed tends to have an exceedingly powerful impact on the person whose experience is being represented. When the empathic representation is both spontaneously rendered and on target, the Expresser usually feels understood at a very deep level. More often than not, that person also experiences deepened self-understanding. Part of the reason for this powerful impact is that the experience of seeing oneself portrayed by someone else gives the person whose experience is being represented the opportunity to observe him- or herself in a qualitatively unique way that creates a form of self-distancing, not unlike the effect created by the psychodrama technique of role reversal (Moreno, 1985). At the same time, the person whose experience is being represented in this way frequently reconnects with the experience in a deeper, more immediate way: "It was as though I could see myself there again," reported one man who had a trancelike experience after having his childhood experience represented to him via the Identification Mode of empathy. It is not uncommon for people to have totally new insights or revelations, or to genuinely *feel* the experience in a qualitatively richer way when they have their experience represented back to them in this way, as reported by one woman, "When my husband told my story back to me, I could see myself as a little girl, and I started to cry."

At its most profound level, the person whose experience is being represented in this manner may also experience a release from negative emotions. This is because he or she is able to apprehend the experience in an emotionally neutral way that has the effect of transforming the person's relationship to the experience and robbing it of its lingering emotional residue. One woman described how, in a rather complex fashion, she found herself empathizing with the therapist's empathic representation of her experience and that this form of self-empathy was very healing for her in that it helped her release some of the feelings that she had been carrying for many years. What happened, in effect, was that she experienced a kind of detachment from her experience that was emotionally liberating. The Identification Mode of empathy thus has profound benefits for both the Empathizer and the person whose experience is being represented. For the Empathizer, it tends to deepen the quality of the empathic connection and thereby enables that person to better represent the experience of the other party; for the person whose experience is being represented, it tends to deepen the quality of the connection with one's own experience in a manner that is generative of new self-understanding or emotional healing.

Becoming

Becoming is one of four special RE therapy techniques and represents a distinctive application of the Identification Mode of empathy. It involves the therapist temporarily assuming the identity of one of the partners during a couple's intimate dialogue for the purpose of representing that person's experience more deeply than he or she is able to do at that moment. This typically involves giving voice to the unexpressed experience, feelings, concerns, or desires of the Expresser. The therapist's ability to represent the unexpressed dimension of that person's experience presupposes that the therapist has made an empathic connection with that person. This is accomplished by the therapist continuously monitoring the Expresser's self-expression during a couple's dialogue and reading between the lines to identify elements of that person's experience that he or she may not fully be in touch with or be able to express adequately.

The therapist can use Becoming for one or more of the following reasons: to help a client break through an impasse involving an internal conflict, to unlock blocked emotions, to speak for a client who is emotionally overwhelmed, to balance power inequalities in a relationship, or to promote insight. Sometimes I resort to Becoming less out of a desire to assist the Expresser than out of a desire to help break through an emotional impasse in a dialogue because the Empathizer is not able to connect empathically with the Expresser's experience (usually because of some form of defensiveness or emotional reactivity). Alternatively, the therapist can ask the person who is having difficulty empathizing to use the Identification Mode of empathy in order to "become" the partner for the purpose of making an empathic connection with the partner's experience. (For a helpful analysis of Becoming and its various applications, see Snyder, 1995.)

When the therapist uses Becoming to represent either person, the therapist speaks to that person's partner as though the therapist were the Expresser. (It is helpful, in this context, for the therapist to think in terms of following the Expressive skill guidelines when representing that person's feelings, concerns, and desires.) Whenever the therapist uses Becoming, the person being represented should be told that he or she may immediately correct the therapist if anything is said that does not accurately represent that person's experience. It is also advisable to turn periodically to the person being represented—in particular, at an especially important point in the representation, in order to reinforce its effect on the listener—to confirm that the therapist is accurately representing that person. At the conclusion of the therapist's representation, the person in the role of the Empathizer is then asked to empathize directly with the partner whose experience was represented, as though everything said by the therapist had been verbalized by the Expresser.

An important consideration arises relative to the respective merits of using Becoming versus Therapist Troubleshooting when the therapist wants to help one partner better understand, for example, issues of gender and power in the couple's relationship. Under the rubric of Therapist Troubleshooting (see chapter 1), the therapist in principle could choose to share a value perspective on gender and power for the purpose of broadening a husband's sensitivity to those issues in his relationship with his wife. However, the therapist probably runs a certain risk in following this path in that the husband could perceive the therapist to be taking sides with the wife and against him. This risk can perhaps be alleviated somewhat by (1) carefully inoculating the couple against perceived side taking by the therapist (see chapter 7) and (2) carefully presenting this value perspective as ultimately being in the service of the relationship. However, the same end can be achieved more efficiently, and at lower risk, by the therapist using the technique of Becoming to give voice to the same value perspective by tying it in to what the therapist is empathically picking up as the feelings, concerns, and desires of this unique wife. This has two additional benefits. First, it keeps the focus on the uniqueness of these two individuals as opposed to invoking men or women in general, which tends to provoke defensiveness. Second, it preserves the integrity of the couple's dialogue process as the primary means for the couple to work through their issues because the partners will immediately resume their dialogue once the therapist's act of Becoming is completed. The therapist, and the couple, will often be better served by the therapist using Becoming in preference to Therapist Troubleshooting. For an example of the therapist choosing to use Becoming in preference to Therapist Troubleshooting, see clinical vignette 3, chapter 12.

Notes

1. The four categories of experience, feelings, concerns, and desires represent a useful frame of reference for conceptualizing any person's (global) experience in its breadth and depth. The categories of values and goals could be added to this set, but in many contexts they remain implicit. Nonetheless, it often is possible to identify a person's values and goals on the basis of his or her concerns and desires.

2. Alternatively, one could make reference, in this context, to the Christian concept of kenosis, which also signifies an emptying of the self and making oneself available to God and to one's fellow human beings.

3. The concept of reading between the lines also suggests the notion that the Expresser's communication contains a "subtext" that he or she may not be fully in touch with. From this point of view, the act of empathizing represents a hermeneutic act that seeks to go beyond the explicit words of the Expresser in order to connect with and "distill" both the essence of the Expresser's experience and its implicit meaning in all its subtle nuances. For further elaboration on the notion of Hermeneutic Empathy, see Keil (1996), cited in Watson (2002). Watson's essay, by the way, provides an excellent discussion of the concept of empathy relative to its Rogerian origins and more recent research.

PART II
Beginning the RE Therapy Process

CHAPTER 4
Conducting the Clinical Intake with Couples in RE Therapy

Typically, the therapist's initial contact with the couple is by telephone. Sometimes the person initiating therapy indicates that the partner is either reluctant to come in or is adamantly opposed to the idea of therapy. In these cases I explain that while I would be willing to meet with that person alone, nonetheless, because relationship issues are involved, it would be preferable for both parties to participate in couples counseling and to do so from the beginning. I also stress, in response to the explicitly stated or implied distrust of "therapy," that my focus is on teaching relationship skills focused on improving communication, problem solving, and behavior change. Most people respond very favorably to this frame of reference. I then inquire whether the person who called would be willing to talk with his or her partner about coming in for a first appointment. I also suggest that the partner call me in order to ask me any questions he or she might have.

In those cases in which the person who initiated the call indicates that it is unlikely that the partner would be willing to come in, or that he or she would simply prefer to come in alone, I explain that I would be happy to meet with him or her, and that I would envision a dual purpose to our working together: first, to help that person address issues of concern in the relationship and, second, to teach that person skills that would most likely help him or her approach the partner more skillfully and with greater confidence. This is referred to as Unilateral RE Couples therapy, which involves working with a single person for the purpose of leveraging positive change in a significant relationship. The initially reluctant partner will often be prompted to join the therapy when he or she begins to notice positive change in the partner who has been coming to therapy.

One final preliminary consideration: It is recommended that the therapist set aside a minimum of 90 minutes for a couple's intake. The dynamics and potential complexity of the issues that need to be covered in an initial couple's session make it advisable to allow at least that much time. Moreover, some couples will present with a crisis, in which case the therapist will want to have enough time to be able to respond effectively and compassionately. This will be especially true if the therapist needs to resort to any extensive use of Troubleshooting or Doublebecoming.

Objectives of the Clinical Intake

The objectives of a clinical intake can be classified into content objectives and process objectives, as follows:

1. The primary content objective is to learn enough about each client's perspective on the partner and the relationship—including each person's experiences, feelings, concerns, desires, and goals for the relationship—so that the clinician can gain an initial understanding of why the couple is presenting for therapy. This in turn presents the basis for being able to make a cogent recommendation to the couple for the plan of therapy (see objective 5 below). Equally important, this also enables the therapist to accomplish a number of process objectives, including the following.

2. Perhaps the most important process objective is to instill in the couple a sense of trust and confidence in the clinician. This is accomplished on several levels, but the most immediate way in which client trust and confidence is achieved is by the therapist's ability to empathize with each person in such a way that it leaves each person *feeling* understood and accepted as a person.

3. A complementary component of a couple's ability to place trust in the therapist is for each person to have confidence that the clinician will be evenhanded and not take sides. This is accomplished by the therapist's ability to show equal, nonjudgmental, and empathic understanding to both members of the couple.

4. Confidence and trust in the clinician's competence also is promoted by the therapist's ability to maintain productive control over the therapy process in a manner that allows both parties to feel emotionally safe. This is accomplished by how the therapist structures the intake session and how client emotions are managed over the course of the intake.

5. Yet another dimension of the clinician's ability to engender trust and confidence is his or her ability to generate and instill hope in the couple that their issues can be addressed in a manner that holds out the promise for healing and reconciliation in the relationship. This is accomplished both by how the intake session is conducted, and by the therapist's ability to make and explain recommendations in a manner that allows the partners to feel that their concerns will be addressed and can be met.

6. A final dimension of the clinician's ability to bring about trust and confidence is his or her ability to avoid objectifying either partner in terms of diagnostic categories. People want to be treated as human beings with real-life issues, not as exemplars of abstract categories, and most especially not as carriers of pathology.

7. Nonetheless, a complementary (content) objective is to assess the couple for potential mental health issues that might call for making a referral for psychiatric evaluation or complementary (or alternative) referrals to address specific issues that might subvert the therapy or fall outside the therapist's own area of expertise.

8. Another process objective has to do with establishing appropriate client expectations for the therapy by explaining how the therapist conducts couples therapy.

9. It is important to establish an informal (i.e., approximate and flexible) time contract with the couple.

10. Finally, it is important to motivate and structure the couple to complete home assignments.

Each of these objectives will be addressed further in the course of outlining the sequence of a clinical intake with couples in RE therapy.

Obtain Basic Client Information

The two-page clinical intake form used with couples is designed to provide a quick snapshot portrait, not a detailed history, of each person. Basic demographic information is obtained on each person, including names, address(es), phone numbers, place of birth, age, marital status, how long married (or living together, or engaged), whether previously married and, if so, for how long and how long ago the separation(s) or divorce(s) took place. Information on previous marriages (or significant relationships) can provide useful reference points for understanding someone's general life experience or what might have been brought into this relationship. Information is sought on each party's educational background and current employment for the same reasons, and in the case of employment, in order to identify any potential instability in current life circumstances. Religious affiliation (if any) reveals whether there might be significant differences in background and orientation that might be the basis for issues in the relationship. Information about children is important, and in the case of divorce (or death) and remarriage, with whom the children reside and who has primary (or joint) custody. Finally, the parties are asked if either has been in therapy previously, either individually or jointly (whether with their current or former spouse/partner) and, if so, a brief summary of when, for what reason(s), and whether medications were used. Obtaining this basic information typically takes between 5 and 10 minutes.

This initial information gathering is kept quite limited for several important reasons. First, from an RE perspective, a protracted question-and-answer format for an initial session creates a less than ideal atmosphere in that the focus is on information gathering rather than on relationship building, which may cause some people to react negatively or become defensive. It can also contribute to a kind of client passivity that disconnects people from their emotions. This points to the second reason for limiting the scope of the initial information gathering: to provide the couple with maximal opportunity during the initial meeting to share as directly and as fully as possible their experience, feelings, concerns, desires, and goals; in other words, to share the reasons that motivated them to come into therapy in the first place. Most people come to therapy because something is of great concern to them, and they want to have the opportunity to talk about that. If the couple leaves the first session without having had the opportunity to express their concerns and feel understood about them, they are less likely to want to return.

Structure the Intake for Success

One of the reasons most frequently given by therapists as to why they "hate" couples therapy is because of the sometimes highly contentious and even out-of-control nature of the couple's interaction during sessions, leaving many clinicians feeling helpless in the face of an emotional tidal wave that short-circuits any effective therapeutic process. This probably also represents the number one reason for clinician burnout with respect to conducting couples therapy. A variation on this is the comment made by many clinicians who attend RE therapy training workshops to the effect that they can't believe that most clients—and what they really mean by this is their own clients—are anything like what they observe in RE therapy training tapes or live workshop demonstrations in which there is a relative (though by no means absolute) absence of such highly contentious, out-of-control dynamics on the part of the couple.

The response to both of these observations is that it is the therapist's responsibility to structure the intake session in such a manner as to minimize (not eliminate) the likelihood of such out-of-control outbursts, which indeed have a tendency to subvert both the therapist's ability to create a therapeutic environment and the therapist's sanity. But such effective structuring in reality is fairly easy to achieve once one understands the principles and techniques by which to establish an atmosphere and a set of expectations on the part of the couple that more likely than not will result in a relatively manageable unfolding of the session, even in the face of intense emotion. And when emotional outbursts do occur, the advance structuring provides the therapist with a firm basis for responding in a manner that is likely to result in the clients being able to contain their emotions and comply with the ground rules for the session.

The key to effective structuring is to establish with the couple a contract of the ground rules that are to govern the intake session. I do so in the following way:

Before we begin, I'd like to talk with you for a moment about how I would like to structure our time together today. I want to give both of you ample opportunity to share with me, each from your own perspective, what brings you here today. I want both of you to be able to express to me your experience, your feelings, your concerns, your desires, and most importantly, your goals for your relationship (or marriage). To help accomplish this, I would like to ask that each of you direct your comments only to me and not to one another. I'd also like to ask that neither of you interrupt the other person while he or she is talking, nor make any side comments. This way, I'll be able to better understand each of you, and both of you will have ample opportunity to share your experience, including commenting on what you hear the other person say, if you choose. Is that acceptable to you? [*Looking at one person, wait for an explicit "yes" or a nod of the head.*] And is that acceptable to you? [*Ditto with the second person.*] Good.

With the couple's consensual "yes," several things have been accomplished. First, and most importantly, a contractual agreement has been established with each individual client. This contractual agreement has the psychological effect of the couple now feeling that they have obligated themselves to the therapist. This tends to translate into most clients making a genuine effort to abide by the ground rules because they want to be "good" clients. Indeed, Guerney is fond of saying that it is the therapist's role in RE therapy to create good clients by virtue of structuring, modeling, and, when necessary, enforcing constructive behavior during the therapy session. This is not to say that every client will comply all the time. Of course not. However, by virtue of having made this contractual agreement at the beginning of the intake session, the therapist has gained incalculable "moral" leverage to more easily coax whoever violates the ground rules back into voluntary compliance, thereby enabling the session to proceed as desired.

Sometimes coaxing this person back into compliance with the ground rules can be accomplished with a simple raising of the therapist's hand in a quasi "stop sign" signal that in effect serves to remind the person of the contractual obligation. For many people that will prove sufficient. However, if that proves to be insufficient, the therapist is faced with the first occasion for Troubleshooting. Then, in response to the client's continued out-of-turn self-expression, the therapist would focus on empathizing with that person by saying something like, "I recognize this is very hard for you to hear, but I would like to request your cooperation [*indirectly appealing to the contract*]. You'll have an opportunity to speak in a moment." Alternatively, the therapist might use praise combined with an implied request and say, "You've been doing a really good job. I really appreciate your cooperation." Oftentimes either statement will prove sufficient for those who were not able to respond to the raising of the hand in a stop sign signal.

Of course, there will be those residual number of cases where even that is not sufficient to get the person to emotionally self-contain. This usually is a function of the person becoming emotionally flooded with negative affect in a manner that short circuits his or her (usual) ability to emotionally self-contain. In those instances, the therapist will resort to a more intensive form of Troubleshooting. This would entail temporarily suspending empathizing with the other partner (saying to him or her, "I'll be back with you in a moment"). The therapist then turns his or her full attention to the emotionally flooded partner and continues to empathize with that person until, by virtue of feeling understood, the ability to recontain emotionally and comply with the request to not interrupt has been regained.

The therapist's ability to successfully maintain and (when necessary) enforce the contracted session structure in turn points to another important accomplishment of successful structuring, namely, that the couple is shown that the therapist *can* maintain effective control of the session in the face of either party's emotional flooding. This is an important metacommunication that says to the couple that the therapist is committed to creating and maintaining an emotionally safe container that will permit them to engage their issues without fear or threat that the session will degenerate into a shouting match or worse. This is absolutely essential to fulfilling one of the crucial goals of the clinical intake, namely, to instill in the couple hope and confidence in the therapist's competence and ability to be genuinely helpful to them in working through their difficult issues. If, conversely, the therapist were to fail to instill such confidence, then the couple would have little or no motivation to continue with the therapy; even worse, the partners might conclude that because the therapist could not help them, they were incapable of being helped, which could cause the couple to give up on the relationship or settle for a life of being miserable together.

An important clarification: This structuring of the intake session to restrain out-of-control expressions of highly charged emotion is *not* designed to suppress the (sometimes intense) expression of authentic feelings and emotion. On the contrary, the premise and conviction of RE therapy is that it is precisely through such structuring for emotional safety that people's authentic, deeper, and more vulnerable feelings and emotions are enabled to come to expression, often for the first time.

Announce in Advance the Intention to Meet With Each Person Alone

It is important to announce in advance the therapist's intention to meet with each person alone as part of the couple's intake process. The reason for this is to avoid creating a transference response by suddenly announcing that the therapist would like to meet with each person alone, which could cause suspicions for some people who might wonder, "Why is the therapist wanting to talk to me (or my spouse) alone?" By announcing these intentions in advance, this potential problem is avoided. At the same time, it normalizes for the couple that this is simply part of the standard intake process. I usually announce my intention in the following way:

> I also want to let you know that I will want to spend a little time with each of you alone. Even in the context of couples counseling I feel it is important for me to connect with each of you as individuals and to ask each of you certain questions that I believe are important for me to ask in my role as a therapist. If we have time, we'll do that as part of today's session. If not, I will plan to do that at the beginning of our next session.

Address the Issue of Confidentiality

There is one additional piece of structuring that it is vital to address before turning things over to the couple, namely, the issue of confidentiality.

There is more or less universal agreement on the general principle of confidentiality with respect to preserving client privacy relative to the outside world, except for the legally mandated exceptions in cases of perceived harm to self or others. However, there are different schools of thought on the issue of confidentiality with respect to whether or not it should apply *between* the members of the couple in the context of individual interviews within the larger framework of couples therapy.

One school of thought argues that the principle of confidentiality should also apply between the partners. The most important reasons given in defense of this position are that there should be no additional constraints placed on the principle of confidentiality than those that are legally (and, by implication, morally) mandated, and that preserving the principle of confidentiality between the partners promotes the vitally important therapeutic value of openness and honesty in the therapy process. In other words, the argument goes, it would be counterproductive to inhibit any client from divulging things that would be relevant to the therapy process. This also helps minimize the likelihood of the therapist being kept in the dark about anything that might impact the therapy.

The other school of thought argues that the principle of confidentiality should not apply between the partners. The most important reason given in defense of this position is that if the principle of confidentiality is adhered to between the partners, then the therapist can be placed in the triangulated position of being compelled to preserve a secret that not only is relevant to the therapy but also has the potential to subvert the therapy process. In other words, the argument goes, it would be better to accept the possibility of less than full disclosure by one or both parties than it would be for the therapist to be placed in the position of being the holder of a secret that could compromise his or her ability to navigate the therapeutic process freely.

One immediate issue over which this disagreement comes to a head is the issue of an undisclosed current affair. Those who advocate maintaining the principle of confidentiality between the partners argue that it is preferable to know about the affair than not, so the therapist can work with that individual for the purpose of either giving up the affair (often in the face of resistance or indecision), coming clean, or exiting the therapy or the relationship. Those who advocate not following the principle of confidentiality between the partners argue that it is preferable for the therapist not to be placed in a compromised position of withholding information that is of vital importance to the unsuspecting partner.

I believe that either principle is theoretically defensible. In either case, however, and regardless of the stance the clinician chooses to adopt,

I believe that *it is ethically mandatory to explain in advance to the couple the therapist's policy on confidentiality between the partners so that there is no potential for misunderstanding.* If the therapist does not explain his or her position in advance, and is confronted by the revelation of an undisclosed affair by one of the partners, he or she will be caught on the horns of an impossible dilemma. On the one hand, if the therapist attempted to explain after the fact that he or she would not be the holder of such a secret, the person having the affair is likely to say, "What are you talking about? I assumed everything I told you was confidential." On the other hand, the other partner is almost certainly going to complain, "How could you keep such a thing from me?" when he or she later finds out both about the affair and that the therapist was aware of it. The former dilemma can be avoided by clearly stating in advance that the principle of confidentiality does *not* apply between the partners. Then, if someone chooses to reveal an affair, that person does so knowing full well that it will (at some point) be shared with the partner in the therapy. This may have the added benefit, by the way, of encouraging some people to come clean about an affair, in particular because they will now have the assistance of the therapist in breaking the news. The latter dilemma can be avoided by clearly stating in advance that the principle of confidentiality *does* apply between the partners. Then, once the unsuspecting partner has discovered the affair (or had it revealed), and learns that the therapist knew about it, he or she can legitimately reply that they were informed about the principle of confidentiality between the partners and they had agreed to it. *To reiterate, the most important thing is to clearly state in advance the individual therapist's policy on confidentiality between the partners.*

This is a serious issue, and each clinician will have to come to his or her own decision about how to handle it. It is important to take into account professional codes of ethics and any applicable state legal codes, which may vary from profession to profession and from state to state. Shirley Glass, one of the leading experts in the field of treating affairs, is one of the few to have explicitly acknowledged the clinical and ethical dilemma of a tension between the principle of confidentiality versus potential implications for a legal or ethical principle of a "duty to warn." Glass (2002, p. 501) observes, "Duty to warn in cases where unprotected sex occurs is an unresolved legal/ethical issue." She also observes the dilemma of withholding information about an ongoing affair from a suspecting spouse in the face of repeated denials because of its "crazy-making" impact on the suspecting spouse and the implied complicity on the part of the therapist. Glass also observes that there is a lack of consensus in the field about how to handle secrets in the case of couples therapy (p. 500). She notes that the prevailing view is to not conduct conjoint sessions when there is an undisclosed ongoing affair. On the other hand, some clinicians argue that the involved partner deserves confidentiality with respect to the partner and should not be subjected to "coercive" conditions for treatment.

Glass does not explicitly advocate a specific position on this issue. She does state that "secret information" should not be revealed in violation of the principle of confidentiality (2002, p. 501). On the other hand, she writes about the clinical and ethical dilemma in a manner that indicates she recognizes the difficulty faced by clinicians who adopt a stance of maintaining confidentiality between the partners in couples therapy. She then goes on to observe that the best way for this dilemma to be handled by those clinicians who choose to adopt a position of no confidentiality between the partners, is for the therapist to clearly explain his or her policy on confidentiality to the couple "at the outset of treatment and obtain informed consent." This implies that it would be wise for a therapist who chooses to adopt a policy of no confidentiality between the partners to have the couple sign a release of information or consent statement acknowledging their understanding and acceptance of the therapist's policy.

I have adopted a policy of *not* maintaining the principle of confidentiality between the partners when I conduct couples therapy. This is not an official position dictated by RE therapy, but a personal professional decision. I explain my policy to couples at the very beginning of the first session, before I invite them to begin sharing with me their principal issues. I do so in the following terms:

> There is one final issue I would like to address before we begin. With respect to the outside world, you are entitled to confidentiality around whatever takes place here with me, with the legally mandated exceptions of perceived harm to self or others, in which case I am required by law to take certain steps. The other possibility would be if I were compelled to testify in a court of law. I would like to clarify one other thing with respect to confidentiality so that there is no misunderstanding. The two of you are here as a couple, so I regard the relationship between you to be my primary client. That doesn't mean I'm not interested in you as an individual [*looking at one person*], because I am. And that doesn't mean I'm not interested in you as an individual [*looking at the other person*], because I am. But I'd like you to understand that from my point of view I have three clients in this room. There's you as an individual; there's you as an individual; and there's the relationship between the two of you. And, from one point of view, it's the relationship

between the two of you that is my primary client. As a consequence, when I meet with each of you individually, it is important
that you both understand that the principle of confidentiality will
not apply between the two of you within the couples therapy. In
other words, anything that either of you shares with me will be
open to the couples counseling.

I have adopted this position so that I am not placed in the position of holding any secrets between the two of you. The reason is
that I believe that would compromise my ability to be of maximum
service to your relationship, which, again, from my point of view, is
my primary client. If either of you wishes to share something of a
sensitive nature with me, I will use my discretion and my clinical
judgment about how to help you with that, including when and
how to bring it into our joint work. But please be aware that in
the end anything shared with me will be made available to the
couples counseling. Is that acceptable to you? And is that acceptable
to you? Do you have any questions? I'd like to have you sign a form
acknowledging your acceptance of these terms.

If either person were to voice a concern, I would empathize with the
stated concerns (as a form of Troubleshooting). Having done so, I would
then reiterate and reexplain my policy. In the event that either person were
to refuse to accept my conditions for doing clinical work, I would politely
explain to the couple that I am sorry but I cannot agree to work with
them. I would then provide a referral to another clinician.

Solicit the Major Issues and Positive Goals

Once the therapist has explained his or her policy on confidentiality
and the couple's acceptance has been secured, it is time to turn to the
couple to solicit their major issues and their positive goals for their
relationship. Understanding the major issues in the relationship, from
each partner's distinct point of view, is important to understanding the
immediate reason(s) for their decision to initiate therapy. But inquiring
about a couple's positive goals for their relationship also is important, and
easy to overlook. By asking the couple to think in terms of their positive
goals, the therapist is already intervening to help them begin to move away
from a past-oriented problem focus to a future-oriented solution focus by
encouraging them to envision the kind of relationship that they would like
to have, perhaps even once had, or have been longing to have. The couple
can be invited to begin their sharing in the following way:

So what I'd like to do now is to turn it over to the two of you to share with me what brings you here, what the issues are from each of your points of view, and, most importantly, what your desires and goals are for this relationship. Whoever would like to begin may begin.

Notice that a specific person is not asked to begin. It is left up to the couple to decide who will start, in order to avoid creating any transference response. Also note the invitation for the couple to share their take on the issues from each of their points of view. This indirectly validates that each person's point of view is legitimate and deserves respect, without in any way invalidating the experience of the other person.

Show Equal Empathic Understanding

Now the real work of the initial session begins. The therapist's most immediate goal is to show equal, nonjudgmental, empathic understanding to both partners so that they both *feel* understood and accepted by the therapist. As already observed, this represents one of the most important process objectives of the initial session in that the aim is to build the couple's capacity to trust and have confidence in the therapist's ability to be fair and to be helpful.

The session will now unfold in the following schematic way. The wife, for example, may begin to share her experience, perspective, and goals for the relationship while the therapist listens empathically. The therapist then empathizes directly with the wife in order to help her feel understood, but with a special emphasis on reading between the lines to identify unstated feelings, concerns, and desires in order to deepen the wife's self-understanding and perhaps even bring greater clarity to the issues than she may have been able to do for herself. The wife may express herself again in light of the empathy, in which case the therapist empathizes with the new content. At some point the therapist turns to the husband and invites him to share his experience by saying something as simple as, "And from your point of view." The therapist then empathizes directly with the husband, again reading between the lines, and does so in response to each expressive statement by the husband. At some point the therapist turns back to the wife and says, "What would you like to add?" And so the process continues, giving each person two or three opportunities to talk about the issues and their goals for the relationship, until the therapist has a good understanding of the basic issues in the relationship. With less verbal or lower functioning couples, there may be an increase in the number of back-and-forth exchanges because either or both partners share less information each time they speak.

In terms of therapist technique, questions are only rarely (and preferably not) asked during this phase of the intake process. Instead, energy is invested in using empathy to help each person go deep into his or her experience. If either person is reticent when speaking or has difficulty verbalizing much real content, then the therapist can resort to a prompt or, as a last resort, ask specific questions designed to engage that person. However, an ideally unfolding intake session would involve the therapist asking no questions at all during this portion of the session. One reason for this is to not interfere with the client's spontaneous internal process, because once a question is asked, then the client is potentially side-tracked out of his or her experience by having to serve the therapist's (misplaced) need to know. Brazier (1995), in his comparison of Carl Rogers's ideas with Zen thought, talks about the importance of a therapist stance of emptiness, or what has also been referred to as a stance of patient "not-knowing." In this context, that translates into the therapist being willing to sit with not-knowing this or that specific detail about the client's experience and instead placing trust in the client knowing what needs to be shared. The RE therapist's job, on this level, is to follow the client's lead and to allow the client to lead the therapist where the client wishes to go. The therapist is therefore encouraged to exercise discipline and not ask questions and to instead channel energy into empathizing as deeply as possible, trusting in the power and efficacy of empathy to elicit from each person what needs to be elicited. This is a deeply Rogerian stance that stands in marked contrast to other models of couples therapy where the therapist has a predetermined agenda of questions (or range of questions) that are put to each couple, regardless of their presenting issue(s). In my experience, however, this Rogerian stance pays huge dividends at several levels of the therapeutic process, not least in that it demonstrates respect and trust in the couple while also avoiding the "under the microscope" feeling that unsolicited and probing questions can generate in clients.

Employ the Technique of Laundering (as Needed)

It is not uncommon in a couple's first therapy session, especially for highly conflicted couples or those whose relationship is seriously fractured, for one or both partners to engage in extremely inflammatory language and highly negative personal attacks on the other person. From the point of view of the Expressive skill, such personal attacks would be regarded as technically unskillful and would not be permitted later in the therapy process because such attacks cause defensiveness and contribute to the development of emotional impasses. However, there is no presumption that people speak skillfully during an initial intake session. Indeed, such a presumption would be counterproductive in that many people are carrying deep and perhaps long-suppressed feelings that need to be expressed and that the person deserves to have validated. As previously indicated, one of the therapist's primary objectives in the intake session is to provide that empathic validation of each person's perspective and feelings.

However, providing that empathic validation does not mean that you need to verbally repeat any inflammatory language, negative personal attacks, or character assassinations made by either party. To the contrary, to do so would indirectly have the effect of validating those attacks, which not only runs counter to everything the RE model is designed to teach and model for couples but also would contribute to deepening the potential defensiveness of the person who is on the receiving end of those attacks. Let me be clear. I am not saying that the therapist should downplay or minimize the authentic experience, feelings, or concerns of an angry partner. Not at all. What I am saying is that part of the therapist's job is to read between the lines of the angry partner's inflammatory language or negative personal attacks in order to disentangle the legitimate core of that person's experience, feelings, and concerns from the unskillful language that is being used to express it. The presumption here, to generalize the point, is that behind every unskillful communication there is an authentic experience and legitimate feelings, concerns, or desires that deserve to be expressed and receive validation. It is the therapist's job to help clarify and validate each of these things, but to do so in a manner that does not contribute to or reinforce the partner's potential defensiveness in hearing it.

This means that the therapist will utilize the special RE therapy technique of Laundering to "clean up" either party's unskillful communication in order to make it easier for that person's partner to hear. Laundering may be defined as a special technique by which the RE therapist empathically represents the experience of either or both members of a couple by eliminating any inflammatory language or negative personal attacks in order to reduce defensiveness and promote receptivity to hearing one another's legitimate points of view. This is accomplished by simply editing out and not repeating inflammatory language or negative personal attacks while nonetheless accurately representing the authentic feelings, concerns, and desires of each partner. (The therapist's ability to do this itself involves a direct application of empathy, including reading between the lines.) In this way, the therapist helps reduce levels of hostility and defensiveness between the partners and thereby paves the way for increased receptivity and more open lines of communication. At the same time, good interpersonal behavior is being modeled by how the therapist verbally represents each partner to the other. Finally, the therapist demonstrates his or her ability to create and maintain an atmosphere of safety and respect in the therapy, which helps the couple gain trust and confidence in the therapist.

Look for and Draw out Underlying Positives

The metaphor of laundering can be taken a step further. In cleaning up unskillful communication, the therapist is making it more presentable not just by eliminating unnecessary negatives, but also by drawing out implicit positives about the partner or the relationship. So in addition to eliminating the unnecessarily inflammatory language and negative personal attacks, the therapist can go deeper into the implied meaning of the person's communication and look for clues that suggest the presence of positive feelings toward the other person (or the relationship) even in the midst of the overtly negative form of the communication. As a consequence, the therapist should always be on the lookout for (often unstated but implicit) underlying positives and then make them explicit by verbalizing them as part of the empathic representation of each partner.

Once again, imagine a highly conflicted or fractured couple. It may be difficult for either partner to explicitly verbalize the positive feelings each has for the other (but that in reality are there) because they are so focused on their anger, their pain, and their unmet needs that all they can do is verbalize the negative dimensions of their relationship. Recall, however, the point made in the Introduction that it is important to operate with the working assumption that the couple has come to therapy because they want help with their relationship, even in the midst of all the anger, pain, and hurt. The further implication is that there still are positive feelings between the partners or a valuing of the relationship, even if those feelings have become largely submerged because of their conflicts. Part of the therapist's goal, then, is to read between the lines of the anger and the negativity. The purpose of this is to bring out the genuine underlying positives that neither person may have been able to express, but which each would readily accept as true, with respect to their underlying positive regard for their partner or their desire for healing and reconciliation in the relationship.

In practice, this reading between the lines to draw out implicit underlying positives is a very delicate dance. On the one hand, the therapist is constantly on the lookout for opportunities to gradually infuse more and more underlying positives into the empathic representation of each partner. In this sense, the therapist is constantly attempting to push the envelope in reaching for deeper underlying positives. On the other hand, the therapist must be cautious never to cross the line into representing either partner in a manner that either would not immediately accept as true. In other words, the last thing the therapist wants to have happen is to empathically represent someone in a manner that would result in that person saying, for example, "No, I'm not at all certain that I still love him (or her) after what's happened," when the therapist had attempted to verbalize that person's continued love for the partner after, say, that partner has had an affair. Such a response by either person would be highly counterproductive to forward progress in the intake session, and indeed could well set the process back quite significantly.

On the other hand, it often is precisely because the therapist pushes the envelope with respect to one or both partner's underlying positive feelings, that each person is helped to reach beyond the anger and the pain to recognize authentic positive feelings and reclaim his or her positive motivation and desire for healing in the relationship. So the therapist's challenge is to be so empathically attuned to each person's experience and feelings *in the moment of the unfolding process* that the therapist can at each moment represent each person authentically and in a manner that each would readily accept as true for him or her. This usually will translate into the therapist gradually increasing the volume on the underlying positives, perhaps beginning with a quite minimalist statement about the one person "not wanting to lose the relationship," and moving on to "wanting to preserve the marriage," to still "caring" for the other person, to "wanting for there to be healing between the two of them," and, if and when it feels empathically appropriate, to explicitly verbalizing that person's love for the partner. Before daring to risk naming that deepest positive feeling of love, the therapist should be absolutely convinced in his or her empathic bones that the person being represented that way will indeed accept the attribution of feelings of love.

If the technique of Laundering and the principle of drawing out underlying positives are viewed as two sides of the same coin, it is possible to observe a kind of hierarchy of feelings that provides a useful frame of reference in terms of which the therapist can calibrate the empathic representation of each party as he or she seeks simultaneously to diffuse the negative language and gradually infuse more positive feelings into the empathic representations. The hierarchy proceeds from anger →frustration→irritation→fear→pain→disappointment→sadness→longing→caring→love, with other possible shades of feeling in between. Moving through this hierarchy enables the therapist to move from one level of feeling to the next as one moves from the more negative feelings to the more positive underlying feelings. In moving up the ladder of underlying positive feelings, the therapist will tend to experience a shift in the emotional energy in the session to a kind of softening characterized by decreased defensiveness and increased receptivity. As that shift occurs, the therapist can feel relatively confident that he or she has brought the couple to the minimal point of what I call "buy-in" to the therapy and an accompanying commitment to at least work on the relationship for the purpose of exploring their issues and the potential viability of their relationship or marriage. From one point of view, that is the therapist's most immediate and minimal goal for the couple's intake session. The therapist's ability to accomplish this important goal is intimately tied to the ability to instill hope in the couple about the future of their relationship, and the therapist's ability to be helpful to them in pursuit of this goal. And the therapist's ability to instill hope is intimately tied, in the more severe cases of estrangement between the couple, to the ability to uncover and make explicit the underlying positive feelings that at least one partner (and usually both) still has for the other. This also points to how absolutely fundamental to the success of the therapy process is the ability to empathize well and empathize deeply with each person, and why deep empathy indeed constitutes the true foundation of RE therapy.

Make Explicit the Love–Pain Connection

There is a complementary angle that also can contribute to a deepening of the process and forward movement in the intake session. It involves what Guerney refers to as the "magic confluence of feelings" that occurs when one partner experiences in the other the deep pain caused by his or her own actions, together with feelings of love, caring, and concern that the other partner has despite the pain (see Cavedo & Guerney, 1999, p. 98). It is, according to Guerney, one person's ability to see this magical confluence of emotions in the other that causes even a previously unresponsive partner to want to do everything possible to overcome the other person's pain, because no one, deep down, wants a loved one to be in pain.

It is important, therefore, that the therapist be alert to opportunities to empathically represent either partner in such a way that highlights precisely such a combination of feelings of deep love toward the partner and deep pain with regard to something that the partner has done (or not done). Interestingly, a golden opportunity to do this presents itself when either partner expresses anger or other related emotions. When anger is expressed, you can read between the lines in two distinct ways. On the one hand, you can reach for what Jacobson and Christiansen (1996, pp. 162–163) refer to as the "softer" emotions, such as fear and sadness, that usually coexist with the "harder" emotions, such as anger. As Jacobson and Christiansen observe, it is easier for people to respond with caring and concern when they are presented with softer emotions. On the other hand, you can read between the lines even more deeply and reach for positive feelings of caring and love that (usually) coexist with—or, from another point of view, constitute the foundation of—that person's overt anger. Guerney's point, in effect, is that the most powerful impact in terms of a motivation to respond with compassion, by changing one's own behavior for the good of the relationship, will occur when one partner observes in the other both feelings of pain (or sadness) and underlying positive feelings of love.

Use Doublebecoming When Necessary (or With Discretion)

There will be those instances when even the therapist's best (or perhaps not so best) efforts at empathizing will not succeed in bringing the couple to the point of buy-in referred to earlier. Alternatively put, the therapist may come to a point in the couple's back-and-forth sharing and his or her own direct empathizing with each partner where things feel emotionally stuck in that there appears to be no tangible evidence of forward movement toward buy-in. When that happens, the therapist can resort to the special RE therapy technique of Doublebecoming to attempt to break through the emotional logjam.

Doublebecoming involves the therapist utilizing the Identification Mode of empathy in order to alternately assume the identity of each partner for the purpose of representing each person's experience to the other. The goal is to elicit the deeper positive feelings and motivations of each partner in order to help the couple either connect more deeply or bridge an emotional gap between them. It is usually advisable that the therapist begin Doublebecoming with the person who the therapist believes is more deeply blocked emotionally or more in need of receiving empathy; the hope is that this will begin to reduce that person's defensiveness and increase his or her receptivity to the partner. I introduce the initiation of Doublebecoming to the couple in the following way:

> I'd like to shift gears and try something different. What I'd like to do, to the best of my ability, is to represent each of you in turn to the other. What that means is that, Alex, I'd like to begin by representing you to Beth, and I'd like to do that by pretending to be you. So, Beth, that means I'm going to talk to you as though I were Alex, and then I'll give you an opportunity to respond to what I've said on Alex's behalf, and to talk to me as though I were Alex. Then, Beth, I'll do the same for you and represent you to Alex as though I were you. Alex, you'll then have an opportunity to respond to what I've said on Beth's behalf. Then I'll continue representing each of you back and forth in that same manner. If at any point I say

something that does not represent either of you accurately, please let me know immediately and I will modify my representation of you so that you feel accurately represented.

When using Doublebecoming, the therapist will employ each of the techniques and principles identified in the three preceding sections: Laundering, drawing out underlying positives, and looking for ways to simultaneously represent either partner's pain and love. In this way, the therapist launders out any inflammatory language and negative personal attacks while also seeking to represent as deeply as possible each partner's feelings of anger and pain in juxtaposition to his or her positive feelings of caring and love. The therapist is thus simultaneously attempting to help the person being represented feel understood and empathized with while also representing that person to the partner in a manner that reduces defensiveness and thereby more readily allows the partner to connect with that person's pain—and love. This in turn begins to dissolve the emotional blockages that have been keeping the couple emotionally disengaged or alienated and fosters the initial stages of an emotional softening and rapprochement that it is hoped will bring the couple to the point of buy-in to the therapy process and to the potential for relationship healing or reconciliation.

In my experience, the use of Doublebecoming in the face of an emotional impasse involving entrenched anger or disengagement almost always results in a significant shift in energy between the partners. Implemented effectively, Doublebecoming begins to break down the emotional barriers that have kept either or both partners locked in their rigid stance (typically motivated by a desire for emotional self-protection). A good deal of the reason for its effectiveness, I am convinced, is the power of the Identification Mode of empathy to create a dynamic experience for both partners by virtue of having either partner's anger, pain, and the more positive feelings of caring and love represented with energy, emotion, and conviction. (Using vivid metaphors and adding emotional tone or inflection to one's voice helps generate this dynamic experience.) Seldom does a client who, up until that point, was entrenched in a self-protective stance not respond with some degree of emotional softening.

Conversely, the therapist's representation of that person usually also genuinely touches the other (typically not quite so emotionally entrenched) person in such a manner that the partner is able to respond to the representation with at least some understanding and compassion. That person is thereby enabled to respond verbally in a manner that represents a positive reaching out to the withdrawn person, usually with some warmth of tone or words of caring, concern, guarded hopefulness, and sometimes even love. The therapist then turns around and represents the second person via the Identification Mode of empathy and reads between the lines as deeply as possible in order to draw out whatever (additional) level of positive emotion the therapist is convinced that person will readily accept *at that moment in the unfolding process*. This second person should then experience the benefits of being represented via the Identification Mode of empathy, while at the same time the first person who had previously been represented should also experience a powerful effect from seeing his or her partner being represented in as positive a manner as possible. It is this back-and-forth representation of each partner via the technique of Doublebecoming that enables the process to go deeper and to generate more positive feelings on both sides in a manner that fosters emotional softening and, in turn, promotes the beginnings of emotional rapprochement. The process of Doublebecoming may be brought to a close when an emotional rapprochement has been achieved sufficiently for the couple to buy in to the therapy—at least at the level of being willing to commit to working on the issues in the relationship with a view to determining whether or not relationship healing or reconciliation is possible.

The classic reason to resort to the technique of Doublebecoming during the clinical intake is to overcome an emotional impasse, as just described, or to deal with a crisis situation that leads the therapist to decide to shift into Crisis Intervention format. However, it also is possible for the therapist to choose to employ the technique of Doublebecoming during the intake for one or more of the following reasons: to facilitate a deeper empathic connection on the part of the therapist with each partner's experience; to enable the therapist to better represent each partner by virtue of the power inherent in the Identification Mode of empathy; to deepen the client's trust and confidence in the therapist by virtue of feeling more deeply understood by the therapist; or to model to the couple what skillful communication looks like, both in terms of skillful expression and in terms of conducting a couple's dialogue. Such a discretionary use of Doublebecoming can indeed foster multiple benefits in the context of a clinical intake, so much so that some therapists may wish to incorporate it as a standard part of their intake process. This is the approach taken by Snyder (1996), as illustrated in a videotaped demonstration of her use of Doublebecoming (what the tape refers to as Laundering) in the context of a clinical intake.

Provide Separate Interviews

Once the therapist has gained sufficient understanding of the couple's issues and has achieved buy-in to the therapy on the couple's part, including a commitment to working on the issues in their relationship, then it is time to move to the separate interviews for each partner. If time permits, this can occur during the first session with the couple; if not, then this becomes the first order of business at the second session. In either case, the individual interview time is regarded as part of the couple's intake process. The individual interviews can take as little as 10 minutes apiece, or as much as a complete session for each person in more complicated cases. In my experience, most individual interviews take most or all of an entire session for the two interviews. However, in cases where domestic violence or the revelation and aftermath of an affair is part of the presenting problem, following the recommendations of experts in each field, it is advisable to schedule a full session with each person alone.

There are several objectives in conducting the individual interviews. The first (content) objective is to ask certain very focused questions to determine whether there are any mental health or diagnostic considerations that need to be addressed, either within the couples therapy or by means of referral to a specialist. Included here would be questions about depression or anxiety, alcohol or drug use, potential physical violence in the relationship, and the state of sexual intimacy in the relationship. (The form of these questions is addressed below.) The second (content) objective is to create an opportunity to learn additional information about either partner's family of origin (including history of physical or sexual abuse), either person as an individual or the relationship. (These questions can also be found below.) The third (process) objective is to further cement a therapeutic alliance with each member of the couple. This is accomplished both by how the content-focused questions are asked and by how the therapist relates to each person as an individual during the separate interview time.

It is worth noting, in this context, that RE therapy does not rely on a battery of written questionnaires as part of its intake and assessment process as do some models of couples therapy. Some clinicians do, for example, combine the use of Gottman's "Sound Marital House Questionnaires" (1999) with the practice of RE therapy as described in this book, and that is entirely acceptable. However, the RE therapy model is not built around the use of written assessment tools per se; instead, the focus is placed on making a more personal connection with the couple in and through the couple's intake and the individual interviews. On the other hand, the therapist always has the option of including the use of written assessment tools in the context of the RE clinical intake process, depending on the setting within which he or she works, the population the therapist is working with, or out of personal professional convictions. So, for example, the therapist could choose to use any of the standard assessment tools designed to assess for domestic violence if it is felt that the recommended questions listed below are not sufficient to address this question with a particular population.

I introduce the individual interview time to each client in the following way:

> As I explained previously, there are a few questions that I feel it's important for me as a therapist to ask of each person I see, even in the context of couples counseling. These are standard questions I ask of everyone, so please don't read anything into my questions in terms of your specific relationship.

The purpose of this introduction is to set people at ease and reduce any potential anxiety about this part of the intake process.

There are seven content areas around which initial and follow-up questions are asked during the individual interviews. In each case, you may ask additional follow-up questions depending on the nature of the response(s) to the initial questions.

1. Do you have any concerns, either for yourself or _____ [*the partner's name*], about depression or anxiety? Is there a history of either in your family?
2. Do you have any concerns, either for yourself or _____ [*the partner's name*], about alcohol use or drug use? Is there a history of alcohol or drug abuse in your family?
3. How do the two of you deal with conflict? Has there ever been any pushing or shoving between the two of you? Has either of you ever slapped the other? Has there ever been any hitting between the two of you?
4. What is the state of sexual intimacy in your relationship? How has that changed over the years?
5. Is there anything else about your family of origin or _____ [*the partner's name*] family of origin that might be helpful for me to know? Has there been a history of physical or sexual abuse in your family? Have you ever been sexually abused?
6. What else do you think it would be helpful for me to know, either about you, about _____ [*the partner's name*], or about your relationship?
7. Is there anything you might have been reluctant to say in your partner's presence or anything else that is important for me to know?

The formulation of the first two questions is designed both to be neutral with respect to the two partners and to provide an opportunity for each person to share observations or concerns about the other person as well as him- or herself. Not infrequently, important information is shared that did not come out during the initial joint interview (e.g., about depression or drinking). The formulation of the third set of questions is important and is preferable to asking, "Has there ever been any violence between the two of you?" The reason is that some people will be hesitant to respond "yes" to a direct inquiry regarding "violence," but will be less defended in responding to questions about how they deal with conflict or whether there has been pushing or shoving (see Stith, Rosen, & McCollum, 2003, p. 422). Depending on the answers to this set of questions, you can follow up with additional questions, working your way up the scale of severity with regard to potential violence. It also is recommended that you ask questions about the safety of children if either mild or severe physical aggression is revealed during the interviews (see Bograd & Mederos, 1999, p. 299).

The fourth question is easy to overlook but very important to ask. One reason is that the responses can provide valuable insight into a vitally important dimension of any couple's relationship. An active, satisfying sex life does not mean that there are no significant issues in the relationship, but a mismatch in libido or an inactive sex life may serve as a useful barometer as to how severely the couple's attachment bonding has been impacted. Indeed, approximately 20% of marriages fall in the category of nonsexual marriages; that is, the couple is sexually intimate less than once per month (see McCarthy & McCarthy, 2003). McCarthy and McCarthy (2003) is an excellent resource for clinicians working with couples having sexual problems involving low or nonexistent desire or other forms of sexual dysfunction. In addition, explicitly raising the issue of sexual intimacy sends an important dual message to the couple: first, that this is an important area of the relationship to explore and, second, that the couple is being given "permission" to address the issue openly in that the therapist has conveyed openness to talking about it.

The fifth question is specifically focused, but open-ended in its formulation; it sometimes yields significant information. The follow-up questions about family and personal history regarding physical and sexual abuse are important areas to explore, both on their own terms and because of potential implications for the couple's sexual intimacy. The final two questions are open-ended and are designed to give each person the opportunity to put on the table anything else that is important. In cases where the therapist has doubts about the level of commitment to the marriage or the relationship on the part of one or both partners, he or she can ask how committed each person is to the relationship, or at least to exploring the possibility of healing and reconciliation in the relationship. The therapist can also add additional questions that he or she believes should be part of the intake screening process. For example, depending on the population the therapist tends to work with, or personal convictions about important questions, it could be important to ask whether either person as a child witnessed physical abuse of a parent. Or each person could be asked to describe what his or her parents' marriage was like, or how each person's family dealt with conflict. However, resist the temptation to turn the separate interview time into an extended history intake. The idea is to learn potentially significant information while avoiding the appearance of medicalizing or pathologizing the clients.

Make Recommendations

Once the two separate interviews have been completed, it is time to bring the other person back into the room in order to make recommendations to the couple. In those cases where it is not possible to conduct the individual interviews during the first meeting with the couple, 10 minutes at the end of the first session should be reserved in order to make initial recommendations for the therapy and to discuss the couple's first home assignments. The most important consideration in making a recommendation to the couple is to avoid the appearance of offering Relationship Enhancement as a prepackaged program and to instead explain in detail exactly how the therapist can help the couple address their issues constructively and improve their overall relationship satisfaction through what the RE model has to offer. So, for example, I might say to a couple:

> I'd like to talk for a moment about where we might go from here, and how I believe I can be helpful to the two of you. You both talked about communication being a problem in your relationship and how you'd like to be able to talk with one another without things degenerating into a verbal fight. I can help you with that by teaching you how to better manage conflict situations when they arise and by teaching you some core communication skills, including how to express yourselves to one another more skillfully. I can teach you how to listen more effectively, how to empathize with one another better, and how to conduct a constructive dialogue so that you both can come to understand one another better. On the basis of that, I can help you in determining how to go about resolving whatever residual differences there may be between the two of you. I can teach you how to do this in a manner that ideally leaves both of you feeling satisfied because you both feel that your feelings and concerns have been taken into account.

Whenever I do couples therapy, I operate on two levels. First, I teach couples these core communication, problem solving, and behavior change skills in order to help couples learn how to interact better. Then, as a result of teaching you those skills and their accompanying dialogue process, we are able to address the very specific content issues in your relationship, such as the affair and how to deal with your estranged son [*or whatever the issues may be*]. In addition, learning these skills will enable you to better address and resolve future relationship issues on your own, which is one of the primary goals of this kind of couples therapy. I'll also check in with you periodically to ask for feedback on how the therapy is going, and please feel free to let me know if something is not working for you. I will do my best to be responsive to your concerns.

I always include in any recommendation the explanation that I work with couples on the two levels described. In part it helps couples understand how I work and what to expect from the therapy; in part it helps set the stage for me to transition into the discussion of the first home assignments. Finally, it helps create the larger context for the couple to understand that there will be (when the therapist follows the Time-Designated format) a temporary postponement in dealing with the couple's substantive content issues in order first to address the process level of their relationship through the skills-training component of the therapy. The therapist can alternatively choose to follow the Experiential format, in which case the couple's substantive issues would be engaged in the very next session after a brief orientation to the RE skills and dialogue process (see chapter 8 for a detailed description of the Experiential format). The statement about how learning these skills will help them deal more constructively with future issues in their relationship helps increase the couple's investment in the therapy, while the final statement, about checking in with them about the therapy and giving them permission to voice concerns, is important both as an element of respect to the couple and as a means of deepening their trust and confidence in the therapist's openness.

If, in my clinical judgment, a referral to a specialist is in order, I would also address that at this time. If I had previously done so with either person during the separate interview time, I would inform the other partner of the referral, unless there were compelling reasons not to do so, such as in cases of severe domestic violence. So, for example, if there were issues of substance abuse, untreated depression, sexual impotence, or domestic violence (in those cases where it was out in the open and both partners were already receptive to the idea of treatment), I would make an appropriate referral. At the same time, I would also make a decision and recommendation as to whether the couple's therapy can legitimately proceed concurrently or whether it would be better to place it on hold until the other issue(s) had been sufficiently addressed. Each situation must be dealt with on a case-by-case basis, using one's best clinical judgment, but the mere presence of an issue such as drinking, for example, ought not in and of itself rule out concurrent couple's therapy. Indeed, several studies have shown that marital therapy is the treatment of choice in cases of alcoholism (see McGrady, Stout, Noel, Abrams, & Nelson, 1991; O'Farrell & Rotunda, 1997), while RE therapy has been used successfully in the treatment of alcohol related issues (see Waldo & Guerney, 1983; Matter, McAllister, & Guerney, 1984). The general point is that there is a preference in RE therapy toward proceeding with concurrent treatment unless there is a very clear reason not to do so, such as in cases of severe domestic violence or severe substance abuse.

Another reason for making a referral to a specialist is if one of the partners is dealing with individual issues that fall outside the therapist's areas of competence. For example, I tend to refer an individual to a specialist when there are issues involving eating disorders. However, RE therapy's preferred approach is to integrate so-called individual therapy issues into the framework of the couple's therapy whenever possible. There are several reasons for this. First, it better preserves the unity of the therapeutic process by not needlessly involving more than one clinician. Second, it permits some or all of the individual therapy work to be done in the context of the conjoint sessions. This has the dual benefit of permitting the partner both to provide support to the partner who is working on his or her issue(s) and to gain new insight into that person's experience by virtue of observing or participating in that person's work. Third, it permits the clinician to take advantage of the real-time intersection of the intrapsychic and interpersonal dimensions of people's lives, in particular how aspects of the interpersonal relationship may provide a window of access into either or both partner's intrapsychic issues. Finally, in those cases where the decision is made (with the consent of both parties) for the therapist to meet with either partner individually, then it is much easier to bring the results of the individual work back into the conjoint sessions. There always is an agreement made for that to happen as one of the conditions for the individual sessions to take place, which helps preserve the primacy of the conjoint therapy. For all these reasons, it is regarded as vastly preferable for individual therapy work to be conducted either as part of the conjoint sessions or privately with the therapist who is working with the couple conjointly.

Teach Restraint (as Needed)

Chapter 5 will address more fully the teaching of Conflict Management skills to couples, typically as part of the first postintake session. However, there are times when the therapist will be faced with the reality of a highly conflicted and contentious couple who are fighting frequently and who clearly are in need of assistance at the very first meeting to help them (at minimum) disengage from their highly charged interactions. In these instances, and even in the face of severe time constraints, the therapist should negotiate with the couple to exercise restraint with respect to any controversial issues that may come up prior to the next time they are to meet with the therapist. The request might be made to the couple in the following way:

> One of the things that's become clear from our time together today is that things frequently get out of hand and the two of you end up in a major verbal fight that leaves both of you feeling pretty awful. I'd like to teach you more systematically in a session or two some basic strategies that will help both of you be able to manage such conflict situations more effectively. In the meantime, what I'd like to request is that each of you makes a concerted effort to exercise restraint with one another and that you both attempt to avoid particularly controversial issues. And, if any difficult issues do come up and it begins to feel like things might get out of hand, I'd like to request that each of you simply agrees to postpone dealing with the issue until we've had an opportunity to cover some of the skills that will enable you to deal with those difficult issues more skillfully. Is that agreeable with you? [*Looking at one person, wait for a head nod or a "yes."*] And is that agreeable with you? [*Ditto.*] I'd also like to request that each of you make an effort to treat your partner for the next several weeks as though the other person were a guest in your home. This doesn't imply that either of you has no place in your home. It's simply to say that, out of caring and consideration for our guests, we tend to treat them with the utmost respect when they are in our home. That's how I'd like each of you to treat one another for the next several weeks, until we've had a chance to establish a framework for addressing your issues more constructively. Is that agreeable with you? And with you? Great.

This intervention is designed to be a stopgap measure when there is not enough time to cover Conflict Management skills more thoroughly. The effectiveness of this intervention is in no small measure a function of the therapist going beyond simply explaining the concepts and, in addition, securing a contractual agreement with the couple to abide by the recommendations.

Negotiate an Informal Time Contract

In response to a couple's inquiry about how long they can expect the therapy to last, my standard response is that RE therapy is a short-term therapy model and that RE couples therapy typically involves between 10 and 20 sessions and lasts somewhere between 3 and 6 months. If a couple expresses concern about the potential number of sessions or length of time, I empathize with their concern (as a form of Troubleshooting). Then I inquire what they would be comfortable with as an initial informal time contract (ideally, from my point of view, a minimum of 6 and preferably 10 sessions), with an opportunity to evaluate and renegotiate the time frame and contract at that point.

With many couples I propose that we work either a session-and-a-half or a double session whenever we meet. I explain my rationale to couples like this:

> I'd also like to raise the question as to whether the two of you would be open to our meeting for a session-and-a-half or a double session whenever we meet. The reason is that the traditional 50-minute therapy session was invented for individual therapy, not for couples counseling. In my experience, 50 minutes goes by very quickly in the context of couples work, and oftentimes that is exactly the point at which the issues are just beginning to be engaged in a deep way. Also, my experience has been that when couples are able to meet for a session-and-a-half or a double session, then the work tends to go much deeper much faster, and the therapy tends to be of shorter duration.

Many couples are not in a position to afford a double fee each time we meet, but some are. The time is prorated according to one's baseline session fee, or the therapist can choose to discount an extended session. The other circumstance where this can be useful, however, is when people's schedules are such that meeting weekly is difficult (due, for example, to frequent travel). Then, when we do meet, the sessions are more meaningful and forward progress in the therapy is more easily maintained. As another variation, if a couple's preference is for biweekly double sessions, I will still try to negotiate for weekly sessions for the first three to 4 weeks in order to jump-start the therapy process, and then shift to a biweekly format. Yet another possibility, if the timing is right, is to have a couple attend a weekend version of the psychoeducationally oriented Couples Relationship Enhancement Program for the purpose of learning all the RE skills in a concentrated format. This has the advantage of then allowing the couple to begin addressing the deeper issues in their relationship right from the beginning of the therapy.

Motivate and Structure for Home Assignments

One of the more easily overlooked issues in RE therapy is the importance of motivating and structuring for home assignments in order to increase the likelihood of the couple's cooperation. Many therapists think that clients simply are not interested in or will not follow through on home assignments in therapy, so why bother? Unfortunately, this attitude creates a self-fulfilling prophecy in that the couple predictably matches the therapist's low level of expectation. It is the job of the therapist in RE therapy to properly motivate the couple and structure for the success of home assignments. I believe the single most important factor in the therapist's success in motivating the couple to complete home assignments is simply his or her commitment to talking to the couple about the importance of home assignments and doing so with conviction. I begin my discussion of home assignments by introducing the *Relationship Enhancement* Client *Manual* (Guerney & Scuka, 2005) to the couple. There also is an audiotape version of the *RE Client Manual*, the *Relationship Enhancement Audio Program* (Guerney, 1994b). I do so in the following way:

> In order to facilitate our work together, I would like to have the two of you purchase a copy of the *Relationship Enhancement Client Manual*. It was written originally by Dr. Bernard Guerney, who created the Relationship Enhancement method to help couples and families improve and have more satisfying relationships. There is considerable research that demonstrates its superior clinical effectiveness, so this is a proven method for doing couples therapy. Please take a look at the Table of Contents. You will notice that each chapter is devoted to one of the Relationship Enhancement skills that Dr. Guerney and I have identified as being important in helping intimate partners improve how they relate to one another. Each week I'll ask you to read a chapter or two. This will help speed up our work together because then I won't have to take as much time to explain things to you. Is that agreeable? [*Presuming a "yes," then continue with:*] Good. What I'd like to ask you to do for next time is to read the first chapter on the Empathic skill. In the appendix you

will also find a set of guidelines for each of the skills. I suggest that you review the corresponding guidelines after you read a chapter on one of the skills. This will reinforce your learning of what you read in the chapter. By the way, there is an audiotape equivalent of this manual if you prefer to listen to tapes instead of reading. Any questions?

This statement accomplishes several things. First, it directly conveys the message, and the expectation, that this is how I conduct couples therapy, and that the manual is a standard part of the therapy process. As a result, in 10-plus years of conducting RE therapy with couples, fewer than a handful of clients have declined to purchase and use the manual. Second, I refer to the research that validates the clinical efficacy of RE therapy as a way of building the partners' confidence in the method and thereby increasing their motivation to actively participate in the process of their own therapy. Third, I explain how the manual will be used and that they will save themselves time (and by implication money) if they do the requested assignments. Fourth, I establish a contract with the couple to do home assignments by securing their agreement. Fifth, I give them a specific assignment in order to establish the importance of home assignments from the very beginning of therapy. Finally, I offer an audiotape equivalent for those who are not likely to read the manual. Addressing each of these points should greatly increase client acceptance and completion of home assignments, to the benefit of the couple's therapy process.

Explain the Use of the Relationship Questionnaire

There is one additional part of the couple's first home assignment, but it deserves its own special attention: the Relationship Questionnaire (see appendix A). I simply continue explaining to the couple in the following way:

I'd also like you to turn to the Relationship Questionnaire in appendix A. I'd like to ask each of you to fill it out independently, without consulting one another, and to respect one another's privacy. Then I'd like to ask you to bring it to me next time. You may keep a copy for yourself. There are five categories on the Relationship Questionnaire. Let me explain each one. The first category is "Positive Issues" or "Partner Appreciations." These are things you like or admire about your partner as a person, or things you appreciate that your partner does, either for you, for the family, for themselves, or even the world at large. The second category is

"Enhancement Issues." I need to explain this category clearly, because to qualify as an enhancement issue, it must meet three criteria. First, it is something that you wish were different about your relationship—that, from your point of view, would improve the relationship. But, second, it is not a source of conflict between the two of you, because then it would no longer qualify as an enhancement issue. In other words, you genuinely believe that it's something that your partner is at least in principle open to, because if it's something you want but you know you're partner doesn't, then by definition it's a conflict issue. The third criterion is that the change not involve a one-time event but something that would represent a sustained change in your relationship over time. The third and fourth categories are pretty straightforward: the minor issues and conflicts in your relationship and the major problems in your relationship. The final category is "Life Goals." This includes your dreams for the future as well as your personal goals and your goals for this relationship. Again, I'd like to ask each of you to fill it out independently of one another and bring it to me next time. Then I'll review them and look for correlations as well as issues unique to each of you, and I'll use them as something of a road map to help us define what issues we'll address in the therapy.

The Relationship Questionnaire indeed plays a very important role in RE therapy with couples. Not only does it provide a road map for identifying and selecting issues for the couple's dialogues later in the therapy, it also engenders a deeper involvement by the couple in their own process.

This brings us to the conclusion of the clinical intake with couples in RE therapy. It is, from one point of view, a major undertaking in that it demands of the therapist much in terms of concentration and skill. On the other hand, if executed well, the clinical intake will launch the couple's therapy process in a positive direction and with the prospect of longer-term success. (For an example of the joint portion of a clinical intake, see clinical vignette 4, chapter 16.)

Looking Ahead to the Expanded Role of Home Assignments in RE Therapy

In order to provide a foretaste of the later stages of the RE therapy process and the expanded role home assignments will play, it should be noted that home assignments involve more than simply reading chapters in the *RE Client Manual* and filling out questionnaires. Much more important, in the long run, are the skills-practice exercises and home dialogues that will be negotiated. This is true whether following the Time-Designated or the Experiential format. The reason is that these practice exercises and home dialogues are instrumental to the couple's longer-term integration of the skills learning and to their ability eventually to conduct skilled dialogues on their own without the assistance of the therapist. They also further deepen the couple's investment and involvement in their own therapy process. Moreover, home assignments are instrumental in facilitating the couple's ability to generalize their use of the basic RE skills both into their daily lives with each other and into other important relationships in their lives, such as those with their children, parents, siblings, friends, and coworkers. Finally, home assignments also foster the couple's responsibility for their own therapy process and increase the likelihood that the couple will maintain their gains once the therapy is completed. As Boegner and Zielenback-Coenen observe (1984, p. 27), "One main strategy for fostering maintenance of change is the gradual shift from therapist control to self-management during the course of therapy. The concept is that couples increase expertise and autonomy during treatment, gaining the competence to cope with their own problems during and after therapy." The strong emphasis in RE therapy on home assignments fosters the maintenance of change virtually from the beginning of the therapy. For all these reasons, home assignments should not be deemed an optional, dispensable part of the RE therapy process; instead, home assignments should be seen as an absolutely integral part of what contributes to the efficacy of RE therapy.

There also is an important general principle regarding home assignments that should always be followed: If the therapist has negotiated a home assignment with a couple, he or she should then follow up and check to see whether the assignment was completed. Following up on home assignments conveys to the couple the seriousness with which the therapist regards them, and doing so in a consistent manner is the best means of increasing the likelihood that the partners will actually complete their home assignments. The therapist's judicious use of the principle of positive reinforcement in the form of praise can also increase the couple's commitment to completing home assignments. Conversely, the therapist's failure to follow up on home assignments indirectly conveys to the couple that they are not that important, in which case the couple becomes less and less likely to complete home assignments over time.

PART **III**
Teaching the Core RE Skills and Launching a Couple's First Dialogue

CHAPTER 5
First Session Postintake: Introducing the RE Model and Teaching Effective Conflict Management

Deciding how to Proceed

Once the clinical intake is complete, the therapist's next task is to decide whether to follow the Time-Designated format (chapters 5–7) or the Experiential format (chapter 8) to teach the core RE skills and launch the couple's first dialogue. The therapist may legitimately choose either format, and his or her decision can be made on a case-by-case basis depending on the needs of any given couple. However, a therapist's ability to utilize the Experiential format well is dependent upon having first mastered the more structured Time-Designated format and the special RE therapy techniques, because the Experiential format involves a more concentrated and faster-paced application of the RE therapy process. The advantage of the Time-Designated format is that it provides a highly systematized and structured frame of reference for conducting RE therapy so that in principle the therapist knows exactly what to do at any given moment in the unfolding process. Therapists new to the RE model may therefore wish to first follow the Time-Designated format and then experiment with using the Experiential format. As therapists become more familiar with both formats, they will be better positioned to use the Experiential format with greater confidence and fluidity. Therapists will also discover the great flexibility that is possible within the RE therapy model, including the flexibility to combine elements of both formats or to move back and forth between them.

The Time-Designated Format

The first session postintake in the Time-Designated format is devoted to introducing the RE model and to teaching effective Conflict Management strategies. The latter have always been part of the RE model, but they are here being brought together and expanded under a newly created Conflict Management skill. The teaching of Conflict Management is being introduced at the beginning of the RE therapy process in its Time-Designated format for several reasons. First, Conflict Management represents a kind of metaskill that in some cases needs to be introduced in order to create more favorable conditions so that a couple can proceed constructively with the rest of the RE therapy process. Second, teaching the Conflict Management skill can serve as the first of a two-pronged approach to dealing with cases of domestic violence involving mild physical aggression or common couple violence (see chapter 2 for a fuller discussion). In this context, teaching the Conflict Management skill can be used as a violence prevention and violence management intervention.[1] Finally, two of the Conflict Management scenarios and strategies flow directly out of the demonstration audiotape or CD that is customarily used to introduce the RE model (Guerney & Vogelsong, 1981b).

The therapist can use his or her discretion as to whether and how much of the Conflict Management skill to introduce to a couple. In those cases where the focus of the therapy is primarily on enrichment, and there is little overt conflict in what is basically a sound relationship, there may be little need for introducing Conflict Management into the therapy. However, in those cases where it is called for, including cases of domestic violence involving mild physical aggression, the therapist will usually have perceived that need on the basis of the clinical intake. In those cases, it is recommended that the therapist begin the first session postintake by explicitly addressing Conflict Management. Alternatively, it may be introduced at any point in the therapy when it becomes clear that it would be beneficial to the couple.

Objectives of the First Session Postintake

There are three objectives for the first session postintake in the Time-Designated format:

1. The first objective is to introduce the RE model in a way that helps couples understand the difference between unskilled versus skilled communication. This is usually facilitated by playing brief portions of the RE demonstration audiotape/CD in order to portray and then analyze the typical interactional patterns that contribute to couples

fighting versus an alternative skilled way of interacting that permits the constructive engagement and resolution of difficult issues.

2. The second objective is to teach Conflict Management strategies that will enable couples to better regulate their emotions and to manage conflict situations more effectively and in a manner that preserves emotional safety and respect for the relationship. This can be accomplished by using the scenarios portrayed on the RE demonstration audiotape/CD to talk about how the couple can preventatively prepare themselves to deal with such scenarios if and when they occur in their relationship. Extra emphasis and attention may be given to Conflict Management strategies when dealing with cases of common couple violence.

3. The third objective is to provide a brief overview of the RE skills in terms of the basic purpose of each skill. This will provide the couple with a general picture of what they will be learning and how the skills will help them begin to transform their relationship.

Follow-Up on Home Assignments and Collect Relationship Questionnaires

The therapist should collect the Relationship Questionnaire from each person at this point and check on any other home assignments that may have been negotiated. If the separate interviews with the couple occurred at a second meeting (a frequent occurrence), then the couple's Relationship Questionnaires likely would have been collected at that time. If the separate interviews were held as part of the first meeting with the couple, then the Relationship Questionnaires would be collected at the beginning of the first session postintake.

Introduce and Process the RE Demonstration Audiotape or CD

The conventional way of introducing the RE model to couples is to play a portion of each of two parts of one of the RE demonstration audiotapes/ CDs. While there are multiple topics that could be used for this purpose, there is one topic in particular that is especially useful both to contrast unskilled versus skilled communication and to set the stage for teaching the Conflict Management skill: "Wife Is Upset Over Husband's Driving Style." This vignette can be found on the *Relationship Enhancement Program: Leader Demonstration Tape* or CD (Guerney & Vogelsong, 1981b). The vignette could be introduced in the following way:

> I'd like to set the stage for our work together by playing two portions of an audiotape [or CD] for you. The first part of the tape

portrays a couple having what we technically refer to as an un-skilled interaction. Most people would simply call it a fight. But I'd like you to begin to make the association in your mind between being unskilled and fighting. Then we'll listen to the second part of the tape and hear the same couple deal with the same issue, but now using the Relationship Enhancement skills. As you listen to the first part of the tape, I'd like to ask that you *not* focus on the con-tent of the issue and that you *not* think in terms of who's right or wrong, or whose side you'd take or who started it, because in the end none of those things matter. What I'd like you to pay attention to instead is the process of the couple's communication and why it deteriorates. You can do this by asking yourself what each person is doing, or not doing, that contributes to them having a fight. I'll play about 3.5 minutes of the tape. Then we'll talk about it.

After playing the first portion of the audiotape/CD (ending where the husband says, "That would be a blessing!"), the therapist should ask the couple, "So, if you had to analyze the couple's pattern of communication and what makes it unskilled, how would you describe it?" Many couples will be able to describe at least some of the elements that contribute to the couple's negative pattern of communication. Ideally, the therapist takes the partners' responses and interweaves them together (and fills in the missing blanks) to make the following sequential observations:

1. The husband is already defensive before a word has been said, and his defensiveness comes across as a quasi-attack on the wife. ("All right, what's the matter? Carol, come on. I've seen that look before. What's the matter?")

2. The wife, for her part, launches into an attack on her husband's driv-ing style and, by implication, his character. ("I'm just so relieved to be alive. You nearly killed us again in that car. It's a miracle we're back in this house alive!")

3. The husband, now feeling personally attacked, becomes even more defensive. Whenever someone experiences himself to be under attack, that person will almost automatically become defensive. This often takes on the quality of a self-protective wall that goes up to protect oneself from the verbal volleys. Behind the wall, the person tends to shut down emotionally and loses touch with his own inter-nal experience. The reason is that the person is focused on the exter-nal threat to his survival. Some people respond to this perceived threat by engaging in "flight" in order to preserve safety. Other peo-ple, however, engage the "fight" response and begin to counterattack

(the latter is what is portrayed on the audiotape). So now we have both people engaging in personal attacks, and both parties feeling defensive. A vicious, self-perpetuating cycle has been created.

4. In addition, because both people are feeling defensive and have shut down emotionally, with the exception of the communication of anger and related emotions, neither person is able to listen. Consequently, neither person feels listened to. This generates an internal frustration in both partners over not feeling heard, and this frustration in turn leads each person to raise his or her voice or intensify the attacks on the other person out of the hope that, "If only I raise my voice, then (maybe) you'll finally hear what I have to say." But since both are feeling the same thing, and they both raise their voices, this merely creates a deeper vicious cycle of escalation.

5. At the extreme, this vicious cycle of escalation can eventually lead to physical violence between the couple. This may happen only in a minority of cases (in the general population), but violence in the form of mild physical aggression between the couple can be seen, from one point of view, as the ultimate expression of frustration over feeling ignored and not feeling heard.

After processing and explaining this dynamic, the therapist may introduce the second vignette with:

Now let's listen to the second part of the tape. It's the same couple with the same issue. It even starts the same way. But then something happens. Pay attention to that. Then observe what makes this interaction different from the previous one.

After playing the second part of the audiotape/CD (about 3.5 minutes, ending where the husband says "…when I don't have any control over it, and it frightens me"), the therapist should ask the couple, "So what makes this interaction different?" Once again, the therapist takes their responses and interweaves them together (and fills in the blanks) to make the following observations:

1. The conversation starts the same way, reflecting the reality of life that feelings are spontaneously generated when something unpleasant happens. But one of the partners, in this case the husband, recognizes that they are about to start one of their typical fight patterns, and requests that they stop and shift into a dialogue to address the issue by using the RE skills. This represents an example of Conflict Management, which will be revisited later.

2. Instead of attacking and criticizing the other person, the partners take turns in speaking out of their own subjective experience, and communicate their feelings about what the other person had said or done, or what had happened.

3. In the absence of negative personal attacks, neither person is feeling a high level of defensiveness. Given the relative absence of defensiveness, there are no counterattacks.

4. As a consequence, each person is able to listen attentively to the other and to empathize with the partner's feelings and concerns.

5. In addition, each person feels emotionally free to go deeper into the experience and to reveal his or her deeper feelings. Case in point: The husband is able to reveal that he, too, was scared, something he in no way would have been able to recognize, let alone admit, when he experienced himself being attacked by his wife in the first vignette.

6. Finally, the therapist should observe to the couple that he or she will teach them how to conduct that kind of skilled dialogue so that they can address issues in their relationship more constructively, and then resolve them to their mutual satisfaction, which is one of the primary goals of the therapy.

Some readers may be thinking, "I can't imagine playing an audiotape or CD like that as part of the therapy process. I think the couple would get bored, and it's just not my style." If this objection were raised in a training workshop, my first response would be to empathize with that person's concerns (as a form of Troubleshooting). Then I would respond in the following way:

> As the therapist, you could simply decide to talk to the couple about the differences between unskilled and skilled communication, or you could solo role-play minivignettes to illustrate the differences. There are, however, some distinct advantages to using the RE demonstration audiotape or CD. Far from boring couples, the role-played vignettes' very vividness actually captures their attention. Moreover, most couples instantaneously see themselves in and identify with the negative interactional pattern portrayed in the first vignette, because many couples have their own similar pattern. There is also a distinct advantage to hearing the negative dynamic so clearly laid out and yet in a depersonalized form because it doesn't directly involve the couple themselves. As a result, it helps avoid activating the couple's defensiveness. This in turn opens the couple to analyzing exactly what contributes to the

negative interactional pattern in a manner that allows them to recognize and admit its dysfunctional nature. Then, hearing a contrasting skilled interaction, the couple immediately gains a sense of what an alternative might look like; the partners also are provided with a context for understanding what to expect from the therapy and what the therapy will expect of them. The role-played vignettes thus serve as a very effective and efficient introduction to the RE model. Sometimes, I even find that when a couple does not hear the vignettes, most typically in the context of using the Experiential format, they sometimes struggle over the structure of the dialogue process, and we may end up spending more time trying to help them sort that out than if they had listened to the vignettes to begin with. I therefore would like to urge you to experiment with using the demonstration audiotape or CD as a way to introduce couples to the RE model.

Teach Conflict Management Skill

Yet another reason for therapists to use the RE demonstration audiotape or CD to introduce the RE model is that it provides the perfect context for teaching couples the principles and techniques of effective Conflict Management. And an ideal time to teach the Conflict Management skill is immediately after the therapist has introduced the RE model by means of processing the RE demonstration audiotape/CD.

The purpose of the Conflict Management skill is to help couples learn how to better regulate their emotions and to manage conflict situations more effectively and in a manner that preserves emotional and physical safety and mutual respect. The key here is that the teaching of Conflict Management is designed to equip couples *preventatively* to self-regulate emotion and behavior and to manage future conflict situations skillfully. This may be done with engaged couples in order to help them learn how to deal with future conflicts in a safe manner. But it is even more important for highly conflicted and emotionally distraught couples whose patterns of interaction are dominated by intense verbal arguments, or for couples who are caught in a web of mild physical aggression.

For both of these kinds of couples, teaching Conflict Management is tantamount to a crisis intervention. Indeed, in the absence of learning how to self-regulate emotions and behavior and how to manage conflict more effectively, such couples often are unable to engage the therapy process well, and sometimes not at all. From this point of view, Conflict Management represents a metaskill that makes possible the use of the other RE skills.

This is why it is important, with many couples, to teach the Conflict Management skill early in the RE therapy process, preferably at the beginning.

Background: The Biology of Emotional Flooding

Regulating emotion and behavior and managing conflict is such an important issue because of the phenomenon of emotional flooding, or what has also been referred to as "emotional hijacking" (Goleman, 1995). What is known about emotional flooding is that when a person's neural system is so overwhelmed by negative affect that he or she is unable to process and manage it, then that person either shuts down emotionally or becomes emotionally hijacked. When that happens, the person's typical means of processing information and experience, including his or her rational faculties, is short-circuited. The person is then rendered helpless in the face of emotional freezing or out-of-control emotions. This can manifest either as a kind of implosion into inertia or as a tempest that sweeps all before it. At its worst, it can lead to mild physical aggression between the couple or to severe physical violence by a batterer toward an abuse victim. In either case, the person (or the couple) loses the ability to constructively engage and navigate his or her environment—and most especially the interpersonal environment.

The goal of Conflict Management, then, is to help couples learn how to (1) preventatively inhibit emotional flooding from taking place at the first signs of its potential emergence, either in oneself or one's partner; (2) respond constructively to emotional flooding in one's partner; (3) safely extricate oneself from interactions where an emotional hijacking has already taken place; and (4) recover from an emotional hijacking after one has successfully extricated oneself from it, or been extricated from it by one's partner, in order to reengage one another in a skilled dialogue. A couple's ability to regulate emotion, manage conflict, or recover from an emotional hijacking constitutes a precondition for their ability to engage each other in a positive way. It also constitutes a precondition for the partners' ability to engage the therapy and the RE dialogue process effectively, most especially with regard to being able to empathize with the other person's feelings, concerns, and desires.

The Four Scenarios for the Application of Conflict Management Skill

It is helpful, for both the therapist and the couple, to conceptualize four distinct scenarios for the application of the Conflict Management skill. The first scenario, which is portrayed on the second part of the RE demonstration audiotape/CD discussed earlier, involves an interaction that has become too emotionally charged or a conflict situation in which there is potential for emotional flooding. The second scenario involves one partner recognizing the presence of strong negative emotion or the beginnings of emotional flooding in the other partner. The third scenario, which is portrayed on the first part of the RE demonstration audiotape/CD discussed earlier, involves a full-blown emotional hijacking, which has overtaken one or both parties; in the latter case, this typically manifests itself in the form of an intense verbal argument that is characterized by the inability to be verbally skillful or empathic. The fourth scenario involves either person recognizing the presence of strong negative emotion and the potential for emotional flooding or aggressive or violent behavior in oneself. In terms of time management, processing the RE demonstration audiotape/CD and teaching the four Conflict Management scenarios generally takes almost a full session, or perhaps longer when the therapist is first acquiring skill in teaching Conflict Management. When the fourth Conflict Management scenario is being applied to cases of mild physical aggression, it may take up to another full session to cover it fully.

Treat the Teaching of Conflict Management as the Negotiation of a Contract Between the Couple

One of the keys to the successful application of the Conflict Management skill to the first, third, and fourth scenarios is that it involves the principle of establishing in advance a contract between the couple so that both partners know exactly what to expect and what is expected of them in the future when they are faced with any of these three scenarios. This contractual component of the teaching of Conflict Management goes to the heart of the preventative nature of this skill. As a consequence, the therapist should never simply teach the content of the Conflict Management skill. *Instead, at certain strategic moments in teaching the principles and strategies of Conflict Management, the therapist should always explicitly ask the couple to agree to accept and abide by the terms of the recommended contract.* This increases the likelihood both that the couple will take what is taught with greater seriousness and that they will feel themselves obligated to make a genuine effort to follow the principles and strategies that they have learned. If either partner raises concerns or objections, be certain to first empathize (by way of Troubleshooting) and then reexplain the rationale for the recommendation or negotiate modifications to the contract that will satisfy that couple's concerns. In addition, it also is advisable to incorporate behavioral practice of some of the Conflict Management strategies described below. In the case of a highly conflicted couple who engage in frequent verbal fights or mild physical aggression, make a special point of checking in with them at the session following the teaching of the Conflict

Management skill as to how their week went and whether or not the strategies they had learned made any difference. This represents another application of the principle of following up on a home assignment in order to reinforce for the couple the importance of using what they have learned.

First Scenario for Conflict Management: Preventing Emotional Flooding as a Conflict Emerges

Once the therapist has processed the two portions of the RE demonstration audiotape/CD with the couple, he or she may immediately proceed to teaching the Conflict Management skill by discussing more fully the implications of the husband's intervention at the beginning of the second portion of the audiotape/CD. This may be done in the following way:

> Let's shift our focus a little bit, because what I'd like to do now is to teach you the principles and strategies of effective conflict management. In fact, it's referred to as Conflict Management skill because being able to manage conflict effectively is a distinct skill of its own. There are several different scenarios requiring the application of Conflict Management skills. The first scenario was portrayed at the beginning of the second audiotape [or CD]. Recall what happened. One partner did something, then the other partner said something, and emotions began to flare. The general principle is that when a conflict emerges and it becomes too emotionally charged, then someone, and it doesn't matter who, needs to recognize what is happening and request the other person to pause and then shift into dialogue mode. This can be done by first using an agreed-upon hand signal or by saying, "Can we pause for a moment, please." Then make a request to enter a structured dialogue using the RE skills by saying, perhaps, "I'd like to request that we deal with this by having a dialogue. Would you be willing to do that?"
>
> Whenever the two of you are faced with the beginnings of a verbal fight, I'd like you to imagine that it's as though the two of you are at a fork in the road. If someone doesn't recognize that emotions are flaring and there is potential for an emotionally charged and unskillful argument, then you are more likely to end up going down the one fork in the road that leads to what was portrayed in the first part of the tape, where the couple ended up in a nasty verbal battle. The alternative is for someone to recognize that emotions are flaring and that there is potential for a serious verbal argument, and for that person to identify what is happening and then make a request to shift gears into a structured dialogue where each

of you commits to following good expressive skills and good empathic skills.

The key, here, is that someone has to be aware of the interaction instead of just getting caught up in it. There's a difference between having an experience and being aware of the experience you are having. If you have no awareness of your experience, then you run a high risk that your experience will end up having you. The alternative is to bring awareness to bear on the interaction you are engaged in, because having awareness is what allows you to make a different choice, such as requesting that you both shift into a dialogue. The first application of the Conflict Management skill, then, is to bring awareness to your interactions and ask for a shift into dialogue mode whenever you find yourselves facing emotionally challenging circumstances. I'd like to encourage both of you to begin to apply this in your relationship. Would you be willing to do that? [Looking at one person, wait for a nod of the head or a "yes."] And would you be willing to do that? [Ditto with the other person.] Good. Any questions?

Second Scenario for Conflict Management: Generalizing the Use of Empathy in Response to Partner's Strong Emotions

The therapist may then move directly to the second scenario calling for the application of the Conflict Management skill. It may be introduced in the following way:

There's a second distinct scenario calling for Conflict Management. One variation of this scenario picks up right where the previous scenario left off. One of you recognizes that you are at that fork in the road and that you are facing an emotionally challenging situation. You identify the situation to your partner and make the recommended request for a dialogue. However, your partner is already too emotional to be able to shift into a dialogue at that moment, and your partner continues to display strong negative emotion. Alternatively, it could be any circumstance in which you recognize that your partner is emotionally upset. In either circumstance of your partner experiencing strong emotion, the most helpful thing that you can do is simply to empathize spontaneously with those strong emotions. Now, we'll discuss the specifics of how to empathize next time, but what's important to observe today is that choosing to empathize spontaneously when you experience your partner having strong negative emotion is itself an important—and distinct—strategy of Conflict Management. From a practical point of view, empathizing spontaneously is an alternative to requesting a dialogue, and in the instance of your partner experiencing strong negative emotion may make more sense because your partner may be unable to participate in a dialogue right at that moment.

Moreover, receiving empathy in the context of strong emotion almost inevitably has a calming or soothing effect. The reason is that the person experiencing strong emotion begins to feel acknowledged and understood, and this allows that person to begin to relax and regain composure. You will recognize that this is happening because you will observe the intensity in your partner's speech begin to subside. Ideally, you would continue to provide empathy until your partner's strong emotion disappears and he or she returns to emotional baseline. Sometimes, that is all that is necessary because, in feeling understood, your partner is enabled to let go of his or her strong emotion. On other occasions, however, regaining composure may become the prelude to the initiation of a structured dialogue because there is a relationship issue yet to be resolved. In either case, the spontaneous use of empathy in response to your partner's strong emotion represents a distinct intervention for effectively managing conflict. It also represents, by the way, a preventative intervention that can help prevent the experience of strong emotion from devolving into an even worse state of emotional flooding. Any questions?

With certain couples, the therapist, at his or her discretion, may choose to demonstrate and have the couple practice unilateral empathy in response to a simulated scenario involving the partner being upset. This follows the behavioral principle that supervised skill practice is important to the internalization of a new skill and to developing a new habit that can be relied on when certain circumstances present themselves.

Third Scenario for Conflict Management: Disengaging From Conflict When Both Partners Have Become Emotionally Hijacked

The therapist may then immediately proceed to discuss the third scenario for the application of the Conflict Management skill. Notice, in this application, how important it is to explicitly negotiate a contract with the couple as to how they will deal with these conflict situations in the future. This third application of Conflict Management can be explained in the following way:

The third scenario calling for Conflict Management also has two variations. The first variation picks up where the previous scenario ended. One of you attempts to empathize with your partner's strong negative emotion in the midst of an emerging conflict, but your partner doesn't respond by calming down and you begin to feel unsafe because the interaction has become too emotionally difficult. The other variation goes back to the first part of the audiotape [or CD] where the couple was having an emotionally charged argument. In effect, that couple went down the first fork in the road because no one recognized what was happening and very quickly both partners became emotionally hijacked. But what can happen, even in this heated scenario, is that it finally dawns on one of you, "Oh, my goodness, look at what we're doing again!"

If either of you find yourself in either situation in the future, here's what I recommend. First, I recommend that you both agree right here and now on a nonverbal signal that either of you could use to signal to the other person that you want to stop either kind of emotionally charged interaction between the two of you. The general principle here is to disengage from an emotionally charged interaction where you are feeling unsafe because one or both of you has become emotionally hijacked or is being verbally unskillful. If you don't disengage, you run a high risk that things will continue to escalate until they become destructive and hurtful. Therefore, it is a sign of respect for yourself, your partner, and your relationship to be willing to agree to this principle of disengaging when things have become too heated.

To facilitate this disengagement, I recommend you use the time-out signal. [*Demonstrate using a hand signal.*] What this nonverbal signal means is something like this: "Here we are again having a fight and not listening to one another, and I don't want to be doing this any more. [Or,] I'm not feeling safe any longer. I'm therefore requesting that we both stop and that we agree to disengage from one another for the purpose of calming down, but with a promise that we come back to deal with what just happened." Now, it might be very difficult to say all of that in the midst of an intense verbal argument or if the other person remains intensely upset even after you have attempted to empathize spontaneously. That is why it is important to have an agreed-upon nonverbal signal that both of you recognize and that both of you would agree to abide by, no questions asked, if your partner uses the signal with you in the midst of an emotionally charged interaction. Would you be willing to make that commitment? [*Looking at one person, wait for a nod of the head or a "yes."*] And would you be willing to make that commitment? [*Ditto with the other person.*] Good.

Now, an important part of this agreement is that you both are also making a promise to come back to deal with what happened. This is to prevent the person who makes the request for a time-out from using it as a means of avoiding dealing with the issue. This also helps the other person accept the request for the time-out by forestalling the fear that the person making the request will only stonewall the issue. To facilitate this, we recommend, after the verbal arguing has stopped, but before you actually separate, that the person initiating the time-out say that he or she wants to continue to work on the issue constructively by means of a skilled dialogue following a cooling-off period, and that you would like to try to do so after a specific period of time that you would propose for the two of you to come back together. It is recommended that you propose a time frame between 20 and 90 minutes. If that time frame appears unrealistic, perhaps because it is already too late at night, then negotiate and agree on a time when you both will come back together for the purpose of having a skilled dialogue. Is that agreeable with you? And with you? Great. So you've now both agreed that if your partner uses the time-out signal with you in the midst of an emotionally charged interaction, you have obligated yourself to immediately stop and then disengage in order to prevent any further harm to the relationship. You've both also agreed that you will come back together to deal with the issue at an agreed-upon time in order to engage in a skilled dialogue. Any questions?

This establishes the first part of the contract with the couple. There are two additional parts to the contract. They have been separated out from the first part in order to help both therapist and couples better understand the principles and strategies of this complex intervention.

Teach the Importance of Self-Calming   The second part of the contract involves a commitment on the part of the couple to not just sit passively holding onto their negative thoughts and emotions after they have disengaged from one another. Instead, a contract is negotiated for the couple to commit to actively work on self-calming for the purpose of preparing themselves to reengage one another in the form of a skilled dialogue. It may be explained in the following way:

Now there's an important assumption that's also part of this contract. After you have disengaged from one another, the assumption is that you're not just going to sit around stewing in your negative emotional juices, but that you're both going to do whatever is necessary to help calm your emotions so that you can reengage your partner in a skilled dialogue to discuss what happened and to address the substance of the issue at hand. There's an interesting piece of research, by the way, that says that once strong negative emotion has become activated, it takes a minimum of 20 minutes for that negative energy to dissipate. That's why it is suggested that you agree to disengage for at least that long.

The further point, though, is that you can facilitate the process of reducing that negative emotion by actively engaging in self-calming strategies. One element of self-calming involves recognizing and directly counteracting the "hot thoughts" about your partner's character or motives that tend to run through your head when you are intensely upset with your partner. The point, however, is that you have to specifically challenge such negative thoughts because otherwise they will perpetuate your negative emotions. This involves noticing the negative thoughts and saying to yourself, "I need to stop thinking that way." This will help reduce the intensity of the negative emotion that usually accompanies such negative thoughts.

The other element of self-calming involves a wide variety of possible strategies to calm oneself physiologically. Some people calm themselves by sitting quietly and meditating, praying, or engaging in deep breathing or other forms of bodily relaxation. Some people like to listen to music, while others like to write out their feelings in the form of journaling, which represents a form of self-empathy. Others like to go for a walk, a run, or engage in some other form of physical activity such as yoga or tai chi. What's important is that each of you develop one or more strategies to help calm yourself after you have disengaged from an emotionally charged interaction. Also, these same strategies can, over time, help you reduce the likelihood that you become emotionally flooded or hijacked to begin with. So there's a double benefit here.

The purpose of self-calming is to help you prepare to reengage your partner in a skilled dialogue to deal with what happened constructively. But to be able to reengage your partner means that you each must meet two conditions. First, you have to be able to honestly say to yourself, "I believe I can participate in a skilled dialogue and remain calm enough that I will not say anything that would cause my partner to feel defensive because of my verbal unskillfulness." It can also be helpful to rehearse what you want to say to increase the odds that you express yourself skillfully. Second, you have to be able to honestly say to yourself, "I believe I can listen to my partner empathically and acknowledge his or her feelings and concerns without becoming overly reactive." These are the two conditions that must be met in order to be able to engage successfully in a skilled dialogue.

Now we haven't yet discussed the guidelines for being a good Expresser and a good Empathizer, or how to conduct a structured dialogue; that will come over the next two sessions. But in the meantime, what's important is that you begin to employ these Conflict Management strategies at least for the purpose of disengaging from emotionally charged and verbally unskilled interactions. In the future you will be able to take the next step of being able to reengage one another in order to have a skilled dialogue. So, is each of you willing to commit to actively working on self-calming after you disengage from a difficult emotional situation? Are you willing to do that? [*Looking at one person, wait for a nod of the head or a "yes."*] And are you willing to do the same? [*Ditto with the other person.*] Great.

In the case of couples who tend to be highly reactive or lack internal resources for emotional self-calming, the therapist may elect to take additional time to teach specific methods for self-calming, including helping them build a new habit through repetition and "overlearning."[2] Three resources that therapists might find useful in helping clients with self-calming strategies are Davis, McKay, and Eshelman's *Relaxation and Stress Reduction Workbook* (2000); McKay and Rogers's *The Anger Control Workbook* (2000); and Ortwein's *ER: Emotional Regulation in the Relationship Enhancement Tradition* (in press-b). A distinct advantage of Ortwein's program is that it combines RE skills with relaxation, emotional awareness, and impulse management techniques.

Teach the Couple how to Approach One Another Following Self-Calming
The third part of the contract involves teaching the couple how to initiate approaching the other person when self-calming has been achieved and that person is now ready to engage in a skilled dialogue. It may be explained in the following way:

> The last piece of the contract involves how it is recommended that you approach your partner when you are ready to engage in a skilled dialogue. When the agreed-upon time has arrived and you

are feeling ready to dialogue, here's what I recommend you do. I'd like you to approach your partner and say something like this: "I just wanted to let you know that I'm ready for us to have a dialogue about what happened, and I wanted to check in with you to see whether you feel you're ready to do that as well." The important point here is that you can't simply assume that your partner is ready to start a dialogue just because you are. That's why it's important that you check it out with your partner, because your partner may say, "I'm sorry, but I still need more time before I'll be ready to dialogue." If your partner indicates that he or she needs more time to complete self-calming, respect that. Giving your partner that additional time is a sign of respect for your partner and your relationship.

However, if the second person indicates a need for more time, then it becomes that person's responsibility to give the first person an approximate time frame as to when he or she will be ready to have a dialogue. If necessary, negotiate, and agree on when the two of you will come back together to have a dialogue if it no longer appears realistic to do so that day. But don't forget, you've already both committed to not just passively harboring your angry and resentful emotions. You've both committed to work actively on self-calming for the purpose of being able to reengage one another skillfully in a dialogue. On the other hand, there can be a certain advantage to a longer period of disengagement because it can help you go beyond physiological recovery to a deeper psychological recovery that is more conducive to dialoguing. Are you willing to follow these guidelines? [*Looking at one person, wait for a nod of the head or a "yes."*] And are you willing to follow these guidelines? [*Ditto with the other person.*] Great.

By the way, if either of you per chance experience the other person stonewalling an issue by seeking to disengage from it by using this intervention, or if either of you experience the other person resisting reengagement after the request for a disengagement, that would represent a misuse of this skill, and you could identify that as an issue in the relationship that would need to be addressed by means of a dialogue. Any questions?

In my experience, taking the time to teach this admittedly complex intervention of Conflict Management helps many highly conflicted couples begin to decrease the frequency of their verbal arguments and to pull back from their intensity because they now feel that they have a framework for regulating their own emotions and managing conflict situations more effectively. Part of the effectiveness of the Conflict Management skill is that it creates a level playing field and helps both parties know exactly what to expect and what to do when faced with a specific conflict situation. In this sense, teaching Conflict Management gives clients the skill and the confidence they have previously lacked to deal with this treacherous terrain. This represents a form of client empowerment, and I urge therapists to incorporate the teaching of Conflict Management into their repertoire of interventions with couples in distress.

Fourth Scenario for Conflict Management: Recognizing Strong Emotion in Oneself and Regulating One's Behavior Accordingly

This final scenario comes out of the literature on domestic violence and is most directly relevant to couples engaging in mild physical aggression. As a consequence, including this scenario in the teaching of Conflict Management is at the discretion of the therapist, though it can be used with nonviolent couples as well. The therapist should be aware that including this intervention in its comprehensive form will likely require an additional session to cover it fully. In cases where mild physical aggression has been reported and is being explicitly addressed in the therapy, the therapist would begin teaching the Conflict Management skill by having the couple make a "no violence" contract with one another and with the therapist. In cases where no violence exists, the therapist may still choose to negotiate such a contract with the couple as a preventative measure. This may be especially helpful with couples who are receiving premarital counseling.

The following presentation of the fourth scenario for Conflict Management borrows in part from the outline provided by Holtzworth-Munroe, Meehan, Rehman, and Marshall (2002, pp. 456–458). It may be introduced in the following way:

> Let's take a look at the final application of Conflict Management. This involves each of you recognizing in the moment that you are experiencing strong emotion and that you are at some risk for emotional flooding or aggressive or violent behavior. The key to being able to effectively manage this situation is to recognize that you are having this experience when it is happening, before it is too late. To facilitate this, I'd like to process with each of you how you experience anger so that you can increase your awareness of the point at which you become vulnerable to emotional flooding or aggressive or violent behavior. That way, each of you will be able to regulate your own emotion and behavior more effectively.

The therapist then has each person identify physical cues involving physiological changes such as tenseness or increased heart rate; cognitive cues involving "hot thoughts" such as labeling, hostile attributions, or catastrophizing; and behavioral cues such as increased emotion in one's voice or slamming doors. Then the therapist has each person construct a personalized anger continuum using a scale from 1 to 10 that would include a graduated listing of physical, cognitive, and behavioral cues from "frustrated" to "angry" to "furious" to "in danger of losing control and resorting to violence." Then the therapist negotiates with the couple for each partner to keep an anger log for briefly describing episodes involving strong negative emotion and for rating each one on the scale of 1 to 10. The purpose is to help each person become more aware of his or her typical patterns, with the hope that this increase in self-awareness will help each person better regulate both their emotions and their behavior. Holtzworth-Munroe et al. (2002, p. 456) discusses this component of the intervention in greater detail; and Ortwein (in press-b) discusses this from the perspective of the RE model.

The second part of this intervention involves having the couple negotiate a contract around self-initiated time-outs. It may be done in the following way:

Recall how in the third scenario either of you could initiate a time-out after it has finally dawned on you that the two of you have gotten into an intense verbal argument and you want to end it before it gets any worse, or if you're simply not feeling safe and you want to disengage from an emotionally charged interaction. Well, in this scenario, the focus is on each of you using your personalized anger continuum in order to monitor yourself preventatively so that you can initiate a time-out for yourself when you recognize that your emotions are getting heated and you are at an increased risk for becoming emotionally flooded or acting out physically in a manner that would be harmful to your partner and your relationship.

If you find yourself in this position and decide to initiate a time-out for yourself on a preventative basis, then I recommend that you commit to doing the following. First, let your partner know that you are experiencing strong negative emotion and that you wish to take a time-out as a preventative measure and out respect for your relationship. Second, give your partner a time that you are committing to return for the purpose of having a skilled dialogue. This is important to help prevent your partner feeling either stonewalled or abandoned by your request for a time-out. Again, try to limit your time-out to between 20 and 90 minutes. If that time frame appears unrealistic, then negotiate and agree on a time when you both will come back together for the purpose of having a skilled dialogue. Third, during the time-out, separate physically and respect the other person's request for the time-out. Fourth, as in the previous scenario, actively engage in self-calming strategies during your time-out, including monitoring your negative thoughts to avoid perpetuating negative emotions. Fifth, if at the end of the designated time you still need more time, inform your partner, and provide a new time for having a dialogue. Finally, let your partner know that you are ready to dialogue and address the issue at hand by using all the RE skills. Are you willing to commit yourself to following these guidelines as appropriate? [*Looking at one person, wait for a nod of the head or a "yes."*] And are you willing to commit yourself to following these guidelines as appropriate? [*Ditto with the other person.*] Great.

If either person raises concerns or objections, the therapist should be certain to empathize and, if necessary, renegotiate the contract in a manner suitable to that couple's needs. With this intervention, it also is advisable to practice elements of this time-out procedure in session. The therapist should also follow up in future sessions on whether the couple had occasion to use this intervention and what their experience of it was. The therapist then troubleshoots and problem solves as necessary. Continued monitoring is an important part of the therapist's role. If the therapist were to determine that this Conflict Management intervention was not sufficient for a particular couple, then he or she would readdress the issue with the couple and provide even more intensive emotional and behavioral self-regulation training or, if necessary, make a referral. One useful resource is the empathy-based Compassion Power program of Stosny (1995, 2003), which helps people achieve better self-regulation by helping them understand the "core hurt" that underlies their anger, which in turn fosters a compassionate approach toward self and others.

Provide a Brief Overview of the RE Skills

The therapist's final task is to provide a brief overview of the remaining RE skills. This typically is done simply by referring to the descriptions of the purpose of each of the RE skills provided in chapter 1 (see pp. 14–15). This could be done either at the end of the session(s) devoted to teaching Conflict Management or, if there's no time, the overview of RE skills can be provided at the beginning of the next session, which will be devoted to the Empathic skill.

Home Assignments

In the case of highly conflicted couples or couples engaging in mild physical aggression, the therapist should request that they begin immediately to apply the principles and strategies of Conflict Management to their relationship as needed. In addition, the therapist should inquire as to whether the couple has read the first chapter in the *RE Client Manual* (Guerney & Scuka, 2005) on the Empathic skill. If not, the therapist should ask that they commit to reading it for the next session. If they have read it, it can be suggested that they review it, perhaps simply by reviewing the "Empathic Skill Guidelines" in the appendix of the *RE Client Manual*.

There is an additional recommended home assignment that may prove useful to some couples. The couple can be invited to listen to the second (skilled) part of one or more demonstration audiotapes or CDs at home for the purpose of reinforcing both how to redirect an emerging conflict into a dialogue and how to conduct a skilled dialogue. There is a nine-topic, five-audiotape/CD set titled *Relationship Enhancement Demonstration Tapes: Solving Marital Problems* (Guerney & Vogelsong, 1981a) that serves as an excellent resource for this purpose. This additional home assignment could prove to be especially useful to highly conflicted or physically aggressive couples, or couples who the therapist suspects may have some difficulty adjusting to the structured RE dialogue process. The simpler form of the assignment would be to have the couple simply listen to the audiotape or CD, either alone or together. The alternative form of the assignment would involve having the couple, either alone or together, pause the audiotape or CD after, say, the wife on the audiotape/CD finishes expressing herself, and the husband attempt an empathic response to the recorded wife's expressive statement. Then, the husband would listen to how the husband on the audiotape/CD empathized with the wife, and in this way be able to compare his own response with the modeled response on the audiotape/CD. The wife would do the same thing with the recorded husband's expressive statements.

Notes

1. In cases of domestic violence involving severe physical aggression and likely harm to the victim, referring the abuser to a batterers' treatment program and referring the victim to a support group and community support services is the appropriate first-step intervention. In addition, an interim safety plan for the victim should be developed.

2. For an illustration of the literally life-saving importance of overlearning, see Zander & Zander (2000, pp. 5–6) for an example of how white water rafting guides teach novices how to recover from falling out of a raft by repeating the phrase "toes to nose and look for the boat" dozens of times before they ever get in a raft. The point is that in a moment of crisis "you cannot think your way back [because] you have no point of reference. You have to call on something that has been established in advance" and is simple to access.

CHAPTER 6
Embracing the Other: Teaching Empathic Skill

The Empathic skill plays two important roles in RE therapy. First, it anchors the RE dialogue process by reducing undesirable emotional reactivity and creating an atmosphere of safety that encourages the exploration of difficult relationship issues. Second, the Empathic skill is the principal tool for creating deepened mutual understanding and emotional connection in the couple's intimate dialogues. Because teaching empathy also involves demonstrating it and having the couple practice it, it is advisable to allocate an entire session just to teaching the Empathic skill when following the Time-Designated format.

There are two approaches to teaching the Empathic skill. The first approach includes introducing the concept and form of a structured dialogue, explaining the goals and benefits of empathy, and explaining the two components of empathy and the two modes of verbal empathy. If a couple has read the chapter on the Empathic skill in the *RE Client Manual* (Guerney & Scuka, 2005) some version of this first approach would be sufficient. The alternative approach, either at the therapist's discretion or when the couple has not read the material, is to do an abbreviated version of the first approach (including the form of a structured dialogue and the goals and benefits of empathy) and to then use the Empathic skill guidelines as a framework for explaining empathy to the couple. Regardless of which approach is chosen, the therapist would also demonstrate empathy and then have the couple practice it with the specially designed practice exercise described below.

121

Introduce the Concept and Form of a Structured Dialogue

It is helpful to provide a context for teaching the Empathic skill by explaining the concept and form of a couple's structured dialogue. I introduce the concept of a structured dialogue with a theater-based metaphor:

> Today we're going to turn our attention to the Empathic skill. But first I'd like to place empathy in the context of conducting a structured dialogue. The purpose of a dialogue is to enable the two of you to be able to discuss potentially difficult issues in a manner that creates emotional safety for both of you. In order for this to be accomplished, it is important that certain guidelines be followed. I'd like to share with you a metaphor to help you understand what's involved in conducting a structured dialogue. I'd like you to imagine a two-person play. And like any play, there are roles. And in this metaphorical play there are two roles. We designate one role the Expresser, and we designate the other role the Empathizer. Now, in order for the play to go on, someone has to be in each role at every moment; otherwise, the play collapses. Practical translation: You can't have two Expressers on stage at the same time. If you do, even if you're polite enough to take turns and not talk over one another, something vital is not happening. What's not happening? [*Pause for the couple to respond.*] What's not happening is that no one is really listening, and no one is providing verbal empathy. Hence, the play collapses. Further practical translation: The person in the role of the Empathizer is not permitted to say anything from his or her point of view while in that role. Because if the Empathizer does that, then the Expresser is going to feel cheated, and the play collapses. Now the burden of the dialogue process clearly falls on the shoulders of the person in the role of the Empathizer, precisely because that person is not permitted to say anything from his or her point of view while in that role. So it would be unfair to keep either person in that role for too long. So what's unusual about this two-person play is that you are going to change roles on stage. However, the roles must be changed according to specific guidelines so that both of you know who's in what role at every moment of the dialogue. I'll teach you later how to change roles. At the moment, I want to focus on the Empathic skill.

Explain the Goals and Benefits of Empathy

The therapist begins by checking whether the couple has read the chapter on the Empathic skill in the *RE Client Manual*. Then the Empathic skill is introduced by explaining that there are three goals of empathy and four benefits. This may be done in the following way:

> There are three goals of empathy. The first goal of empathy is to leave your partner *feeling* understood and accepted. The second goal of empathy is to deepen your partner's self-understanding. The third goal is to help you, the Empathizer, better understand your partner's feelings, concerns, and desires. When these three goals are accomplished, empathy has four benefits. The first benefit of good empathy is that it encourages your partner to go deep in exploring and sharing his or her experience. A second benefit is that in feeling understood your partner will be more receptive to hearing your point of view and to resolving issues constructively. A third benefit is that it helps you, the Empathizer, dissipate negative feelings and increases receptivity to hearing your partner's point of view. A final benefit of empathy is that it fosters a deepened sense of intimacy, compassion, and emotional bonding in your relationship.

Explain the Concept of Empathy and Its Two Components

The concept of empathy is introduced by the therapist who explains that there are two components to empathy: the experiential act of becoming empathic and the giving of good verbal empathy. Then empathy is defined, the concept of selflessness is introduced, and a visual image is provided for understanding the process of becoming empathic. I introduce empathy in the following way:

> I'd like to provide you with a context for understanding empathy that goes beyond what you have read in the *RE Client Manual.* There are two parts to empathy: the experience of becoming empathic with another person's experience, and then the giving of good verbal empathy. What does it mean to become empathic with another person's experience? Recall the old saying about walking in another person's moccasins: One person cannot understand another's experience unless he or she first walks in the other's shoes, and then walks around in that person's world, imaginatively being that person, having that person's experience. Notice that empathy is *not* about you imagining yourself in the other person's place, imagining what *you* would feel, or how *you* would respond to a situation. Instead, empathy is about experiencing things from *the other person's* point of view, not from your own point of view.

Empathy thus involves embracing the other person on his or her terms, rather than on your own terms.

One way to understand this is through the concept of selflessness. To be selfless means to be able to be fully present to the experience of another person without your own feelings and concerns getting in the way; without your own preferences and desires getting in the way; and without your own values and goals getting in the way. Now, there's nothing wrong with any of those things per se, until they become obstacles to our being able to understand another person from that person's point of view. At that point, however, they become a real problem, because then, in effect, I am looking at you from the outside in, through the lenses of my own point of view. At its worst, this can take the form of me making negative judgments about you and your experience. But to be selflessly present to another person's experience means that I am not filtering your experience though my lenses and making judgments about it. To be selflessly present to your experience means that I have imaginatively entered into your experience in such a manner that I can identify with your experience from the inside out, rather than looking at you from the outside in.

I have an image that may help you grasp what it means to become empathic. It's as though you were to dive off a diving board into the water, and as you hit the water and plunge to the deepest point you can go, you begin to shed your ego, just like a snake sheds its skin. And as you begin to rise back toward the surface, you continue shedding your ego until you reach the surface, at which point you emerge from the water having metaphorically become the other person. At that point, you are able to experience things the way the other person experiences things, from the inside out, as though you *were* the other person. And, in doing so, you are enabled to embrace the other person on his or her own terms.

Then there's the process of giving good verbal empathy. Now empathy is not a memory game, nor does it involve simply mirroring or repeating back what your partner has said. That's not empathy, that's parroting, and it will not leave your partner *feeling* understood. Instead, empathy involves reading between the lines of what your partner has said in order to identify what else your partner is feeling, concerned about, and desiring that he or she may not have been able to put into words. And you want to include your reading between the lines in your verbal empathy. In doing that, you are giving a powerful gift because you will actually help your partner gain deeper self-understanding, and that's one of the essential goals of good empathy.

Explain the Two Modes of Verbal Empathy

Next the therapist explains the two forms of verbal empathy:

> There actually are two forms of verbal empathy. The first form is referred to as the conventional You Mode of empathy. In the conventional You Mode, the Empathizer simply uses the pronoun *you* to represent the other person's experience. If I were to use the You Mode of empathy, and you were sharing with me a childhood experience of yours, I would simply begin by saying, for example, "You were really upset when your parents ignored your complaints …." But there's another form of empathy called the Identification Mode of empathy. In the Identification Mode, the Empathizer uses the pronoun *I* to represent the other person's experience. If I were to use the Identification Mode of empathy, I would empathize with your childhood story by pretending to be you and retelling your story as though I were you. In that case, I might empathize by saying, "I was really upset at my parents for ignoring me. They never listened to me, especially when there was something wrong." But in using the pronoun *I* in this way, I am not being myself; I am temporarily assuming the identity of the person whose experience I am trying to represent. The reason for choosing to use the Identification Mode of empathy is that it often helps the Empathizer connect with the other person's experience more deeply.

Review the Empathic Skill Guidelines

Each of the Empathic skill guidelines is followed by explanatory comments in order to provide an alternative approach to teaching empathy. These guidelines and comments also provide a framework for coaching couples on the finer points of empathizing and answering client questions about empathy.

1. *Put your own feelings, concerns, and desires on hold so that you can become fully present to your partner's experience.*

    When you are in the role of the Empathizer, it's not about you. Ideally, your focus is exclusively on your partner. Empathy involves emptying your mind of all thoughts and self-preoccupations and surrendering yourself into your partner's experience. This self-emptying represents the precondition for making yourself truly available to your partner's experience.

2. *Listen intently and connect as deeply as possible with your partner's feelings, concerns, and desires from his or her point of view.*

This can be accomplished by simply focusing your eyes very intently on your partner at the same time that you listen patiently and nondefensively. The more intently you focus on your partner, including his or her facial expressions and body language, the more you fade into the background. This is how one actually becomes fully present to the experience of another person, because as you fade into the background, you are no longer focused on your own feelings and concerns, and you become available to enter imaginatively into your partner's experience.

3. *As you listen to your partner share his or her experience, imagine yourself as your partner, having your partner's experience.*

As you focus your attention ever more intently on your partner and what he or she shares with you, simply imagine yourself being your partner, having your partner's experience. Recall the metaphor of walking in someone else's moccasins. That metaphor perfectly captures what empathy is all about. So allow yourself, if you will, to walk around in your partner's world wearing your partner's shoes, experiencing things as he or she experiences them.

4. *As you imagine yourself being your partner, "read between the lines" of what your partner shares to identify deeper dimensions of his or her experience and the meaning or significance it holds for your partner. This can be facilitated by asking yourself:*

Given what I am hearing my partner share about his or her experience,
What would I, as my partner, be feeling?
What would I, as my partner, be concerned about?
What would I, as my partner, be in conflict about?
What would I, as my partner, desire?
What would I, as my partner, be thinking about doing?

As you are imagining yourself being your partner, having your partner's experience, ask yourself these kinds of questions as a way of facilitating your reading between the lines of what your partner actually says. This will enable you to identify what your partner is also trying to say that he or she is not quite managing to put into words.

5. *In giving verbal empathy, be certain to include insights gained from reading between the lines that your partner would immediately accept as true and that would deepen his or her self-understanding.*

Empathy is not a memory game. It's not just about repeating back to your partner what he or she has said to you. Unfortunately, that's what some therapies teach, but that's not genuine empathy. Remember, one of the goals of empathy is to deepen your partner's self-understanding. You accomplish that by reading between the lines of what he or she says to you in a manner that allows you to give to your partner an enhanced or deepened version of what was said. Every time you are able to do that, you are giving a precious gift to your partner, the gift of enhanced self-understanding.

6. *When using the more specialized Identification Mode of empathy, use the pronoun "I" to represent your partner's experience as though you were your partner. To signal that you are using the Identification Mode, you would begin by saying, "As Alice [using the name of your partner as you represent his or her experience], I am feeling…."*

Typically, you would use this more specialized Identification Mode of empathy only with your partner. But the advantage in choosing to use the Identification Mode of empathy is that it can help you connect more deeply with your partner's experience. The reason is that using the pronoun *I* helps you put your own feelings, concerns, and desires on hold because it encourages you to imagine yourself being your partner, having your partner's experience. This helps you better connect with your partner's experience from his or her point of view. It also encourages a more spontaneous reading between the lines that helps you uncover the deeper dimensions of your partner's experience and the meaning or significance it holds for your partner.

7. *When using the more conventional You Mode of empathy, provide your empathy in the form of direct declarative statements, such as "You're really angry with me about…."*

In this more conventional mode of empathy, the Empathizer uses the pronoun *you* to represent the partner's experience. Empathy given in this form is best given as directly as possible. For example, "You really get frustrated when I…," "You really wish I wouldn't…," "You would feel a lot happier if I would…," "You really love it when I…."

8. *Avoid introductory phrases such as "What I think I hear you saying is …" because they weaken the force of your empathy. They also draw attention to yourself when the focus is supposed to be on your partner.*

Listen to the difference between "What I think I hear you saying is, you're really angry with me for yelling at the kids this morning" and "You're really angry with me for yelling at the kids this morning." Can you hear how weak the first statement is compared to the second? It weakens the force of the empathy, so it's best to avoid all such introductory clauses. Besides, notice how such introductory clauses draw attention to yourself twice before you get around to acknowledging the other person, exactly what empathy is not supposed to do.

9. *Avoid qualifiers to your empathy such as "It seems like you're feeling…," "You're probably feeling…," "You're maybe feeling…," or "You're perhaps feeling…"; they also weaken the force of your empathy.*

Again, simply make your empathic statements as direct as possible, and without any qualifiers. This will increase the power and the force of your empathy. And don't worry about getting it wrong. If you get part of it wrong, your partner will correct you.

10. *Avoid putting your own thoughts, feelings, or opinions into your empathy.*

When you are in the role of the Empathizer, you are not permitted to say anything from your own point of view. The reason is that it would interfere with your ability to empathize with your partner from his or her point of view. This would almost certainly leave your partner not feeling understood, and perhaps even judged.

11. *Avoid giving advice or asking questions while empathizing.*

In addition to being presumptuous, giving advice obviously originates in your ego, implying you think you know how to solve the person's "problem." This betrays a nonempathic stance. The same thing is true of asking questions, which come out of your need to know, and thereby also betrays a nonempathic stance. Even if you are curious about something, you are encouraged to channel that energy into empathizing more deeply with what has been said and to trust that good empathy will lead your partner to disclose more to you about his or her experience, including what you wanted to know. And even if that doesn't happen, a truly empathic stance accepts that what the other person wants you to know is what's important for you to know. Also, it's not that you can't ask questions; it's simply that you can't ask questions while in the role of the Empathizer. Once roles have changed and you have become the Expresser, then you can ask all the questions you want.

There is one qualification to this guideline: If you truly do not understand what your partner has just said, you are permitted to state that and to request that your partner say what he or she was trying to say in different terms. The reason, obviously, is that you can't empathize with something that you don't understand.

12. *Graciously accept any corrections your partner makes to your empathy by verbally empathizing with the correction.*

One of the wonderful things about empathy is that it's a naturally self-correcting process. If a portion of your empathy happens to be off target—and I wager it will be off target by a shade or two of meaning rather than being way out in left field—then that will almost automatically prompt your partner to realize what is true, and he or she will tell you. So you needn't be concerned about having to get your empathy 100% exactly right. That doesn't mean you shouldn't make your best effort, because you should. But it also means that as long as your empathy is largely on target, your partner will both feel understood and will have his or her self-understanding enhanced by you reading between the lines. And if you happen to get a piece of it wrong, graciously accept any correction by verbally empathizing with the correction.

One last point: Empathizing with your partner does not entail agreement with what has been said. Empathizing with your partner simply says, as an indirect (or metalevel) communication, that you respect your partner enough to acknowledge his or her experience as simply that. And, of course, the hope is that you both will show this kind of respect to one another, even and most especially when you do disagree with one another. Moreover, you will have a chance to express any disagreements you do have when you become the Expresser.

Demonstrate the Empathic Skill

Once the therapist has explained empathy, he or she will next demonstrate it so that the couple can experience both what is involved in becoming empathic and what it feels like to receive empathy. During this demonstration, it is important that the therapist use the Identification Mode of empathy in order to accomplish two goals: first, to demonstrate one person imaginatively "becoming" another person by empathically identifying with that person's experience; and second, to demonstrate how to give good verbal empathy. In the Identification Mode of empathy, the Empathizer uses the pronoun *I* to represent the other person's experience, including imaginatively reading between the lines. The demonstration may be introduced in the following way:

> What I'd like to do now is to demonstrate to you what empathy involves and what it feels like to receive empathy. To do that, I'd like to ask each of you to come up with a childhood experience of yours, or perhaps one from adolescence, that you'd be willing to share. It can be either a happy memory of something positive in your life or a sad memory of something that wasn't very pleasant. It can be either; it doesn't matter which. The only thing I ask is that it not be some random event of little significance, but an event that really meant something to you in that it carried a lot of emotional weight for you as a child. Whoever's ready first can go first.

The choice of a childhood experience for the demonstration of empathy is designed to serve two purposes simultaneously. The first reason for specifically choosing a childhood experience is to avoid activating negative energy between the couple during what is designed to be a positive learning experience. The second reason a childhood experience is chosen is because it helps the couple to get in touch with a more vulnerable part of themselves. This, in turn, increases the likelihood that one or both parties will be touched by their partner's experience, the hope being that the demonstration and, even more importantly, the couple's subsequent practicing of empathy (by means of their sharing additional stories and empathizing directly with one another), will foster an attachment bonding experience between the partners. One final note: In those instances where the couple knew one another as children, specify that the experience shared should not involve the partner or the partner's family. The reason is to avoid generating any negative emotion between the partners, even inadvertently.

When the first person indicates he or she is ready to share a story, then it is important that the therapist carefully structure the experience. It may be done in the following way:

> Before we begin, let me ask you [*the person not telling the story*] to sit over here [*either next to or behind the therapist, but facing the person telling the story*]. Now, I'm going to be the person to provide your partner with verbal empathy, but what I'd like you to do is to imagine yourself being your partner, having his (or her) experience as he (or she) relates the story. And one thing for you [*to the person who is about to share their story*]: If, after I empathize, you come to have new insights or simply want to say more about your experience, feel free to do so. If not, that's OK, too. Often good empathy will prompt the desire to say more, but not always. Sometimes people feel complete with their original statement and the empathy received. One last thing: When I empathize, I will use the Identification Mode of empathy and use the pronoun *I* to represent your experience. But in doing that I'm not going to be myself; I'm going to be you and represent your experience as though I were you.

As the first person shares his or her story, the therapist attempts to identify as deeply as possible with the experience of the child by imagining him- or herself being the child, having the child's experience. When the client is finished, the therapist would then proceed to empathize with the story by assuming that person's identity and retelling the story as though the therapist were the client. Make a special effort to read between the lines in order to verbalize feelings that the client had not been able to verbalize but clearly are implied in what that person has shared. If the person is prompted to say more after receiving the initial empathic representation, you would empathize again. If the person still talks about the experience in terms of how it was experienced by that person as a child, you would continue to use the Identification Mode of empathy. If, instead, the person shifts focus and now talks about the impact the experience continues to have on his or her life today, you can elect to shift into using the You Mode of empathy.

Once the demonstration is complete, the therapist briefly processes the experience with the couple in order to reinforce their learning. The therapist begins by asking the person who shared the experience what it was like to receive empathy in that way. Depending on the person's response, the therapist can also make an observation about the benefits of the Identification

Mode of empathy. Most importantly, and assuming the therapist has done a good job, he or she should look for an opportunity to say, "I take it that you feel understood." When appropriate, the therapist may also observe, "It appears that you came to have a deeper understanding of (or connection with) your experience as a result of the empathy." These comments help reinforce the benefits of giving and receiving empathy.

Then the therapist should turn to the partner who also had been listening and ask, "What did you observe me to do?" Following the partner's observations, the therapist makes a point of emphasizing that he or she read between the lines and, if true, that emotional tone or feelings were added that were not verbalized but that the therapist imagined to be true given his or her identification with the partner's experience. The therapist may also ask the partner whether there were any dimensions of the storyteller's experience that he or she picked up on that were not verbalized. This is useful both to validate (when appropriate) the partner's ability to read between the lines and to make the point that different people will pick up on different nuances when listening empathically. This permits another useful observation, namely, that there is no one correct way to empathize with someone's experience; instead, there is a range of plausible readings between the lines, any number or combination of which can result in perfectly adequate empathy in terms of the desired goals of leaving the Expresser feeling understood and deepening the Expresser's self-understanding.

When the processing of the first person's sharing is finished, the entire sequence would be repeated by having the second person share a childhood experience. The reason both people are invited to share a story is that it is important that both people have the experience of receiving empathy and that both people observe empathy being given by the therapist.

Example of a Therapist's Demonstration of Empathy Using the Identification Mode

The following is a transcript of an actual demonstration of empathy using the Identification Mode in response to a client relating an experience from adolescence. Notice how I begin the empathy by reaching for a deep underlying positive feeling, and note the impact it has on the client. Also notice how I read between the lines to bring out deeper dimensions of her experience that were not explicitly stated by the client in her initial statement, but which she immediately accepted as true for her. Also observe that I shift from Identification Mode of empathy to You Mode of empathy, and then back again. When the client shifts into talking about relating to the experience in the present, as opposed to talking about the experience itself, it can be more natural to use You Mode of empathy. But when the client shifts back to talking about the experience itself, you can revert back to the Identification Mode.

Cindy [*a female in her early 50s*]: "When I was 18 years old, my father died at a young age. And I wasn't prepared for that. I was the beneficiary, and had to handle things. But mostly, I felt cheated out of life with my father. There's a part of me that has always felt alone. I lost a part of me when he died. I don't feel complete because I lost him." [*Cindy was exhibiting tender emotion by the end, quasi-suppressing some incipient tears.*]

Rob [*using Identification Mode of empathy*]: I loved my father *very* much. [*Cindy visibly heaved a deep breath.*] So I wasn't prepared for his death when I was only 18. [*Tears started to flow from her eyes, as did a few from mine.*] He was *way* too young, and so was I. It was really unfair. I wasn't ready to lose him. I felt very alone. Plus, it was way too much responsibility, having to handle all the details of the funeral and the estate at that age. I wasn't ready for all that. It was too much responsibility, especially on top of losing Dad. I couldn't even grieve properly because I had to handle everything myself. I still miss Dad a lot. It's like it happened yesterday. I feel cheated by his death. I'd give almost anything to have him back again.

Cindy: That's it. You got it.

Rob [*after patiently waiting to see if she would choose to say more*]: What was that like for you, to receive empathy in that way?

Cindy: I've never felt understood before by anyone about this.

Rob [*shifting to You Mode of empathy to process the experience*]: So, you feel less alone with the experience.

Cindy: Yes. I feel really understood. Like someone finally understands me, after all these years, including therapy.

Rob: And that feels good. It's been a heavy burden to carry all alone.

Cindy: Yes. I can feel a sense of relief.

Rob: It feels lighter now.

Cindy: I was the beneficiary because he was alone. My parents divorced. That's why I was the beneficiary. I was sad about his being alone.

Rob [*shifting back to Identification Mode of empathy*]: The reason I was the beneficiary was that my parents had divorced, and he was all alone. I was really sad about that, about his being alone. I wish he'd had a happier life.

Cindy: Yes. That's right.

Rob [*shifting back to You Mode of empathy*]: So, you're feeling understood, and that feels good.

Cindy: I've never felt understood like that before. I've been in therapy for years, and I've never felt empathized with in this way. Next time I see my [individual] therapist, I'm going to watch and see what she does; see if I feel any different.

Rob: You want to see if you feel empathized with by her.

Cindy: You bet.

As a result of the empathy she received, Cindy *felt* understood, and she experienced a deeper sense of connection to her own experience. These are two of the key goals of empathizing.

Have the Couple Practice the Empathic Skill

Once the therapist has explained empathy and provided a demonstration of empathy with a story from each partner, he or she would then invite each person to share an additional story from childhood (or adolescence). This time, however, the couple will provide the empathy to one another. It is important to have the couple use the Identification Mode of empathy for this practice exercise so that they can experience empathy in the form of imaginatively identifying with and assuming the identity of their partner. This will involve coaching the couple to use the pronoun *I* to represent the experience of the other person. While each person shares his or her story, it's important that the therapist tune in empathically in order to imaginatively identify with each person's experience so that the therapist can coach the Empathizer to go deeper in his or her empathy as necessary.

However, following the principle of positive reinforcement, positive feedback should always be offered for whatever level of empathizing the Empathizer is able to provide before coaching the Empathizer to go deeper in his or her empathy. For example, the therapist might say to the Empathizer, "That was great. You really captured aspects of Alice's experience well, and I could see her nodding her head, which is a sign that you were on target. I picked up one additional piece, though, which I'd like to model for you so that you can add it to your empathy." Then the therapist would model an additional empathic statement in the exact form in which he or she would like the Empathizer to verbalize it, namely, by using the pronoun *I* to represent the person whose experience is being empathized with. Then the therapist would say to the partner providing the empathy, "Say something like that, in your own words." This conveys to the Empathizer that he or she need not repeat exactly what the therapist has said, but may take it as a model of the kind of thing that could be said by way of providing additional empathy. This both lowers potential performance anxiety and encourages the Empathizer to be creative in finding his or her own way of empathically representing the partner's experience.

Have the Couple Share and Empathize With Partner Appreciations

There is one additional piece to the couple's practice of empathy, and that involves the couple sharing partner appreciations. This also serves as another attachment bonding experience between the partners, and adds to the couple's emotional bank account as well. This sharing of partner appreciations reappears throughout the therapy process in the form of home assignments and as a way of anchoring subsequent therapy sessions (see below and the next chapter). The more immediate point, however, is that this part of the exercise is not just about each person giving an appreciation; it's also about the recipient of an appreciation having to empathically acknowledge it back to the giver. Partner appreciations may be introduced in the following way:

> There's one additional thing I'd like to have you do. I'd like each of you to share a partner appreciation. Giving appreciations is important because they are a way of expressing gratitude to one another. They also help build your relationship's emotional bank account, from which you can draw when things are less than ideal. But since we're doing this in the context of practicing empathy, it's not just about giving one another an appreciation. It also involves the person receiving an appreciation having to empathically acknowledge it back to the giver. That means the recipient of the appreciation can't just say, "Thanks for saying that," because that technically is an expressive statement, as in "*I* thank you for saying that," and if this were a dialogue, the Empathizer wouldn't be permitted to say anything from his or her point of view. Let me give you an example. Let's say my wife said to me, "I really appreciate it when you make lunch for me to take to work, because if you didn't do it for me, I certainly wouldn't do it for myself, and then I'd end up going to the cafeteria and eating food that isn't very good and certainly isn't good for me. So, I really appreciate it when you do that." One way

of empathizing with that appreciation would be for me to say—and here I am going to use the conventional You Mode of empathy— "You really like it when I make lunch for you. It leaves you feeling cared for and loved when I do that." Or, if I wanted to be playful, I could say, "You think I'm a pretty nifty guy for doing that for you." Do you see how that captures the spirit of the appreciation, even though I didn't repeat its content? Good. So, now, I'd like the two of you to share partner appreciations.

After the couple has shared and empathized with their partner appreciations, it is useful for the therapist to briefly process the experience with them. Often, one person may say something to the effect that it was hard to do or felt awkward. This offers an opportunity to make the following observations:

We all have a certain tendency psychologically to minimize or downplay an appreciation or compliment. This is manifested by our saying things like, "Oh, it was no big deal. It didn't really take much effort." I think our culture has fostered that attitude with messages like, "Now, don't let compliments go to your head, because it will just get you in trouble," or "Be careful of false pride; you should always be modest." The impact of those messages is that we tend to keep compliments and appreciations psychologically at a distance. There's a triple tragedy here. The first tragedy is that it keeps us from really taking in appreciations and compliments when they are given to us, and so we don't really experience the intended positive effect. The second tragedy is that the giver of the appreciation often is left feeling as though the gift of the appreciation has just been handed back, because the minimizing statements that we use leave the giver feeling as though the appreciation indeed was not received, that is, was not really taken in, which is not a good feeling for the giver of the appreciation. All of this has a direct and unfortunate impact on couples' relationships in that it inhibits people from feeling truly appreciated by their partner, not because appreciations aren't given, but because even when they are given, they're not really taken in emotionally by the recipient. That's the third tragedy, this time for the relationship, because the relationship is indirectly robbed of the nurturing benefits to be had from the giving and receiving of partner appreciations.

In addition to the obvious attachment bonding aspects of sharing partner appreciations, having each person empathically acknowledge an appreciation also indirectly helps people build their ability to receive love. For people with deep narcissistic injuries, poor self-concept, or low self-esteem, being able to receive love can be a major challenge, so having couples share and empathically acknowledge partner appreciations in this way can help validate a sense of self-worth and open previously blocked channels to genuinely receiving love.

Home Assignments

While the giving of a home assignment is here being identified as a distinct piece of the therapy process in order to highlight its importance, in practice the therapist can simply continue from the preceding explanation and move directly into the home assignments, as follows:

> So what I'd like to ask that each of you do between now and our next session is that you give one another a partner appreciation, ideally daily. Would you each be willing to do that? Great. You can do it spontaneously, or at an agreed-to time such as when you go to sleep. But it's not just about the giving of the appreciations. I also want each of you to empathically acknowledge any appreciation you receive, so that you really take it in. And, by the way, it's precisely the fact that you verbally acknowledge the appreciation in the form of empathy that helps you take it in emotionally. The reason is that when you verbalize out loud the content of your partner's appreciation of you it goes more deeply into your neural pathways and thus into your heart. And I also want to encourage each of you to hold your partner's feet to the fire and request that he or she empathically acknowledge your appreciation if your partner forgets to do it. That way, you'll help each other take in your appreciations. I'd also like to request that you each share at least one more childhood experience and that each of you empathize with your partner's experience by using the Identification Mode of empathy. That will give each of you some additional practice at making an empathic connection and giving verbal empathy. Would you each be willing to do that? Great.

Another valuable resource that the therapist might wish to use with couples is to invite them to view at home the *Demonstration of Identification Mode of Empathy Within the Relationship Enhancement Model* videotape (Scuka, 2003). The advantage of this videotape is that it demonstrates the use of the Identification Mode of empathy in the context of a couple's dialogue. While the idea of using the Identification Mode of empathy while dialoguing typically is explained in the following session devoted to the Expressive and Discussion/Negotiation skills, nonetheless this can be offered as a home assignment at this time in order to accomplish two purposes simultaneously. First, viewing the demonstration videotape will reinforce the couple's understanding and use of the Identification Mode of empathy following their Empathic skill practice in the current session. Second, it will prepare them in advance to feel better prepared to conduct their couples dialogues using the Identification Mode of empathy.

Finally, clients could also be asked to begin to read between the lines empathically with people other than their partner, either in their own minds or in reality. This would indirectly represent an early application of one of the principles of the Generalization skill, and is a valuable way of having couples reinforce their use of empathy with one another by encouraging them to use it with other people. When the couple has children, strongly encourage them to begin applying this skill immediately with their children.

CHAPTER 7

Communicating Respectfully and Dialoguing Constructively: Teaching Expressive and Discussion/Negotiation Skills

The next session in the Time-Designated format is devoted to teaching the Expressive and Discussion/Negotiation skills for the purpose of initiating the couple's first dialogue. If the therapist has a high level of confidence in a given couple's ability to communicate skillfully and to follow the dialogue process well, he or she may elect to review these two skills in a more condensed manner. This could amount to a shift into the Experiential format (see chapter 8), which has the benefit of enabling the couple to initiate their first dialogue in the same session. However, if the therapist has any questions concerning the couple's ability to be skillful and to follow the demands of the dialogue process, the couple will be better served by reviewing these skills more thoroughly. In this case, it is likely that the couple's first dialogue will not be engaged until the next session.

Begin All Subsequent Sessions by Having Couples Share Partner Appreciations

Once the couple has been introduced to them, I recommend that the therapist begin all subsequent therapy sessions by having the couple share partner appreciations. This should involve the recipient of an appreciation empathically acknowledging it back to the giver in order to deepen its internalization. There are several advantages to beginning a couple's therapy session in this manner on a consistent basis. First, and most especially with highly conflicted couples, it helps the couple develop the habit of looking for something positive about a partner even in the midst of having intense feelings about a difficult issue. The hope is that over time this will begin to generalize into helping the couple learn how to keep things in perspective even when they are dealing with difficult issues on their own. Second, the sharing of appreciations helps anchor the couple back into the dynamics of the dialogue process, because each person is having to empathize with what his or her partner shares. Third, each time the couple shares partner appreciations, they are given the opportunity to have a minibonding experience fueled by positive feelings.

I never begin a therapy session without having the couple share appreciations. However, if a person has difficulty providing one or, on rare occasions, says that he or she simply can't that day, then I treat that as an occasion for exploratory Troubleshooting and I inquire as to whether there is an issue that the couple is needing to turn their attention to during that session. So, in an interesting way, how the couple responds to the invitation to share partner appreciations can become diagnostic of the couple being in a difficult place emotionally or having a particularly difficult issue that has come up and needs to be explored.

Follow Up on Home Assignments

The therapist should follow up on whether the couple practiced empathy at home by sharing stories and partner appreciations with one another. Then the therapist inquires as to whether the couple has read the chapters in the *RE Client Manual* (Guerney & Scuka, 2005) devoted to the Expressive and Discussion/Negotiation skills. This may well influence the therapist's decision about how much of these two skills to teach in session.

Explain the Goals of the Expressive Skill

The Expressive skill should be introduced by explaining that there are three principal goals whenever either person is attempting to communicate his or her experience. I do so in the following way:

> There are three primary goals in being a skillful Expresser. The first goal is to promote a spirit of cooperation in order to facilitate open communication and foster cooperative problem solving. The second goal is to communicate all your experiences, feelings, concerns, and desires to your partner openly, honestly, and clearly. The third goal is to express yourself in a manner that minimizes defensiveness

in your partner and maximizes receptivity to hearing your point of view. I could summarize all three goals by saying that it is your responsibility as an Expresser to create the receptivity that you are wanting your partner to have in listening to your point of view.

Explain Two of the Values Embodied in the RE Model

The therapist then proceeds to explain two of the values that are embodied in the RE model. This may be done in the following way:

There are two important sets of values embodied in the RE model: openness and honesty, and caring and compassion. The RE model promotes openness and honesty in that if something is important to you, or bothering you, it advocates that you share that with your partner. Otherwise you are cheating yourself and your partner of the opportunity to address and resolve the issue constructively. Over time, ignoring issues in a relationship generally leads to resentment, and that gradually tears away at the fabric of the relationship. On the other hand, the values of openness and honesty need to be balanced by the values of caring and compassion. Otherwise, the first set of values alone can lead to ill-considered statements that cause defensiveness. So it's your responsibility to express yourself skillfully so that you do not cause your partner to feel defensive. It's your job as an Expresser to make it easier for your partner to be receptive to hearing your point of view. If we combine the values of openness and honesty with the values of caring and compassion, then I believe that you can say virtually anything you wish to say to your partner because you will say it caringly and compassionately. Let's take a look at the guidelines for being a skillful Expresser.

Review the Expressive Skill Guidelines

Each of the Expressive skill guidelines is followed by explanatory comments.

1. *Be respectful. Let your partner know you have an issue before you begin to discuss it, and request that he or she agree to join you in a skilled dialogue.*

There are two elements of respect involved here. The first element of respect involves simply letting your partner know in advance that you have an issue you wish to discuss. This helps reduce defensiveness simply by virtue of eliminating, or at least minimizing, the element of surprise. Just barging in on someone and saying, for example, "Hey, I've got to talk to you about..." and launching directly into the issue is almost guaranteed to cause defensiveness, and therefore reduce receptivity to hearing your concerns, clearly a counterproductive result. The second element of respect involves requesting your partner's agreement to have a dialogue, with the implicit recognition that your partner has the right to say, "I'm sorry, but this isn't a good time for me to have a dialogue." If you are the person initiating the request, you should be prepared to accept the possibility of such a response, because the reality is, not all times are good times, and your willingness to hear that response is a sign of respect toward your partner.

On the other hand, if your partner elects to exercise the right to say that this is not a good time, then that person incurs an obligation to the person who made the request to say when would be a good time, preferably within 24 to 48 hours, so that the person making the request is not left feeling stonewalled. What this dual-sided approach accomplishes is to balance the emotional needs of both of you in a fair manner, regardless of who happens to be in either role. Moreover, explicitly requesting and obtaining your partner's agreement to have a conversation or dialogue on an issue you are concerned about helps create a positive atmosphere of common expectations about how the interaction will proceed. The reason is that in agreeing to have a dialogue, you both are also agreeing to follow all the guidelines for having a skilled dialogue.

2. *To help build a spirit of cooperation, begin your expressive statement with an underlying positive. Let your partner know how important he or she is to you, or express something positive about your partner related to the issue you wish to discuss.*

How we begin expressing ourselves about a potentially difficult issue goes a long way toward shaping the tone and the tenor of the subsequent interaction. It's all too easy to get caught up in the negative feelings we are experiencing in the moment and forget that there are genuinely positive things about the other person and the relationship as well. It therefore is very important that, in initiating a dialogue about a difficult issue, you make an effort to express something positive about your partner relating to the issue at hand or how and why the relationship is important to you. This will reduce your emotional reactivity and help you develop a more positive frame of mind for the ensuing dialogue, which in turn will help you be more verbally skillful. In addition, you indirectly communicate to your partner that you are not intending to drop a verbal bomb in order to destroy the bridge between you, but that you are wanting to build a bridge of cooperation between you, even though there is this difficult issue that you are hoping to address and to resolve. This indirect message (or metalevel communication) is as important as the explicit content of your underlying positive statement. The reason is that it ought to reduce your partner's anxiety about the interaction and thereby make your partner more receptive to hearing your concerns. By the way, it never hurts to continue adding underlying positives over the course of your dialogue. Indeed, it can have a very positive effect.

3. *When possible, use "preemptive" empathy to acknowledge your understanding of your partner's feelings, concerns, or difficulties relating to the issue.*

    Giving your partner preemptive empathy as part of your expressive statement is different from giving an underlying positive, but it too can facilitate making your partner more receptive to hearing your point of view. By verbalizing in advance your understanding of at least a part of your partner's side of the issue you wish to discuss, you can help reduce your partner's defensiveness and you likely will further increase his or her receptivity to hearing your feelings and concerns.

4. *Express all your relevant feelings, concerns, and desires relating to the issue.*

    One of the purposes of the Expressive skill is to empower people to feel confident that they can say what needs to be said, and to do so in a manner that will result in as positive an interaction as possible. It's important, therefore, to try to identify in advance exactly what it is you want to say, and how you want to say it. Realize, also, that it's usually better to bring up an issue sooner rather than later, before resentment begins to build, at which point it only becomes more difficult to deal with the issue.

5. *Be subjective and speak from your own point of view. Avoid all claims about what "really" happened, or what supposedly is or is not true, accurate, normal, right, or good. Also avoid implying that your way of*

thinking, memory, insight, values, or morals is superior to those of your partner. Instead, frame everything your partner might see differently in terms of your own perception, memory, personal commitments, values, etc.

Avoid unhelpful (and unwinnable) diversionary arguments over presumed "facts" by speaking subjectively. Avoid framing things in terms of presumed objective states of affairs, and instead frame things in terms of your own subjective experience by using phrases such as, "In my experience...," "From my point of view...," "It seems to me...," "As I recall...." In this way, you indirectly communicate that you recognize and respect that your partner may see things differently than you do. You are not presuming that your way of seeing things, your way of thinking, your memory, or your values or moral standards are somehow superior to those of your partner. The reason, of course, is that saying or implying any of these things would immediately cause your partner to become defensive, which would only cause the communication between the two of you to shut down or lead to an intractable and unwinnable argument over who is "right." So it's important that you frame anything your partner might see differently in subjective language. The indirect message (or metalevel communication) is that you respect your partner enough to not talk in a way that implies that your point of view is superior, and that you respect your partner enough to accept the legitimacy of his or her point of view and to have it acknowledged as such, even if it differs from your own.

6. *Avoid implying that there is something "wrong" with your partner as a person because you are unhappy with your partner's behavior. Instead, keep the focus on your own experience and describe the impact that your partner's behavior has on you.*

This represents yet another angle on speaking subjectively. When you're upset with your partner, it's all too easy to turn being upset over your partner's behavior into a personal attack on your partner's character, what I refer to generically as "character assassination." This would immediately cause your partner to become defensive and lead either to an emotional shutdown or to a verbal fight like the one we observed on the RE demonstration audiotape. Now, you have to be able to refer to what it was that your partner said or did that upset you. But the challenge is to avoid pointing your finger at your partner in a manner that implies that there is something wrong with your partner because of what your partner said or did, and instead to keep the focus on your own subjective experience and feelings about what your partner said or did and the impact that has had on you.

7. *Be specific when referring to your partner's behavior. Avoid generalizations about your partner's character ("I think you're lazy"), behavior ("You always..." or "You never..."), motives ("You did that to hurt me."), or commitment to the relationship ("You don't care about our relationship.").*

Clearly, any of these statements would cause your partner to feel defensive, and therefore should be avoided at all costs. Take, for example, the statement, "You don't care about our relationship." That is almost automatically going to elicit a defensive response such as, "What do you mean I don't care about our relationship? How can you say such a thing?" So, instead, be specific about what your partner said or did that upset you, and keep the focus on your own experience and the impact it had on you.

8. *When relevant, make a specific request for a change in behavior. Be certain to explain the benefits of your requested change to yourself, your partner, and the relationship.*

If there's something that's upsetting you, then there's almost certainly something you wish your partner would do differently. But rather than leave it for your partner to figure out, it would be much better to make a specific request for a change in behavior, or for the implementation of an agreement or a plan of action. In addition, be certain to explain how your partner agreeing to your request would make you feel (presumably better) and what the benefits would be for you, your partner, and your relationship if your partner were to agree to your request. In explaining the benefits, you in effect are creating the motivation for your partner to want to agree to your request. This not only increases the likelihood that your partner will agree to your request, but also increases the likelihood that your partner will follow through on the changes being agreed to.

One final comment. If you think about it, many of the Expressive skill guidelines represent a form of preventative Conflict Management by helping you avoid some of the most common things that tend to cause defensiveness in relationships.

Model an Ideal Expressive Message

Having explained the Expressive skill guidelines, and following the principles of learning theory that are at the heart of the RE model, the therapist next models for the couple an ideal expressive message in order to provide a concrete example of how the guidelines are applied. Here is one example I use to model an ideal expressive message:

> I'd like to model for you an example of an ideal expressive message. Let's say, just for the sake of illustration, that an issue I had with my wife was that I was upset with her for yelling at the kids a lot, that is, to put it subjectively, more than I was comfortable with. As I model this expressive statement, notice how I follow all the Expressive skill guidelines.
>
> "Mary, there's something relating to you and the children that's been bothering me that I really would like us to talk about. Would you be willing to have a dialogue with me about that? [*Assuming she agreed, I would continue as follows:*] First of all, I want you to know how much I appreciate everything you do with and for the children. I think you're great with the children, and I know they feel loved and secure because of what you do. I also recognize that they can be a real challenge, and that sometimes they may feel like more than you are able, or want, to handle. I get that it's not always easy. What's bothering me is that you appear to me to be raising your voice at the kids a lot more lately. When I hear you yell at them, I cringe, and I get really tense. It makes me feel really uncomfortable, and it's very difficult for me to feel relaxed around that. Then, too, I get worried that you'll get upset with me because you appear to be so tense. So, I'd really appreciate it if together we could come up with a solution so this doesn't happen so often. I recognize that it's going to happen sometimes, but I would certainly feel better if there were less of it, and I have to imagine that you and the children would feel more relaxed and would enjoy yourselves more as well."
>
> That's an example of a complete expressive message. Let's tease apart the various components of my expressive message. Can you identify how I followed each of the guidelines? [*I involve the couple in reviewing my modeled expressive message point by point in order to reinforce each of the Expressive skill guidelines. Then I continue with the following observation:*]

We ought to note that what I modeled technically was a monologue, not a dialogue. In an actual dialogue, I would probably pause at the point of expressing my feelings and concerns, allow my wife to empathize with me, and then allow her an opportunity to express herself on the topic. If this were an actual issue, by the way, I would almost certainly learn something about her feelings and concerns. This might include that she feels as though she is carrying too much of the burden in caring for the children, and that she really would appreciate and welcome my doing more by way of caring for them. I'd probably also be told that if I were to do so, that in itself would help her yell less because she wouldn't feel so stressed. At that point I'd empathize with her, and then either modify what I was going to say in light of her response, or proceed to verbalize my request for a change in behavior and the benefits that I believe would follow. But the specifics of the example aside, the point is that the person who initiated the issue should at some point in the dialogue make a specific request for a change in behavior or the development of an agreement or a plan of action if that continues to be relevant.

The modeled expressive message provided here is offered simply as an example of the kind of modeling that the therapist should aim to provide in order to make the Expressive skill guidelines more concrete for the couple. Therapists are encouraged to develop their own modeled expressive message for the purpose of illustrating the Expressive skill guidelines. The more creative and potentially relevant the example, the better.

Have the Couple Practice Developing an Ideal Expressive Message (at the Therapist's Discretion)

In principle, and again following the tenets of learning theory, the therapist would now have the couple practice developing an ideal expressive message. In practice, the therapist often dispenses with that and proceeds to teach the Discussion/Negotiation skill so as to be able to initiate the couple's first structured dialogue more quickly. The structure of the dialogue process and the therapist's coaching are relied on to help the partners express themselves as skillfully as possible. However, it is wise to monitor each couple to determine whether the partners may have difficulty expressing themselves skillfully. If that is the therapist's judgment, then he or she would be well advised to take the time to have the couple practice developing an ideal expressive message by means of a carefully designed exercise that avoids any actual issues in the couple's relationship.

The exercise is derived from the educational version of the RE model as found in the RE Program (see Scuka, Nordling, & Guerney, 2004). It may be introduced in the following way:

> I'd like to have the two of you practice developing a good expressive message before we move on to the next skill. What I'd like each of you to do is pick a real issue you have with someone in your life other than your partner or a member of your partner's family. It could be an issue you have with a member of your own family of origin, a friend, a colleague at work, or a member of your faith group. Take a moment to think of an issue you'd like to address. [*Pause.*] Do you both have an issue? Good. Then what I'd like each of you to do is to talk to your partner as though your partner were this other person. All you have to do is tell your partner who the person is you're talking to, and then go ahead and to the best of your ability follow all the Expressive skill guidelines in developing your expressive message to this person. Please be certain to begin with an underlying positive. I may coach you along the way. What I'd like the other of you to do in pretending to be the other person is to not say anything, other than to say "yes" to the request for a conversation. But I would like you to monitor your partner's expressive message, both with a view as to how well your partner follows the guidelines and with respect to any points at which you feel yourself becoming defensive while imagining yourself being this other person to whom your partner is talking. Then you will provide your partner with feedback on those two points. Then the person practicing will express a second time, taking it from the top, and incorporate any feedback from your partner and from me. I wager that each of you will experience that it goes more smoothly the second time through. Any questions? Who'd like to begin?

The therapist has each person enact this role-played conversation with an imaginary interlocutor, provides appropriate positive feedback, and suggests any improvements that come to mind. Then each person is asked to enact their role-played conversation a second time. This practice exercise can be concluded with the following observation to the couple:

> There's an important lesson in this exercise, namely, that it's important to identify in advance, and if necessary rehearse, exactly what it is you want to say and how to say it before you initiate an actual dialogue with your partner or with someone else. That way, you increase the odds that you express yourself both thoughtfully and

skillfully, and that increases the likelihood that you will have a positive interaction with the other person.

Introduce the RE Dialogue Process by Explaining the Goals of Discussion/Negotiation

The therapist would next proceed to introduce RE dialogue process by explaining the goals of the Discussion/Negotiation skill. If the therapist has not previously used the theater-based metaphor for a couple's dialogue (see p. 122), this is another place where it can be introduced.

> Let's move now to the Discussion/Negotiation skill. This is where we put the Expressive skill and the Empathic skill together for the purpose of having a structured dialogue. There are three goals of the Discussion/Negotiation skill. The first goal is to encourage both of you to explore and communicate all your feelings, concerns, and desires relating to a specific issue. The second goal is to enable you to dialogue in a manner that fosters emotional safety and promotes deepened mutual understanding, compassion, and acceptance. The third goal is an extension of the first two: to help both of you build a commitment to finding an appropriate solution to a problem when that is called for. I could summarize by saying that the purpose of dialoging is to open up channels of communication between the two of you in order to foster greater emotional engagement and a more satisfying sense of connection.

Explain That Each Dialogue Has Two Phases

The therapist continues by explaining that there are two phases to a dialogue.

> It is helpful to think of each dialogue as having two phases. Phase 1 is Discussion/Negotiation, which is the third RE skill, and phase 2 is Problem/Conflict Resolution, which is the fourth RE skill. The purpose of phase 1 of a dialogue is to foster mutual understanding. The purpose of phase 2 of a dialogue is to create a solution, agreement, or plan of action that leaves both of you feeling satisfied because each of you feels that your concerns and desires have been taken into account in the formulation of the solution. But for that to happen, each of you must first have expressed fully everything that is important regarding your experience, feelings, concerns, and desires relating to the issue at hand, and each of you must

empathize with the other for the sake of deepening mutual understanding. That is the sole purpose of phase 1 of a dialogue, so much so that there is an implicit contract during phase 1 that no specific solutions will be proposed—though the general outlines of a desired solution might be shared. The reason is that if you focus on coming up with a specific solution too quickly, you run a high risk of short-circuiting—going deeper into what is really important to you about the issue at hand [*looking at one person*], and what is really important to you [*looking at the other person*]. The point of phase 1 is to go as far as possible in uncovering deeper levels of the issue, so that when you do turn to working out a specific solution in phase 2, you will be solving the issue at a deep level rather than superficially. That tends to increase the odds of your solution being a successful and enduring solution because both of you will more likely feel as though your feelings, concerns, and desires have been heard and are being incorporated into your solution. Now let's take a look at the guidelines for conducting a structured dialogue.

Review the Guidelines for Conducting a Structured Dialogue

Each of the dialogue guidelines is followed by explanatory comments.

1. *Limit each dialogue to a single topic. However, allow yourself to go as deep as possible. This may involve redefining the issue in different terms.*

It's not possible to deal effectively with more than one issue at a time. Each issue deserves its own dialogue. That said, two things may happen during the course of a dialogue. First, as a dialogue unfolds, the issue may get redefined. That's perfectly acceptable because that represents a deepening of the issue. The second thing that may happen is that a tangential or related issue may surface. If that happens, then one of several things must be decided. The first option is to identify that a new issue has arisen and suggest that it be tabled for a separate dialogue at another time. The second option is to agree that the new issue is part of the original issue, and agree to fold it into the present dialogue. The third option is for either of you to propose that the new issue takes logical precedence over the original issue in that the resolution of the original issue is dependent upon the resolution of the new issue. That too is perfectly acceptable, so long as both of you agree to postpone and eventually return to the original issue.

2. *Be certain that at all times one of you is in the role of the Expresser and the other is in the role of the Empathizer. The designated Empathizer is not permitted to interrupt the Expresser. The designated Empathizer also is not permitted to say anything from his or her point of view.*

This guideline should be followed absolutely rigorously because preserving the integrity of the dialogue structure helps anchor your dialogue process and keeps it emotionally safe for both of you. Part of the reason for that is that having to empathize with your partner without saying anything from your own point of view serves to reduce undesirable emotional reactivity. The structure of the dialogue process thus helps to slow things down, and that helps both of you feel safer emotionally.

3. *Decide who will be the initial Expresser. The person who is more emotionally invested in the issue, or experiencing stronger emotion, should be the initial Expresser.*

With an enhancement issue around which there is little emotional energy, it may not matter who begins the dialogue as the initial Expresser. But with a conflict issue it probably will make a big difference. Now, you may both be itching to speak your mind, but it does not serve either of you or the dialogue process between you for either of you to insist upon being the initial Expresser if your partner is the one who is more emotionally invested in the issue or more emotionally upset at that moment. The reason is that person is not likely to be able to listen and empathize well with you at that moment anyway, so there's no point in insisting on being the initial Expresser. It would be better for you to allow your partner to become the initial Expresser, with the prospect that he or she will be better able to listen to you and empathize after he or she has received some empathy from you. And I wager that under most circumstances, both of you will know who the first Expresser should be. As a last resort, if you simply can't agree, flip a coin. In the end, there's no point in fighting over the role of the Expresser because both of you will have ample opportunity to say what is important to you.

4. *There are two ways to change roles. The preferred method is for the current Expresser to invite the Empathizer to change roles after you have expressed what is most important to you. Alternatively, the Empathizer*

may request a change in role after you have empathized with what your partner has shared.

The preferred method for changing roles is for the Expresser to invite the Empathizer to now become the Expresser. The current Expresser may express several times, and the Empathizer may empathize several times. At some point, the Expresser will have said what he or she wants to say for the moment, and that person probably also is wondering what his or her partner is thinking and feeling about what has been shared. That's the perfect time for the current Expresser to move the dialogue forward by inviting his or her partner to now become the Expresser. This may be done by saying, "I'd like to know what your thoughts are about what I've expressed," or by motioning with the palm of your hand up. On the other hand, it is acceptable for the designated Empathizer to make a request for a change in role. This may be done either by saying, "I'd like to become the Expresser now," or by placing your hand over your heart. However, we recommend the following to the person in the role of the Empathizer.

5. *The person in the role of the Empathizer is encouraged to remain in that role as long as he or she feels comfortable doing so. However, you may request a change in role to become the Expresser when you have something to say that might favorably influence your partner. You may also request a change in role when you are experiencing difficulty continuing to empathize because your own feelings are getting in the way.*

The reason the person in the role of the Empathizer is encouraged to remain in that role as long as is comfortable is that each time you allow your partner to express and you empathize, you are giving a gift to your partner. In effect, you are choosing to be of service to your partner's emotional process, and that's a good thing both for your partner and for you because you are helping your partner gain deeper self-understanding while you also learn more about your partner's experience. Doing that for each other is one of the principal ways of deepening intimacy in your relationship because you both are sharing more with your partner and learning more about your partner.

On the other hand, there will be times when the Empathizer, if he or she has not yet been invited to become the Expresser, will want to do so and deserves that opportunity. However, the designated

Empathizer may not interrupt the designated Expresser to make the request while the Expresser is expressing, because that would be disrespectful. Also, because the designated Empathizer is obligated to empathize, he or she must first empathize with what the Expresser has shared before making the request. When you have finished empathizing, you may then simply say, "I'd like to become the Expresser now," or you may place the palm of your hand on your heart as a nonverbal signal indicating your desire to become the Expresser. You may use either the verbal request or the nonverbal signal to initiate a change in role.

6. *Once a change in role has been requested by the Empathizer, the request cannot be refused so long as the Expresser has received adequate empathy and feels understood.*

The reason for this is that the Empathizer has been empathizing, perhaps for several rounds, and it's only fair that he or she be given the opportunity to express. So once a request for a change in role has been made by the Empathizer, the request cannot be refused, even if the current Expresser has more he or she would like to say. The caveat is that the designated Expresser deserves to feel understood concerning what had been said before a change in role takes place. The designated Expresser may not feel understood for one of three reasons: First, the Empathizer may have omitted something from the Expresser's message that the Expresser wishes to have explicitly acknowledged; second, the Empathizer may have misrepresented, even inadvertently, part of the Expresser's message; finally, the Empathizer's empathy is simply experienced by the Expresser as inauthentic. This feeling of inauthenticity arises most likely because the Empathizer's feelings have gotten in the way of being able to empathize in a genuine way. Under any of these three conditions the Expresser is permitted to reiterate what was omitted, correct the misrepresentation, or make a statement about not feeling genuinely empathized with. The designated Empathizer would then be required to empathically acknowledge the reiteration or correction, or would have to empathize again from the beginning. However, the designated Expresser may not under any of these three scenarios add new content to what had been previously expressed because then the Empathizer technically would be obligated to empathize with the new content, and that would be to deprive the partner of the request to change roles.

7. *Be cautious that you do not move too quickly from phase 1 discussion mode into phase 2 problem-solving mode. Give yourselves enough time to go as deep as possible into your feelings, concerns, and desires so that you can better understand each other regarding the issue at hand.*

There is a certain temptation to think that you are ready to move from discussion mode into problem-solving mode after a few exchanges back and forth. The reality is that there often is more to be said in terms of going deeper into your feelings, concerns, and desires, and it is important that you give yourselves the opportunity to uncover those deeper dimensions. If you don't, you run a high risk of "solving" the issue at a relatively superficial level, and thereby depriving yourselves not only of understanding one another more deeply, but also of being able to resolve your issue in a truly satisfying and meaningful way.

Inoculate Against Perceived Side-Taking by the Therapist

One of the risks of couples therapy is that either person may sometimes feel as though the therapist is taking sides with one partner, leaving the other partner feeling ganged up on. Of course, either person could have this experience because the therapist seriously missteps by actively taking sides with one person against the other. But sometimes a client may have these feelings when a therapist is simply doing his or her job by intervening in the dialogue process in a legitimate and expected manner. This is most likely to happen when the therapist intervenes to help either partner express himself more deeply or when the therapist coaches the Empathizer to go deeper in empathizing with the partner's experience, most especially when the content of the partner's expression cuts against the grain of the Empathizer's own concerns, feelings, and desires. Once such feelings surface for either person, it may become difficult for that person to let go of the feeling that the therapist is taking sides against him or her, even with the therapist's skillful use of Troubleshooting to empathically acknowledge that person's negative feelings and suspicions regarding the therapist. It would be much better, then, in terms of promoting success for the therapy process, for neither person ever to have those feelings to begin with.

The best way to accomplish this goal of minimizing the likelihood that either person would interpret the therapist's expected intervention(s) as a form of taking sides is to proactively explain to the couple the therapist's role in facilitating the couple's dialogue process. The therapist may make this preventative intervention at any number of points in the therapy process. It is included here because it represents a prelude to commencing the couple's first dialogue. However, it could be introduced toward the conclusion of the clinical intake, or at the conclusion of the first session postintake, following discussion of the Conflict Management skill. The therapist's decision about the timing of this intervention may be influenced by an intuition of the need to provide reassurance to the couple earlier rather than later concerning the role of the therapist and the therapist's neutrality with respect to not taking sides with one person against the other. I typically address the potential issue of perceived side-taking in the following way:

> I'd like to discuss my role in your dialogues for a moment so there is no misunderstanding. From this point forward the focus of our work together will be the two of you dialoguing with one another. My role will be that of a facilitator. That means that there will be times when I coach one of you or the other to go deeper in expressing yourself. I'll be able to do that because I'll be tracking each of you empathically during your dialogues. I might even take on one of your identities and "become" either of you momentarily in order to give deeper voice to your experience, either to help you understand your own experience better, or to help you understand your partner's experience better. And there will be times when I will encourage and coach either of you to go deeper in empathizing with your partner. What I'd like both of you to understand is that if I do any of these things and you experience discomfort or even resentment toward me for more sharply representing your partner's experience, that doesn't mean I'm taking sides with your partner. It simply means I'm doing my job in facilitating your dialogue process so that it goes as deep as possible, which is one of my primary responsibilities, even if it takes either or both of you into uncomfortable territory.
>
> Recall the point I made in our first meeting that I actually have three clients in this room with me. There's you, and you, and then there's the relationship between you. And in a very real sense, it's the relationship between you that is my primary client. That doesn't mean I don't care about each of you as individuals, because I do. But if I am going to do my job well, I have to serve your relationship first and foremost. And one of the most important ways I can do that is to serve the communication process between the two of you, even if it causes you to experience some discomfort. You have my commitment to do my best to be of service to your relationship while I am coaching your dialogues. Having said that, I also invite you to let me know if at any time either of you feels as though I am

siding with your partner against you. I want you to bring that to my attention, because if you have those feelings I want to hear about them, and I want to be as responsive to your concerns as I can be.

I should also indicate that there may be times, relatively rarely, that I may express something from my own point of view. In the nature of the case, if I do that it would almost certainly involve my own values, particularly with regard to how I view being in a relationship. If I do that, you again have my commitment that I will do so from the vantage point of trying to be of service to your relationship, and I will also do my best to express my point of view as skillfully and as subjectively as possible. However, in doing that, I can't promise that my values might not conflict either with your values [looking at one person], or with yours [looking at the other person]. If that happens, I want you to know, and I hope to feel, that I am respectful toward your values and that I'm not taking sides so much as I am giving voice to something I regard as important. But again, if you become uncomfortable with what I say, I invite you to voice your concerns, and it will be my job to be as responsive to your concerns as I can be.

Such a proactively given message should help ease potential client concerns about the therapist taking sides, and in this way serve as a kind of inoculation against such fears. This intervention will not eliminate all such reactions, but it should help structure the RE therapy process for success by minimizing the likelihood that those fears get needlessly activated.

Explain the Options and Rationale for Choosing a First Dialogue Topic

The time has now arrived for the therapist to initiate the couple's first dialogue. Prior to this session, the therapist should have examined each person's Relationship Questionnaire and looked for linkages on commonly shared issues as well as for issues that are unique to each individual. On the basis of that, the therapist creates a tentative game plan (or two) in his or her own mind of what issues the couple might take up, and in what potential sequence. When addressing the issues unique to each person, the therapist should be mindful to balance things in such a way that the therapy alternates over time from addressing one person's issue to addressing the other person's issue.

There are several options and rationales for choosing a first dialogue topic. My preference is to be as open with the couple as possible about the options and to give them an active role in helping to make the actual decision(s). I base this in part on my own clinical experience, which has taught me that one standard approach to choosing issues does not work well for all couples because the needs and abilities of one couple are unique relative to the needs and abilities of other couples. But this approach also empowers couples to take responsibility for their own treatment and fosters a collaborative approach to the couples therapy. The options and rationale for the couple's first dialogue may be explained in the following way:

> You're now ready to begin your first dialogue. There are several options as to how we might proceed, and I'd like to discuss those with you for a moment. One option is to begin with an enhancement issue from your Relationship Questionnaires. The advantage of this way of proceeding is that it allows the two of you to focus more on learning and getting comfortable with dialoguing without a lot of negative emotion getting stirred up, as would more likely be the case if you were to begin with a conflict issue. The tradeoff is that you would postpone for a session or two tackling one of your conflict issues. Another advantage, however, is that selecting an enhancement issue should give you a sense of accomplishment and a feeling of success over being able to use the skills and the dialogue process. That might make it easier for you then to tackle a conflict issue. The other option is to begin with a conflict issue. The advantage here is that we get to one of your more serious relationship issues sooner rather than later. The potential disadvantage is that it might make your learning and getting comfortable with the dialogue process somewhat more difficult. The first option is a slower but more methodical approach. The second option engages your deeper issues more quickly. What's your sense as to how you'd like to proceed?

Some couples will prefer the first option; others will prefer the second option. In my experience, couples tend to prefer the first option when they are particularly concerned about their own or their partner's tendency to become highly emotional, when there has been a history of negatively charged interactions between the couple, or when either person is feeling uncertain about his or her ability to easily engage with the dialogue process. Conversely, couples tend to prefer the second option when they feel confident about their ability to engage the dialogue process well or they have a sense of urgency about wanting to tackle the difficult issues in their relationship. My inclination is to trust people's self-assessment, while always reserving the right in any particular instance to make a contrary recommendation. If either person expresses reservations about choosing the second option, I recommend to the couple that we begin with an enhancement issue.

Once a decision has been made as to whether to proceed with an enhancement issue or a conflict issue, the choice of a specific issue has to be made. Here, too, I like to enter into a collaborative process with the couple to select an issue for their first dialogue. I will initially propose an enhancement issue or a conflict issue from the Relationship Questionnaires, but I then ask the couple if that feels to them like a good issue to start with or whether they would like to pick a different issue. In the case of a conflict issue, it generally is preferable to begin with one of the couple's minor conflict issues, rather than one of their more intense, core issues. However, even this is not a hard and fast rule within the Time-Designated format. As always, good therapeutic judgment is required in making this collaborative decision with the couple, taking into account both the couple's needs and their abilities.

Encourage the Couple to Use the Identification Mode of Empathy While Dialoguing

Traditionally, whether in the RE model or other models of couples therapy (or psychoeducational programs that focus on couples' communication), couples would dialogue using the conventional You Mode of empathy. However, as we observed in chapter 3, the Identification Mode of empathy has the potential to create an even deeper experience for both the Empathizer and the person whose experience is being represented. For the Empathizer, the advantage of the Identification Mode of empathy is that it helps deepen the quality of the empathic connection and thereby enables the Empathizer to better represent the partner's experience. For the person whose experience is being represented, the advantage is that it tends to deepen the quality of the connection with one's own experience in a manner that is generative of new insight or emotional healing. This has been repeatedly confirmed to me experientially when I demonstrate empathy to couples using the Identification Mode and when couples then practice empathy for the first time by also using the Identification Mode.

As a consequence, and on the basis of a suggestion made to me by Guerney in a private conversation, I have experimented over the last several years with having couples use the Identification Mode of empathy even while conducting their dialogues. My experience has been that when couples do this on a regular basis, they not only more readily *get* what empathy is and involves, but their ability to empathize with a partner's experience and provide quality verbal empathy is greatly enhanced. This has led, in my experience, to a more rapid breaking down of emotional barriers and a quicker reestablishment of a deepened sense of emotional connection. This, in turn, has more readily promoted a shift away from the estranged attitude of "me versus you" that characterizes many couples in therapy toward a more cooperative attitude of "we're in this together," which has facilitated more rapid healing and more effective and long-lasting problem solving (when that has been relevant).

Not all couples will feel comfortable using the Identification Mode of empathy while dialoguing, and their decision should be respected. However, the results have been so impressive when couples have used the Identification Mode of empathy while dialoguing that my standard clinical practice is now to recommend and encourage all couples to experiment with using the Identification Mode while dialoguing and to use it regularly while conducting most or all of their couple dialogues if they are comfortable doing so. (For an extended clinical case example of a couple whose process benefited from using the Identification Mode of empathy while dialoguing, see clinical vignette 2, chapter 9.) This represents a shift in therapeutic practice and an expansion of the use of the Identification Mode of empathy within the RE model. But my experience with using the Identification Mode of empathy in this innovative manner has convinced me to now actively train and encourage all therapists using the RE therapy model to in turn encourage the couples they work with to experiment with using the Identification Mode while dialoguing and to continue to do so if they find it to be helpful in deepening their dialogue process. I encourage therapists to do the same.

Initiate the Couple's First Dialogue

Once the couple's first dialogue topic has been selected, the therapist asks the couple to sit facing each other in order to promote eye contact. The reason is that eye contact facilitates making an empathic connection with the other person. Also, the therapist determines who will be the initial Expresser and structures the couple into their respective roles. This involves reminding the designated Empathizer that he metaphorically "go on vacation" in order to focus all his attention on connecting empathically with his partner, that he not interrupt his partner, and that he provide good empathy to the best of his ability. Also the therapist alerts the Empathizer that he or she may coach him to go deeper in his empathy and then reminds the designated Expresser to keep the focus on her own experience and to be certain to speak subjectively and to begin with an underlying positive in order to help build a spirit of cooperation. If the initial Expresser omits an underlying positive, the therapist immediately steps in and reminds her to do so.

Introduce the Use of a Transitional Object to Clearly Demarcate Roles in the Dialogue

The last piece to introduce to the couple before they begin their first dialogue is the use of a transitional object such as a pen or a "talking stick" to clearly demarcate who is in the role of the Expresser. Symbolically, the notion of a talking stick derives from its use in the Native American tradition, where the talking stick represents the authority of the tribal council and is given to the person who is authorized to speak to the council. Only the person in possession of the talking stick is permitted to address the council. By implication, everyone else is obligated to remain silent and to listen attentively. Only when the talking stick has been officially passed can someone else speak to the council.

When couples are first learning the RE skills and dialogue process, it can be helpful to have them use a talking stick (or other object) in order to help anchor for them who is in the role of the Expresser. By implication, the person not in possession of the talking stick is in the role of the Empathizer. In order to receive the talking stick, and with it the right to become the Expresser, the Empathizer must first provide acceptable empathy to his or her partner. While receiving empathy, the designated Expresser retains possession of the talking stick. The Expresser then gives the talking stick to his or her partner when roles are exchanged. Some couples dispense with the talking stick after they become comfortable with the RE dialogue process. Other couples choose to use it permanently because it helps keep them anchored in their respective roles. For some it even lends an air of ritual to the dialogue process whereby they come to regard their time together in dialogue as a kind of sacred space for the relationship.

Coach the Expresser to Be Verbally Skillful

In the early rounds of the couple's initial dialogue, the therapist typically will devote a considerable amount of attention to monitoring the Expresser's level of skillfulness in expressing herself and to coaching her as necessary to say things more subjectively. It is important that the therapist be very vigilant in this regard and not allow any unskillful statements to go uncorrected. There are two reasons why. First, coaching the Expresser to be more verbally skillful is a form of teaching that will help both partners gradually become more truly subjective in how they think and speak. Over time, this will help the couple's dialogues go more smoothly because they will have created new habits of mental and verbal skillfulness that will make it easier for them to initiate and complete dialogues about difficult relationship issues. Second, vigilant coaching of the Expresser's verbal skillfulness is important in minimizing the potential for the Empathizer to become defensive in response to the Expresser's lack of verbal skill. The Empathizer becoming emotionally defensive is the number one reason why a couple's dialogue breaks down, so it is incumbent upon the therapist to help ensure that this does not happen. This is one of the prime examples of how and why the role of the therapist in the RE therapy process is so active.

When I facilitate a couple's dialogue, I am vigilant like a hawk to not allow even the most seemingly innocuous unskillful statement to go by uncorrected. Of course, it is important to take a nonjudgmental approach to this kind of corrective coaching, and to use an even, neutral tone of voice. I might introduce my intervention in the following way: "Terry, let's find a different way of saying that." I would then model an alternative statement that I believe captures the authentic feeling, concern, or desire behind the unskillful statement; then I would have the Expresser verbalize my modeled statement in her own words by saying, "If that is accurate, say that," or "Say something more like that." There may be times when the Expresser, because she is feeling highly charged around the issue, may let slip a truly major "character assassination" statement against her partner. In such cases, I may elect to specifically identify, for example, that she's calling into question his motivation, and that it is important to avoid doing that. Again, this represents a form of continued teaching and reinforcement on the part of the therapist while facilitating and coaching a couple's dialogue. This kind of intervention will be a significant portion of the therapist's coaching during a couple's first several dialogues. Over time, however, couples tend to gradually become more skilled in expressing themselves, and not infrequently will even begin to catch and correct their own mistakes as they are making them.

Coach the Empathizer to Remain Empathic and to Go Deeper Empathically

The therapist will also need to exert a considerable amount of energy early in the couple's dialogues to help the Empathizer both remain empathic and go deeper in empathizing with his partner's experience. Probably the greatest challenge for the Empathizer early on in dialoguing is to keep himself and his own feelings, concerns, and desires out of the empathy. There is a strong tendency in all of us as human beings to want to express ourselves, in particular in response to something with which we disagree. But the role of the Empathizer in a structured dialogue requires that the person in that role exercise a serious level of self-discipline in order to fulfill the obligations of that role. In particular, this means that the Empathizer must exercise discipline to not say anything from his own point of view while his partner is expressing herself to him in a dialogue. This is where the empathy guidelines become helpful, because in part they are a set of practical tools to help the person in the role of the Empathizer be able to shift his attention away from himself and onto his partner's feelings, concerns, and desires. This also helps explain why in the Time-Designated format an entire session is taken to teach, demonstrate, and have the couple practice the Empathic skill, because that constitutes a kind of dry-run simulator training to help prepare the couple to be able to enter into a structured dialogue with the right frame of mind and an understanding of what is expected of them when in that role.

But even with the benefits of the couple having previously practiced the Empathic skill, there remains a strong possibility that the Empathizer will have some difficulty not expressing from his own point of view, especially when he is being emotionally reactive. Therefore, the therapist should be prepared to engage in corrective coaching to help the Empathizer refrain from expressing his own point of view while in the role of the Empathizer. The Empathizer will also need help in refocusing his attention on making an empathic connection with his partner's experience so that he can provide good verbal empathy. This intervention also needs to be made in a nonjudgmental manner, and with an even, neutral tone of voice. The therapist might say to the Empathizer, "You're speaking out of your own experience there. Remember, you don't exist right now." Or, "Let's keep yourself out of the empathy." Or, "You'll be able to express your own feelings after you change roles. Right now, I'd like you to stay focused on your partner's experience." If the Empathizer is not able to shift gears back into empathizing, and continues to express himself, the therapist may have to engage in Troubleshooting in order to help the Empathizer to be able to contain himself emotionally for the purpose of reentering the role of the Empathizer.

In addition, the therapist must be prepared to coach the Empathizer to go deeper in empathizing with what his partner has shared by helping him read between the lines. This presumes, of course, that the therapist has been empathically tracking the Expresser, which is one of the primary therapist responsibilities while coaching a couple's dialogue. In helping the Empathizer go deeper in his verbal empathy, positive reinforcement should always be offered for what the Empathizer was able to empathize with on his own. The therapist might say, "That was great. But let's add this to your empathy." Then the therapist would model additional empathy in the very form in which he or she would like the Empathizer to provide it. So, assuming the Empathizer was using the Identification Mode of empathy, the therapist would model an additional empathic statement using the pronoun *I*, but representing the experience of the Expresser. For example, "'What I'd also like you to understand is that I get really scared when you withdraw from me the way you do. It leaves me fearing that you're going to leave me.' Say something like that as part of your empathy."

The couple's first dialogue is now launched, and the therapist continues to monitor the dialogue and coach both partners as necessary while the dialogue unfolds. The goal is to take the couple as deep as possible, as quickly as possible, into the core of the issue being discussed. The therapist's active coaching often plays a significant role in this happening, though some people's ability to read between the lines quite deeply all on their own never ceases to amaze. In chapters 9 and 11, we will examine further aspects of the therapist's role as coach. We will also take a deeper look at the dialogue process in action in chapter 9 through two clinical vignettes.

Special Considerations With Respect to a Home Assignment

There are several important considerations for the therapist to keep in mind relative to a home assignment at this point in the therapy process. One of the key principles of home assignments is never to assign a task unless the therapist has a very high level of confidence in the couple's ability to carry out the assignment successfully. The reason is that the therapist wants to minimize the potential for the couple to experience frustration or, worse, an emotional setback because they were not ready to take on a particular task. In the present case, it is ill-advised to consider asking the couple to conduct a structured dialogue at home at this point in the therapy process. Generally speaking, couples are not asked to conduct a structured dialogue at home until two conditions have been met. First, the couple should have successfully completed at least one dialogue of similar difficulty in session with the assistance of the therapist. Second, the therapist should have first taught the couple how to use the Facilitation skill to help keep their dialogues on track when either person makes a mistake that has the potential to derail the dialogue (see chapter 10). It is even advisable to explicitly discourage the couple from attempting to dialogue at home at this point in time.

All that said, some couples will spontaneously attempt to conduct dialogues on their own at home anyway. Some will even manage to do a fairly creditable job the first time out. This can represent a significant psychological achievement for the couple, of which they may be quite proud. This should be responded to with support and positive reinforcement. Other couples will make a point of asking explicitly whether or not they should attempt to dialogue if a difficult issue emerges between sessions. My standard response is that it would be advisable for the couple to use the

Conflict Management strategies they have learned if they encounter a situation or issue that is too difficult to handle, and save the issue for the next therapy session. If pressed further by the couple, I respond to the effect that if a difficult issue emerges that they are not able to postpone or refrain from addressing, it certainly would be preferable for them to use what they have learned so far and attempt to do their best in having a dialogue as opposed to dealing with the issue in their old (i.e., unskillful) manner. There have been couples who have had initially frustrating experiences in their attempts to dialogue on their own but who have kept at it and have improved over time because they recognized that their old ways of interacting were doomed to failure and they were doggedly committed to making the dialogue process work for them. As is so often the case for therapists, I have learned much about the nuances of conducting couples therapy from the many couples I have worked with over the years.

There are several options for home assignments following this session. One option is to ask the couple to read the chapters devoted to the Facilitation and Problem/Conflict Resolution skills. (It is a good idea to have the couple continue reading through the *RE Client Manual* until they have read all the skill chapters.) For something more experiential, encourage the couple to continue giving one another daily appreciations (along with empathic acknowledgments), and also to dialogue about concerns or events that happened during the day that do not involve one another, for example, an issue that one partner has with a colleague at work. If the latter is suggested as a home assignment, advise the couple to refrain from offering advice unless it is specifically asked for, and instead to simply focus on understanding and empathizing with the partner's experience, feelings, and concerns. Assuming they had not already seen it following the previous session, the couple could be asked to view the *Demonstration of Identification Mode of Empathy Within the Relationship Enhancement Model* videotape (Scuka, 2003). As appropriate, a couple can be encouraged to continue to treat one another with respect and to continue to use the Conflict Management skill. Alternatively, and as appropriate, a couple can be encouraged to spend more quality time together to nurture their relationship.

CHAPTER **8**

Using the Experiential Format to Launch a Couple's First Dialogue

The Experiential Format

The Experiential format involves the therapist teaching just enough of the basic RE skills to allow a couple to initiate a substantive dialogue as quickly as possible. In practice, this includes the Empathic, Expressive, and Discussion/Negotiation skills, because these are the skills necessary for a couple to begin dialoguing. But in the Experiential format these skills are taught in a highly condensed, abbreviated manner. The advantage is that this enables the couple to more quickly engage an issue through dialogue than typically would be the case in the Time-Designated format. The tradeoff, however, is that the partners will not have been able to practice empathy in order to get accustomed to the demands of being a good Empathizer before initiating their first dialogue. As a consequence, it is vitally important that the therapist be proactive in carefully structuring the partners into their respective roles in their first dialogue. It will then become equally important to monitor the couple's dialogue during its early phases in order to steer the couple in constructive directions. This will include helping the person in the role of the Expresser translate unskillful statements into more subjectively appropriate language, while also initially demonstrating and continuing to model good empathic responses for the person in the role of the Empathizer. The success of RE therapy in its Experiential format is highly dependent upon the skill of the therapist in structuring and coaching the couple's process of intimate dialoguing (see the relevant sections on coaching in chapters 7, 9, and 11).

There are several reasons why a therapist might choose to use the Experiential format. First, this format would be appropriate if the number of sessions available for the therapy is limited and the couple desires to address a specific agenda within that limited time frame. Or perhaps frequent travel means that sessions will take place on an irregular basis, increasing the relative importance of each meeting in terms of accomplishing something concrete for the relationship. In such instances, the therapist may negotiate with the couple to meet for multiple hours at each meeting, in what is referred to as a minimarathon (3 to 4 hours) or marathon (5 to 8 hours) format.

Second, the couple might respond impatiently to the Time-Designated format or wish to move into their issues more rapidly. Many couples actually prefer the Time-Designated format because it allows them to postpone dealing with their intense issues while also giving them the opportunity to become more comfortable with the RE skills and dialogue process. Other couples, however, are able to pick up the basics of empathy, skillful expression, and the RE dialogue process quite rapidly and they wish to start dialoguing as quickly as possible.

A related but distinct reason is that the couple may be experiencing a sense of urgency to get to the core relationship issue(s) as quickly as possible, perhaps because there is a sense that the very viability of the relationship is hanging in the balance. In this instance, there may be a fine line between conceptualizing the therapy work as falling within the Experiential format or the Crisis Intervention format. The key difference between the two, in terms of process, is that within the Experiential format the therapist is teaching the couple, albeit in abbreviated form, how to dialogue between themselves, with the therapist in the role of a dialogue facilitator. Within the Crisis Intervention format, the therapist typically dispenses with trying to teach the couple how to dialogue and instead serves as the intermediary through whom all communication is directed, much as would happen during a standard RE clinical intake. This involves the therapist using Doublebecoming to alternately represent each partner to the other, in effect conducting the couple's dialogue for them in the role of an alternating surrogate for each person.

The final reason for using the Experiential format simply has to do with therapist preference. Some therapists prefer this format precisely because of its less structured and more fluid nature compared to the Time-Designated format. This gives some therapists more of a sense of freedom in applying the RE therapy model and might be especially attractive to therapists more accustomed to working within the framework of other therapy models. In principle, that is a perfectly legitimate reason for using the

Experiential format. For an example of a case utilizing the Experiential format, including an explanation of the rationale for its choice, see clinical vignette 1, chapter 9.

A Streamlined Approach to Teaching the RE Skills for Launching a Couple's First Dialogue

The initial challenge in using the Experiential format is to decide how much of the first three skills to introduce as a prelude to having the couple initiate their first structured dialogue. In principle, there are a number of ways it can be done, from the exceedingly brief to the slightly more elaborate. On the briefer side, the therapist can briefly orient the person who will be the first designated Empathizer about how to think about and how to approach being empathic, while inviting the designated Expresser to begin to express his or her point of view, with the therapist being prepared to coach the Expresser on how to express more skillfully if necessary. The success of this briefer approach is dependent upon the therapist's ability to effectively do two things. First, the therapist must be able to demonstrate and model ideal empathic representations of what the Expresser shares so that the Empathizer can begin to provide good empathy to the Expresser. Second, the therapist must be able to coach the Empathizer effectively in such a manner as to maximize that person's felt success with empathizing since this will be the very first time that this person will have attempted to empathize with his or her partner. Guerney's (1999a) videotape effectively models this abbreviated approach to introducing the RE skills and dialogue process. The relevant segment is to be found near the beginning of the first videotape of this five-tape set of a live workshop demonstration illustrating the Experiential format.

My own preference is to provide a brief introduction to the principles and a few of the guidelines of the first three RE skills. This can be done in about 10 minutes, and, to my mind, it is well worth the time and effort to help provide a somewhat fuller context for the couple to better understand the nature of the process they are being asked to embark upon. This way of introducing the RE skills and dialogue process within the Experiential format is analogous to allowing someone to look at a map before beginning a journey; it almost certainly will give that person a better perspective on where he or she is headed and how to get there. Intrinsically, that is a good thing, and I highly recommend it to therapists who choose to experiment with using the Experiential model.

I would like to model one way of introducing the RE dialogue process in the Experiential format that covers the basics of what I think is important for a couple to understand before initiating their first dialogue.

Scuka's (2003) videotape models this approach to introducing the RE dialogue process, in the context of a couple using the Identification Mode of empathy while conducting their first dialogue (involving an enhancement issue).

> Before you start your first dialogue, I'd like to take a few minutes to orient you to what is involved in having a structured dialogue. It's helpful to think of a dialogue as having two phases. The purpose of phase 1, which is referred to as Discussion/Negotiation, is to give each of you plenty of opportunities to share your respective points of view, your feelings, your concerns, and your desires, for the primary purpose, initially, of simply coming to understand one another better. That's the purpose of phase 1 of a dialogue. Then, on the basis of that, during phase 2, which is referred to as Problem/Conflict Resolution, the two of you will attempt to negotiate a solution or come up with an agreement that I hope will leave both of you feeling satisfied because you both feel your concerns have been heard and incorporated into the agreement.
>
> It's also helpful to think of a dialogue as involving two roles. We designate one role the Expresser, and we designate the other role the Empathizer. In order for a dialogue to work, it's important that each person stay in role and follow certain guidelines. For example, the person in the role of the Empathizer is not permitted to interrupt the Expresser, and is not permitted to ask any questions. The Empathizer also is not permitted to say anything from his or her point of view while in the role of the Empathizer. Once roles switch—and they must switch according to specific guidelines, which I will teach you later—then, as the new Expresser, you can ask all the questions you want; you then are also permitted to express your own point of view on the issue at hand. This way, everyone knows who is supposed to be in what role at all times.
>
> The person in the role of the Expresser is permitted to say whatever he or she wants, so long as it is said skillfully and subjectively. This means that it is the responsibility of the Expresser to communicate his or her point of view in a manner that does not cause the listener to feel defensive. That means that the Expresser must avoid saying things that imply that his or her way of thinking, memory, or values are superior to those of the partner. It also means no personal attacks on your partner's character, no questioning of his or her motivation or commitment to the relationship, and no saying anything that implies that there is something wrong with the other person. The Expresser can refer to what his or her partner has said

or done, but the trick is to keep the focus on your own subjective experience about what was said or done, without implying that there is something wrong with your partner. It's also helpful to begin your expressive message by sharing an underlying positive, something you appreciate about your partner or the relationship related to the issue you wish to discuss, to help establish a positive atmosphere between the two of you in the dialogue.

It's also really important when you are in the role of the Empathizer to give your complete attention to your partner, because that will allow you to really tune in to your partner's experience, which is what empathy is all about. Empathy is about connecting with your partner's feelings, your partner's concerns, and your partner's desires, but from your partner's point of view, as opposed to your own. That's the experiential part of empathy, where you focus your attention on your partner's experience, not on your own. One way to think about empathy is that you put your own feelings, concerns, and desires on hold so that you can become fully present to your partner's experience, without your own preoccupations getting in the way. Then there's the verbal part of empathy. That's where you verbally empathize with your partner by empathically acknowledging your partner's experience. There are two forms of verbal empathy. There's the conventional You Mode of empathy where one of you would express your point of view and the other person would empathize by saying, "You feel such and such." But there's an alternative form of empathy, the Identification Mode of empathy. This involves you identifying with your partner's experience by simply imagining yourself being your partner, having his or her experience, as you listen to your partner share his or her experience with you. What this looks like in terms of verbalizing your empathy is that you temporarily assume your partner's identity by pretending to be your partner, and you use the pronoun *I* to represent your partner's experience as though you were your partner.

This way of empathizing has several benefits. First, it helps the person who is doing the listening and the empathizing connect with the partner's experience from the inside out, as though he or she was having the partner's experience. The second benefit is that the person whose experience is being represented has this powerful sense of encounter, and a deeper sense of connection, with his or her experience by virtue of it being enacted by someone else. The reason this is so important is that the primary goal of empathy is to leave the Expresser *feeling* understood, which I believe is one of the most important things that most people want from one another in an intimate relationship. And when people feel understood by an intimate partner, they tend to feel good and feel positive about the relationship; and when they don't feel understood by an intimate partner, they tend not to feel so good about the relationship.

Let's take this a step further, because empathy is not just about repeating back what you've heard your partner say. That's a pretty simplistic view of empathy that sometimes gets taught, but it really doesn't help very much just to repeat back what your partner has said. It's much more powerful to read between the lines of what your partner says and to imagine what else, given what you are hearing your partner say, you can infer he or she is feeling or is in conflict about, what else he or she might be concerned about, and what else he or she might be wanting or desiring. That's what you want to verbalize as part of your empathy, by reading between the lines and trying to draw out the implied meaning that your partner didn't quite manage to put into words. And that's the golden gift that empathy has to offer: You not only help your partner feel understood, but you also help deepen your partner's self-understanding. The third thing that empathy does is help the Empathizer better understand the Expresser's feelings, concerns, and desires and in that way promotes compassion toward your partner's point of view. In this way empathy helps bridge the gap between two people. It's also one of the ways of deepening intimacy between two people. I think that's enough of an introduction to enable the two of you to begin your first dialogue.

With that as a general introduction to the RE dialogue process, the therapist can now have the couple initiate their first dialogue. However, the therapist will have to monitor the dialogue closely on two levels. First, the therapist will have to monitor the Expresser and help that person express as skillfully and as subjectively as possible in order to avoid causing defensiveness in the listener. Second, he or she will have to demonstrate and model good empathy and coach the Empathizer frequently in the early stages because neither party will have had the benefit of having been able to practice empathy with nonrelationship issues before conducting their first dialogue, as they would in the Time-Designated format.

Blending the Time-Designated and Experiential Formats

This last consideration points to yet another variation on how to initiate a couple's first dialogue. This would involve combining elements of the

Time-Designated format with elements of the Experiential format. The Time-Designated format would be followed in order to teach, demonstrate, and have the couple practice the Empathic skill (as outlined in chapter 6), followed by a shift into the Experiential format in order to teach the Expressive skill and the basics of the RE dialogue process (as outlined in this chapter). The virtue of this combination is that it retains the rigor of solidly grounding the couple in the Empathic skill while also enabling the couple to initiate their first dialogue one session earlier than would otherwise be the case. This variation might be used when the therapist has concluded that there is no need to cover the Conflict Management skill with a particular couple and he or she would like the couple to begin dialoguing sooner rather than later, yet the therapist wants to ensure that the couple is well grounded in the empathic process. Alternatively, devoting a full session to teaching, demonstrating, and having the couple practice the Empathic skill might also be advisable when the therapist wants the couple to use the Identification Mode of empathy while dialoguing, although I have successfully introduced couples to the use of the Identification Mode of empathy within the context of using the Experiential format. For an example of a blended application of the Time-Designated and Experiential formats, see clinical vignette 3, chapter 12.

What these different formats, combination of formats, and options for implementing RE therapy demonstrate is the great flexibility and versatility of the RE model relative to its clinical application. This flexibility also makes it possible for clinicians to tailor and adapt their use of RE therapy to their own individual stylistic preferences. What remains common in all these variations, however, is the use of deep empathy to anchor a dialogue process that fosters intimate sharing, mutual understanding, and a deepened sense of emotional connection, compassion, and acceptance. Let's now turn our attention to the RE dialogue process in action, with the understanding that it could be initiated either via the more structured approach of the Time-Designated format, the briefer and more condensed approach of the Experiential format, or a blended application of the two.

CHAPTER 9

The Heart of the Matter:
The RE Dialogue Process in Action

The RE dialogue process is the principal framework within which most of the couples work is done in RE therapy. The process of intimate dialoguing enables couples to reach deeper levels of understanding than would otherwise be likely to happen. This in turn fosters increased compassion and acceptance, while also creating a crucible for emotional healing and a deepening of intimacy. This chapter presents two clinical vignettes to bring the RE dialogue process to life. In preparation, coaching tips on how to effectively manage the couple's dialogue process are reviewed.

Coach From "Behind" the Clients: The Preferred Method for Interacting With a Couple While Coaching a Dialogue in RE Therapy

Recall that during the clinical intake in RE therapy, the therapist requests that each person direct his or her comments solely to the therapist and not the partner. The primary reason this is done is to help maintain a safe structure and atmosphere for the initial interview so that the couple can have confidence in the therapist's ability to keep each of them emotionally safe. There is a secondary positive benefit to this way of structuring the clinical intake; it helps strengthen the therapist's relationship with each person individually by giving each person the experience and confidence of being well understood by the therapist.

In many forms of couples therapy, this pattern of therapist–client interaction, where the therapist interacts directly with each client in turn, continues even past the clinical intake. For example, the therapist first listens to and then responds (empathically or otherwise) to the first partner, and then in similar fashion to the second partner. This way of interacting with the couple has the effect of continuing to strengthen the therapist's individual relationship with each member of the couple. When this becomes the therapist's dominant mode for conducting couples therapy, this strengthening of the therapist's relationship with each member of the couple arguably comes at the expense of strengthening the relationship between the partners themselves, which, after all, ought to be the focal point and purpose of couples therapy.

In RE therapy, however, the explicit goal, once the clinical intake is completed, is to have the partners interact directly with one another through the format of structured dialogues. The role of the therapist during these dialogues is best conceived as that of a coach or facilitator. This coaching will most typically take two forms: helping the Expresser more completely express his or her feelings, concerns, and desires, and helping the Empathizer empathize more deeply with the core experience of the Expresser. This is best accomplished, in the latter instance, by modeling for the Empathizer how she might empathize more deeply with her partner's expressive statement. She then would provide the empathy to her partner, rather than the therapist turning to the partner and providing the deeper empathy him- or herself.

This way of facilitating a couple's dialogue has the important effect of preserving the primacy of the couple's interaction through their dialogue process, while also promoting the obvious benefit of strengthening the couple's relationship with each other (rather than the therapist's relationship with one or both members of the couple). The therapist should therefore aim, as much as possible, to coach the couple's dialogues from "behind" the clients (or through the back door). This is most especially true when coaching the Empathizer, as in the example above. But this principle also applies when coaching the Expresser. Therefore, it would in general be preferable for the therapist to prompt the Expresser to share more about his feelings, concerns, or desires—or for the therapist to make a specific suggestion and then encourage the Expresser to express it more fully for himself—than it would for the therapist to express extensively on the Expresser's behalf. The exception would be when the therapist believes that the Expresser is not able to express as deeply or as richly as the therapist believes he or she could on the Expresser's behalf, or when the Expresser is either out of touch with his own experience or is otherwise blocked from expressing it fully. In those cases, the therapist will want to use Becoming in order to more fully represent the Expresser's experience than he may be able to do for himself.

Additional Tips for the Therapist on How to Coach a Couple's Dialogue

1. *Exercise caution to not insert yourself into or disrupt a couple's dialogue.*

As an extension of the previous point, it is important that the therapist learn to exercise restraint in not inserting him- or herself into a couple's dialogue too casually or too frequently. The couple needs to be given space to unfold their own dialogue because the real work of the therapy is between the couple, not between the therapist and the couple. The therapist's principal role, once the couple has begun to dialogue, is that of a dialogue coach or facilitator. The therapist will have many more thoughts and opinions about the issue being discussed by the couple than he or she would ever verbalize, other than by coaching the clients through the back door. But even here it is important that restraint is exercised by giving the couple the opportunity to come to the same insight the therapist is having, because it will be more powerful for the couple if it first comes from one of them. The paradox of the coach/facilitator role in RE therapy is that the therapist must be very active in terms of monitoring the couple's dialogue *process* but more reticent when it comes to the *content* of the couple's dialogue, except for the purpose of deepening it (see 4 and 8 below). A skilled therapist thus masters the fine art of knowing when to remain silent and stays out of the couple's way.

2. *Coach the Expresser to begin his or her initial expressive statement with an underlying positive.*

Especially in the couple's first few dialogues (but continuing throughout the therapy), it is exceedingly important to coach and train the couple to begin their initiation of a dialogue with an underlying positive in order to help establish a positive atmosphere of cooperation. There are three benefits to couples getting in the habit of beginning their initial expressive statements with an underlying positive. The first benefit is that it encourages couples to keep things in perspective when dealing with a difficult issue, which tends to reduce the intensity of negative feeling around the issue. The second benefit is that it tends to reduce defensiveness in the Empathizer, which in turn tends to increase receptivity to hearing the Expresser's concerns. The third benefit of beginning with an underlying positive is that it encourages couples to get in the habit of thinking through in advance what they want to say about an issue. This increases the likelihood that the Expresser will express in a verbally skillful manner, to the benefit of the couple's dialogue.

3. *Constantly monitor the Expresser's communication to help ensure that he or she expresses as skillfully and as subjectively as possible, and model alternative expressive statements as necessary.*

   Monitoring the Expresser to help ensure skillful communication is one of the most important ways in which the therapist monitors the process of the couple's dialogue. It is the therapist's responsibility to help preserve the Empathizer's emotional safety by minimizing the likelihood that he or she comes to feel defensive due to unskillful communication by the Expresser. The therapist should therefore be prepared to model alternative ways of helping the Expresser say whatever he or she is trying to communicate. In this context, it is helpful to remember that behind every unskillful expressive statement there is a legitimate feeling, concern, or desire that deserves to be expressed, but in a skillful manner. It is the therapist's job to help the Expresser achieve that dual purpose by helping that person say what he or she is trying to say using skillful language. This will most often take the form of helping the Expresser restate an accusation about the partner into a subjective statement about the Expresser's own feelings or experience. For example, coach the Expresser to translate the accusatory statement, "You don't even notice me!" into the more subjective statement, "I feel invisible to you." It can be helpful, in this context, to point out to couples that accusatory expressive statements, which often have an active voice formulation, can be effectively "translated" into a skillful subjective statement by turning the active tense into a passive voice formulation. For example, if one partner were to say "You did that to hurt me!," which is both an accusation and an unskillful attribution of negative motivation, coach that person to instead say "I felt hurt by what did."

4. *Continue to coach attentively by tracking the issue and look for ways to clarify or deepen what the Expresser is saying in order to advance the couple's dialogue.*

   In addition to monitoring the dialogue process, the therapist should also closely monitor the content of the issue being dialogued about. In this context, the therapist should be on the lookout for opportunities to help clarify what the Expresser is saying or to help the Expresser express more fully or deeply. Clarifying what the Expresser is saying can help avoid potential misunderstanding on the part of the Empathizer if the Expresser has not been clear. Helping the Expresser express more clearly or deeply can help advance the dialogue by helping both partners understand more fully what the Expresser's feelings, concerns, and desires are. This may be done either by saying to the Expresser, "I think you are also trying to say that ..." or by using Becoming in order to give a more extended and deeper representation of what the therapist is empathically identifying is part of the Expresser's experience.

5. *If the Expresser begins to look at or direct comments to the therapist, redirect the Expresser to address his or her partner instead.*

Sometimes subtly, sometimes more overtly, the Expresser will begin to address his or her comments to the therapist. This sometimes happens because the Expresser is looking for confirmation or moral support for his or her point of view. Whenever that happens, gently but firmly redirect the Expresser to address his or her comments to the dialogue partner. This can be done unobtrusively and nonverbally by the therapist simply pointing an index finger across his or her body in the direction of the Empathizer. Alternatively, the therapist might say to the Expresser, "Please speak directly to your partner." A variation on this is that the Expresser will sometimes speak of the partner in the third person, as though he or she was speaking to the therapist about the partner. In those cases, the therapist gently coaches the Expresser by saying, "Please speak directly to your partner."

6. *Monitor the Empathizer closely to ensure that person does not begin to speak from his or her point of view while in that role.*

This is perhaps the single most important thing the therapist can do to help prevent a breakdown in the couple's dialogue process. It is the therapist's responsibility to ensure that the integrity of the structure of the dialogue process is preserved at all times. This does not mean that the therapist has to pedantically correct the Empathizer if that person makes an innocuous passing comment that, strictly speaking, is not empathic in nature. That would be more disruptive of the dialogue than allowing such a comment to pass. However, do make a point early on in the couple's dialoguing to emphasize that, technically speaking, the Empathizer is not even permitted to express agreement with what the Expresser is saying until roles have been exchanged. The real point, however, is that the therapist must be vigilant like a hawk never to allow the Empathizer to begin to express reactively from his or her point of view instead of empathizing with what the Expresser has just said. This, in practice, is how the integrity of the structured dialogue process is preserved, and it is indeed the single most important thing the clinician can do to prevent a dialogue from breaking down. (I explain my rigor in maintaining the integrity of the structure of the dialogue process by saying that the dialogue process is the couple's friend, and that if they treat it well and follow the process rigorously, then it will serve them well in turn.) The therapist might say to the Empathizer something like this: "You're expressing from your point of view, and at the moment your job is to empathize with what your partner has said." Or the therapist might say, with a playful tone, "You don't exist right now. Your focus should be on empathizing with your partner." Or, very simply, "It's not about you right now. Your focus should be on your partner."

7. *Be certain the Empathizer begins by empathizing with the partner's underlying positive.*

It's all too easy for the Empathizer to forget, overlook, or otherwise not take in the underlying positive(s) with which the Expresser (let us hope) began his or her expressive statement. Because it is so important that the Expresser begin his or her first expressive statement with an underlying positive, and because the therapist (ideally) has made such a big point of the Expresser doing so, it is equally important that the Empathizer empathically acknowledge any underlying positive(s) that were given. This is both to ensure that the Empathizer genuinely takes in the content of the underlying positive(s) and to help reinforce the Expresser's attempt to establish a positive atmosphere between the couple, especially when they are addressing a difficult relationship issue.

8. *Help the Empathizer read more deeply between the lines of what the Expresser is saying in order to help both partners better understand what the Expresser is saying.*

Here the therapist focuses on the empathy provided by the Empathizer in order to help him go deeper in reading between the lines so that the Empathizer can connect more deeply with his or her partner's experience, and in turn provide deeper empathy that will help the Expresser understand him- or herself better. This presumes that the therapist has been monitoring both the content of the issue being dialogued about and the Expresser's current statement so that the therapist can read between the lines in the service of helping the Empathizer empathize more deeply. However, it is important to first offer positive reinforcement for whatever level of empathy the Empathizer was able to provide and then go on to model additional empathy as the therapist would like the Empathizer to provide it. For example, the therapist might say, "That was good. There's one additional piece I picked up on." Then, after modeling the additional empathy, the therapist could say, "Say something like that, in your own words."

There are two specific ways of reading between the lines that are especially useful. The first involves picking up on internal conflicts that the Expresser may be experiencing that he or she is not fully aware of or giving explicit voice to. It can be especially helpful to the Expresser to name such internal conflicts. One effective of way of doing this is to use "parts" language, where the therapist might model empathy for the Empathizer by saying, "Part of you is feeling…, but another part of you is feeling…." The therapist can also simply prompt the Empathizer by saying, "What do you imagine your partner's internal conflict around this is?" Richard Schwartz's *Internal Family Systems* model (1995) provides a useful framework for working with a person's internal "parts" when working with either partner at the intrapsychic level.

The second helpful way of reading between the lines is to point out to couples that they can take a negative complaint being voiced by the partner and in effect flip it around to the implied positive state of affairs that person is desiring. For example, if someone is upset about feeling ignored and unattended to emotionally, then clearly implied in that is the desire that the partner pay more attention to and engage more meaningfully with the person who is feeling neglected. This is a very simple but powerful way for both the therapist and the couple to learn how to read between the lines. In addition to explaining this general principle of reading between the lines, the therapist can also verbally prompt the Empathizer to read between the lines in this manner by simply asking "What's the implied desire there?" or "What is he [or she] wanting from you?"

9. *Encourage the new Expresser to begin by stating what makes sense to him or her about the partner's feelings, concerns, and desires.*

Coaching the partners to begin their new self-expression by sharing what makes sense to them about the partner's experience, before expressing their own point of view, serves several important purposes. First, it helps the couple avoid talking past one another, which can happen if the new Expresser fails to address some of the specific points raised by the previous Expresser before going on to his or her own points. Second, when one person says, "It makes sense to me that you would feel [or be concerned about, etc.]...," that conveys to the partner a deeper level of acceptance than simply receiving good empathy (where no agreement is implied). Third, it also represents the beginning of potential bridge building between the partners because encouraging them to think in these terms encourages them to also think in terms of what they may be able to agree on with each other. The other person's experience "making sense" and agreeing with the other person are not identical, but becoming conscious of the former can help promote the latter. This, in turn, can help create a positive sense of building common ground, which can expedite the couple's discussion and resolution of an issue. The new Expresser can also be coached to continue expressing by responding from his or her point of view to what had been shared by the partner and to share his or her own distinctive concerns about the issue at hand.

10. *Troubleshoot breakdowns in the dialogue process (as necessary).*

The therapist should be prepared to intervene at the earliest possible moment when it appears that the dialogue process is beginning to go awry. This could happen because the Expresser is being verbally unskillful, in which case the therapist must help that person express more skillfully (see 3 above). By itself, however, this usually will not result in the dialogue process breaking down. What is more likely to cause a breakdown is if the person in the role of the Empathizer were unable (or unwilling) to empathize. This will often manifest itself as the Empathizer beginning to express reactively from his or her point of view to what the Expresser has just said. The therapist's first response should be to redirect the Empathizer back into empathizing with his or her partner (see 6 above). However, if this fails to bring the Empathizer back into empathizing, then the therapist is faced with an obstacle to forward movement in the dialogue process, at which point the therapist must engage in

Troubleshooting with the Empathizer. This involves the therapist continuing to empathize with that person as long as necessary until that person is able to reenter the role of Empathizer for the purpose of empathizing with the partner and continuing the dialogue.

11. *Use Therapist Troubleshooting sparingly, and choose more often to use Becoming on behalf of one partner to indirectly help the other partner better understand an important consideration.*

The therapist can often use Therapist Troubleshooting and Becoming toward the same end of helping one partner better understand an important consideration. However, the very indirectness of the technique of Becoming, compared to that of Therapist Troubleshooting, gives it a certain advantage in that it lowers the risk of triggering a defensive response. The therapist is therefore well-advised to channel the (sometimes not infrequent) temptation to intervene in the couple's dialogue via Therapist Troubleshooting into looking for an opportunity to use Becoming on behalf of one partner in order to address the other partner indirectly. Using Becoming in this way has the added advantage of better preserving the integrity of the couple's dialogue process, which is where the primary focus of the work belongs.

12. *Use Becoming to help cut through misunderstandings between the partners.*

One of the essential purposes of dialoguing is to help couples overcome the layers of misunderstandings that have accumulated over time as a result of poor communication, partial or unclear communication, and outright unskillful communication. The therapist can often rapidly cut through such misunderstandings by using Becoming to help clarify what one partner had been trying to communicate while also addressing the concerns of the other partner that may have fed the misunderstanding. As a consequence, the therapist should never hesitate to clarify the meaning of what one partner is trying to communicate if it appears that the other partner is misunderstanding the intended meaning.

13. *Consider using Doublebecoming if the dialogue process becomes stuck and there is little forward movement on the issue.*

In those cases where none of the above interventions is sufficient to move the couple's dialogue forward, the use of Doublebecoming can be tried to achieve a breakthrough to the emotional impasse. By using the Identification Mode of empathy to represent each member of the couple, the therapist would seek to read between the lines deeply and positively enough to help each person begin to feel more deeply understood and in turn to be able to hear each other's feelings, concerns, and desires in a more favorable light.

Clinical Vignette 1: Dialoguing for Enrichment Purposes in a Stable Marriage

In this clinical vignette we observe the RE dialogue process being used by a couple in a stable marriage in which there is no crisis and the couple is not highly distressed or conflicted (though they have their moments), but the couple does have important issues—including issues from the past—that they would like to address for the sake of improving their marriage. This represents a case where RE therapy is being used primarily for enrichment as opposed to reparative purposes, though the line between enrichment and reparative therapy work is not absolutely fixed or clean in that nondistressed couples seeking enrichment may still have conflicts to be resolved (as is illustrated in this vignette) while couples with troubled relationships may still desire and have their relationships enriched in a manner that transcends the resolution of overt conflicts.

This vignette also shows that even when a couple does not have a troubled or highly distressed relationship and the partners are primarily seeking enrichment, they can still benefit immensely from the process of intimate dialogue because of what it makes possible in terms of the couple's communication process. Specifically, it is the very structure of the RE dialogue process that makes possible the uncovering of dimensions of people's feelings, concerns, and desires that are unlikely to emerge simply through normal day-to-day conversation, even when such conversation is positive and nonconflictual. The two key factors that foster this enriched experience are a rigorous adherence to respecting the two distinct roles of Expresser and Empathizer and the emotional safety that this creates. Along with this is the fact that couples are encouraged to go beyond mere paraphrasing into the more challenging but interpersonally more rewarding experience of deeply empathizing with one another's experience. This benefit holds true whether the couple seeking to enrich their relationship has been married for a number of years or is engaged or only recently married. The point is that it is the very nature of intimate dialogue that opens emotional doors in the relationship, and this in turn permits a new level of communication and connection that otherwise often eludes couples.

Mike and Lisa[1] were both in their early to mid-60s, and had been referred to me by another couple. Lisa had already retired several years prior, while Mike, at the point at which we began working together, was about a year away from retirement. Their purpose in coming to see me, according to Mike, was to enlist my services to help "coach" them in their retirement planning, the biggest issue of which was whether to stay in the area or move away, possibly closer to their adult children. Lisa expressed concern that retirement would be a challenge for Mike because he was so committed to and involved in his policy-related career. She feared he might not be able to disengage from his work world and truly embrace retirement. Lisa also expressed concern about their years of living in orbits that were independent of each other, and how she wanted that to change. Most important to Lisa was the process by which they would go about making their decision as to whether to stay or leave the area, because she wanted to ensure that they would make a genuinely sustainable decision. Finally, Lisa indicated that she recognized that she, in years past, had held unrealistic and unfair expectations that "if only Mike were different, everything would be fine," and that she did not want to go down that path any longer. They both were clear that their marriage was sound, that they loved and were committed to each other, and that they had come to therapy to sort out important issues so that the final phases of their life together would be built on a solid and jointly constructed foundation.

My assessment was that Lisa and Mike were a stable couple who were seeking to enrich an already good marriage, and that they were approaching Mike's impending retirement with intentionality and the desire to make it as positive an experience as they could, both for him and for them as a couple. I explained to them that the way I could be most helpful to them would be to teach them a process on how to communicate in a manner that would enable them to get to their core feelings, concerns, and desires so that they could come to understand one another better. Then, on the basis of that, they would be able to make decisions that they could feel comfortable with and have confidence in because they both would feel that their feelings, concerns, and desires had been taken into account and incorporated into their joint decisions. They both indicated that they felt that was exactly what they needed.

On the basis of my assessment and their acceptance of my proposed therapeutic contract, I made several decisions about how I would proceed with the therapy. First, I decided that I did not need to take time to teach this couple Conflict Management skills because they gave me no reason to think that this was necessary. I also decided that I would not use the RE demonstration audiotape to introduce the RE model to them, but that I would instead employ the Experiential format and (following in general terms the outline provided in chapter 8) introduce the RE dialogue process. I would talk to them about what it means to be empathic and how to use the Identification Mode of empathy, and cover the basics of the Expressive skill in terms of communicating subjectively and avoiding ways of communicating that tend to cause defensiveness in the other person. I also would introduce the ideas of partner appreciations and underlying positives and have them share partner appreciations before they began their first dialogue. I also would have them begin each subsequent session with partner appreciations.

A number of the early sessions, and many thereafter, focused not just on helping Mike and Lisa sort through how they would approach the prospect of joint retirement and planning for the future, but also on helping Mike come to terms with how he would actually make the break from a 20-year career that was both demanding and emotionally draining. (He admitted that he was close to burnout and looking forward to retirement with a certain sense of relief.) It did not take long, however (the second session postintake), before aspects of their marital relationship and their respective personalities began naturally to come to the fore in their dialogues. And it did not take much longer than that, at Lisa's prodding, for them to begin to tackle more emotionally laden relationship issues. These issues included looking at old problems and unhelpful patterns of interaction between them that no longer necessarily generated intense fights between them but that still held an emotional sway over them in a manner that sometimes would trip them up and cause them to reexperience some of the old pains and hurts. So while the therapy focused, on one level, on planning for the future in order to enrich their relationship, it also focused, on another level, on emotional issues that involved them looking at themselves and their relationship in a deep and probing manner. Some of that I think would perhaps have been inevitable, given this particular couple, but I also believe that the unfolding of Mike and Lisa's dialogues over time, including my use of Becoming to help clear away misunderstandings and my coaching each of them to go deeper in empathizing with each other, also created the conditions of safety and experienced success that encouraged them to go into emotionally deeper territory relative to their intimate relationship.

Over the course of the therapy, Lisa and Mike covered many issues relating to the history and the present state of their marriage that went well beyond planning for their retirement. Indeed, as Lisa explicitly stated, from her point of view, their sessions had as much to do with their sorting out their relationship issues so that they could get truly comfortable with each other, as they did with planning for the future. More to the point, Lisa felt that the success of the former was essential to the success of the latter. Over time, Mike and Lisa dialogued about a wide variety of relationship issues, including their differing approaches to spirituality and how each of them relate to the world around them; preparing for and communicating their experiences after holiday events involving family; and their individual sexual histories, the various phases of their own sexual relationship, and the current state and challenges of being sexual with each other in their later years. But perhaps the most significant relationship issues addressed by Lisa and Mike involved a series of dialogues held intermittently over the space of a year and a half. These particular dialogues typically focused on their disentangling old, negative patterns of interaction that had set a certain tone in their marriage and that continued at times to trip them up, though with less frequency and with some increased ability on their part to disengage themselves from a pattern after it reappeared. On the other hand, they both recognized that they could still all too easily get caught up in the same negative cycles of interaction, and they wanted both to learn to interrupt the cycles sooner and to recover from them more quickly so that they would not continue to impact their relationship negatively.

One such issue involved a pattern that included Mike feeling upset and defensive around believing that certain "facts" were being misrepresented by Lisa, or that he was being misunderstood or misinterpreted by Lisa, and Lisa either "going ballistic" (her own description) or totally shutting down around feeling as though Mike was presenting his perceptions as facts. This would leave Lisa feeling totally discounted in terms of her perceptions about the issue being discussed or the event that had transpired between them. Lisa first made reference to this dynamic between the two of them in the fourth session postintake. On another occasion she observed that this dynamic continued to dog them in their lives. This dynamic, not unsurprisingly, also reared itself several times during our couples work together. Each time, the overtly visible part of the pattern would be that Mike would get upset at something Lisa had said and would insist on his need and right to present the "facts" as he "knew" them to be. The challenge for me, the first few times this dynamic presented itself in session, was that it had seemed to me that what Lisa had said was technically skillful and fell within the allowable limits of the Expressive skill guidelines. (It is imperative that the therapist constantly monitor the Expresser for the skillfulness of his or her expressive statements precisely so that the Empathizer does not become needlessly defensive over unskillful communication by the Expresser.)

More specifically, it seemed to me that Lisa had been very careful to speak subjectively so as to convey that she was speaking from her point of view, and not making claims to "facts" which, had she done so, clearly would have been in violation of the Expressive skill guidelines. On several occasions when this happened, I found myself resorting to a combination of Troubleshooting on the one hand, because Mike would sometimes break out of role as the Empathizer when he had become upset, and attempting to explain to him that he was not entitled, as an Expresser, to state things as though he had special access to the "truth" or the "facts" about what had happened. Rather, he was only entitled to state things in terms of his perceptions and his recollections, because that was all he really had access to. This latter point represented a major bone of contention for Mike emotionally, despite his ability to understand the Expressive skill guidelines in the abstract. However, the intensity of his feelings around this indicated that there was some deeper emotional issue for Mike that appeared to leave him feeling as though his very sense of self was at stake in these interactions with Lisa.

After perhaps the third or fourth dialogue where this dynamic had played out in session (over the course of over a year of mostly biweekly sessions, to put things in perspective), Lisa ventured to raise this dynamic itself as an issue for them to dialogue about. Lisa began by referencing a recent dialogue in which she had experienced Mike presenting his perspective "in objective terms that leave me feeling that my subjective experience is being invalidated. That's still a place of great vulnerability for me in our relationship, because it leaves me feeling wiped out [as a person]." She chose to raise this issue, she explained, precisely because she had finally come to realize through their work in therapy that the issue of their retirement was not at all about where they would choose to live. She had finally come to realize that the issue of their retirement was instead "about you and me, and about our adventure together," and that she needed them to sort this issue out so that she could feel truly safe at an emotional level about their decision to move away from their home of 20-plus years. The reason this felt so pressing to her was that "the new possibilities between the two of us also raise the stakes in terms of my vulnerability [to you and with you] … because our moving away also means that we will become more reliant on one another," implying that on one level that prospect had been scary to her up until now, but that she was willing to embrace the risk because he had "demonstrated such an openness to [their] process" in the therapy. Lisa then returned to the issue of the negative dynamic between them and invited Mike to "please talk about what happens [for you] when we get into that locked space and you become insistent on things being a certain way. It would help me understand how it reflects a threat and a need [for you] to survive.... Do you fear that you'll be obliterated in some way?" Mike responded to this perceptively phrased observation and question:

> Mike: It's difficult to generalize. There are several different circumstances. Sometimes it's about a special decision. Other times it's about a reaction you have toward a behavior of mine. I think the answer to your question is "yes" [I do fear being obliterated in some way]. What makes me most fearful is that I haven't been heard, understood, or acknowledged, or that what I've said has been totally misunderstood, or negative motives have been attributed to me. I then fear that there's no way to sort it out, and it feels like absolutes have been laid on me that I don't recognize. It feels like there's been a breakdown in our dialogue process, and there's no way to resolve it.

> Lisa [as Empathizer]: You do fear being obliterated. You feel very unheard. It feels as though motives are attributed to you that are erroneous. It feels like there's no place for a dialogue that can have a redemptive effect. That leaves you feeling frantic and desperate and gives you a sense of urgency.

> Lisa [as Expresser, parenthetically]: Boy, do I hate that place!

> Mike [as Expresser]: It [the fear] becomes most intense when I feel that my behavior is being criticized [implying that this leaves him feeling attacked as a person, and therefore unable to defend himself, hence vulnerable to being obliterated as a person].

Interestingly, or perhaps almost predictably, Lisa and Mike then played out the very dynamic they had up until now been able to dialogue about with relative dispassion. Lisa reverted to a content issue that had been the occasion for the most recent appearance of this negative dynamic, and Mike immediately became reactive. I resorted to Troubleshooting and empathized with Mike feeling defensive. I then helped him disentangle what had just transpired in terms of his emotional defensiveness on the one hand and his becoming verbally insistent about the "facts" of the matter on the other. I then observed to Mike empathically, "You have a real fear of being falsely accused." When he agreed with that statement, I observed to him that when that happens he appears to go into a kind of authority stance with regard to what he sees as the "facts" in order to attempt to reestablish order to his emotional world. Mike indicated that made sense to him, and then he made an interesting statement about himself: "I do keep on identifying with those who are falsely accused." This prompted Lisa to observe that Mike's father used his authority in an arbitrary manner and regularly made false accusations toward people in general, and that this had been his pattern with Mike when he was growing up. I observed to Mike that his entire life had been spent defending people who had been falsely accused (or otherwise deprived of their sense of humanity). I then observed that he also feels a need to do that for himself when he experiences himself being falsely accused, in this case by Lisa, who also represents his father. Lisa then volunteered, somewhat sheepishly, that she realized she probably had said something in their mini-interaction a moment prior that came across as an accusation and triggered Mike's defensiveness, just like his father would have done. This prompted a further self-realization on Lisa's part that when she gets triggered by becoming upset with something that Mike has done, she ends up doing the very thing with him that she objects to from him with respect to her, "and then a power struggle ensues between us." Mike concurred with everything that had been said, and expressed appreciation to Lisa for owning her part in the interaction that had just taken place.

I closed the session by reminding Mike and Lisa about the Facilitation skill (which I had taught to them many months earlier) and suggesting to Mike that one thing that could help break the cycle from his end would be for him to become more aware in the moment that he was feeling falsely accused and for him to use the stop sign signal to inform Lisa that he was feeling defensive because he was experiencing her communicating to him nonsubjectively. At the following session, we briefly reviewed what had happened in the previous session. Mike reiterated his appreciation to Lisa for acknowledging her part in their negative dynamic and indicated that he realized his tendency to adopt an authoritative stance with regard to presumed facts (what Lisa characterized as his tendency to speak as though he was in possession of the truth, which violates the Expressive skill guidelines) left Lisa feeling unsafe emotionally. He also indicated that he would attempt to use the stop sign signal to communicate his defensiveness so that he would be less likely to slip into that authoritative stance and in this way perhaps be able to keep the focus on his subjective experience of feeling falsely accused.

At the next session, Lisa made a statement that summarized not just her feelings about their ability to disentangle the difficult issue that had occupied much of the preceding two sessions, but her feelings as well about the entire therapy process and where it had brought her and them as a couple:

I felt really understood by you with regard to my feelings the last two times. That has been my experience time and again here, that I've been able to open up issues that I've felt blocked on in the past in trying to communicate with you. Our coming here is not primarily about our retirement plans. It's about the core of our relationship. In the process of these sessions, I've actually come to understand my feelings really for the first time because of this dialogue process. I understand myself more deeply, as well as feel understood by you.

Lisa's statement represents, to my mind, forceful testimony to the power of the process of intimate dialogue to facilitate couples going more deeply into themselves and the issues that confront them in their relationships. Time and again, in my experience, the process of intimate dialogue brings couples to a place of self-encounter and encounter with one another that is quite remarkable and, I believe, unlikely to be attained through conventional day-to-day conversation. I also question how much of this kind of deeply interpersonal encounter is likely to happen in other models of therapy where the emphasis of the work is not placed on the couple engaging each other directly in dialogue. In some of these alternative models, the emphasis is instead placed on the therapist interpreting, analyzing, or directing/orchestrating the couple's process as an external observer. In RE therapy the therapist occasionally interprets or analyzes (as evidenced above), but this is a very small proportion of the therapy work in the RE model. Also, the therapist is very directive in RE therapy relative to the structure, rules, and guidelines of the dialogue process *as a process*, whereas the therapist is very nondirective relative to the content of the couple's dialogues (though the therapist does help clarify the meaning of each person's communication as necessary). But, in the end, what distinguishes RE therapy with couples is that the heart of the work is done by the couples themselves through dialoguing directly with one another about their core issues, under the facilitation of the therapist. The emotional safety and experienced success that is engendered by the RE dialogue process enables couples to explore themselves and their issues more deeply than otherwise would be the case. In turn, this enables couples to reach a place of mutual understanding, acceptance, compassion, and genuine healing in the relationship. As this vignette demonstrates, even nondistressed couples in stable marriages can benefit immensely from the RE dialogue process because it facilitates the couple becoming more open with each other in a collaborative process of exploration and discovery.

Clinical Vignette 2: Dialoguing to Process a Traumatic Experience That Was Emotionally Painful for Both Partners

In this vignette we will observe how a couple use intimate dialogue to process a traumatic event experienced by the female partner that also had a significant emotional impact on the male partner. We will also observe the couple use the Identification Mode of empathy as their standard mode of empathizing while they dialogued. The early stages of the therapy will also be reviewed, both to illuminate the unfolding of the therapy process and to help set the stage for their decisive dialogue.

Anna and Jim were in their mid-30s and both were divorced; they were living together but were not married, though they intended to marry; both had several children, his with them part time, her youngest with them full time, while her older child (with a different father) had been living with the father for the past year. Several issues brought them into therapy, but the most immediate issue was one of trust, more specifically, Anna's lack of trust in Jim. This was not because he had an affair but because of what she regarded as poor judgment on his part during a business trip that to her reflected poor interpersonal boundaries that put him at risk for being taken advantage of by conniving females (who she really did not trust). They had an argument about it 2 weeks prior to the session that brought up "old wounds" for Anna and caused her to have doubts both about the relationship and Jim's love for her. She acknowledged Jim's gestures of love and responsiveness toward her concerns, but also admitted "I don't know how to make the demons go away." For his part, Jim described the wrenching nature of his own divorce, how he and Anna had gradually become fond of each other and then decided to live together, how much he wanted not to harm their relationship in any way, and the adjustments he had tried to make in his behavior in light of understanding Anna's sensitivities. On the other hand, he was concerned about the emotional wall that Anna had put up between them of late. He also made reference to an incident where Anna had gotten together with her ex one time after they had started living together, and how hurt he had been by that, but that she felt bad about it, and he worked to get past it emotionally, despite the fact that its impact on him had been quite significant.

I decided that it would be advisable to follow the Time-Designated format with this couple, so I introduced the RE model with the demonstration audiotape and talked about Conflict Management strategies. Then, after teaching Anna and Jim how to empathize by using the Identification Mode of empathy and how to conduct a structured dialogue, I encouraged them to experiment with using the Identification Mode of empathy while conducting their couple's dialogues. They agreed, and very quickly began to make progress on several issues. They first spent several sessions dialoguing about parenting issues, which I recommended as their first issue, both because it was a genuine issue of joint concern relative to their budding stepfamily, and because it was less intense than some of their other issues. My hope was that this would allow them to get comfortable with the dialogue process before addressing the more challenging issues in their relationship. Moreover, both Anna and Jim had identified multiple angles on parenting issues on their Relationship Questionnaires: All three of Jim's "minor conflict issues" related to parenting and stepfamily issues, while Anna had one enhancement issue, one minor conflict issue, and one major relationship issue relating to parenting and stepfamily issues. So it appeared, all the way around, that parenting would be a good place to have them begin to dialogue.

Anna and Jim then segued quite naturally (at Jim's suggestion) to Anna's negative feelings about Jim's positive relationship with his ex-wife, with whom he maintained an active dual-parenting relationship with regard to their children. This gave Jim an opportunity to explain why it was important to him for the sake of his children that he and his former wife be able to be cordial and have a good working relationship concerning the children. He also emphasized that this was his only interest relative to his ex, and that he was fully committed to his intimate relationship with Anna. For her part, Anna was able to express her frustration about not being kept better informed about conversations with his ex and her perception that his ex took advantage of Jim financially and that he did not set limits with her. Through their mutual empathizing back and forth, Anna was able to come to see the importance of her accepting, and not feeling threatened by, Jim's relationship with his former wife for the sake of the children. Jim, for his part, was able to come to see the importance of setting boundaries with his ex around time and keeping Anna informed of what was happening. In her final expressive statement, Anna said,

> I think a lot of my feelings have been due to a lack of information. I feel as though I've gotten a lot of important information tonight. I understand about needing to put things in the past. And, yes, we're doing better than ever. I may need some time to adjust to accepting her as the mother of your children. I want to try to make peace with all of this, and I trust that you will do what you say. I've seen a slight shift in your interactions with her, and I appreciate that. I would appreciate you coming to me more to share about issues with her. I don't want to feel left out of the process.

Jim empathized, using the Identification Mode, as follows:

I, Anna, do trust you, Jim, but it may be hard for me at times. I need you to be patient with me about that. I will do my best to be patient and accepting of your relationship with your ex-wife. But it would help me a whole lot if you would talk to me more so that my anxieties don't get stirred up unnecessarily.

In the following session, Anna and Jim addressed the original issue that had prompted them to initiate couple's therapy: Anna's feeling vulnerable in her relationship with Jim because of her perceptions about his relationships with other females. It is not unusual, in the Time-Designated format, for the therapy to gradually work its way toward the central presenting problem. One reason is that some couples either are hesitant to approach the issue too quickly or want to feel more confident about their ability to tackle the core issue more constructively. Moreover, the therapist wants the couple to feel skilled in their use of the RE dialogue process before tackling the major issues in the relationship. That is why the therapist often will recommend a less intense issue for the couple's first dialogue, as I did with Anna and Jim. On the other hand, it was no accident that Jim proposed his relationship with his former wife as their second dialogue issue, because it indirectly connected with Anna's feelings of vulnerability with regard to his relationships with females in general. Their successfully addressing and resolving these two issues set the stage for them to address the issue that first brought them into therapy.

In this particular case, however, there was an interesting but unanticipated twist. When I proposed the issue, Anna queried, "What if I've already let the issue go?" I responded, "That's good," but I suggested that it could still be helpful to their relationship for them to dialogue the issue through by her sharing where she had been with the issue and where she was with it now. Anna began, in the form of a dialogue, with a deep underlying positive:

The therapy has really opened things up between us. I've seen changes in you, and I've seen your commitment to this relationship. My trust in you has grown. So I'm not scared anymore about you and other women. My concern was all rooted in my loving you so much, and not wanting to lose you.

That Anna could come to this place of peace, acceptance, and trust after addressing just two issues in four and a half extended sessions is, to my mind, powerful testimony to the power of the process of intimate dialogue to help couples transform their relationship in positive ways. What's equally noteworthy is that the very nature of the RE dialogue process, through its structured format and its tendency to encourage couples to become open and honest in their communication (because they feel safe), enabled Anna to resolve her original presenting issue without the issue even being directly engaged. The reason she was able to come to this place, as Anna went on to explain, is that

> I've seen you grow and evolve into a person who is taking this relationship as seriously as I do. Now it's like, "He really gets it. He's really my partner."

This new experience of how Jim was being in the relationship with her allowed Anna to surrender her anxiety over the future of their relationship. What Anna's statement signifies is that the dialogue process worked at a metalevel of communication in that how they communicated with one another was as important, and perhaps even more important, than what they dialogued about.

Part of what enabled the rapid progress, in my judgment, was Anna and Jim's use of the Identification Mode of empathy during their dialogues. My perception was that their using the Identification Mode in a sense compelled both of them to reach beyond their own self-preoccupations surrounding the issue at hand and enter imaginatively into their partner's experience in a way that permitted genuine empathic identification with the other person's deeper concerns about the relationship. This in turn prompted each person to become more responsive to the feelings, concerns, and desires of the other person. As a result, Anna and Jim were able not just to work through two significant issues in their relationship, but they were able, even more importantly, to come to a new and deepened understanding about, commitment to, and trust in their relationship. This, in turn, had dissolved yet another issue between them, indeed, the most immediate issue that had been the reason why the therapy had been initiated.

However, this was not the end of the couple's therapy work. Indeed, the success of the therapy work up to this point created an overall atmosphere of safety and trust in the therapy and in their process of intimate dialogue. This permitted the couple to venture into the deepest and darkest issue in their relationship, an issue that both had alluded to but neither had tackled head on. The issue this time was a trust issue that Jim had with Anna, specifically his anger and pain over what he believed to have been a sexual liaison that Anna had with the father of her youngest child after Jim and Anna had started living together. From Anna's point of view, however, it had been an involuntary seduction and rape when he cornered her in his house while she was dropping off their child for a custody visit. What the ensuing dialogue yielded was that Jim was able to express his anger in a manner that did not leave Anna feeling attacked and that permitted her to enter empathically into his pain at feeling betrayed. Jim's feeling genuinely empathized with by Anna in turn allowed Jim to put aside his preoccupations about the issue and to identify with Anna's deep feelings of pain and shame over not having been strong enough emotionally at the time to resist or fight off her former husband. Jim also was able to understand the further complicating factor of her child being in the next room and her not wanting to frighten or alarm him by screaming. Jim was so able to identify with Anna's experience that it brought tears to his eyes and utterly dissolved whatever residual feelings of anger or pain that he had been carrying because he had so completely entered into Anna's pain. As the session drew to a close, Jim reached over to hold and comfort Anna, and she accepted his empathic embrace with gratitude as she visibly released her own tension in light of feeling herself understood and totally accepted by Jim.

What I'd like to do here is present portions of the transcript from the extended session devoted to this issue. One of my reasons for doing this is that I want to provide a fuller example of a couple using the Identification Mode of empathy while conducting their dialogue in order to convey its power in taking the partners deep into each other's feelings, concerns, and desires. This dialogue sequence also illustrates how the safety of the dialogue process can facilitate one of the partners going into a trancelike state that fosters a cathartic experience that brings to the surface previously buried emotion. The result of this cathartic experience, which was facilitated by Jim's empathic representation of Anna's experience via the Identification Mode of empathy, was that Anna gained deeper insight into her own experience. This deepened insight, together with Anna's sensing of Jim's identification with and acceptance of her, in turn permitted Anna to let go of the emotion around the trauma in a way that was redemptively healing.

> Jim: I don't feel about this [issue] the way I did back when we started therapy. It bothered me back then because our relationship was less secure than it is now. It's not that I haven't believed you, but I'm not confident I know the whole story, though I'm also not certain I need or even want to know [the whole story]. It probably had as much as anything to do with what I felt criticized for by you. Also, now I see it as something that happened before our relationship really became the committed relationship we now have.

Anna [*after empathizing, as Expresser*]: That event was the tip of the iceberg of a long-standing psychologically abusive relationship that I don't know how I stayed in as long as I did. I've lots of hostility toward him for this and other similar incidents. I don't know how people get used to abuse. I had a first marriage that was abusive. [*She shifted her focus back to her second husband and the signal event:*] He took advantage of me emotionally. I cried. Then he took advantage of me physically. Something snapped. My mind drifted. I thought of suicide. But there were my children. [*By this time, Anna was in a quasi-trance-like state.*] "Why am I being punished?" I asked myself. "Why was he acting this way?" The legacy of [sexual abuse in] my family was always denied. So I just put it away. "Just be civil to your son," I told myself, "and I won't tell anyone [what you're doing to me]." Then, when he told me that he'd tell you what happened, laughing as he said it, I knew he was obsessed and insane. I should have reported him, but I didn't have the strength to fight. I felt all alone. I couldn't tell anyone, not even you, because I felt so ashamed. I live with this anger and wish every day that he would die. But, then, there's my son [*implying that he needs his father*]. When you started using it …, it was like being raped all over again. It also put up the first wall in our relationship, and you became one of "them" [in my mind]. It [the experience] may fade for you, but it won't fade for me so easily. It's hurting me too much.

Jim [*as Empathizer, using the Identification Mode of empathy*]: That event was the tip of the iceberg of the kind of abuse that happened to me at his hands. It's something that continues to haunt me and crush me internally for many reasons. He is my son's father, but I hate to think I had to have a son with someone like that. I also felt bad that I wasn't strong enough to fight for myself, and that I wasn't modeling for my children that I could take care of myself. So it's going to take a long time before I can make peace with this, and I'll need help. My typical reaction was to bury all this and forget it. The abuse carried over from my first marriage, so I had no positive expectations for my second marriage. So I put on a happy face for my kids, and put off his crime as something that was in him, not in me. But I was ashamed, and had thoughts of suicide. I kept it from you because I couldn't easily talk to you about it back then. It was only when he threatened to tell you that I had to admit to myself that it happened. It's a constant source of anguish for me because I can't get away from him because of my son. I can't believe how much I hate him. I can't compel you to believe me as to how it happened, but it's burned into my memory that it happened that way. It may fade for you, but the memory of it won't be easy to fade for me.

Anna was deeply entranced by Jim's empathic representation of her experience via the Identification Mode of empathy. Jim unquestionably had imaginatively entered into Anna's experience and had succeeded in giving voice to it from the inside out, as though he were Anna, in an exceedingly powerful way. Anna clearly felt completely understood by Jim, and I could sense in her the beginnings of an emerging peacefulness that came from her feeling genuinely understood by Jim. I could also sense Jim's coming to terms with the event and Anna's experience as he was representing Anna in the first person, because he would not, I believe, have been able to give such a powerful and compassionate representation to her experience if he were still caught in his own (former) feelings about what had happened. In other words, despite Jim's history of negative feelings about what had happened, he was able to put them aside and open himself to receiving and entering into the depths of Anna's pain about what had happened. Anna did not add anything else to her statement, but, feeling well understood, invited Jim to express.

Jim [*as Expresser*]: I could see back then [when it happened] how it affected you, and I can see it now. It's potency for me [as an issue] has faded. I hope you don't continue to push it away, but work through it for yourself. We can't wish the source of your pain away. I want to tell you that for me my previous negative feelings and defensive posture are gone.

Anna [*as Empathizer, using the Identification Mode of empathy*]: For me, Jim, my previous doubts have all but vanished. I hope you won't allow it to fester so it comes back to haunt you and us. My hope is for you and your healing, and I want you to know you have my complete support.

Jim [*continuing as Expresser*]: Also, for me, in my teenage years, I felt I was on the short end of the stick when, as a teenager, females did similar kinds of things to me. So this [event of yours] rekindled my feelings associated with those experiences. I was scared I'd lose you, too.

Anna [*as Empathizer, using the Identification Mode of empathy*]: When I was a teenager, females I was seeing would sleep with someone else. I was scared someone would come between us. My past experience shaped my experience in the present.

Anna [*as Expresser*]: I know I have to work at this. I've started. I've opened up to my sister. It's helped a little bit. But I'm still really angry. But when I look at the anger, it's really about me, that I put up with it, and did so for so long. That's why I preach to my daughter about this. I hope I can move to a place of acceptance, and not let the anger consume me. I can talk with you, but you can't understand the pain and humiliation of rape. I love you so much. I hope this fades for me, so it doesn't hurt us. So if I just know you're there for me and understand, that's a start.

Jim [*as Empathizer, using the Identification Mode of empathy*]: For me the deepest pain is... I don't know how I put up with it as long as I did. The pain I feel about knowing what happened, and wanting to tell my daughter how to stand up for herself, causes me pain. Talking with my sister has helped some, because she can understand. I hope I can dissipate some of the hate. I love you very much, and knowing you love me and that you're there for me will help me heal.

Anna [*continuing as Expresser*]: To be perfectly honest, whenever you referred to the event, not only did I have to relive the event, with a buildup of hate toward him, I [also] felt you had no idea what this event meant to me: that I was the victim of a crime, and here you were raising it as a question about me. This was a crime committed on me, to my person, to my soul. [*Anna was shedding tears now.*] I didn't know about your teenage experiences. If I had, I might have been able to bring you in earlier. I'm so glad we are where we are now.

Jim [*as Empathizer, using the Identification Mode of empathy*]: I was so angry at you, too, for bringing up what happened and questioning me about it when I was raped and I was an innocent victim. He assaulted my body and my soul, and you couldn't see it. I wish I had known about your teenage experiences. If I had, perhaps I would have understood better where you were coming from, and perhaps I could have reached out to you, and then perhaps we could have shared the pain together. But I'm glad we're talking about it now. Maybe we can finally put this behind us.

Jim [*as Expresser*]: You couldn't know about my past. I responded defensively and caused collateral damage back on you. I was scared because I thought we had a special relationship unlike any I had ever had. And then this happened, and all of a sudden it felt like this relationship was no different than any of the others. And I was scared I would lose you.

Anna [*as Empathizer, using the Identification Mode of empathy*]: So what happened was my pain, too.

Anna [*as Expresser*]: I clung to the pain back then as my pain, but I've come to see that it was your pain, too, and that what happened happened to both of us. But it hasn't been until today that I really faced it. Because, until now, I haven't known what to do with the pain.

The therapy concluded very soon after this powerful session. In a brief recap of the final issue they had dialogued about, Anna indicated that an article that I had given her at the intervening session on the issue of forgiveness and whether or not it is necessary to forgive in order to heal, was extremely helpful to her.

Anna: It cemented my feelings that I need not forgive and yet still be able to heal. So I'm OK with not forgiving.

Jim [*after empathizing, as Expresser*]: I'm glad you've made some peace with this. I needed some closure around this, too, and for you to see my pain around this incident. I feel at peace with this issue now in terms of our relationship.

Anna [*as Expresser*]: It was really helpful to me to come to see that the event was something that happened to both of us and that it affected our relationship. I hadn't been able until now to see your pain around what happened.

When I suggested that we might be close to the end of the therapy (and this would indeed prove to be the final session), I asked for their evaluation of our work together and their progress.

Jim: I feel we've done really well with our issues here. It's exceeded my expectations about what we would accomplish in the therapy. We've made huge amounts of progress in our relationship. I don't fear being able to bring up issues with you any longer. I've felt so much closer to you since we've been coming here.

Anna: I agree.

I then asked them their opinion of the role that the Identification Mode of empathy played in their dialogue process and in helping them break through impasses and emotional blockages.

Anna: When I became Jim, I would experience a series of "Aha!" realizations about his experience. It really made a big difference.

Jim: I agree. It helped me understand Anna's experience in a new way.

To my mind, the work of Anna and Jim on the deepest, most painful issue in their relationship is a testimony not just to the power of the process of intimate dialogue, but to the power of the Identification Mode of empathy as well. Moreover, it has been my experience over the past few years that those couples who have embraced and successfully employed the Identification Mode of empathy while conducting their dialogues have on the whole made better progress more rapidly when compared to couples who have not. This may in part be due to the fact that those couples who are most desirous of making progress on their issues, or are more emotionally invested in their relationship, may more readily embrace the logic and the benefits of using the Identification Mode of empathy. Be that as it may, I now encourage all the couples I work with, whether in couples therapy or in RE educational programs, to utilize the Identification Mode of empathy while dialoguing their serious relationship issues. I strongly recommend that other therapists do the same.

Note

1. Names and identifying information in all clinical vignettes have been changed to preserve anonymity.

PART IV

Integrating the Other RE Skills
Into the Couple's Dialogue Process

CHAPTER 10

Keeping Couples' Dialogues on Track: Teaching Facilitation Skill

Now that the therapeutic process has been launched so that couples are able to conduct structured dialogues as their primary vehicle for engaging issues in session, the therapist will look for opportunities to introduce the remaining skills that make up the RE model. These include Facilitation, Problem/Conflict Resolution, Self-Change, and Helping-Others Change, Generalization, and Maintenance. When following the Time-Designated format, each of these six skills is introduced in a structured and systematized way in order to maximize the benefits for the couple, including increasing the odds of longer-term use of the skills and dialogue process after the couple terminates of therapy. This typically involves the therapist recommending that the couple initially dialogue on an issue that would likely result in one partner or both agreeing to make a change in behavior. This permits the therapist to introduce the Problem/Conflict Resolution and Self-Change and Helping-Others Change skills in the context of the couple's first dialogue.

By contrast, when following the Experiential format, there is a certain elasticity as to when and in what sequence a particular skill might be introduced. In general terms, Facilitation and Problem/Conflict Resolution tend to be introduced first, though even here either could be taught first depending on the circumstances. But it would be quite conceivable, for example, for the Generalization skill to be introduced before either of those two skills if the couple's first dialogue involved parenting issues. But there is one absolutely firm principle that applies in either format: The therapist must first teach Facilitation before assigning a dialogue to the

204 • Relationship Enhancement Therapy

couple as a home assignment. The reason, as will soon become clear, is that this skill permits a couple to monitor and regulate their own dialogues in order to keep them on track when mistakes get made and there is no therapist present to help them deal with that. It is both for that reason and the fact that Facilitation has to do with the effective management of the dialogue process that it is being presented here before Problem/Conflict Resolution.

Explain the Purpose of the Facilitation Skill

When the therapist is ready to introduce the Facilitation skill, check to see whether the couple has read the relevant chapter in the *RE Client Manual* (Guerney & Scuka, 2005) That may dictate whether the therapist provides a more thorough or a summary explanation of the skill. This chapter provides a model for a more thorough presentation. The therapist may also use it as a framework for devising a more abbreviated presentation. The purpose of the Facilitation skill may be explained in the following way:

> The purpose of the Facilitation skill is to enable you to keep your dialogue on track when someone fails to be skillful and I'm not around to help you correct it. You also want to be able to do this in a way that reduces the risk of disrupting your dialogue. The reality is, when the two of you begin to dialogue on your own, mistakes are going to happen. So, it's important that both of you recognize and accept that, and that you both are prepared to deal with mistakes effectively so that you can keep your dialogue on track and not allow it to get derailed. The Facilitation skill enables you to identify that a mistake has been made and get it corrected as expeditiously as possible so that you can continue with the dialogue, which, after all, is the point. You want to have your dialogue, not get hung up over the fact that someone has made a mistake. Having compassion toward one another when a mistake is made, by the way, is part of what makes this skill work.

Explain the Three Principal Applications of the Facilitation Skill

The therapist continues by explaining that there are three principal applications of the Facilitation skill:

> There are three principal mistakes that may get made while you are dialoguing. The first is that the Expresser may say something, even inadvertently, that is unskillful in that it violates one of the Expressive skill guidelines. Now, if that were to go uncorrected and, even

worse, happen repeatedly, that likely would cause the Empathizer to become defensive; and if that were to go too far, then your dialogue likely would break down, which we obviously don't want to happen. So you need to have a way to correct those kinds of mistakes when they happen so that the dialogue can continue.

The second mistake that may happen is that the Empathizer, instead of empathizing with what the Expresser has said, simply starts expressing, perhaps because feelings have gotten stirred up and that person wants to respond to what had been said, or sometimes simply because that person forgets to empathize. Now, if that were to be allowed to go unchecked, the designated Expresser is almost certainly going to feel cheated and be resentful because he or she rightfully is expecting to receive empathy, in terms of the guidelines for having a dialogue. So, again, you need to have a way to correct that mistake when it happens, because otherwise the dialogue is likely to get derailed.

The third mistake that may occur is that one of you begins to talk in terms of solutions when no agreement has been made to move from the discussion phase to the problem-solving phase of your dialogue. When that happens, you need to have a way of reminding your partner of the need to remain in discussion mode until both of you have finished sharing all your feelings, concerns, and desires about the issue at hand. Let's take a look at the guidelines for correcting a mistake when one gets made while conducting a dialogue. To be clear, I would like to add that this skill is used most often when the two of you have agreed to have a structured dialogue. However, even here it is possible to generalize the use of this skill beyond formal dialogues into your day-to-day interactions, especially if you experience your partner speaking to you unskillfully in a way that is causing you to feel defensive.

Review the Facilitation Skill Guidelines

Each guideline for the Facilitation skill is followed by explanatory comments.

1. *Agree with your partner in advance on a nonverbal signal (e.g., the stop sign signal with a simple raising of the hand) and a verbal phrase (e.g., "Please stop").*

It's important that you have a nonverbal signal that you both agree on in advance that either of you can use when you believe a mistake has been made in your dialogue. I would recommend simply raising your hand in the form of a stop sign. Are you willing to agree to that [*looking at one person*]? And are you [*looking at the other*]? Good. It's also a good idea to have a verbal phrase to use when you are having a dialogue on the phone or in the car. I would simply recommend "Please stop." Is that acceptable to both of you? Good.

2. *When either of you observes that a mistake has been made, use one of the stop signals.*

As soon as you observe that your partner has made a mistake, simply raise your hand or say, "Please stop," to signal your perception that a mistake has been made. And don't hesitate to do so, because this is a way that each of you can coach the other to be more skillful in your interactions.

3. *If your partner uses one of the stop signals, stop speaking immediately. You may resume speaking if you recognize your mistake and you can readily correct it.*

If your partner gives you the stop sign signal, you are immediately obligated to stop speaking, even in midsentence. If you immediately understand the mistake you made and you are able to correct it, you may then proceed as though the mistake had not been made and the dialogue simply continues.

4. *If your partner is not able to correct it, skillfully identify the mistake. Then request that your partner revise the statement so that it better conforms to Expressive skill guidelines.*

If you observe that your partner perhaps has a quizzical look on his or her face or does not immediately correct the expressive mistake, then you have several options. You may simply identify the offending statement or word as being unskillful or as violating one of the Expressive skill guidelines. Or you might state that you feel defensive when your partner speaks to you in that manner, identifying the offending phrase. Or you might make a request for your partner to please say what he or she is trying to say differently, in more subjective language. Here are some examples of what you might say to your partner. For example, you might say, "I believe you are not supposed to frame things in terms of 'always' statements." Or you might say, "It's hard for me to listen when you represent something as a fact rather than as your way of seeing things." Or you might say, "I start feeling defensive when you tell me what I 'should' do. I would really appreciate it if you would simply tell me what it is you would like me to do." Or you could simply say, "I would appreciate it if you would say that more subjectively," in effect invoking one of the Expressive skill guidelines. It's important that in each case you use an even, neutral tone of voice. The point, again, is to identify the mistake and get it corrected, and avoid turning the mistake into an issue. So, notice, you would never say to your partner anything like, "There you go again calling into question my motives." That would only add fuel to the fire, so you would never say something like that.

5. *If your partner remains uncertain how to correct the mistake, model a more skillful statement.*

If after identifying the mistake or requesting a change in language your partner still is unable to correct the mistake, then you may model a more skillful version of what you believe your partner is trying to say to you. After all, you are in the role of the Empathizer, so you should be tracking what your partner is saying and you probably have some idea of what your partner is trying to say, even though it is being expressed unskillfully. By the way, one very important assumption of this skill is that behind every unskillful statement there is a legitimate experience, feeling, concern, or desire; it simply is being expressed unskillfully. One way of understanding this skill is that it is designed to enable the legitimate content behind the unskillful language to get expressed, but in a skillful manner. So, for example, if your partner said to you, out of frustration, "You don't care about our relationship!" you would raise your hand and say something like, "I feel defensive when you say things like that. Could you please say that more subjectively?" And if your partner is not able to self-correct, then you could model a skillful statement such as, "I think what you are trying to say to me is that you don't feel cared for by me when I...," and then fill in the blank as appropriate. Assuming you were accurate, then your partner would pick it up and say, "That's right, I don't feel cared for when you...." Again, it is important that these comments are made in an even, neutral tone of voice.

6. *Use a stop signal only if you are confident that an actual Expressive skill guideline has been violated.*

If you are feeling defensive while your partner is speaking to you, that may be a clue that your partner is speaking unskillfully and nonsubjectively. But it is not an infallible clue. You have to be able to distinguish between two different kinds of defensiveness. You may be feeling defensive because your partner is indeed speaking unskillfully, but you may be feeling defensive instead because of the content of what your partner is saying. The Facilitation skill is designed to eliminate the first kind of defensiveness, when your partner is speaking to you unskillfully. But we can't do anything about you feeling defensive because you don't like or don't want to hear what your partner is saying. That kind of defensiveness simply means that there is a significant difference between you, and that is precisely why you are having this dialogue. That kind of defensiveness you work through as you dialogue. It would be unfair to use this skill to try to keep your partner from saying what your partner wants to say. This skill is designed solely to ensure that mistakes in your dialogues are identified and corrected so that no one feels needlessly defensive because someone is verbally unskillful.

7. *If a disagreement arises about whether a guideline violation has occurred, turn to the Expressive skill guidelines or the RE Phrase Finder. If you cannot identify a violation, allow the designated Expresser to continue. Then look for ways through your empathy to more skillfully express your partner's experience.*

Again, the point is to not get caught up in a debate about whether a mistake has been made, but to have your dialogue.

8. *If your partner expresses when he or she is supposed to empathize, use one of the stop signals. Then gently request that your partner first provide you with empathy before expressing.*

If your partner forgets to empathize with you, for whatever reason, make a simple request for your partner to return to role by saying something like, "I would appreciate receiving empathy from you before you respond to me as an Expresser." Again, this should be stated in an even, neutral tone of voice.

9. *If your partner begins to propose a specific solution before you have agreed to move into phase 2 of your dialogue, use one of the stop signals. Then make a request that you remain in phase 1 discussion mode until*

both of you finish sharing all your feelings, concerns, and desires about the issue.

It's important that you both have ample opportunity to share everything important to you about the issue at hand before moving into problem solution mode. Otherwise, you run the risk of not understanding one another sufficiently well, and this could undercut your ability to negotiate an effective solution to your issue.

10. *Once a mistake has been identified and corrected, return to your respective roles as designated Expresser and designated Empathizer and resume your dialogue.*

To summarize, this skill is designed to help you manage your dialogues effectively so that you don't get sidetracked into arguments when someone makes a mistake.

Demonstrate the Facilitation Skill by Using the Relationship Enhancement Phrase Finder

Once the therapist has explained the Facilitation skill, the use of the stop-sign signal would be demonstrated along with some examples of the kinds of things the Empathizer can verbalize in the context of pointing out that a mistake has been made by the Expresser. Even though this follows the principles of learning theory previously described (see chapter 1), the reader may be imagining, "This skill doesn't seem very difficult, so what's the point in taking the time to demonstrate it?" Experience has taught me that since the application of this skill involves the adoption of a new behavioral tool, one cannot presume a particular individual's ability to implement this intervention. This is especially true in those instances where a person might feel self-conscious about interrupting the partner or there has been a significant power differential in the relationship that would inhibit one partner from being assertive. The therapist may, of course, use his or her best therapeutic judgment as to whether to proceed with a demonstration of this skill, but I recommend being cautious about simply assuming that it is unimportant to demonstrate this skill.

One convenient way to demonstrate the Facilitation skill is to utilize the RE Phrase Finder found in the *RE Client Manual* (see appendix B). A case could be made that it would be beneficial to introduce the RE Phrase Finder earlier in the therapy in the context of teaching the Expressive skill because it represents a useful compendium of unskillful language that would be good for couples to learn to avoid using sooner rather than later.

That is an option. I introduce the Phrase Finder under the Facilitation skill because of its usefulness in demonstrating how to implement this skill. The demonstration of the Facilitation skill might be introduced in the following way:

> I'd like to briefly demonstrate how to use this skill. Let's take a look at the Relationship Enhancement Phrase Finder in the back of your *Client Manual* to facilitate that. Notice that the left column is headed "Incite..." while the right column is headed "Insight...." The left column represents some of the most frequent phrases that people commonly use, but they are phrases that are technically unskillful. The right column represents, in effect, skillful translations of the legitimate intent behind the unskillful language of the left column. So, for example, it's not, "You make me angry," which is an accusation, but, "When you act (or talk) that way, I get really angry at you," which is a subjective statement about my feelings about your behavior. Or, "You should..." or "You need to...." Well, nobody "needs" to do anything, and nobody likes to be told what they "should" do. That almost guarantees defensiveness, so ideally it never gets said. Or, "Most men or women think or feel..."; or, "The right, or correct, thing to do is..."; or, "A good father or mother would or would never...." In each case, the person is speaking nonsubjectively, and in each case it basically comes down to what that person is wanting or desiring the other person to do. Ideally, then, the Expresser owns and directly communicates that subjective desire. The examples get more complicated, so notice under the section headed "Underlying Positives" that the left column is technically not unskillful, but simply less skillful than the version on the right column because the version on the left omits an underlying positive.

What I then do is invite one of the partners (at their choice), or both, to role-play being unskillful with me so that I can demonstrate both the use of the stop sign signal and some of the kinds of things that can be verbalized in identifying an unskillful statement and making a request for it to be stated in more subjective language. To reinforce that this skill is used by two people who both know the RE model and who have agreed to have a structured dialogue, I suggest that each client and I pretend that we are siblings who have been trained in the RE model and who therefore understand the purpose of this skill. I then suggest that each person (in turn) initiate a fictitious dialogue with me, their "brother," about not spending enough time with that person or with mom and dad, but that each person should then quickly begin to make a series of unskillful statements to me, simply by borrowing phrases from the left column of the first page of the RE Phrase Finder, so that I can demonstrate how to implement this skill. I have each person make four or five unskillful statements, and in response I look for a variety of ways to verbalize how to identify an unskillful statement and how to make a request that it be stated more skillfully.

Have the Couple Practice Facilitation Skill

The therapist would next have the couple practice this skill by similarly having them engage in a fictitious dialogue by pretending to be someone else, again perhaps siblings. It is very important in this practice exercise to have the couple role-play being someone other than who they really are. The reason for this is to avoid the exercise even inadvertently triggering real-life issues and feelings in the relationship. Have one person role-play being the Expresser and have that person make four or five unskillful statements for the purpose of allowing the partner to practice using the stop sign signal, and to practice verbally identifying the mistake and making a request for a more skillful statement. Then have the couple switch roles so that the other person has the opportunity to practice using this skill. In both the demonstration and the couple's practice, I introduce an air of humor around role-playing being siblings and having a fictitious dialogue. Being able to laugh during the course of therapy is a positive thing.

Home Assignment

Once the couple has learned how to use the Facilitation skill, the therapist may now assign the couple their first home dialogue. There are several reasons for having couples begin to conduct dialogues on their own at home. The first reason is to increase their facility in using the skills. This in turn will have a positive rebound effect on the therapy process in that the couple should be able to dialogue even more effectively in session. It should also increase the couple's confidence in their ability to use the RE dialogue process on their own. This is connected with the second and, in the long run, even more important reason to have couples begin to conduct dialogues at home: to increase the odds that the couple will continue to dialogue on their own even after the therapy has been terminated. This dovetails with one of the essential preventative goals of RE therapy: to help couples become better equipped to more skillfully address and more successfully resolve future problems that may arise in their relationship.

In negotiating with the couple about their first home dialogue, it is recommended that the therapist advise the couple to choose an enhancement issue rather than a conflict issue. The reason is to minimize the possibility that the couple has difficulty conducting their first home dialogue and to maximize the likelihood that they have a positive experience. The chosen issue can either be one of the issues on the couple's Relationship Questionnaire, or it can be a newly identified issue. It is a good idea to have the couple agree in session on a specific time when they will have this dialogue, in order to increase the odds that the dialogue will actually take place. It's also important to tell the couple that if their dialogue becomes difficult or emotionally overheated, it would be better for them to end their dialogue and agree to bring the issue to the next session.

One final wrinkle in the timing of when to have the couple conduct their first home dialogue is whether or not the couple has been introduced to the Problem/Conflict Resolution skill. If the Facilitation skill has been introduced but Problem/Conflict Resolution has not, the therapist might elect to wait before assigning the couple's first dialogue until after the couple has been introduced to that latter skill as well. The reason is that most enhancement issues that the couple might dialogue about at home likely would have a problem-solving component, so in principle it would be better for both skills to have been taught before assigning a home dialogue. On the other hand, it is not uncommon for couples to start dialoguing spontaneously on their own at home even before the therapist has asked them to do so. If that happens, immediately introduce the basics of Facilitation and Problem/Conflict Resolution in order to increase the couple's ability to conduct their home dialogues skillfully and successfully.

In addition (or as a substitute) to assigning a home dialogue, the therapist can ask the couple to read the chapters on the Problem/Conflict Resolution and Self-Change and Helping-Others Change skills in the *RE Client Manual* if they have not already done so. Even though these latter skills may not be introduced in the next session or two, it's always a good idea at this stage in the therapy to ask the couple to continue (and complete) reading the *RE Client Manual* so that they will have some orientation to each of the skills when the opportunity naturally presents itself to introduce a particular skill into the therapy process.

CHAPTER 11
Getting to Win-Win: Teaching Problem/Conflict Resolution Skill

Not every dialogue needs to proceed from phase 1 Discussion/Negotiation to phase 2 Problem/Conflict Resolution. Some issues can be addressed simply by conducting an extended phase 1 dialogue that helps clear away misunderstandings and fosters better understanding and a deepened sense of connection and intimacy. However, whenever the issue involves a request for a concrete change in behavior, a solution to a problem, or an agreement or the adoption of a plan of action, then the dialogue needs to move explicitly into phase 2. The purpose of the Problem/Conflict Resolution skill is to enable a couple to learn how to approach developing a solution, agreement, or plan of action in a manner that is most likely to lead to a satisfying result for both partners.

This skill is formally introduced into the therapy at the first opportunity where the issue being dialogued about clearly calls for a concrete change in behavior or other solution. This may happen with a couple's first issue, or with a subsequent issue. In a more rigorously applied Time-Designated format, the therapist recommends as a first issue one that would clearly require a solution-oriented phase, for the express purpose of teaching Problem/Conflict Resolution as soon as possible in the therapy process. My preference is to allow the couple to have a strong influence on the choice of a first issue, regardless of whether the issue would involve having the couple move into Problem/Conflict Resolution. This also reflects a more flexible approach in applying the RE model in a manner that helps increase its utility and its relevance to meeting the unique needs of each couple.

Monitor the Couple's Dialogue to Determine When a Shift to the Problem/Conflict Resolution Phase Is Appropriate

When a couple is for the first time dialoguing an issue that is likely to require a shift into phase 2 in order to come up with a specific solution, agreement, or plan of action, the therapist should actively monitor the process in order to identify when a shift into phase 2 appears to be called for. There are three indicators that a couple is ready to move into Problem/ Conflict Resolution. First, each person appears to have said everything that needs to be said about the issue at hand in terms of feelings, concerns, and desires, and each person is feeling understood. Second, the couple appears to be on the same page in terms of wanting the same thing. Third, the couple is already beginning, quite naturally, to drift into solution mode. When the therapist detects that any of these conditions apply, he or she should explain that these are indicators that the couple is ready to move into phase 2 of a dialogue. The therapist then inquires whether each person is feeling understood and feels ready to move into solution mode. If both agree that they are feeling understood, have said what they wanted to say, and are ready to move into solution mode, then the therapist helps them initiate the transition to phase 2 of their dialogue. If either person indicates that he or she has more to say at the level of feelings, concerns, or desires, then the couple remains in phase 1 of the dialogue until everything that needs to be said has been said. Then the therapist reinitiates the transition to phase 2 of the dialogue.

Explain how to Transition From Discussion/Negotiation to Problem/Conflict Resolution

Once the therapist has determined that the couple is ready to move into phase 2 of their dialogue, he or she should explain how to make the transition from the Discussion/Negotiation phase to the Problem/Conflict Resolution phase. It is important for the therapist to be aware that this is the first time the transition from one phase of a dialogue to another is being explained. Therefore, the explanation is as much designed to structure for the couple how they will do this on their own in the future, as it is designed to make the transition in the present dialogue. The transition may be explained in the following way, incorporating the content of the first two Problem/Conflict Resolution skill guidelines from the *RE Client Manual* (Guerney & Scuka, 2005):

> Since you are now ready to move into the Problem/Conflict Resolution phase of your dialogue, I'd like to explain how to make the transition from Discussion/Negotiation, phase 1, to Problem/Conflict

Resolution, phase 2. And I'd like to explain it in a way that will allow you to apply this on your own when you begin to dialogue at home. By the way, these are the first two guidelines under the Problem/Conflict Resolution skill in your *RE Client Manual.*

1. *When you are ready to move into problem-solving mode, tell your partner that you are ready and ask whether your partner also is ready. If your partner is not ready, continue with Discussion/Negotiation.*

The first guideline in effect states: When one of you feels as though you have said everything you want to say about your feelings, concerns, and desires about the issue at hand, and you believe your partner may have as well, then indicate your own readiness to move into Problem/Conflict Resolution and, equally important, inquire whether your partner also is ready. You could indicate your readiness by saying something like this: "I've said everything I want to say about this issue, and I'm feeling understood by you. I'm ready to move toward developing a solution, and I wonder if you feel ready to do that as well." Checking with your partner as to whether he or she is ready to move into Problem/Conflict Resolution is important, because you can't just assume that your partner is ready because you are. If your partner indicates that there is more that he or she would like to say, then remain in phase 1 of the dialogue and your partner automatically becomes the Expresser to continue to share his or her further concerns, feelings, or desires. Of course, you always have the right to comment on anything new that your partner may share. When the second person finally feels complete, then he or she indicates readiness to move into Problem/Conflict Resolution.

2. *When both of you are ready to shift into problem-solving mode, discuss whether this is a good time to continue the dialogue. If not, agree on a specific time to resume your dialogue.*

Once you have agreed that you both are ready to move into phase 2 of your dialogue, then you also need to check with each other whether this actually is a good time to continue the dialogue. The reason is that sometimes it might not be a good time to continue, for any number of perfectly valid reasons, such as it being late and one of you needs to go to bed because you have to go to work the next day, or because one of you has a prearranged activity. If either person indicates that this is not a good time to continue the dialogue, then agree on a specific day and time when you will resume the dialogue. Treat it like a formal appointment, and put it on your calendars. Because if you don't, you run a high risk that you will forget to continue the dialogue until one of you says to the other, perhaps a week later, "Remember that dialogue we had that we never finished?" If that happens, the reason will almost certainly be because you didn't make an appointment and treat it like any other appointment you might make.

Explain the Goals of Problem/Conflict Resolution

The therapist then explains that there are three principal goals of the Problem/Conflict Resolution process.

> There are three primary goals when you are aiming to come up with a satisfactory solution to your issue or problem. The first goal is to use what you have learned during phase 1 of your dialogue to create a win-win solution that each of you feels is fair and that meets each of your needs and desires as much as possible. The second goal is to work out the details of your solution to maximize the likelihood that you implement it. The third goal is to provide an opportunity to evaluate your solution and make changes if necessary.

The therapist would next review the Problem/Conflict Resolution skill guidelines, which have been divided into three categories in order to highlight three distinct steps in the Problem/Conflict Resolution process: (1) arriving at a mutually satisfying solution or agreement, (2) implementing solutions and agreements, and (3) evaluating and revising solutions and agreements. Each guideline is followed by explanatory comments.

Arriving at a Mutually Satisfying Solution or Agreement

1. *When making suggestions about how to resolve your issue, aim for a win-win solution by proposing ideas that will meet your partner's concerns and desires as much as your own.*

> The goal of Problem/Conflict Resolution is to create a solution, agreement, or plan of action that will leave both of you feeling genuinely satisfied because you both feel that your feelings and concerns have been heard and have been incorporated into your agreement. This is what is meant by a win-win solution. We could

put this in the context of both of you being committed to the good of the relationship as something that transcends either of you as individuals. Moreover, from a practical point of view, if you've conducted Discussion/Negotiation well, then by the time you are ready to move into phase 2 of your dialogue you should no longer be feeling as though it's "me versus you." Ideally, by this time you're now feeling "We're in this together, and we need to find a way to make this work for both of us, out of a commitment to doing what's good for the relationship." If phase 1 of your dialogue has gone well, then the outlines of a solution or agreement often will emerge quite directly from that and be relatively clear to both of you. Whether or not that is the case, it is important that you only propose solutions that you genuinely believe will meet your partner's concerns and desires as well as your own. It can even be a good idea to explicitly state why and how you believe your proposed solution would meet both of your concerns and desires.

2. *Be creative and imaginative when you offer possible solutions. Avoid compromising too quickly. Try to come as close as possible to meeting both of your needs as fully as possible.*

I could say, tongue in cheek, that "compromise is a dirty word." In reality, there are two meanings to the word *compromise*. The negative meaning involves surrendering something that is fundamental to your self-identity, and ideally that is something that neither of you ever would do. We don't want you to compromise if it means giving up something that is essential to your sense of yourself or your core values. On the other hand, there is a positive meaning to the word *compromise* in the sense of accommodating yourself to another person. In this sense, compromise is an essential ingredient in healthy relationships because the reality is that you both have to be happy with a solution or it won't be a genuine solution. The only solutions that work are win-win solutions. If either person feels that he or she is on the losing end of the agreement, then in reality it's a win-lose solution, which translates into a lose-lose proposition for the relationship, which means it's no solution at all. So compromise in the sense of accommodation is a good thing. Indeed, having a spirit of accommodation, and being willing to be influenced by your partner's desires, represents a commitment to the well-being of the relationship that transcends your own personal desires. On the other hand, we don't want you to settle for a 50/50 compromise where you both settle for half of what you want. That may be a good business proposition, but it's a poor intimacy proposition. That's where being creative and imaginative comes in. We want you both to get more like 70 to 80% of what you want. It helps to realize that creating a solution need not involve a zero-sum game where when one person wins and the other person loses. Being creative and imaginative means being guided by the principle that both of you can win at the same time if you are creative about it.

3. *Continue to follow all the requirements of the dialogue process. Be certain to have a designated Expresser and designated Empathizer, and empathically acknowledge all suggestions.*

Even during phase 2 of a dialogue, always continue with one of you being the designated Expresser and the other being the designated Empathizer, and continue to follow all the RE skill guidelines. This also means that you should always empathically acknowledge all the details of your partner's proposed solutions. That may sound unnecessary, but there are two reasons why it's important to do that. The first is that you don't want to lose sight of the details of a potentially complex proposal, and it's easy for that to happen. So it's important to empathically acknowledge the details of all proposals. On the other hand, empathizing during phase 2 of a dialogue will come closer to paraphrasing since presumably there are few feelings to decipher at this point in the dialogue. The second reason for empathically acknowledging the details of a proposed solution is that all proposed solutions should be treated by both of you as suggestions, and suggestions should always be open to amendment.

4. *Whenever possible, respond to your partner's proposed solution by first indicating what you agree with. Then proceed to what you would like to modify or what you disagree with. Feel free to propose alternative ideas for a solution.*

The point here is that you first want to let your partner know what you do agree with about his or her proposal before you go on to address points you may want to modify or object to. The reason is one of simple psychology. If you begin with what you disagree with, then you will leave your partner wondering if there's anything you do agree with or, even worse, your partner may conclude that there's nothing you agree with about the proposal, which may leave your partner with negative feelings. So it's always a good idea to begin by acknowledging what you do agree with or what you can accept from your partner's proposal. That makes it easier for your partner to hear what your proposed modifications or alternative suggestions might be. It also helps build and reinforce an atmosphere that the two of you are gradually working your way toward a workable solution, because you begin by identifying the points of commonality while gradually whittling away the residual points of divergence. You may wish to write down your final agreement for future reference.

5. *If new feelings or concerns emerge about the issue, suspend problem solving and return to Discussion/Negotiation.*

If, per chance, either of you experiences a significant negative reaction to your partner's proposal during phase 2 of your dialogue, that likely is a sign that not everything that needed to have been said during the Discussion/Negotiation phase was said. If that happens, temporarily suspend problem solving and return to talking at the level of simply trying to understand one another better. That should include a renewed effort to read more deeply between the lines empathically in order to go as deep as possible into what your partner's feelings and concerns might be. When you both acknowledge that you have said what needs to be said and you feel understood, then explicitly agree to resume Problem/Conflict Resolution so you both are on the same page in terms of the process.

Implementing Solutions and Agreements

1. *Once you have agreed on the outlines of a solution, assign responsibility to who will do what, how often, when, and where.*

If aiming to create a win-win solution is the most important principle of Problem/Conflict Resolution, then assigning responsibility is the most important principle for helping to ensure the implementation of solutions. Indeed, the failure to assign responsibility as to who is going to do what, when, where, and how often, is the number one reason why agreements that are made fail to get implemented. For example, if you are agreeing to go out to dinner on Friday evenings without the children, then who's taking responsibility for getting the babysitter, and who's taking responsibility for making the dinner reservation? Because if you don't, you may be looking at one another early Friday evening frustrated because you didn't agree on who would do what, and so what needed to happen didn't happen, and you're not going to go out to dinner that night. So always be clear as to who is taking on responsibility for what in your agreements.

2. *Avoid future disappointment by anticipating special circumstances or potential obstacles to implementing your solution or agreement. Make modifications as necessary.*

It's also helpful to identify special circumstances or potential obstacles that could get in the way of you being able to carry out your agreement. To continue the preceding example, let's say your son Johnny gets sick on Friday. Are you still having the babysitter come to the house, or are you going to take Johnny to Grandma's, or are you going to stay home and postpone going out to dinner to the next available opportunity? There's no abstract correct answer to that question. Each couple has to make its own decision about how to handle that situation. The point is to identify that as a possibility in advance. You want to avoid suddenly being confronted with the situation, one of you arguing that there's an agreement to go out and so you should go out, whereas the other person argues that you can't go out because Johnny is sick. The point is to decide the issue in advance, when emotions are not in play, and come to a mutually acceptable solution for the special circumstance.

3. *Consider whether reminders would help you implement your solution or agreement.*

Reminders fall under the Self-Change and Helping-Others Change skills, but this is where they have their place within the Problem/ Conflict Resolution process. We'll take a closer look at those two skills at another time.

Evaluating and Revising Solutions and Agreements

1. *Establish a trial period and set a date to evaluate how well your solution or agreement is working.*

Whenever there is a change in behavior or a new agreement or plan of action being adopted, you should always establish a trial period. The trial period will vary in length depending on the nature of the behavior change or plan of action being adopted, but it should be long enough to gather a reasonable amount of data on the basis of which you can meaningfully evaluate how well your solution or agreement is working. Set a date at the end of the trial period to conduct an evaluation of your solution or agreement.

2. *When evaluating your solution or agreement, follow all the requirements of the dialogue process.*

When conducting the evaluation, treat it as a dialogue and follow all the guidelines for conducting a structured dialogue. Have a designated Expresser and a designated Empathizer, and empathize with each other's evaluations.

3. *Make any needed changes by again following the steps in the Problem/ Conflict Resolution process.*

There are two helpful attitudes to take toward agreements. Once an agreement has been made, take it seriously and follow through because, after all, you have made a commitment. On the other hand, if you learn during the evaluation dialogue that the agreement is not working out as anticipated and your partner is dissatisfied, then be open to modifying the agreement. To take a stand that you already have an agreement and therefore you should stick to it would, in effect, be to ignore your partner's feelings and concerns; this would only leave your partner feeling dismissed and would result in a lose-lose proposition for the relationship. So, once made, take your agreements seriously, but be open to modifying them if you learn from your partner that it is not working out as anticipated. If you do find yourselves wanting to make changes to your solution or agreement, then be certain to follow all the relevant steps in the Problem/Conflict Resolution process.

A final observation: These Problem/Conflict Resolution guidelines may be utilized in one of two ways. The therapist may either (1) review these guidelines with the couple up front and then have the couple begin phase 2 of their dialogue or (2) work through the guidelines one by one as he or she walks the couple through their first Problem/Conflict Resolution process. I personally prefer the former method because it gives the couple a global grasp of how to approach problem solving. In either case, it is important that the therapist ensure through active coaching that the couple follow all the steps in the Problem/Conflict Resolution process.

Address the Difference Between a Solvable Problem and a Perpetual Problem, and When Relevant, the Possibility of Irreconcilable Differences

In addition to explaining the Problem/Conflict Resolution process, it also is important to provide some perspective to couples regarding the reality that there may be some issues for which there may be no ready resolution. Gottman (1999) refers to these as "perpetual problems," a useful notion that captures the reality that not every relationship problem is solvable in the conventional sense. It's also helpful, in this context, for the therapist to help couples distinguish between less important issues and issues that may be less amenable to change, (such as character traits) versus more serious issues that in principle are amenable to change but that, despite the couple's best efforts, elude resolution.

With regard to perpetual problems for which there may be no ready resolution, it becomes important that couples learn three complementary approaches to dealing with what could otherwise become a longer-term emotional drain on the relationship. The first is simply a commonsense reminder: "Don't sweat the small stuff." When couples are struggling with all sorts of issues in their relationship, and everything has become equally charged because of the spillover of one unresolved issue onto other unresolved issues, such a reminder can serve a useful purpose in helping couples to put certain things in perspective and to realize that not everything is important enough to fight over. The second approach is to help couples understand the importance of developing an attitude of acceptance toward things that may be different from the way one wishes them to be. Christensen and Jacobson (2000) provide a useful perspective on "reconcilable differences" and the important role that the acceptance of such differences plays in any relationship.

The third approach involves the couple dialoguing about both minor and major issues in the relationship. This, of course, is the whole point of the RE therapy process. When the couple is faced with a difficult or potentially gridlocked issue, it is important to assist the couple to get to the deeper underlying concerns, values, or life goals that may be at stake for each person in the issue. This may also include identifying the implicit or symbolic meaning that each person attaches to the issue or the significance that the issue holds for each person, including what Gottman refers to as the "dreams" that each person is carrying and which are embedded in the issue (1999, p. 234). In some cases, by means of extensive dialoguing, this may open up new and unforeseen avenues of mutual understanding, acceptance, or resolution of a previously intractable and gridlocked issue. This might also involve one partner or the other voluntarily and in good faith (i.e., without holding any resentment toward the other partner), coming to have a genuine change of heart that allows one to embrace the other partner's dream as one's own. But the additional point is that when resolution appears out of reach, couples must maintain open lines of communication, specifically with reference to continuing a periodic dialogue about these perpetual problems. This involves checking in with each other about the issue in order to prevent erosion in the relationship. It also involves acceptance at the level of valuing the relationship as a good that transcends the unresolvable differences. For some, this may manifest as a commitment to the institution of marriage that transcends any particular preferences, desires, or differences in the relationship.

However, this also points indirectly to another possibility for some couples, namely, the differences are such that they do not become "reconcilable differences" leading to acceptance, but they instead become irreconcilable differences that, at the extreme, have the potential to threaten the very sustainability of the relationship. A couple's own values will inevitably come into play here; for example, for some people, divorce simply is not an option under any or under only the most dire of circumstances. For other couples, however, there may not be an intrinsic religious or moral barrier to the possibility of divorce. (For some married couples, the presence or absence of children may change the calculus.) Then, again, there are a not insignificant number of intimate relationships where partners are living together in a committed relationship without being married. For the latter two groups, certain irreconcilable differences may become the basis for rethinking one's commitment to a partnership or marriage. This is another place where the difference between minor and major relationship issues is relevant, because for some couples it may be easier to cultivate an attitude of acceptance around less important issues as compared to major issues that go to the very core of a person's sense of self and the kind of relationship he or she wants to have. The major issues that are most likely to threaten a relationship for some couples will be those involving fundamental differences in core values or life goals. Examples include whether or not to have a child (or more children), where to live, or how to handle money and finances. Sexual difficulties also are a common cause of relationship dissolution, especially in the early years of a marriage or after a couple that is not married has lived together for several years (see McCarthy & McCarthy, 2003).

The issue of potentially serious irreconcilable differences interestingly has perhaps its greatest clinical utility in the context of premarital counseling. By helping unmarried couples take a serious look at their relationship, including having them focus their attention on potentially serious areas of disagreement or incompatibility with regard to core values, dreams, and life goals, a therapist (or minister or educator) can help couples identify issues in the relationship that are better identified and worked through prior to getting married. It would be better in the long run, in the case of premarried couples, for them to come to a determination that they are not able to sustain a mutually satisfying relationship with each other because the conditions for mutual happiness are not present (i.e., what one person wants is fundamentally incompatible with what the other person wants) before they tie the knot, when things become infinitely more difficult because more is at stake. The stakes, of course, become even greater when children have become part of the equation. As a consequence, helping couples come to terms with their potential incompatibility before getting married, and even more importantly before having children, has the potential to spare many people unnecessary grief later in life. This represents, in effect, a preventative approach to potential irreconcilable differences.

Coaching the Couple During Problem/Conflict Resolution

One of the important (Rogerian-based) assumptions of the Problem/Conflict Resolution process is that each person and each couple ultimately knows what the best solution is for their issue and their situation. This means, generally speaking, that the therapist should not interject him- or herself into the content of the couple's solution. Instead, the therapist should have confidence that the partners will find appropriate solutions for themselves and be able to work out the details in a manner satisfactory to them. I typically make a point of telling couples that I am not a miracle worker when it comes to coming up with solutions, and that in the end they will know best what will work for them. The reason, I go on to explain, is that there really isn't some abstract right or wrong solution to their issue. Each couple is unique, and what will work for one couple is not necessarily going to work for another couple. I believe that this message is empowering to the couple in that it conveys my confidence that they can come up with their own satisfying solutions. It also conveys respect for their autonomy and their right to self-determination.

There are two important exceptions to this general principle. The first is if the therapist experiences genuine concern over one or more of the specifics of the couple's emerging solution. If that happens, the therapist has the right, under the rubric of Therapist Troubleshooting, to express his or her concerns to the couple. Of course, in doing so, the therapist is obligated to communicate the relevant points as skillfully and as subjectively as possible. Moreover, in many instances, a therapist's concerns will likely be rooted in values that may be different from those of the couple. If that is the case, it is important that the therapist be aware that his or her concerns about the couple's proposed solution indeed involve a question of values and this should be explicitly acknowledged to the couple.

To illustrate, let's say that the couple is discussing a parenting issue involving discipline of the children and appears to be comfortable with or is explicitly suggesting corporal punishment as part of their agreement about how to handle the children's unruly behavior. The therapist is permitted, under such circumstances, to express concerns about the wisdom of resorting to corporal punishment as a form of discipline, including concerns about likely negative effects on the children. It would also be wise, however, for the therapist to acknowledge explicitly, especially in those cases where the therapist is from a different ethnic or racial group than the couple, that there may well be some differences in values between him or her and the couple. The therapist needs to emphasize that he or she wants to be respectful of the couple's values but also feels compelled to share his or her own perspective on this question because there is so much at stake, especially with regard to the well-being of the children. In this way, the autonomy of the couple is respected at the same time that the therapist chooses to share his or her concerns.

The second important exception to the general rule that it is better for the therapist to not interject him- or herself into the content of the couple's solution is when the therapist becomes aware that the couple may genuinely be in need of assistance in crafting a suitable solution or a workable plan of action; then interjection by the therapist is appropriate. Some couples may need such assistance for any number of reasons. Some people may suffer from a condition such as depression that limits their ability to think positively or clearly. Other people may have suffered a partially disabling brain injury that limits their ability to devise or craft future-oriented plans. Some people tend toward concrete patterns of thinking, while other people may simply lack experience in effective problem solving. Any of these people may experience limitations that restrict their problem-solving resourcefulness. In such cases, the therapist may indeed need to become more actively involved in order to help the couple craft a solution that is suitable or a plan of action that is workable. However, there is an important principle that should be followed in such instances: The therapist should help craft a solution that follows as closely and as relevantly as possible the couple's own stated feelings, concerns, and desires. In this way, the therapist's proposed solution is less likely to be experienced by the couple as being imposed on them, and it is more likely to be experienced as genuinely meeting their needs. In following this principle, the therapist also respects the autonomy and self-determination of the couple, even while getting involved in the content of their issue.

One final observation. When a couple is focused on a parenting issue and it appears to me that they would benefit from some focused parenting tips or guidelines, I look for an opportunity to share some basic perspectives and insights about parenting strategies. In doing this, I follow the excellent insights and recommendations found in Louise Guerney's *Parenting: A Skills Training Manual* (1995). This short and easy-to-read book represents, in effect, a parenting application of the principles embodied in the RE model, and I often encourage couples with children to read it.

Optional Brainstorming Interlude

Sometimes a couple may want to suspend the demands of the structured dialogue process temporarily (in terms of always having to empathize) in order to explore possible ideas for a solution in a brainstorming mode. I tell couples that it is permissible to do that, though I strongly recommend that someone write down all the ideas. I also more or less insist that when they get to the point of wanting to share their evaluations of the various ideas that they then return to the formal dialogue process. Let me be clear: I am a firm believer in the absolute necessity of the therapist rigorously adhering to the demands of the structured dialogue process while the couple is conducting a dialogue, most especially during Discussion/ Negotiation. The principal reason is that the structured dialogue process creates a safe container within which disagreements can be managed more effectively, and this in turn permits the partners to explore their issue as deeply as possible because they feel safe emotionally.

On the other hand, I also believe that a modicum of flexibility is salutary while conducting this kind of couples therapy in that it is a very rigorous process for the couple, and being able once in a while to depart from the demands of the structured dialogue process can be beneficial—so long as the therapist also is vigilant in returning the couple to a structured dialogue format at the earliest sign of heightened emotion. I find that this kind of flexibility makes the RE therapy process more user friendly in a manner that in no way diminishes its rigor or effectiveness. It also shows the partners that the therapist has confidence in them, itself not an insignificant thing. The therapist should use good judgment and discretion in allowing a couple to step outside the structured dialogue process; not all couples should be allowed to do so, in particular highly conflicted or less skilled couples. But for those couples who are using the process well, there is little harm in allowing such a brainstorming interlude outside the bounds of the normal structured dialogue process.

Home Assignments

At this point in the RE therapy process, the therapist should have the couple continue conducting dialogues at home, but carefully negotiate that they only address issues that match their current level of skillfulness. Indeed, it is wise to counsel couples explicitly to *not* address their most serious issues at home on their own, but to save those for the therapy sessions. Also, the therapist should ask the couple at the next therapy session to report the results of their home dialogues and how well their dialoguing went. Finally, the couple should be encouraged to continue or finish reading the *RE Client Manual.*

CHAPTER 12

The Challenges of Changing Behavior: Teaching Self-Change and Helping-Others Change Skills

The Self-Change and Helping-Others Change skills can be viewed as an extension and refinement of the Problem/Conflict Resolution skill in that they aim to increase the odds for the successful implementation of an agreed-upon change in behavior. The genesis of these two skills, structurally speaking, derives from the recognition that change often is not easy, and that it therefore is helpful to understand both what gets in the way of constructive change and what can facilitate more rapid and more successful change. Practically speaking, their genesis arises from the genuine difficulties that people would encounter in their efforts to make changes in their lives even when they were committed to doing so. The Self-Change and Helping-Others Change skills are thus designed to help people follow through on their decisions and commitments to implement change in their lives. These skills are best introduced at the first opportunity when a solution, agreement, or plan or action is being negotiated that involves a concrete behavior change on the part of one or both partners. If this happens during the couple's first dialogue, so much the better, because then the couple will be armed with the full range of the RE model's tools when they address subsequent relationship issues, whether in session or in practice dialogues at home. What is provided in this chapter is a framework and template for presenting these skills in a meaningful but concise manner.

Explain the Purpose of Self-Change and Helping-Others Change Skills

When the therapist decides it is time to introduce Self-Change and Help-ing-Others Change skills, it is important to check whether the partners have read the relevant chapters in the *RE Client Manual* (Guerney & Scuka, 2005). If not, they should be asked to read those chapters as a fol-low-up to what the therapist will share with them in session.

The purpose of Self-Change and Helping-Others Change skills may be explained in the following way:

> The Self-Change and Helping-Others Change skills represent an extension and a refinement of the Problem/Conflict Resolution skill. The purpose of the Self-Change skill is to enable the person who has agreed to make a change in behavior to do so more quickly and more reliably. The purpose of Helping-Others Change skill is to help that person's partner to be patient and supportive of that person's change efforts. Both of these goals can be accomplished by avoiding some of the common pitfalls that get in the way of suc-cessful change and learning strategies that can increase the odds of successfully implementing a change in behavior.

Explain That Change Is a Gradual Learning Process

I find it helpful, in introducing Self-Change and Helping-Others Change skills, to explain that change is not easy and usually takes time to accom-plish, which helps create a context for understanding that change involves a gradual learning process. An important implicit goal in teaching these two skills is to alter couples' attitudes toward the change process in a man-ner that will be more conducive to positive change. I introduce the theme that change is not easy in the following way:

> The reason the Self-Change and Helping-Others Change skills are important is that we recognize that change is not easy and therefore often takes time to accomplish and implement successfully. Because this is the case, it is important to view change as a gradual learning process. It's important to realize that making a decision to change and successfully implementing that decision are two different things. Unfortunately, making a decision to change does not auto-matically result in the change happening. If only life were that simple. One way to understand why this is the case is to focus on the notion of a habit. What's a habit? [*Solicits responses from the couple.*] A habit involves something that we typically do without

thinking; we do it more or less automatically. There are many benefits to developing habits. But when we want to change a habit, that's another matter, because habits represent what amount to sedimentations of familiar and established patterns of behavior. I imagine a habit as a pattern of behavior that's become sedimented in stone. So to change behavior isn't simply about adding or substituting one behavior for another. It's as though you have to take a jackhammer to the old, established pattern of behavior before you can successfully replace it with a new pattern of behavior. That's one way of understanding why change is not easy and why change often is a gradual process.

One of the important implications of this is that the attitude that both people bring to the process of change can have a significant influence on its course and outcome. Patience is important, both on the part of the person attempting to implement a change in behavior and on the part of the partner who is invested in and hoping that the change in behavior will happen. Compassion also is important, because the reality is that incidental setbacks or "failures to perform" are an almost inevitable part of the change process. How those setbacks are handled, especially by the partner who is hoping the change will happen, can have a significant impact on the eventual success or failure of the change in behavior. Because if the person who is invested in his or her partner following through on the new behavior responds to those setbacks with frustration and impatience, and those feelings then get translated into criticism, accusations, or questioning the other person's commitment to making the change, that will almost inevitably cause the person who has agreed to make a change in behavior to feel defensive and become discouraged. That, in turn, will likely result in a decrease in motivation to make further attempts to implement the change. On the other hand, if the partner instead responds with patience, support, and appreciation for the effort made to change, even in the face of setbacks, then the person trying to make the change is likely to feel supported and encouraged, which likely will strengthen that person's commitment and motivation to following through on the change. So the attitude that each person brings to the process of change can have a significant impact on its eventual outcome. This does not absolve the person who has agreed to make a change of responsibility if he or she fails to do so. But it is to say that the other person in reality wields a considerable amount of influence on the outcome. Let's take a look at the specific Self-Change guidelines.

Review the Guidelines for the Person Agreeing to Make a Change in Behavior

1. *Take responsibility for your own change process.*

   If you have agreed to make a change in behavior, the responsibility to follow through and implement the change is entirely yours. Therefore, do not offer excuses for failing to follow through, but accept responsibility and recommit yourself to implementing the change you previously agreed to.

2. *Visualize the change in behavior you have agreed to make.*

   One way to facilitate the successful implementation of your change in behavior is for you to visualize what it would look like for you to perform the desired behavior (or to stop performing an undesired behavior).

Introduce the Concept of Self-Reminders

3. *Use self-reminders to help implement your change in behavior.*

   One of the things that the person who has agreed to make a change in behavior can do to increase the likelihood that he or she will follow through successfully is to use self-reminders. What are some of the kinds of things that people customarily do to remind themselves to do something? [*Supplement the couple's examples with some of the following:*] Place sticky notes in strategic places, use the alarm on your wrist watch, make an entry in your calendar or palm pilot, tie a string to a purse or briefcase handle. The point is that there are all kinds of things that we ourselves can do to increase the likelihood that we follow through on our decisions and our commitments to change our behavior. In addition, however, we could involve our partner in helping us follow through on making a change in behavior.

Introduce the Concept of Interpersonal Reminders

4. *Consider inviting your partner to help you implement your change in behavior by giving you interpersonal reminders.*

   Now, I imagine your first response to the notion of being reminded by your partner might be, "Are you kidding? Be reminded by my partner? No way." Most people have a viscerally negative response to the idea of being reminded to do something by other people because most people's experience in being reminded by other people has not been a positive one. Indeed, it's usually been experienced in quite negative terms in the form of nagging such as "Don't forget to …," which often elicits the defensive response of "Get off my back already. I said I'd do it." Or, we hear the biting criticism and sarcasm that often accompany being reminded that we didn't do something: "I knew I couldn't count on you to do that." So most people aren't keen on the idea of being reminded by somebody else. But there's a tragedy in that, because reminders in principle are a good thing; and, in principle, interpersonal reminders could be a good thing. I want to show you how we can detoxify the use of interpersonal reminders and retrieve their utility.

5. *Decide what kind of interpersonal reminder(s) you wish to receive—a prereminder and/or postreminder—and whether you wish the reminder(s) to be verbal or nonverbal.*

There are two possible sets of reminders: You can use a verbal or nonverbal prereminder, or you can use a verbal or nonverbal postreminder. You could choose to use both a prereminder and a postreminder, or just one or the other. Now, technically speaking, the person who is agreeing to make a change in behavior is not required to use interpersonal reminders. On the other hand, I would suggest that if that person were smart, he or she would agree to the use of interpersonal reminders. We'll see more clearly why later.

6. *Specify the exact form each reminder is to take so that your partner is comfortable giving it and you will not respond defensively in receiving it.*

It's very important that you specify and negotiate the exact form of the reminder so that both of you will be comfortable with it. The reason is that we want to avoid causing any defensiveness in the person receiving the reminder. This tends to be especially important with verbal reminders, since that is where there is the greatest risk for defensiveness to get generated. Let me give you some examples of the four kinds of reminders previously mentioned. Let's say I agreed to call my wife once a day at work at her request. An example of a nonverbal prereminder would be if she were to put a red ribbon on my briefcase handle in the morning before I went to work. An example of a verbal prereminder would be if she were to say to me in the morning as I left to go to the office, "I look forward to getting a call from you today." Notice the positive formulation, as opposed to "Don't forget to call me today," which I probably would not agree to because of its negative tone and implication that I would forget to call. An example of a nonverbal postreminder would be if she were to tie a black ribbon on the handle of the door from the garage to the house. That way, when I come home and see the ribbon, I am reminded that I forgot to call her that day. The beauty of a nonverbal postreminder is that nothing need be said between us, yet the message is given and received. An example of a verbal postreminder, which is the trickiest kind of reminder to pull off successfully without causing defensiveness, would be if she were to say to me when I got home in the evening, "I look forward to receiving a phone call from you tomorrow." Again, notice the positive formulation, as opposed to "You forgot to call me today," which, because of its negative formulation, I would not agree to because it would leave me feeling defensive.

7. *Do not offer excuses or respond defensively when your partner reminds you in the manner that has been agreed upon. Instead, show appreciation to your partner for giving you the reminder since your partner is doing you a favor.*

If I have agreed to receive a reminder from my wife as part of our negotiated agreement, then I am obligated to not respond negatively if she does remind me because she in fact is doing me a favor. That would be unfair to her. Instead, it would be appropriate for me to show appreciation to her for reminding me.

8. *If your partner reminds you in a manner different from what has been negotiated, and you feel defensive, use Expressive skills to inform your partner.*

If your partner reminds you in a manner that has not been negotiated and you feel defensive, then explain to your partner your desire to be reminded only in the manner agreed upon, but be certain to do so by expressing yourself skillfully and in an even, neutral tone of voice. Also, be certain to express appreciation for your partner's help in agreeing to remind you.

9. *If your behavior has become well established and you no longer need to receive a reminder, inform your partner of your decision to discontinue the reminder.*

    Reminders are not meant to be permanent. Reminders are intended to be a temporary means of helping a person establish a new pattern of behavior. So after the new behavior has become well established, it will make sense to discontinue the use of a reminder. When you are ready to discontinue receiving a reminder, inform your partner of your desire and express appreciation to your partner for having assisted you.

10. *If you are not making adequate progress, set more realistic subgoals without abandoning the longer-term goal.*

    Solicit your partner's input and assistance and, if necessary, renegotiate your agreement so that both of you know what to expect. Consider once again whether self-reminders or interpersonal reminders would be helpful to you.

    Let's now take a look at the complementary Helping-Others Change skill guidelines.

Review the Guidelines for the Person Assisting a Partner to Make a Change in Behavior

1. *Be certain you have a clear understanding of how you are to help your partner.*

    This should include whether you are to provide reminders, what kind of reminders (pre- or post-), and the exact form the reminders are to take. Remind your partner only in the manner agreed to. If no reminders have been negotiated, then you are obligated during the trial period to not give any reminders.

2. *If you have agreed to provide reminders, do not hesitate to give them.*

    If you have agreed to provide reminders to your partner, do not hesitate to do so because you are helping your partner in his or her effort to change. However, avoid giving prereminders at every possible opportunity. The reason is that you would unwittingly create a dependency relationship in that your partner could become dependent on your reminders as a prompt for performing the desired behavior. It is preferable to provide prereminders on an intermittent, unpredictable basis. That is the best strategy to help your partner gradually learn to perform the behavior on his or her own. On the other hand, if a postreminder has been negotiated as part of an agreement, do not hesitate to give it because that will be a useful way to help you deal with your potential disappointment over your partner's failure to perform. This, by the way, is the reason why it is smart for the person who is agreeing to make a change in behavior to agree at least to a postreminder. That way, you are providing a constructive avenue for your partner to be able to channel potential frustration over your nonperformance of the new behavior which, if it were to go on for too long, could well result in your partner's feelings getting expressed to you in a sideways and negative fashion.

3. *Show appreciation when your partner succeeds in performing the new behavior.*

While you should avoid negative comments about your partner's nonperformance during the trial period in order to not discourage your partner from trying harder, expressions of appreciation always are a good thing when your partner does perform as desired. Moreover, that kind of positive reinforcement is the quickest way to increase the likelihood of the new behavior being performed.

4. *Be patient and supportive if your partner fails to perform the new behavior.*

Accept that it will take time for your partner to perform a new behavior consistently, or to stop performing an unwanted behavior. Therefore, be patient and supportive, especially during the early stages of your partner attempting to make this change in behavior. Expressing appreciation for efforts made will have a more positive impact on your partner's motivation to continue with efforts to implement the change than expressing disappointment or criticism. View gradual improvement as a positive sign.

5. *If you feel frustrated or disappointed because of your partner's failure to perform a new behavior or failure to stop an unwanted behavior, request a skilled dialogue to discuss the situation. Be certain to express yourself skillfully.*

If your partner's failure to perform or slowness in changing becomes so pronounced that you become very frustrated or disappointed, you may elect to initiate a structured dialogue to communicate your feelings and discuss the situation with your partner. Be certain to communicate yourself as skillfully as possible, including an underlying positive appreciation for your partner's willingness and/or efforts to change. Assist your partner in setting more realistic subgoals or negotiate new reminders.

6. *Even after your partner's new behavior has become well established, continue to show appreciation to your partner for performing the new behavior.*

Don't allow yourself to slip into taking your partner's new behavior for granted. Instead, continue to express appreciation to your partner for performing the desired behavior so that your partner knows that it continues to be meaningful to you.

Home Assignment

Once the Self-Change and Helping-Others Change skills have been explained and implemented at least once during an in-session dialogue, the therapist should be certain to remind couples to consider whether the use of reminders would be beneficial as part of their behavior-change agreement or their implementation of a plan of action during their home dialogue assignments. If the couple reports that they negotiated a change in behavior as part of an agreement during a home dialogue, the therapist should be certain to ask whether they considered incorporating the use of reminders to facilitate the change process. If they did not, and the therapist (or the couple) thinks it may be advisable to do so, then the therapist should take time during session to help the couple develop self-reminders or interpersonal reminders.

Clinical Vignette 3: Using the RE Dialogue Process to Address a Complaint and Make a Request for a Change in Behavior

The focal point of this vignette is a wife's request that her husband change a behavior that she experiences as demeaning and that causes her to withdraw from him in the relationship. As we shall see, the husband quite readily agrees to the wife's request that he changes his behavior because of the damage it does to her and their relationship. Nonetheless, this vignette illustrates two useful aspects of the RE therapy process. First, it illustrates how the therapist can use the technique of Becoming to redefine the issue at a much deeper level that permits both partners to better grasp the heart of the issue. Second, in the context of this chapter, it illustrates how the therapist can spontaneously bring to bear one or more of the later RE skills—in this case the Self-Change and Helping-Others Change skills—in the context of an early dialogue between partners. More to the point, it illustrates how the therapist can introduce elements of a skill into a couple's dialogue without necessarily covering the entire skill. This also demonstrates the flexibility that the therapist has in introducing and applying the RE skills to the therapy process and the couple's issues. This flexibility within RE therapy is important relative to the evident clinical reality that time often is short, with the obvious implication that it will not always be possible to cover all the aspects of a skill when first introducing it. Yet, that in no way means that the couple cannot meaningfully benefit from the limited introduction of a skill that offers genuine help to the resolution of an issue or the implementation of a change in behavior.

Karen and Edward came to me to attempt to resolve what had been a long-standing emotional rift in the marriage over a change in her life goals relative to wanting to have children when they had previously had a long-standing agreement between them that they would not. Karen and Edward were emotionally estranged from one another because of this and Karen was in deep pain over feeling unsupported by Edward during and after her pregnancy. Edward, for his part, had made peace with having a child, but the depth of Karen's continuing anger and pain was more than he knew how to respond to. Despite all this, they had remained married and were now determined to work through their respective feelings so that they could experience genuine emotional reconciliation in the relationship.

Given the seriousness of their issues, and their difficulty communicating constructively, I recommended, and they agreed, that we follow the Time-Designated format (in my mind, for at least the first two sessions). I did the standard introduction with the demonstration audiotape in the first session postintake, and used that as a platform to segue into the Conflict Management skill. The second session was devoted to teaching, demonstrating, and having Karen and Edward practice the Empathic skill with childhood stories and partner appreciations. I also explained the structure of the dialogue process and the two phases of a dialogue. Then, in the third session postintake, I decided, given that they had read the chapters on the Expressive and Discussion/Negotiation skills, to shift into the Experiential format and provide just the briefest of comments about the Expressive skill so that they could begin their first dialogue. This way of conducting the first three sessions postintake illustrates, in effect, how the therapist can shift from the Time-Designated to the Experiential format or, if you will, naturally blend elements of both formats into the course of the therapy.

The immediate issue that is the focus of this vignette came relatively early in the therapy (the second issue to be engaged via dialogue), and involved Karen's request that Edward stop calling her names because of how hurtful that was to her. After opening the session with partner appreciations, Karen requested to address an issue and began as the Expresser:

> Edward, I need the name-calling to stop. It's very demoralizing to me when you say things like that to me. It takes me a long time to recover, and I withdraw from you. It's gotten to the point where I don't want to live like this anymore. I need for there to be a more positive atmosphere between us. So I need for it to stop. I've even contemplated the possibility of divorce over this. That's how badly it's affected me. You stopping this is a condition for us to be able to move forward. You can have your anger, Edward. But I'm asking you to agree to stop the name-calling.

Edward empathized moderately well, though he distanced himself from the depth of her pain by using the phrase "when I use language that disappoints you." This clearly failed to capture the depth of Karen's experience, so I coached Edward to go deeper in his empathizing and to acknowledge (by reading between the lines) that she not only felt deeply hurt by his language, but that she felt demeaned by it as well, which he did. As an Expresser, Edward acknowledged that he did call Karen names, though he (defensively) tried to explain it away as his muttering under his breadth when he was in another room, saying, "I never intended for you to hear what I was saying. It's a way for me to release my anger and my frustration. But I agree to stop." Despite the defensive, and even disingenuous quality of part of Edward's statement, the fact that he so readily agreed to stop his behavior could be attributed to his having heard his wife's pain and his desire, out of love and caring for her, to not cause her such pain once it had been clearly pointed out to him. I invited Karen to express her feelings more deeply, which she did. I then coached Karen to express appreciation for Edward's willingness to stop this behavior in light of her experience and request, which she did. I then had Edward empathize with Karen's second statement, including the appreciation. By way of educating them about one of the finer points of dialoguing, I explained that when someone has a complaint and makes a request, and the other person hears the pain and agrees to make a change, it is important to express appreciation so that the person who has agreed to make the change is more motivated to follow through.

As they were dialoguing, I was also processing internally that this was a classic case involving a change in behavior where the use of a verbal or nonverbal postreminder would be exceedingly important because it was virtually guaranteed that, despite Edward's agreement to change his behavior and stop calling Karen names, there would be times when his established pattern of behavior would naturally assert itself. As a consequence, I knew that it would be important to structure this agreement in such a way that Karen would be given an agreed-upon signal that she could use to remind Edward gently of his commitment if he were to slip. So I elected on the spot to outline briefly for Karen and Edward the basic principles of Self-Change and Helping-Others Change skills, and then had them immediately move to negotiate whether and how Karen could let Edward know that she was feeling demeaned by something he said if he were to slip. I also observed to them that the latter formulation, in terms of any language that left Karen feeling demeaned, constituted a widened definition of Karen's original complaint that she was feeling hurt by Edward's language, but that it was clearly implied in Karen's request. (This illustrates how the therapist can intervene to clarify and deepen the couple's dialogue and problem-solving process.) Edward agreed both to the widened definition of the issue and to receiving a verbal reminder from Karen if he were to slip verbally. Following guideline 6 from the Self-Change skill, that the form of the reminder needs to be comfortable to the person receiving it so that he or she does not feel defensive when the reminder is given, Karen and Edward negotiated that she could say to him, when he slipped and said something that Karen experienced as demeaning, "Edward, could you please rethink what you just said?"

It then occurred to me—in light of a passing comment that Karen had made in her second expressive statement, but that had not been picked up on by Edward, nor by me initially—that there was a deeper psychological angle to this issue that needed to be addressed with Edward on Karen's behalf. I could have chosen to address Edward myself under the rubric of Therapist Troubleshooting. However, I recognized that using the technique of Becoming would probably be more effective in that it would less likely arouse a defensive reaction on Edward's part. So I informed Edward that I wanted to represent Karen to him because I believed there was a deeper message that she was trying to convey to him. I then represented Karen as follows:

> Edward, as I said earlier, I can accept that you get angry or frustrated or upset with me. And I appreciate you hearing my pain around you calling me names, and I appreciate you agreeing to stop doing that. That means a lot to me. However, there's an even deeper

angle here, because it seems clear to me that behind your calling me names is a certain thought process that you are engaging in that then leads you to verbalize your negative thoughts in the way that you do. So even more than ask you to stop calling me names, I'd like to ask you to make a serious effort to stop thinking of me in those negative terms to begin with. More to the point, I'd like to ask you to change your focus to what it is that's actually upsetting you, without you translating that frustration or anger into an implicit character assassination of me where in effect you end up demonizing me in your mind. That way, I believe you can then communicate to me directly what it is you are upset about rather than muttering under your breath that I'm some kind of awful person.

Notice how in the final two sentences of this Becoming representation of Karen's perspective I invoke Expressive skill guidelines 6 and 7 to help make the point that it would be preferable for Edward to be specific about what is bothering him rather than for him to "translate" those feelings unskillfully into character assassinations directed toward Karen, even if only mentally.

I turned to Karen and asked if that represented her feelings and desires well, and she responded: "I wish I had been able to say that myself. Yes, that's exactly what I'm feeling." I then asked Edward to please empathize with what I had said and to give the empathy to Karen as though she had said it for herself. This time Edward did a very creditable job of nondefensively empathizing with Karen. I then asked Karen if she'd like to add anything for herself. She said, by way of explaining the benefits of such a change, that she could imagine things being very different and much more positive between the two of them if he could change not just his outward behavior but his internal thought process as well, because she imagined she would experience a very different kind of energy from him. After Edward empathized, I invited him to begin as Expresser with what made sense to him about my representation of Karen's desire and request, and for him to then go on to say whatever he would like to say. Without further prompting, Edward was able to acknowledge that what had been said made sense to him, and that he could see the benefits for him as well as for her if he were able to keep his focus on what was actually bothering him instead of thinking that she was "some kind of hopeless case" and thinking "unkind thoughts" about her. Karen empathized with Edward's statement, and then she became the Expresser and stated that hearing that gave her some sense of hope. This concluded the session.

This vignette illustrates a number of things. First, it demonstrates how the therapist can use the technique of Becoming to deepen the couple's

issue in a manner that has the potential both to help the couple understand the issue better and to reinforce the likelihood that genuine change
actually happens as a result of the couple's dialogue. Second, this vignette
portrays how the therapist can helpfully increase the effectiveness of his
Becoming representation by invoking the underlying principles
or guidelines of the Expressive skill. Third, the vignette shows how the
therapist can gradually refine a couple's ability to dialogue effectively by
teaching some of the finer points of dialoguing. Fourth, the vignette illustrates how it is possible for the therapist to shift from the Time-Designated
to the Experiential format, or to blend elements of the two into one seam-
less application of the RE model. Finally, this vignette illustrates how the
therapist can spontaneously introduce one or more of the later RE skills
into a couple's dialogue when a relevant opportunity presents itself. The
last two points also demonstrate the great flexibility available to the therapist in terms of how the RE therapy model can be applied in practice.

CHAPTER 13
Integrating the RE Skills Into Everyday Life: Teaching Generalization Skill

The Generalization skill shifts the couple's focus in applying the RE skills in two ways: First, it moves the focus beyond the context of the couple's structured dialogues into the couple's day-to-day lives; second, it moves the focus beyond the confines of the couple's relationship into other meaningful relationships in their lives, most especially, but not limited to, other family members. Another way of understanding the Generalization skill is that it represents the unilateral use of the RE skills, without the expectation of reciprocity from the other person.

The Generalization skill may be introduced at any point in the RE therapy process, but the earlier it is introduced the better in that one of the benefits of Generalization is that it will have a positive rebound effect on the couple's own relationship. The same "transfer" effect can be achieved by careful and consistent negotiating of home dialogues and other home assignments. The reason is that the more partners use the RE skills with each other in their daily lives and with other people, the more likely it is that they will use the RE skills and dialogue process with each other when they really need to, namely, when a difficult issue or troublesome situation presents itself. In addition, introducing the Generalization skill earlier in the therapy process can also increase the likelihood that a couple will transfer their use of the RE skills and dialogue process from the therapy sessions to the home environment. This is the reason that Ginsberg (1997) introduces the Generalization skill very early into the couple's therapy process.

But there is a deeper, even spiritual, dimension to the Generalization skill that should not be overlooked. There comes a point in a person's use of the RE skills where they no longer represent an artificial set of skills to which a person submits him- or herself; instead, they gradually become second nature as a person consolidates and integrates their use more fully into daily life. In this sense, the RE model holds out the prospect of nothing less than a spiritual transformation of the self to the extent that the RE skills become so fully integrated that they become a natural part of who a person is and how that person relates to other people. Indeed, at its deepest level, the RE model reflects and embodies an attitude and commitment toward living one's life as a compassionate human being, and the RE skills become part of one's philosophy of life.

Explain the Purpose of the Generalization Skill

The purpose of the Generalization skill may be introduced in the following way:

> The Purpose of the Generalization skill is to enable you to consolidate and integrate your use of the RE skills into your daily lives, both with one another and with other people who are important in your lives. This primarily involves following the principles and guidelines of the Empathic and Expressive skills outside the context of your formal dialogues. It's also helpful to think of the Generalization skill in terms of using the RE skills unilaterally to improve communication in virtually any relationship.

Explain the Three Principles of Generalization

There are three principles of Generalization:

1. *Use the RE skills in your day-to-day life with your partner even when you are not formally dialoguing.*

   The principal use of the RE skills so far has been in the context of you dialoguing with each other when there is a potentially difficult or emotionally challenging issue, either here in session or at home. The first principle of Generalization involves applying the principles and guidelines of the RE skills, especially the Empathic and Expressive skills, in your daily lives with one another, even though there is no need, or perhaps no time, for you to have a formal dialogue. So, for example, there may be an issue you want to talk to your partner about, and you recognize there could be some sensitivities, but you do not want to have a dialogue at that moment. Even so, how could it not be to your advantage, and to the advantage of your relationship, to express yourself as skillfully and as subjectively as possible? Obviously, that's a rhetorical question, because the answer is self-evident. And, by the same token, how could it not be to your advantage, and to the advantage of your relationship, for you to be spontaneously empathic to your partner if you become aware that your partner has strong feelings or is upset, especially if your partner is upset with you? Again, the answer is self-evident.

2. *Use the RE skills with as many people and in as many situations as possible.*

The second principle of Generalization involves applying the principles and guidelines of the RE skills in your relationships with other people in your lives. In principle, there isn't a person on the planet with whom you couldn't use the RE skills to your own benefit and the benefit of that relationship. Of course, whether you choose to do that is entirely up to you. If a relationship is not especially important to you, or if you perhaps feel uncomfortable with someone and you don't really want to develop a relationship with that person, that is perfectly acceptable and you are under no obligation to use the RE skills with that person. But if a relationship is at all meaningful to you, whether on a personal or professional level, how could it not be to your advantage and the advantage of that relationship for you to be as expressively skillful and as empathic as you possibly can be with that person? Again, the answer is pretty self-evident. So the point here is to encourage you to begin to use the RE skills with as many people in your life as it makes sense for you to do, whether it's with your children, your parents, siblings, friends, coworkers, or members of your faith congregation. And, by the way, children need and want empathy every bit as much as we adults do, so that's a great place to start.

3. *When using the RE skills unilaterally with people other than your partner, do not expect reciprocity.*

This third principle of Generalization is really a cautionary note. In using the RE skills with people other than your partner, it is important to realize that you will be using the skills unilaterally, and therefore you cannot realistically expect reciprocity from the other person.

But that doesn't mean that it's not worth doing what you can to uphold your end of the interaction. Every time you express yourself skillfully and provide empathy to the other person, you are helping ensure that the net interaction between the two of you will be better than it would have been had you not made the effort to be skillful. That's obviously a net gain both for you and the other person.

There is one final point. Many people hesitate to have what they think will be a difficult conversation with someone because they are convinced that it will only make things worse. I believe the reason we fear this is that we lack confidence in our own ability to initiate and carry on a conversation in a skillful manner. We become anxious that we will say the wrong thing, or say it the wrong way, and that this will result in the other person responding defensively and feeling hurt or angry. To avoid that unwelcome result, we choose to say nothing at all. The tragedy is that is exactly what contributes to long-term resentment and even estrangement from the other person. At its worst, this leads to a sense of powerlessness and, out of frustration, to our expressing negative feelings in an indirect manner that is harmful to the relationship in its own way. It also deprives the other person of the opportunity to know what is bothering you and the chance to make it right. So one purpose of the Generalization skill is to empower you to have confidence that you can successfully discuss a potentially difficult issue with someone who is unfamiliar with the RE skills, and that such a conversation can have a positive outcome.

Review the Generalization Skill Guidelines

1. Observe and analyze conversations among other people. Notice how someone failed to express skillfully, or how a missed opportunity to empathize might have changed the direction of the interaction. You can also learn from people who interact skillfully.
2. Observe and analyze your own interactions with people while they are happening. This enables you to avoid or correct mistakes. It also enables you to monitor your own feelings to reduce the likelihood that you react defensively or unskillfully. This in turn enables you to respond more empathically.
3. Practice for the sake of practice. Regard omissions and mistakes as natural stepping stones to future mastery.
4. Practice with a variety of people and in a variety of situations. Practice first in situations where there is less at stake. As your skills improve, use them with more significant people.

5. Use self-reminders to help you remember to use the RE skills in new situations. Self-reminders include placing Post-it notes in strategic places, setting the alarm on your wristwatch, making an entry in your calendar or palm pilot, tying a string to a purse or briefcase handle, and so on.
6. Set specific goals for practicing skills. Raise your goals as you succeed.
7. Commend yourself silently when you have succeeded in meeting your goals.
8. Anticipate occasions in which your use of the RE skills could help increase the likelihood of having a positive interaction and constructive outcome. Identify in advance what you want to say and rehearse exactly how you want to say it. This will minimize the likelihood that the other person reacts defensively.
9. Review your interactions with other people after the fact to assess your own performance. Identify where you were particularly successful and give yourself a pat on the back. Then identify where you may not have performed as well as you might have so that you learn from your mistakes. Resolve to do better next time.
10. If you had a negative emotion during the day and you responded unskillfully, turn that emotion into a trigger to use skills in the future. Visualize a future scene involving that same emotion and mentally practice using your skills to deal more effectively with the situation.
11. If you had a positive emotion during the day and you did not share it with the person who stimulated it, or you failed to express appreciation, visualize yourself doing so in the future.

Special Considerations in Using the RE Skills Unilaterally
Special considerations in the unilateral use of the RE skills may be introduced in the following way:

Let's return to the idea of using the RE skills unilaterally. There are two goals in applying the skills unilaterally. Your first goal is to respond empathically so the other person feels understood by you. Your second goal is to communicate yourself skillfully so you minimize the possibility that the other person feels defensive or angry. In each case, this will increase that person's willingness to hear your point of view. There are a few helpful guidelines to keep in mind when using the RE skills unilaterally.

1. Always make an effort to give an underlying positive and preemptive empathy when communicating your point of view.
2. If the other person interrupts you while you are speaking, take that as sign that this person is not able to listen to you at that moment. Shift into an empathic posture and attempt to empathize with what this person has to say.
3. Always attempt to respond to negative emotion with empathy.
4. Sometimes it might be better to empathize with the other person indirectly by attributing feelings to the situation rather than directly to the person.
5. If you are responding to a request for advice involving a third party or a solution to an issue which that person has with you, think in terms of that person's feelings, concerns, and desires and look for a solution that would meet the needs of everyone involved.

Integrating One's Use of the RE Skills and the Spiritual Transformation of Human Personality

One of the deeper long-term goals of the RE model is that each person consolidates and integrates his or her use of the RE skills in such a manner that the person undergoes both a transformation of his patterns of interaction with others and, as a result, a transformation of personality. This transformation occurs at two levels: first, a person consistently expressing as skillfully and as subjectively as possible in order to minimize potential defensiveness in another person; second, a person regularly identifying with the immediacy of another person's experience in a manner that permits one to empathize with the other person's feelings, concerns, and desires. Actually, both of these transformations involve at their core an empathic stance of attunement to other people. And it is this generalized stance of empathic attunement, which involves being open and compassionate to the experience of others, that represents, most deeply, the spiritual transformation of self.

The key to realizing this transformation of self is the continued and regular use of the RE skills in a manner that fosters their consolidation and integration. It is noteworthy, in this context, that many spiritual traditions, for example, both Christianity and Buddhism, place such importance on *practice* as the means for developing empathic attunement. It also is no accident, as we shall see in the next chapter, that practice is at the very heart of the RE Maintenance skill. When engaged in consistently over time, such practice allows the building of a new habit of empathic attunement whereby that person is enabled to be more consistently empathic not just in word and deed, but in mind and spirit as well. Moreover, the building of such a new habit (or virtue) of empathic attunement can have a profoundly liberating impact on that person. The reason, as Buddhist spirituality would explain it, is that empathic attunement, in the form of a selfless identification with another person's experience, is the basis of compassion and, by extension, the path to enlightenment, that is, genuine happiness. While the RE model is not itself a religion or a form of spirituality per se, it nonetheless could be said that the RE model, at its deepest level, promotes the development of human virtue in the service of compassion and the development of compassion as a human virtue. In this sense, the RE model embodies and fosters a spiritual quality.

When I choose to address this dimension of the RE model with a couple, I do so in the following (simplified) way:

> There is one other dimension of the Generalization skill that I would like to share with you. It has to do with you consolidating and internalizing your use of the RE skills so thoroughly that they become second nature to you and, as a result, you become a different kind of person by virtue of relating to other people in more positive and more effective ways. Moreover, other people will come to experience you as a different kind of person because they will experience their interactions with you in a more positive way. So, at its deepest level, the RE model isn't just a set of artificial skills to which you submit yourself. Instead, the RE model holds out the promise of a kind of spiritual transformation of the self that allows you to become a different and better person because you come to relate to people across the board with greater empathy and compassion. And when this transformation of the self becomes a mutually shared process between two people in an intimate relationship, then the relationship itself is spiritually transformed into another dimension where the values of caring and compassion balance the values of openness and honesty in a way that allows a couple to experience genuine intimacy. This is the ultimate goal, and the opportunity, that the RE model holds for all couples.

Home Assignment

The introduction of the Generalization skill opens new doors on home assignments. One option is for each person to be asked to initiate a conversation with someone (other than the partner) with whom he or she has a real issue and to do so with intention: thinking through in advance—and even rehearsing with the partner—what might be said and how to say it in order to increase the likelihood of a positive outcome with the other person. Another option, when the couple has children, is to ask that each person make a concerted effort to actively empathize with his or her children in response to a variety of the children's experiences and feelings. When negotiating either assignment with a couple, the therapist should inform them that they will be asked to report on the results of their Generalization assignment at the next session. Then the therapist should begin the following session by processing each person's experience with the exercise. These assignments may be repeated as many times as the therapist and the couple find them to be beneficial.

CHAPTER 14

Fostering Long-Term Success: Teaching Maintenance Skill

The immediate goal of the Maintenance skill is to maximize the likelihood that couples use the RE skills and dialogue process on a long-term basis so that they continue to address and resolve new issues that emerge in the relationship and do so in a constructive manner. The ultimate goal of the Maintenance skill is to create and preserve an environment of emotional safety, intimacy, and positive feeling in the relationship by giving couples the confidence that they can indeed be open and honest with each other because they both have confidence that each person will, to the best of his or her ability in the moment, be open to and embracing of the other's feelings, concerns, and desires. The Maintenance skill also is designed to foster mutual nurturing of the couple's relationship and thereby forestall the possibility of relapse into an emotionally disengaged or highly conflicted relationship pattern. This takes the form, in part, of having the couple use the RE skills and dialogue process more and more for relationship enhancement purposes. From this vantage point, the Relationship Maintenance skill (as I prefer to think of it) simultaneously represents a form of relationship enhancement and a form of relapse prevention.

The Maintenance skill can also be seen as an extension of the Generalization skill. As such, the therapist could choose to introduce it (or elements of it) in conjunction with the latter skill. From yet another point of view, the Maintenance skill points to the closure of therapy in that it is concerned with helping couples increase the likelihood that they take what they have learned about the RE skills and dialogue process and incorporate them into their relationship on an ongoing basis following the termination of therapy. As such, the Maintenance skill can be used as a framework within which to initiate and address the issue of termination.

Explain the Purpose of the Maintenance Skill

The purpose of the Maintenance skill may be introduced in the following way:

> Let's talk about one of the long-term goals of the RE therapy process. The hope is that you take what you have learned here in our work together and continue to use the RE skills and dialogue process, both with each other and with other people in your lives, to address and resolve issues as they come up. Nothing that you've learned here is going to prevent issues from coming up in your relationship; that new issues will emerge is inevitable. The key is that the two of you have the confidence that you can address those issues skillfully and resolve them constructively. That's one of the key variables that makes for satisfying and happy relationships. The Maintenance skill is designed precisely to help increase the odds that you continue to use what you've learned after our work together is finished.
>
> [*In a playful tone, I might continue:*] I can summarize the Maintenance skill in one word. Can you guess what that is? *Practice. Practice. Practice.* Or, *Dialogue. Dialogue. Dialogue.* Yet another variation might be, "Use them or lose them." In other words, either continue to use the skills and dialogue process, or you gradually will lose your ability to use them effectively when you really need them. And the way to avoid that is to continue dialoguing with one another on a regular basis and to use the skills in your day-to-day lives, making them an integral part of your lives.
>
> But using the RE skills and dialogue process are not ends in themselves. They are the means by which the two of you can actively nurture your relationship on a daily and weekly basis for the purpose of promoting a deeper sense of emotional connection and engagement. In doing this, you will also be forestalling the possibility of relapsing into negative patterns of interaction in your relationship. In effect, the RE skills and dialogue process provide a means for continuing to cultivate an atmosphere of safety, emotional connection, and support that will help you not just maintain the gains you have made, but also extend those gains even more deeply into the future. This will include you dialoguing about relationship enhancement issues such as planning fun activities,

upcoming important events or life transitions, and dreams and goals for the future. Dialoguing about your relationship in these ways on an ongoing basis is the one of the best ways to ensure that your relationship remains vital and satisfying.

Introduce the Key Recommendations for Effective Relationship Maintenance

One helpful way to think about the Relationship Maintenance skill is that it represents a set of recommendations for maintaining *and increasing* the well-being of a couple's relationship. Since these recommendations are designed in part as a strategy for relapse prevention, *it is important that the therapist treat the presentation as the negotiation of a contract with the couple in order to increase the odds that they actually implement the recommendations.* The therapist can either have the couple negotiate their agreements in his or her presence, or make this a home assignment for them to negotiate and make decisions about. In the latter case, the therapist would ask the couple to report back on their decision(s) at the following session.

Ideally, the Maintenance skill is introduced well before the point where the couple is ready to terminate because this will increase the likelihood that the partners will take what they have learned and integrate it into their relationship on an ongoing basis. The Maintenance skill can even be used as a framework for initiating termination, or be introduced in response to the couple initiating termination. In the latter case, the therapist should recommend and negotiate with the couple that termination is a process that requires several sessions. If, per chance, these recommendations are being addressed in what turns out to be the final session with the couple (not an ideal situation), then the therapist should have the couple negotiate their agreements in his or her presence in order to increase the odds that they follow through to implement the recommendations. The key recommendations might be introduced in the following way:

There are three key recommendations relative to helping you maintain and deepen the quality of your relationship. The first recommendation has to do with nurturing your relationship on a daily basis. As we shall see in a moment, this has two parts. The second involves dialoguing on a weekly basis to address issues in your relationship. The third recommendation has to do with nurturing your relationship on a weekly basis. Let's take a look at each one in turn.

Explain the Key Recommendations
The recommendations parallel the form of the guidelines of the other RE skills.

1. *Set aside time each day to nurture your relationship by talking with your partner. Share partner appreciations. Talk about how you are feeling and how your day went, a concern involving another person, a concern involving your partner (but not a major conflict issue), or a desire you have for a joint activity.*

This first recommendation has to do with strengthening the sense of connection between you as well as fostering positive feelings about each other, and doing so on a daily basis. It's important that you share partner appreciations with each other each day. And, as you have learned, the person receiving an appreciation should empathically acknowledge it back to the giver so that you both really take in the appreciation you are being given. Then you could continue by taking turns talking to share your feelings, concerns, and desires. Each of you would empathize with what your partner shares. By doing this, you will learn more about what is important to your partner, you will help your partner feel understood, and you will develop a closer sense of connection to each other.

Ideally, the recommendation to share partner appreciations on a daily basis was already made at the time the Empathic skill was taught. However, introducing the Maintenance skill provides an excellent opportunity to reinforce for couples the importance of this daily ritual, and provides them with either a second chance to adopt this into their relationship or the encouragement to pick up this daily practice once again if they had been doing it but had gradually stopped.

2. *Set aside time each day to nurture your relationship with physical touch. Show affection and touch each other physically with kisses, hugs, back rubs, sitting together, and so on.*

The second way to nurture your relationship on a daily basis is to show affection and to touch each other physically. This can involve giving one another a goodbye kiss and hug in the morning, spending time together, sitting next to one another on the sofa, and perhaps cuddling or holding hands while you talk, giving one another back rubs, or giving one another a kiss when you go to bed each night. Do not underestimate the importance of physical touch between the two of you, and commit yourselves to nurturing your relationship in that way. I'd like to suggest that you dialogue at home about how you would like to nurture your relationship on a daily basis in each of these two ways, and then report back to me next time what you decide to do. Is this something you'd be willing to commit to? Great.

3. *Set aside time each week to dialogue about important issues in your relationship.*

This recommendation is designed to increase the odds that you dialogue regularly to address important issues in your relationship. Ideally you would dialogue for at least 1 hour each week. During that time, you would use all the RE skills and follow the structured dialogue process you have learned. There are a number of things you could choose to dialogue about, such as an enhancement issue for the relationship, an issue that came up during the week that you didn't have time to deal with, a newly emerging issue that you would like to address before it becomes a major problem in the relationship, a perpetual problem in the relationship for the purpose of smoothing over any rough edges, a life decision or life transition that could impact you as a couple or your family, or dreams for the future and individual and shared life goals. You could also use your Relationship Questionnaires to periodically take a relationship temperature reading on the issues in your relationship and agree to tackle one issue from each of your forms in turn.

As for scheduling, some couples prefer to set a standard time each week, say 9 P.M. on Sunday evenings. Other couples prefer to negotiate each week on a specific time, but then they agree on a day when that decision will be made. For example, they decide on Friday evenings when they will have their dialogue that weekend. Is having a weekly dialogue something that you would be willing to commit to? Great. I'd like you to work out the details about that at home and report back to me about what you decide.

If the couple has children, stress the importance of setting aside a time when they are not likely to be interrupted by their children.

4. *Set aside time each week to nurture your relationship by having fun and enjoying one another.*

This fourth recommendation is about making your relationship a priority. We all face pressures around time, and it's all too easy to allow our time to get taken up with the minutiae of daily life, and in the process lose focus and lose sight of what is truly most important: our relationships. The possibilities as to what you can do are almost endless, but what is most important is that you make the commitment and follow through on spending time with each other where there is no agenda other than to relax together, have fun, and enjoy each other's company. There's one ground rule: no dialoguing about serious relationship issues during "date" time. That's why a separate weekly dialogue time is recommended. On the other hand, you can use your weekly dialogue time to talk about how you'd like to enhance your relationship in terms of more quality time together and more fun activities together. I'd like to ask that you also dialogue at home this week about how you would like to structure your lives in order to create more quality time and fun activities together, with a primary focus on setting time aside each week for your relationship. But you could also consider whether there are activities that you would like to commit to less frequently, whether monthly, quarterly, and so on. This could include planning regular getaways. Would you be willing to agree to do that and report back to me what you have decided about nurturing your relationship on a weekly basis? Great.

There are two additional recommendations that will help maintain the strength of your relationship.

5. *When you have had a less-than-ideal interaction with your partner, analyze what went wrong and see how you might have avoided the conflict or lessened its negative impact by a more self-conscious use of the RE skills and dialogue process.*

Realize that there may be times when one or both of you will be at less than your individual or joint best, and you end up having a verbal fight and one or both of your feelings get hurt. How the two of you deal with that when it happens will be very important. In a sense, this is another dimension of Conflict Management, and involves a kind of recovery resiliency in and for your relationship. Everything we talked about earlier under the self-calming part of the Conflict Management skill certainly applies here in terms of each of you working to get your own emotions under control to the extent that is necessary. In addition, it also involves a retrospective reflection on what happened in the interaction between the two of you, *and most especially a focus on what you realize you contributed to the negative interaction.* It's all too easy to stay focused on "what the other person did to me" during the argument. It's much harder, but much more helpful in terms of fostering reconciliation, to own your own contributions to the negative interaction and to actually begin as an Expresser by sharing what you realize you said or did that was less than helpful to the interaction. Doing this will almost certainly reduce defensiveness in your partner and increase receptivity. Once you both have owned your piece of the negative interaction, then you can go on to dialogue about the substantive issue between you that almost certainly got sidetracked because of your less than skillful interaction. If you follow this recommendation, you more than likely will recover from your unskillful interactions more quickly and with less of a sense of lingering ill feelings.

6. *Consider getting a periodic booster session to renew and reinforce your ability to use the RE skills and dialogue process* (see below).

When Is a Couple Ready to Terminate Therapy?

Many couples have quite a good sense as to when they are ready to terminate therapy. But I believe it is the responsibility of the therapist to set the stage for termination very early in the therapy process by explaining to couples how they will know when they are ready to bring the therapy to a conclusion. The therapist may explain this either in response to the couple's question about the possible length of the therapy or by initiating the topic, either at the conclusion of the intake or during the first session postintake. Moreover, addressing the issue of termination early in the therapy allows the therapist to plant the seed that termination is a process, and doesn't just happen in the same session it is first broached by the couple. It can be explained in the following way:

> You will know you are ready to terminate therapy when two conditions have been met. The first is that you will have gained sufficient confidence in your ability to use the RE skills and dialogue process effectively on your own that you will no longer feel the need to have me facilitate your dialogues. The second condition is that we will have addressed enough of the truly difficult issues in your relationship through the therapy so you feel confident that the two of you will be able to address the rest of your issues on your own by using the RE skills and dialogue process. When those two conditions have been met, you will know that you are ready to terminate therapy, and you'll come in one day and tell me that.

I will honor your self-evaluation, but I will also give you my feedback if I have concerns about your readiness to terminate at that point. Let me also indicate that the process of termination itself may take several sessions. I will want to make certain that the two of you have done everything possible to take what you have learned here into your relationship on an ongoing basis so that your relationship continues to benefit and improve after the therapy is concluded.

Giving this message to couples early in the therapy process both conveys respect for the autonomy and self-determination of the couple and empowers the partners to feel and assume responsibility for their therapy. This creates a win-win for the couple and the therapist, because the therapist's demonstration of respect for the couple and empowering them to take control of their own therapy has a positive rebound effect on the couple's respect for the therapist.

When couples announce that they believe they are ready to terminate (or prepare to terminate) therapy, I inquire about several things. First, I ask the couple how well and how often they are dialoguing on their own at home, and whether they have truly incorporated dialoguing into the structure of their lives. If they have not, then we talk about what it would take for them to do that or what the obstacles have been, and I continue to monitor the situation until the therapy terminates. Not having met this condition itself becomes a reason for some couples to agree to prolong therapy, because they recognize the importance of this to the long-term health of their relationship. Second, I suggest that the couple examine their original (and any subsequent) Relationship Questionnaires to see whether they feel that they have addressed enough of the truly challenging issues in their relationship so that they feel confident of being able to address the rest of their issues on their own. If they feel they have reached that point, it is a positive indicator that they are ready for termination. If they feel they have not reached that point, then I suggest we contract for additional sessions to address whatever remaining issues they believe are important for them to tackle in therapy before they terminate.

If both the couple and I are satisfied that they have met the two conditions outlined above, then we are in agreement about the couple's readiness to terminate therapy. If I, as their therapist, am not completely satisfied about their readiness to terminate therapy, then I treat that as an occasion calling for Therapist Troubleshooting, and I proceed to share my concerns with the couple, being careful to communicate as skillfully and as subjectively as possible. In the end, however, it is the couple's decision to make, and it is important to be genuinely respectful of the couple's decision. Under either circumstance, I also want to communicate my sense of what the couple has accomplished as a way of reinforcing the value of our work together and as a way of indirectly encouraging them to continue to use what they have learned.

The Importance of Booster Sessions

One of the things that has become clear from research is the importance of building booster sessions into the therapy process in order to increase the likelihood of maintaining the positive effects of treatment. This dovetails with the underlying philosophy of RE therapy in that one of the goals is to equip and empower couples to be able to solve future problems on their own, and for couples to feel confident in their ability to do so. The key to this, as already explained, is for couples to commit to continuing to use the RE skills and dialogue process after the therapy has been terminated. Building booster sessions into the therapy process is one way to foster this continued use of what couples have learned.

There are two ways to approach scheduling booster sessions. The first is a more indirect method and involves gradually tapering the therapy sessions to once every 2, 3, or 4 weeks during a more extended termination phase. This may be especially useful for those couples who have not fully integrated structured dialogues into their relationship on a weekly basis. The therapist would then use part of the time in each of these sessions to monitor and reinforce the couple dialoguing on their own at home. The rest of the time can be used to continue working on issues. The second approach would be to contract with the couple to schedule booster sessions at 1, 3, and 6 months and a final booster session at the 12-month mark. Each session would involve a report by the couple as to their use of the RE skills and dialogue process, the issues they addressed, a review of whatever parts of the process they need a refresher on, and the working through or completing of an issue in session that they may have had some difficulty bringing to resolution. Either approach is likely to reinforce the couple's continued use of the RE skills and dialogue process, and this in turn is likely to maintain the positive effects of treatment over a longer period of time. In addition, either approach also has the benefit of allowing for a more rapid intervention in cases where the couple may experience a relapse, precisely because there is continuity in the therapeutic relationship. This will likely also reduce the level of deterioration and facilitate a quicker turnaround.

Final Parting Thoughts

I also want to make one final point to every couple terminating therapy: My door is always open to them should the need arise in the future. I explain that they might choose to call me simply because they realize they've gotten away from dialoguing and using the skills, and they want a brief refresher to help get them back on track. Perhaps an especially delicate or difficult issue has emerged and they may decide that they want my assistance to help them get to the deeper levels of the issue more quickly than they think they can do for themselves, or because they have gotten stuck. I also suggest to couples that they might want to think in terms of coming in once a year for a kind of couple's relationship checkup and skills tune-up. Some couples have taken me up on that suggestion independently of, or in addition to, formally scheduled booster sessions.

To couples with whom I have had an especially good working relationship, and with whom I feel there is a sufficient level of comfort, I have even been known to jokingly say as they are about to leave for the last time, "Of course, my door always remains open to you should the need arise. But, and I know you won't take this the wrong way, I hope I never have to see the two of you again—except, of course, under favorable circumstances." This has never failed to generate a genuine laugh of appreciation and a warm acknowledgment of the value of our work together. It's moments like these, and others like them, that symbolize the value of my work with couples and make it all feel worthwhile.

PART V

The Application of RE Therapy to the Treatment of Affairs

CHAPTER 15
Using RE Therapy in the
Treatment of Affairs

One of the most important issues for a couples therapist to be knowledge-able about, and one of the most challenging clinically, is the phenomenon of infidelity and the treatment of affairs. A survey of marital therapists and family psychologists (Whisman, Dixon, & Johnson, 1997) identified affairs as the second most damaging problem to relationships and the third most difficult problem to treat. While figures vary, it is estimated that approximately 30% of marital therapy cases are initiated because of a crisis involving infidelity, while another 30% of cases involve a disclosure of infidelity during the course of treatment (see Glass, 2002, pp. 488–489 for this and all the following figures). In one survey, involving 316 married couples, 23% of the wives and 45% of the husbands had been unfaithful, while 57% of the couples had been impacted by an extramarital involvement. However, the stereotypical belief that the principal reason for having an affair is that the involved partner is unhappy in the marriage turns out to be quite misleading. In a nonclinical survey, 56% of married men and 34% of married women who have had affairs reported that they were happily married. This reality has important ramifications for the clinical treatment of affairs, because it belies the established assumption (on the part of some clinicians and treatment models) that problems in the marriage are the principal explanation for why one spouse has an affair.

In this chapter, I provide a synopsis of the central issues in understanding infidelity and treating affairs as well as a foundation for understanding why RE therapy represents an ideal therapeutic framework for the treatment of an affair. In chapter 16, three clinical vignettes that demonstrate how versatile the RE therapy model is in the treatment of affairs. These vignettes will illustrate various phases of the RE therapy process as well as a variety of therapist interventions that permit a deepening of the therapy process. The final vignette will also reinforce the centrality of the RE dialogue process as the principal vehicle for facilitating healing from the trauma of an affair and reconciliation between the partners.

Utilizing the Literature on the Treatment of Affairs

There are a variety of resources available on affairs, from self-help books written by the survivor of an affair (Vaughn, 1998), a psychologist (Spring, 1996), and a psychiatrist (Pittman, 1989) to treatment manuals written by mental health professionals (Brown, 1991; Strean, 2000). Perhaps the best integrative statement on the phenomenon of infidelity and the treatment of affairs is by the late Shirley Glass (2000, 2002, 2003), who brought 30 years of groundbreaking research and clinical experience to her formulation of a model for the treatment of affairs. The following introduction to the treatment of affairs is informed by Glass's framework, but also includes references to the work of other authors, as well as my own insights and formulations. In addition, Spring's latest book, *How Can I Forgive You? The Courage to Forgive, the Freedom Not To* (2004), is an important contribution to the literature and strikes, to my mind, just the right note on this very sensitive and important subject.

Terminological Considerations

There are differences among various writers with regard to the terminology used to describe the three parties to an affair: the two married spouses (or nonmarried but ostensibly monogamous partners) and the third party. Spring (1996) recognizes the difficulty of potential "moral righteousness" in the use of certain terms to describe one party or the other. For this reason, she avoids the use of the terms *betrayed partner,* and *betrayer,* and prefers the use of the term *hurt partner* to designate the noninvolved person and the term *unfaithful partner* to designate the person who is involved in an affair. I share Spring's concern about the undesirable potential for implicit moralizing in the use of certain terms, but to my mind the term *unfaithful partner* carries precisely that undesirable connotation. On the other hand, I believe the term *betrayed partner* accurately captures a core component of the experience of the noninvolved partner, namely, the experience of feeling betrayed. I thus regard the term *betrayed partner* to be both a natural and legitimate term. Furthermore, this term can be used to capture the subjective experience of the noninvolved party without also having to use the term *betrayer* to designate the involved *partner*. On this latter point I agree with Spring. I thus concur with Glass's terminological choices of either *hurt partner* or *betrayed partner* to designate the noninvolved person, *involved partner* to designate the person who has had or is having an affair or "extramarital involvement," and *affair partner* to designate the third party who is sexually entangled with the involved *partner*.

For the sake of linguistic convenience, general references to *marriage* in the rest of this chapter and the following chapter will also be understood to include nonmarital but ostensibly monogamous committed relationships, and *spouse* will also be understood to include nonmarried but ostensibly committed partners. Finally, it should be acknowledged and understood that the phenomenon of infidelity and the emotional difficulties engendered by an affair apply as much to gay and lesbian relationships as they do to heterosexual relationships. In my experience, the underlying emotional dynamics are identical, even while allowing for distinctive elements in gay and lesbian relationships.

Thematic Considerations in Understanding and Treating Affairs

While it lies beyond the scope of this chapter to provide a comprehensive theoretical statement concerning the treatment of affairs (which is effectively presented by Glass, 2002), I do want to provide an integrative overview of some of the essential thematic considerations involved. Like the field of domestic violence, the field of infidelity treatment has been characterized by a kind of ideological division between a moral perspective on the one hand versus a psychological or systems based perspective on the other. I believe either position alone is inadequate and creates difficulties for the treatment of infidelity. The difficulty of a moral perspective alone is that it risks becoming moralistic, and therefore clinically counterproductive. The risk of a purely systems-based approach is that it runs the dual risk of absolving the involved partner of *existential* responsibility for choices made while indirectly blaming the betrayed partner for the involved partner's choice to have an affair.

The challenge, then, is to find the appropriate balance between what I would term an assumption of responsibility framework and a contributing factor framework. The goal must be to hold in balance a framework that stresses individual existential responsibility for choices made, with a perspective that acknowledges that both partners likely contributed to the conditions and issues in the marriage that constituted the backdrop to the affair. The practical clinical challenge is to balance the need to do affair recovery work with the need to work on other major issues in the marriage. The additional clinical challenge is to balance empathy for the hurt partner with empathy for the involved partner. What follows is my attempt at integrating an assumption of responsibility framework with a contributing factor framework relative to the established literature on the treatment of infidelity.

1. Once an affair enters into the equation of issues in a marriage, it changes the equation. The emotional wounds brought about by an affair tend to dwarf any other issues in the marriage, and therefore usually become the number one issue in the marriage, at least for the hurt partner.

2. The feeling of betrayal is at the core of the hurt partner's emotional experience relative to the spouse's involvement in an affair (see Brown, 1991). The reason the theme of betrayal is so central to the experience of infidelity is that it involves "a breach of trust" (Pittman, 1995, p. 295). This is reinforced by the hurt partner often feeling more upset about the lies and deceit involved in an affair than by the sexual involvement per se.

3. As a consequence, a profound sense of loss also dominates the betrayed partner's emotional experience. The losses experienced include a loss of innocence and confidence about the marriage, a loss of previously taken for granted emotional safety, and, most significantly, a loss of the ability to trust (Glass, 2002, p. 489).

4. The revelation of an affair is often experienced by the hurt partner as a kind of trauma, with the hurt partner not infrequently displaying a number of the symptoms characteristic of posttraumatic stress disorder. As Glass observes, "Disclosure of infidelity evokes a traumatic reaction because … the basic assumptions about the committed relationship … are shattered" (2002, p. 489). It can be normalizing and reassuring for the hurt partner to understand his or her experience in terms of a traumatic response to the affair. It can also be helpful to the involved partner to have the hurt partner's experience explained in these terms.

5. Healing from an affair cannot begin until all contact with the affair partner has been definitively terminated (or rigorously protected against if continued professional contact is unavoidable). Healing can be facilitated by the involved partner communicating forcefully and unambiguously to the affair partner that the affair is over and that the involved partner has recommitted to the marriage (see Spring, 1996, p. 178). This can be done in the presence of the betrayed partner by telephone or by a letter written by the involved partner and edited and mailed by the betrayed partner.

6. It is essential to the healing process of the hurt partner and the marriage that the affair be talked about. As Spring observes (1996, p. 167), there is "no substitute for talking out [the] pain and dissatisfaction, and being listened to and understood" by the involved partner. The necessity of talking about the affair must be especially stressed to the involved partner, who often is motivated by the desire (and impatience) to forget about and "just get past" the affair. Talking about the affair includes the involved partner answering the betrayed partner's questions about the affair, the hurt partner talking about the emotional devastation experienced in the wake of the affair, the hurt partner coming to *feel* understood by the involved partner with regard to the emotional devastation caused by the affair, and the involved partner and hurt partner individually and together defining the meaning of the affair.

7. One implication of the preceding point is that the experience of the hurt partner constitutes the primary reference point for the couple's therapeutic work, at least initially. This means, in particular, that the involved partner must be able to come to see the affair from the perspective of the hurt partner.

8. On the other hand, room must also be found for the experience and feelings of the involved partner. This may include giving the involved partner the space to come to terms with or grieve the loss of the affair. The latter may best be accomplished through individual sessions with the involved partner, in part to spare the hurt partner the pain of hearing the involved partner's feelings for the affair partner.

9. The betrayed partner is the judge of how much detail about the affair is to be revealed by the involved partner, and the involved partner needs to be helped to understand that it is important that he or she share whatever information the hurt partner desires (Glass, 2002, p. 501).

10. On the other hand, the therapist may have to help the betrayed partner overcome any obsessive preoccupation with details of the affair that gets in the way of the hurt partner's ability to move past the fact of the affair (see Brown, 1991; Glass, 2002; Spring, 1996). An obsessive preoccupation with the details of the affair, coupled with intense and persistent anger, may represent a defense mechanism that keeps the hurt partner from being truly in touch with deeper feelings of pain, fear, and sadness.

11. An essential step and ingredient in a couple's healing process is that the involved partner must face and accept exclusive responsibility

for the decision to have the affair (Glass, 2002). While there may indeed have been preexisting issues in the marriage that contributed to the involved partner's unhappiness and that deserve to be addressed as part of the therapy in order to improve the quality of the marital relationship, the involved partner needs to be helped to understand that no preexisting issues can be used as an excuse to justify the decision to have the affair. The responsibility for the decision to have an affair belongs exclusively to the partner who made that decision, and owning that responsibility is both an essential part of the involved partner's coming to terms with having had the affair and a prerequisite to the hurt partner's healing relative to the affair. The involved partner's willingness and ability to take ownership of and assume exclusive responsibility for the decision to have the affair may be diagnostic for the possibility of healing between the couple and the survivability of the marriage.

12. As a corollary, it is extremely important that the therapist not slip into scapegoating the hurt partner by implying that he or she is indirectly responsible for the affair because there were preexisting issues in the marriage. This would amount to a retraumatization of the hurt partner by the therapist in that he or she is essentially being blamed for the action of the partner who chose to have an affair. That there are other issues in the marriage that deserve to be addressed is virtually inevitable, and this too needs to be acknowledged in the therapy. However, those issues need to be kept separate from the issue of the involved partner assuming exclusive responsibility for the decision to have an affair, even in the face of unhappiness in the marriage. As Glass observes (2002, p. 494), "Preexisting relationship problems should be addressed without blaming the betrayed partner for the involved partner's decision to have an extramarital relationship."

13. Not only does the hurt partner need to hear an unambiguous assumption of individual responsibility by the involved partner for the decision to have the affair, but the hurt partner also needs to hear genuine feelings of regret and remorse from the involved partner with regard to the emotional pain caused to the hurt partner by the affair.

14. The involved partner also needs to be helped to understand that the hurt partner's healing process will take a considerable period of time (of no predictable duration). The involved partner will therefore need to develop a high level of patience with the hurt partner's questions and a high level of tolerance and acceptance of the hurt

partner's unpredictable eruptions of emotion relating to the affair. Any number of factors, or combination of factors, can result in the hurt partner having spontaneous and emotionally overwhelming feelings relating to the affair. It is the job of the involved partner to genuinely connect and empathize with the hurt partner's pain in order to facilitate the hurt partner's healing process. The involved partner's willingness and ability to do this may also be diagnostic for the possibility of healing between the couple and the survivability of the marriage.

15. The involved partner also needs to be helped to understand that he or she will have to reearn the hurt partner's trust gradually, and that this will necessarily entail his or her exhibiting impeccable behavior with regard to respecting the sensitivities of the hurt partner. Reearning trust will also involve erecting and maintaining solid emotional and sexual boundaries with members of the opposite sex (or of the same sex in a gay or lesbian relationship), thereby giving the hurt partner no reason to have suspicions about the involved partner's behavior. The specific terms for reearning trust need to be negotiated between the couple.

16. Another important element of the involved partner's reearning trust will entail being able to define and explain what it was about the involved partner, including personal vulnerabilities, that allowed him or her to make the decision to have the affair (Glass, 2002, pp. 498–499). This is important for two reasons: first, to help the involved partner be able to erect the necessary emotional boundaries against any possible future affair and second, as a consequence, to give the hurt partner confidence that another affair is unlikely to happen.

17. It is important that the therapist help both partners see the opportunities for healing relative to the affair and for strengthening the relationship in light of and despite the affair. Opening (or reopening) channels of communication is an essential part of the healing process, as is dealing with whatever other marital issues may need to be addressed and learning new and more effective ways of addressing interpersonal problems in the marriage.

18. As part of this process, the therapist may need to help the hurt partner examine his or her role and contribution to issues in the marriage other than the affair. While preexisting issues in the marriage do not excuse the decision of the involved partner to have an affair, they do constitute part of the context within which the affair happened. The hurt partner may need to be helped to see

that healing in the relationship will of necessity also involve an opportunity for the involved partner to have his or her concerns about the marriage addressed.

19. The couple may be regarded as moving toward closure with regard to the affair when the hurt partner can begin to think in terms of forgiveness of the involved partner or to accept of the reality of the affair as part of the fabric of the marriage, when some measure of trust and emotional safety have been reestablished, and when the couple together can begin to focus more on the marriage than on the affair. Continued work on other issues in the marriage will almost certainly be necessary.

20. The therapist must be careful not to retraumatize the hurt partner by insisting that forgiveness is a prerequisite to that person's healing. In addition to being disrespectful of the hurt partner's feelings and experience, this would represent what Spring (2004) refers to as "cheap forgiveness," where the hurt partner grants a pardon to the involved partner without the hurt partner coming to terms with his or her pain and regardless of the involved partner's meaningful participation in the healing process.

21. In cases where the involved partner declines to apologize or become meaningfully involved in the hurt partner's healing process (as described above), the hurt partner may choose to forego forgiveness but nonetheless undertake an alternative, internal path to healing called acceptance. As Spring suggests, the "goal is not necessarily forgiveness. [The] goal is emotional resolution" (2004, p. 114). Acceptance involves the hurt partner processing the emotional pain of the affair and coming to terms with it so that he or she can move on in life without the emotionally debilitating effects of unresolved negative feelings. Acceptance may or may not result in reconciliation, at the discretion of the hurt party.

22. In those cases where the involved partner is apologetic and willing to participate in the hurt partner's emotional healing process in a meaningful way, including reearning trust, but the hurt partner refuses to forgive, then the therapist may need to work with the hurt party to help uncover what is blocking that person from participating in a process of mutual healing and reconciliation (see Spring, 2004).

23. The ideal resolution of an affair when both partners are desirous of authentic emotional reconciliation is what Spring (2004) refers to as "genuine forgiveness." This involves the partner who had the affair making a sincere apology, undertaking genuine acts of contrition

(including being willing to connect with the pain of the hurt partner), and making a sustained effort at reearning trust (along the lines described above). It also involves the hurt partner working to let go of the pain of the affair and forgiving the involved partner in response to an apology and genuine acts of emotional repair and attempts to reearn trust. Genuine forgiveness thus involves a transactional process where both partners are committed to the task of healing and the goal of reconciliation.

Maintaining the Primacy of Joint Sessions

In conducting therapy relative to the treatment of an affair, it is important to maintain the primacy of conjoint sessions in those cases where the couple is committed to rebuilding their marriage.[1] There is a role for individual sessions in these cases, both as part of the clinical intake and on an as needed basis in response to the unique needs of either the hurt partner or the involved partner. Individual sessions may be deemed appropriate for a number of reasons: when emotional support needs to be provided to one or both partners; when the betrayed partner's rage is so strong that it risks overwhelming the involved partner; when the involved partner needs to process grief over the loss of the affair partner; or when either partner would benefit from private coaching—in the case of the hurt partner, to help move past preoccupation with the affair and, in the case of the involved partner, to help that person be more responsive to the needs of the hurt partner (Glass, 2002, p. 493).

On balance, however, individual sessions should be ancillary to and in support of the couple's sessions, which ought to be the primary focus of the therapy process. The reason is that an affair represents an "interpersonal trauma" (Glass's term). The implication is that healing from an affair must take place on an interpersonal basis, involving both spouses. In the long run, this can be accomplished only by means of the couple engaging directly with one another over the affair and whatever other issues in the marriage need to be addressed and resolved in order for the couple to put their marriage back on a positive footing. I believe the RE dialogue process provides the ideal context within which this interpersonal work can be accomplished.

Moreover, Glass recommends (2002, p. 493), as does RE therapy, that individual issues be explored within the context of couples sessions whenever possible in order "to provide insight and intimacy within the couple." In this context, Glass also warns of the potentially disastrous consequences of either partner having individual therapy with an outside therapist while conducting conjoint therapy in the treatment of an affair. The reason is

272 • Relationship Enhancement Therapy

that the outside therapist may not regard the marriage as the primary client and may undermine the goals of the couples therapy.[2] This confirms the position advocated in this book that in most instances it is preferable for the couples therapist to conduct all levels of the therapeutic intervention when relationship issues are the primary reason for the couple being in therapy. I believe this is most especially true in cases involving the treatment of an affair. In those cases involving an affair in which an outside therapist is involved, Glass notes that coordination of treatment is essential.

RE Therapy as an Ideal Therapeutic Framework for the Treatment of an Affair

I believe there are a number of reasons why RE therapy provides an ideal therapeutic framework for the clinical treatment of an affair. These include:

1. The structure and process of the clinical intake in RE therapy help establish an emotionally safe environment within which both parties can feel nonjudgmentally understood and accepted.
2. The special RE therapy techniques of Laundering and Doublebecoming provide the tools necessary to enable the therapist to shift easily into Crisis Intervention mode whenever emotions become too intense or the normal process of empathizing with the couple fails to yield the desired movement toward "buy-in" to conjoint treatment.
3. The special RE therapy techniques of Becoming and Therapist Troubleshooting provide the therapist with additional tools to deepen the therapy process on the one hand, and to manage it more effectively on the other, either in response to client difficulties encountered in the therapy or because the therapist sees an opportunity to intervene in a manner that will advance the process.
4. RE therapy's Conflict Management skill provides couples in the throws of emotional turmoil surrounding an affair with the tools to effectively manage the intense emotion that otherwise can contribute to escalation and out-of-control verbal fights. RE's approach of a prenegotiated preventative contract to use time-outs to disengage from high-conflict situations is especially helpful here.
5. RE therapy's Expressive skill provides a comprehensive set of guidelines to help both partners express skillfully and subjectively concerning their feelings and concerns. This may be especially helpful to the hurt/betrayed partner who often is struggling with intense

feelings of anger that can easily be turned into vicious personal attacks against the involved partner.

6. RE therapy's intensive training of couples in deep empathy provides both partners with the one tool that is essential to the development of mutual understanding and compassion. This may be especially important in that the hurt partner *feeling* understood by the involved partner with regard to the anger, pain, sadness, and fear experienced relative to the affair is an essential element of the healing process in recovering from the trauma of an affair.

7. RE therapy's specialized Identification Mode of empathy is an ideal tool to further deepen the involved partner's ability to connect with the hurt partner's pain and suffering, especially when the involved partner may be having difficulty doing so.

8. The RE dialogue process provides the ideal context within which the really hard work of talking about the affair and other issues in the marriage can be undertaken and successfully accomplished. Moreover, by incorporating the Expressive and Empathic skills into its very fabric, the RE dialogue process creates precisely the "process for compassionate communication" that Glass (2002, p. 492) identifies as one of the therapist's most important goals in creating a framework within which the couple can address the "interpersonal trauma" of the affair.

9. RE therapy's focus on teaching core relationship skills that enable couples not just to address their difficult issues in therapy but also to restructure their basic patterns of relating to one another and communicating on an ongoing basis, provides couples with the positive experience, and therefore the confidence, that they can indeed have a more intimate and more satisfying relationship than they have had in the past.

10. RE therapy's focus on the value of the relationship as an entity that transcends either individual provides a framework within which the ideal goal of reconciliation can be fostered in a respectful manner.

11. Glass's description of what is necessary for conducting effective couples therapy when the primary issue is an affair virtually reads as a precis for everything that RE therapy advocates and implements as a matter of course when conducting couples therapy. For example, Glass states that "improving communication skills is… essential…. The betrayed partner practices expressing pain without attacking, and the involved partner practices empathic listening" (2002, p. 497). She continues by observing that such "compassionate

communication leads to a healing process" between the couple. These two statements represent a perfect description of the two core skills of the RE therapy process and its expected outcome in the form of compassion and healing.

For all these reasons, RE therapy provides an ideal therapeutic framework for the clinical treatment of an affair. In the next chapter we turn our attention to three clinical vignettes that illustrate the versatility and clinical efficacy of RE therapy as a modality for treating affairs.

Note

1. As Glass observes (2002, p. 492), conjoint therapy may also be undertaken to help a couple "obtain closure about the breakdown of their relationship" in the case of "Separation" therapy, or to resolve ambivalence "where one or both partners cannot decide whether they want to stay or leave" in the case of "Ambivalence" therapy. On the other hand, Glass observes (2002, p. 491) that conjoint treatment is contraindicated whenever there is an extramarital involvement that is not known to the noninvolved partner. The implication of Glass's observation is that it would be unethical for a therapist to collude with an involved partner by keeping an affair a secret while conducting couples therapy.
2. Doherty (2002) points to the danger of how a therapist can subvert a marriage by an unacknowledged commitment to the autonomy of the individual as the primary value. Doherty refers to this as "therapist-assisted marital suicide."

CHAPTER **16**
Clinical Examples of the Application of RE Therapy to the Treatment of Affairs

The three clinical vignettes in this chapter are designed to provide an opportunity to observe how the wide-ranging repertoire of client skills and therapist interventions available within the RE therapy model can be brought effectively to bear in the treatment of affairs. They also have been selected to provide a diversity of illustrative material covering different phases of the RE therapy process. Special attention will be paid throughout to the therapist's thought process during a session, including explaining the rationale for the intervention(s) made. The first two vignettes come from the same case. The first vignette focuses on the therapist's calculated use of empathy to help sharpen the core issue in the relationship during a clinical intake with the couple. The challenge here is to do so in a manner that does not alienate either person, because that would be to run an all too high risk of a premature termination to the therapy, obviously an undesirable outcome. The second vignette, involving the same couple, illustrates the use of Therapist Troubleshooting during the individual interview with the involved partner (as part of the clinical intake). The decision to resort to Therapist Troubleshooting was for the purpose of educating the involved partner about the seriousness of the work ahead and what he could expect to have to do in order for the therapy, and the marriage, to have a positive outcome.

The final vignette involves another couple and presents a more extended account of the first 9 months of the couples therapy. This will enable the reader to observe an actual therapy process unfold in its thematic richness and complexity. The vignette also illustrates the use of individual therapy sessions. These are used as an adjunct to the couples therapy sessions. However, the primacy of the couple's dialogues is still preserved as the principal means by which the trauma of the affair is worked through and emotional healing is facilitated. Collectively, I hope these vignettes demonstrate the versatility of the RE therapy process in the treatment of affairs, and the depths to which it can take couples by virtue of it creating a structure through which partners can safely encounter each other and address their issues for the purpose of healing their relationship.

Clinical Vignette 4: Using Empathy to Help Sharpen the Core Issue in the Relationship During a Clinical Intake

In this clinical vignette we have an example of how the therapist can use empathy during a first session to help sharpen the core issue in the relationship and represent one partner with such clarity that it leaves the other partner with absolutely no doubt as to what is at stake. This pursuit of therapeutic "truth" is carefully balanced, however, by the therapist's constant effort to identify and verbalize underlying positive feelings that motivate either or both partners (see chapter 4, pp. 79–82, for a fuller discussion). It also is balanced by the therapist's careful and respectful empathy toward the partner who either may be more on the fence with regard to the relationship or who may be in need of being helped to understand what is at stake in the relationship.

The process of sharpening the core issue in the relationship via the therapist's empathy will tend to lead to one of two results. One possibility is that it will bring one partner or both to face more openly and directly the issue(s) that need to be faced for healing to be possible in the relationship. Alternatively, the one partner is brought to the point of being helped to see that the other partner is not acting in good faith for the sake of healing in the relationship. In the latter case, that person is then empowered to make his or her own decision about the future viability of the relationship. While the general hope is that the sharpening of the core relationship issues will in the end facilitate the deepened work that will enable a couple to reconcile their relationship, that will not always be the case. However, I regard either to be a legitimate outcome of how empathy can be used to help sharpen a core relationship issue if in the process the couple is brought to a place of truth for themselves about their relationship. As always, the ultimate decision about the relationship remains in the hands of the couple.

I received the initial phone call from the wife. Vicky called for marital therapy because she was deeply concerned about the state of her marriage and whether it could survive. She recounted that they had been married for 4 years; her husband had been involved in at least one affair while she was pregnant with their first child (they had a second child, and she had an older child from a previous relationship). They had separated for 1 year, and had been back together for about 4 months. They had trouble communicating, and there were severe trust issues because, from her point of view, he was continuing his pattern of lying that was all too reminiscent of when he had been having the affair(s). They were of different religious faiths, birth control had been an issue between them, and they had ended their previous attempt at marital counseling following the first therapy session because the therapist commented to the husband that he might have a sex addiction.

At the first session with the couple, Vicky asked her husband Dave to begin after I structured the session in the standard manner (see chapter 4). Dave's initial sharing was very brief:

> We are the product of two young people who got married because of a pregnancy and who didn't know one another, and we've grown apart. I acknowledge that things have happened that weren't always right.

I empathized briefly to the effect that they didn't know one another very well when they got married; that it was a marriage essentially forced by circumstances rather than being rooted in love and commitment; that their bonds were not strong to begin with, and they had only grown even more distant; and that he had done some things about which he wasn't necessarily very proud. He nodded in agreement with my empathy. After waiting to give him a chance to continue, I inquired whether there was more he'd like to add, but he indicated there was not.

Here was my internal process at this point in the intake. I was very purposeful in ending my initial empathy to the husband with the admittedly innocuous phrase that he "had done some things about which [he wasn't] necessarily very proud." I did so because I wanted to calibrate my empathy in a way that would not cause him to check out emotionally or abandon the therapy. It could be said, from one point of view, that I treated the husband with kid gloves by not explicitly referring to the affair. But the therapist's job is not to score points against one partner or the other. The immediate point is that the husband had not used the term *affair* himself. I knew about the affair, however, from talking to the wife by phone, and it would be reasonable to suppose that he knew that I knew about the affair because I had talked to his wife. However, it was empathically clear to me in the moment that he was feeling narcissistically vulnerable and needed to approach this subject slowly and gingerly. It was my job, as his therapist and theirs, to be respectful of that need. That does not mean, however, that I was letting, or would let, the husband off the hook. The therapist's initial job is to gradually build a therapeutic alliance with each person so that he or she can hear what eventually must be said and must be heard. Given what Vicky had told me on the phone, I was determined not to repeat the previous therapist's mistake and lose the husband before the therapy even had a chance to get underway. As is so often the case, the therapist must exercise good clinical judgment about the timing as well as the content of an intervention. So my choice of phrase at this point in the empathy was designed to match as closely as possible what I empathically sensed the husband was able to tolerate hearing, knowing full well in the back of my mind that I would look for opportunities to push the envelope with him later on. As we shall see, that opportunity presented itself fairly quickly.

Vicky initiated her round of sharing, which began calmly, but gradually became more animated, and finally more emotionally desperate, by correcting what she regarded as a distortion:

> We had been engaged before I got pregnant. I wanted to get married. I felt I could trust him. I had been hurt before, and [broken] trust for me was a deal breaker. Religion had been a big issue between us. He was baptized in the Roman Catholic Church so we could get married, and even went to church with me before we got married. But he stopped going to Mass after we got married. My mother and aunt, both of whom are very religious, did not respond well to that.

I made two mental notes to myself at that point: There's a possible boundary violation issue here, and if there was a boundary violation by members of Vicky's family, it was her responsibility to have addressed that. Vicky continued:

> I began to have concerns about Dave's truthfulness. He started spending time with another female and staying out late. I'd ask him about it, and he lied to me. I knew something was wrong, but he'd keep denying everything, so I doubted myself. Eventually I couldn't stand it anymore and I started checking phone logs and listening to his messages. One day I heard a vulgar voice mail. It was an explicit message from her to him about sex. I confronted him, but he denied it! He got even more deeply involved with her; he was definitely having sex with her now, even if he hadn't been before. Eight months later I asked him to leave.

Vicky paused briefly, then continued, but backtracking in time:

> They met on the job, while on a special assignment. They continued
> seeing one another for a long time, and he continued the lies. I was
> frantic. I was pregnant with our second child. I felt humiliated.
> When the baby was born, he came home for a few weeks. Then he
> left again. He was effectively living with her even then. [*Now she
> was sounding emotionally devastated.*] Eventually I threw him out,
> and he moved in with her. Then the two of them broke up. She
> actually called me up and admitted the affair, but only to taunt me.
> Then he went out of town to a conference and shacked up with yet
> another female, some bartender, but he never told her he was mar-
> ried and had two kids. I found out by talking to her. He even
> denied he was married. He came back and apologized for the affair.
> But he wouldn't admit to shacking up at the conference until I con-
> fronted him with hard facts.
>
> I got into counseling because I feared I was having a nervous
> breakdown over all the lies and the deceit. When it became clear to
> him that I was serious about getting a divorce, then he asked for a
> reconciliation. I agreed, because I didn't really want to get a
> divorce, but I monitored him carefully. He started a new relation-
> ship [with someone else on the job] 1 week later [after he came
> back home]. I knew something was wrong, but I didn't trust my
> gut. He only admitted it when I cornered him. He'll never admit
> anything; he'll keep lying, until he's pushed to the wall and forced
> to admit something because you've got hard facts.
>
> I want the marriage to work, but I'm scared. There's a new vol-
> unteer where he's working, and he's responsible for her. She's pur-
> suing him, but he's not putting boundaries in place with her. He's
> not telling her that he's married and that he's not available. So
> what's going to happen? He'll start kissing her and then f***ing her?
> But then [when I try to say something to him about it] he gets into
> his "You're not going to tell me what to do." I've asked him to trans-
> fer, but he refuses. I can't take this anymore. I'm scared for the kids.
> [*Almost plaintively:*] I want him to stand up for me and our mar-
> riage.

By this time, I was not exactly having warm and fuzzy feelings about the
husband. But I also recalled Vicky's comment on the phone about how
Dave had bolted from the previous therapy because of the therapist's comment about his possibly having a sex addiction. So I was still acutely aware
of not wanting to do or say anything that would result in Dave bolting

from therapy yet again, because I was not likely to be able to help them as a couple, given the severity of the situation, if he were to bolt. I also reminded myself of one of my most important couples therapy mantras: No matter how seemingly horrible the one person's behavior appears to be on the basis of the other person's account, it is vitally important that I—as a therapist—suspend judgment, keep an open mind, and not close the door to being available empathically to the second person. This attitude is important, both because of the human penchant for presenting things in a singularly self-serving manner, and because there always are two sides to every story, and I must remain open to hearing both sides if I am to do my job as a couples therapist. I also reminded myself of my firm conviction that no matter how seemingly bad a relationship or marriage might be, it's really not my place, ethically speaking, to pronounce that this marriage is dead upon arrival, especially when one partner (Vicky) is still emotionally invested in the possibility of preserving the marriage.

On the other hand, I was also quite well aware of not wanting Vicky to perpetuate her place of self-disempowerment and of my needing to help her say to Dave what I believed empathically she was wanting to say to him, though at the moment she was unable to say directly for herself because of her inner turmoil. Stated differently, I wanted to be certain, through my empathy, to deliver a message on Vicky's behalf that would not mince any words and would delineate what was at stake with such clarity that it would minimize and ideally eliminate any potential wiggle room for Dave to skirt the fundamental issues. I sometimes frame this in my mind as using empathy to "force the issue" by framing things with such clarity that it cuts off emotional escape routes that would only serve to deflect the issue. However, even here, I had to find a way to state things in such a way that I did not alienate Dave, and thereby again run the risk of driving him away from the therapy. Instead, it was more in the nature of finding that narrow path where, in effect, I could help Vicky hold Dave accountable for his behavior in such a manner that, regardless of how he responded, the responsibility for the outcome would clearly fall on his shoulders in that he would be the person who was making the choice. This is no easy task, but it's an important one for the therapist to accomplish. I spontaneously empathized with Vicky in the following way, but note that my empathy repeats little of what she actually said and instead reaches down to the deep underlying layers of her emotion and desire:

> You're in a lot of pain over all of this, and there have been times when you've been close to despair. You want to find a way to save your marriage [*stating an underlying positive*], but you simply can't go on with the way things have been [*effectively drawing a line in the*

sand on Vicky's behalf]. You need to be able to trust your husband, but for that to happen, the lies have got to stop. And his behavior is going to have to change, in some pretty radical ways. And if he's not willing to do that, then this marriage cannot survive. You've been emotionally devastated by Dave's deceitfulness [*a pointed word, deliberately chosen*] and his behavior, and, worse, you feel humiliated. After everything you've been through, you need to have peace of mind. You can't continue worrying about whether Dave is being faithful to you. [*In what follows, I am indirectly talking to Dave while nonetheless authentically empathizing with Vicky in the form of reading between the lines.*] You need for Dave to put up clear boundaries with his female colleagues so that there is absolutely no doubt in their minds about his intentions to remain faithful to you. And then you need for him to follow through and maintain clear boundaries at all times. You also need for him to be willing to be completely transparent in his behavior and to be willing to be held accountable for his behavior, without his reacting defensively. You need to know that he's willing to put your emotional needs above his own at this point, and you need to know that he recognizes that he is going to have to reearn your trust. You want Dave to know that you want this marriage to continue [*another underlying positive*], but it can't continue if his choices and his behavior continue the way they've been [*drawing another line in the sand*]. You need openness and transparency, and you need to feel safe. You're letting Dave know what your needs are in all of this. The rest is up to him. It's his choice.

With these last two statements, I am forcefully emphasizing Dave's responsibility for his decisions in all of this. I did not know how Dave would respond to this empathic representation of Vicky, though I was perfectly willing for the chips to fall where they may. By this I mean that one way or the other Vicky would learn what she needed to know: either that Dave was willing to rise to the challenge and engage with the therapy on truly meaningful terms, or that he was unable or unwilling to be responsive to her emotional needs, at which point she could begin to come to terms for herself with the almost certain end to the marriage. And in saying this, I was absolutely convinced *empathically* that Vicky also was prepared to allow the chips to fall where they may, as difficult as it would be for her if Dave did not rise to the challenge of meeting her emotional needs, because she truly was incapable emotionally of things continuing the way they had been. It was clear to me, empathically, that she had come to the point where something had to give, either his behavior or the marriage, and so I did not hesitate to represent her to her husband in the way I did. So, from one point of view, it could be said that I "forced the issue," while from another point of view I simply represented Vicky empathically in a manner that authentically captured both her complex dilemma and her determination to find resolution, one way or the other.

As already stated, I did not know how Dave would respond. His initial response did not engender a lot of confidence in that it was imbued with a lot of the typical defensiveness on the part of a person who has been involved in an affair. But even this response provided me with another opportunity to choose an intervention, in this case Therapist Trouble-shooting, to respond to what I experienced as his less than open acknowledgment of his role in the problem. Dave responded:

> I know I've done some bad things, but there was a context within which it happened. I told her before the pregnancy we should end the relationship because of differences about religion and finances. Then she got pregnant and all the other issues disappeared. We never had a strong relationship. It wasn't great to come home. There was constant bickering between us, or her ex was a problem. The affair happened in the context of my not getting my needs met. Also, her mother's pushiness on religion drove me away. We can try to fix this, but there's got to be some give and take. [*Then, with a touch of defiance in his tone:*] I don't want to change for her, but for me.

Dave's reference to the "context" within which the affair happened had both a legitimate and a shadow side to it. On the one hand, it was legitimate for him to point to other issues in the marriage that were of concern to him and constituted part of the backdrop to the affair. On the other hand, he was implicitly justifying his affair because his needs were not getting met. The latter did not bother me much because I recognized that there would be plenty of opportunity at some point in the therapy to address the statement's implicit denial and abdication of responsibility for having had the affair. Indeed, that often is a central part of the therapy work in cases involving an affair. However, his final statement about not wanting to change for her, but only for himself, did concern me because of its implication that the relationship was not important and did not deserve consideration on its own terms. I wanted to find a way to address that, but I also recognized that I first needed to empathize with what he had said, especially because he was now beginning to open up relative to his first statement. So I empathized in the following way:

You recognize that your having the affair has had really negative consequences on your marriage. But you'd also like me to know that there were some other complicated issues between the two of you before the affair happened. You didn't have the best of relationships to begin with, and you had even suggested ending the relationship.

Dave interjected, "But she wouldn't hear of it." I continued:

But then she got pregnant, and everything else seemed to go by the board. Yet, you weren't really happy. There was a lot of fighting, and her mother really pushed your buttons about the religion issue. You didn't feel respected by her about that. You're open to working on the marriage, and recognize that there's a lot of pain and hurt that needs to be healed, but you also want it to be clear that you've got some issues in this marriage as well, and you want to have an opportunity to have those issues addressed.

Dave responded, "Yes, that's right."

It appeared that I had succeeded in establishing an empathic connection with Dave in a manner that left him feeling understood by me, and he appeared to be in a less defensive and more receptive posture (which is what good empathy should accomplish). So I decided that I would risk challenging his statement about not being willing to change for Vicky but only for himself. This represents, under the rubric of Therapist Troubleshooting, a decision by the therapist to take the initiative to address a concern of perceived relevance to the therapy. But in choosing to challenge Dave's statement, I knew that I must use good Expressive skills myself in order not to leave Dave feeling attacked by me, because I knew that if I were to do that I would be virtually certain to lose him the same way the previous therapist lost him when she in effect accused him of being a sex addict. So I chose my words very carefully, but nonetheless made the point I wanted to make in terms of challenging the assumption behind his statement.

"So, you're feeling understood by me?" I asked. Dave responded, "Yes." I continued, "I'd like to make an observation, if that's OK with you." Dave nodded and said, "OK." I went on to say:

I'm a bit troubled by your statement about not wanting to change for Vicky, but only for yourself. Now, I recognize that statement can be taken in two different ways [*giving him the benefit of the doubt*]. On the one hand, it can be taken to mean that you are primarily motivated to want to change for yourself, independent of the fact that Vicky is your wife. [*In addition to my genuinely believing that, my statement was also designed to convey additional empathy to Dave so that he would continue to feel empathized with by me.*] And that makes sense to me. [*This statement represents a form of validation.*] On the other hand, that statement could also be taken to mean that you're not interested in changing anything that Vicky might be interested in you changing. I'm not assuming that's what you meant, but it certainly would trouble me if that were what you meant.

Dave responded quite nondefensively and almost in a disarmed manner:

I could see why you would be troubled by that. I see your point, and I agree. I didn't mean to imply that I wouldn't be willing to make changes for her. I know that wouldn't be a good thing.

Given Dave's receptive response, I decided to take things a step further and use this as an opportunity to share my values and perspective about what it means to be in a marriage. I continued:

The reason I wanted to say something about this is that one of the things that I believe is fundamentally important about being married is that each person be open to hearing the complaints of the other person and also be willing to be responsive to those complaints by being willing to make changes that would reduce the other person's painful feelings. Another way I could make the point would be to observe that in any marriage there are actually three entities present, you as an individual, your wife as an individual, and the relationship between the two of you. And from one point of view, the relationship between the two of you takes a certain kind of precedence over either of you as individuals. This is not to say that your feelings and desires, or your wife's, are not important, because they are. But, there will be times, if your marriage is going to be a healthy, happy marriage, when one of you or the other chooses to do something that may not be your first preference but you do it for the sake of your partner and for the sake of your relationship. Does that make sense?

Dave responded, "Yes, it does."

While all the issues had by no means been addressed, I at this point felt as though I had secured what I have previously referred to (in chapter 4) as "buy-in" to the therapy. I felt I had succeeded in two ways. First, I represented Vicky with the strength and clarity that she deserved so that she would have a chance of having her emotional needs met. Second, I established an initial therapeutic alliance with Dave that would lay the foundation for our future work together. In the process, I managed to use empathy to sharpen the core issue in the relationship in a manner that helped define it with clarity while leaving little room for ambiguity as to what was at stake. In addition, by taking the initiative, under the rubric of Therapist Troubleshooting, to address a concern that I had in light of something that Dave had said, I was able to accomplish two further things. First, I was able to address and disarm Dave's defensive posture of defiance, but in a manner that did not leave him feeling attacked and actually helped solidify the therapeutic alliance. Second, I was able to challenge an implicit assumption in Dave's thinking by offering an analysis and a cognitive reframing that permitted him to see the questionable nature of his thinking—or at least the questionable nature of the implications of his statement. In addition, I used the space opened up by Therapist Troubleshooting to do some values teaching in a way that I felt would be supportive of the couple's future work in the therapy. The next vignette continues with my work with Vicky and Dave in the individual interviews.

Clinical Vignette 5: Using Therapist Troubleshooting for the Purpose of Educating the Person Who Had the Affair About What Will Be Required for the Therapy to Be Successful

The framework of Therapist Troubleshooting permits a wide range of potential interventions, allowing the therapist to bring to bear whatever relevant educational or therapeutic resources are available in the therapist's toolbox in order to facilitate and increase the efficacy of the couples therapy. The present vignette, which continues with the same couple, illustrates how this can be done during the individual interview time of the clinical intake for the purpose of laying a more solid foundation for conducting the couples therapy. In particular, it will show how I took an opportunity that became available to do some additional teaching with Dave, this time orienting him to what I believed was important for him to understand about the nature of the issues involved in the therapy given his infidelity, and what he could expect to have to do if he was genuinely interested in healing his wife's emotional devastation and saving his marriage. Whether he would choose to do so would, of course, be entirely up to him.

At the conclusion of the clinical intake, I scheduled a full individual session with each person, as I always do whenever an affair is a major part of the presenting problem. The reason is twofold. First, the hurt partner almost always is in need of an extended opportunity to discharge additional emotion and receive empathy from the therapist. This allows the therapist to solidify the therapeutic alliance with the hurt partner by allowing that person to feel deeply understood about the pain and hurt that has been suffered, as well as the almost universal sense of betrayal that has been experienced. In addition, it provides the therapist with a more ample opportunity to assess the present emotional vulnerability of the hurt partner. It also allows the therapist to begin (very gently) to lay the foundation for helping the hurt partner either to move past the obsessive preoccupation with the details of the affair or to become open to the possibility of healing, both for that person as an individual and, when appropriate, for the marriage. The latter represents another instance of Therapist Troubleshooting, but it also represents one of the most important things that any therapist can do for any client, namely, instill hope.

The second reason for scheduling a full individual session with each person in the context of treating an affair has to do with the involved partner. That is because the involved partner frequently is in some form of denial about fully accepting responsibility for the choice to have an affair as opposed to any of the "reasons" that person might invoke in order to justify having had the affair. It is important that the therapist begin to lay the foundation for challenging this denial and helping the involved partner face and accept full existential responsibility for the choice that person made. This is not necessarily (or even likely) going to be accomplished in one session, but the foundation can be laid in order to facilitate what will be one of the central and continuing themes of the therapy. In addition, the involved partner often is carrying around a high level of defensiveness due to the feeling of being judged for the affair. This defensiveness often translates into resistance to meeting the legitimate emotional needs of the hurt partner, whether it has to do with maintaining good interpersonal boundaries with members of the opposite sex, being willing to be held accountable for one's whereabouts, or taking the initiative to be in contact with the hurt partner during the workday or while traveling. Given these typical forms of resistance, it is important that the therapist begin to explain to the involved partner that the emotional pain from the affair has been so devastating to the hurt partner that the involved partner must be willing to step up to the plate and do more or less whatever it is the hurt partner asks if he or she is genuinely interested in fostering emotional healing for the hurt partner and the marriage. I also always make a point that the hurt partner's sense of betrayal is such that the involved partner has no choice but to face and accept the reality of needing to rebuild and reearn trust, virtually from ground zero—assuming, that is, that the partner who had the affair wants to save the marriage.

In my experience, directly addressing these issues early on in the therapy in an educational or informational mode helps cut through much of the denial and resistance rather quickly. At the same time, this approach recognizes that the hard work of continuing to work through the denial and resistance will inevitably be a significant part of the therapy. This also represents an instance of Therapist Troubleshooting. Of course, the therapist's ability to pull this off successfully will be dependent upon his or her verbal skillfulness in addressing the issues in such a manner that the involved partner's defensiveness is minimally aroused while being made to feel respected by the therapist despite the affair. This last point again illustrates the principle that everything that the therapist does must be in service of the relationship and must be done in a manner that does not arouse feelings that the therapist is taking sides with one partner against the other.

Let us return to Vicky and Dave. Very briefly, my individual session with Vicky (following the standard format outlined in chapter 4), revealed that she had struggled with depression, anxiety, intense crying bouts, and panic attacks at various times over the past several years in the face of Dave's behavior and infidelity. She had been medicated for a time, but was not currently taking medication because things had calmed down for her since Dave's return home 4 months prior. I made a mental note and suggested to her that it would be important for her to self-monitor and that I would check in with her periodically to assess whether or not a consultation for medication might be warranted. (She eventually did go on medication to address her intense anxiety.) She related how she had asked for Dave's cell phone records, and he went off and accused her of having an affair because she played tennis with a mutual male friend. I made a mental note that this constituted a form of emotional abuse and needed to be addressed with Dave. Vicky described both her and Dave's families as "dysfunctional," and herself as "codependent." In addition, her dad had cheated on her mom, and Dave's dad suffered from alcoholism and left Dave's mother. She reported that Dave acknowledged he was acting like his dad. She said he had a habit of saying "mean things" and being "angry and vindictive" toward her. The female bartender he slept with while traveling told her that he was drunk a lot while they were together. Vicky admitted to having slapped him once, though he never hit her.

Sexual intimacy between Dave and Vicky had improved since he moved back home, but she could not shake from her mind the possibility that he was still sleeping with someone else because he was still working in the same place where the affair happened. She did report that he took himself out of a supervisory role with a newer female volunteer that she was uncomfortable with. *One positive sign,* I thought to myself. Because Vicky's speech often was intense and rapid-fire, she spoke most of the time. I therefore focused primarily on simply holding an empathic space for her to say what she needed to say and looked for opportunities to empathize briefly so that she would feel acknowledged and understood. (Patient listening is itself a form of empathy.) At the end, I provided summary empathy and a direct acknowledgment of how much pain she was in and that all she was looking for was peace of mind so that she and Dave could move on with their lives. She said that was correct.

In my individual session with Dave, he confirmed Vicky's depression and panic attacks, but thought they had decreased in frequency. He described himself as a "social drinker" who would have between two and four beers a week. How far to press on something like drinking is a judgment call. I decided in this instance, in light of Vicky's statements, that drinking might be something of an issue, but not necessarily a major issue. I could be proven wrong, but I also had confidence it would come out later in the therapy if it indeed were a major problem. There also is the reality that time is limited, and I had other fish I wanted to fry. He said it was "possible" his dad was an alcoholic. He described Vicky's mother as "obsessed" with religion and with trying to "convert" him and save his soul, which he deeply resented. He reiterated that he and Vicky had a very shaky foundation for their marriage and that, as a result, "even the small problems couldn't be dealt with."

As I had hoped, I still had a decent amount of time left, so after empathizing I decided to begin orienting Dave to what I saw the therapy involving and what I believed would be necessary for him to do if there was to be a chance for healing in the marriage: "If it's OK with you, Dave, I'd like to talk with you about where I see things being with the therapy, the issues, as I see them, and what I believe will need to happen in order for there to be genuine healing both for Vicky and the marriage." Dave appeared to be receptive, and said, "OK," so I continued:

> I recognize that none of this is easy for you [*preemptive empathy, designed to deepen his receptivity*]. I also recognize that there are other issues in the marriage that you deserve to have an opportunity to have addressed [*additional preemptive empathy*]. But as I think you recognize, Vicky is in tremendous pain over you having

had the affair, and the pain is still there, big time. It's almost as though she is having posttraumatic stress disorder–like symptoms; not that she has the full-blown disorder, but she clearly is exhibiting trauma-like symptoms, most especially the anxiety and quasi-obsessive symptoms. She's in shellshock, and it's going to take her quite some time to heal completely from that. Does that make sense to you? [*Dave responded, "Yes."*] And how you respond to her pain and her emotional needs is going to be the single most important factor in whether and how quickly she recovers. Does that make sense? [*Again, Dave responded, "Yes."*] The reality is that both her confidence in herself and her trust in you have been shattered. What that means is that you will need to help rebuild her confidence and you will need to reearn her trust, and that's going to take time, and patience, and consistency on your part. Does that make sense to you? [*Dave responded, "Yes."*]

Part of what that is going to involve is you being very patient with her fears, her doubts, her anxieties, and even her asking you repetitive questions so often that it begins to drive you nuts [*additional preemptive empathy*]. But when she exhibits any of those feelings, or asks you any of those annoying questions, you will need to have the patience of a saint and not react defensively. In order for her to be able to heal from all this, she needs you to be patient and understanding of her need to feel secure. That will mean, for example, that you not try to keep your phone records private and that you make them available to her if she asks. I understand your desire for privacy, and in principle your desire is legitimate [*preemptive empathy*]. Everyone deserves a certain amount of privacy, even in a marriage. But given the affair, you insisting on your right to privacy is untenable if you want to begin to rebuild her trust in you. From this point forward, your behavior will need to be completely transparent and you cannot even allow the appearance of having something to hide. Does that make sense to you? [*Again, Dave responded, "Yes."*]

It also means that it would be better for you not to complain about her putting security software on the computer so that she can track things, because that would simply convey that you don't accept the legitimacy of her fears and anxieties or the legitimacy of her need to ensure your trustworthiness.

At this point Dave spoke up, somewhat in self-defense, and stated that Vicky wanted to have access to all his e-mail accounts but that two of them were organizational accounts and he was prohibited from giving his

290 • Relationship Enhancement Therapy

password to anyone, including her. He also stated, however, that he barely used those accounts and that he understood my point. I acknowledged his point, and continued:

> Then there's another issue altogether, namely, the question of boundaries between you and other females. Vicky told me about you surrendering supervisory responsibility for the new female volunteer. I think that was a very positive thing for you to do and shows that you are capable of being responsive to Vicky's concerns.

This represented a positive acknowledgment and validation of his action. I also took it as a positive sign that Dave heard what I had said to him the previous session about it being important in a marriage that both partners be willing to change in response to the concerns or desires of the other person. However, I also wanted to deliver a direct and unambiguous message to Dave, so I continued as follows:

> But let me very clear about this. When it comes to other females, your behavior will need to be absolutely impeccable, with no wiggle room, and not even the slightest appearance of something amiss that would cause Vicky to have doubts or concerns. Part of what that means is that you will need to put in place and maintain an absolutely solid boundary around the marriage, and put in place and maintain absolutely solid boundaries between yourself and all other females. That means being very clear with them that you are married, that you are committed to your marriage, and that you have no interest in doing anything that would compromise your marriage. You can't control other people's behavior, but you can control your own response and do so in a manner that communicates an absolutely unambiguous message to them about your intentions. Vicky has to be able to have absolute trust in your intentions and your behavior if this marriage is going to have a chance to heal, but it's going to be the consistency and reliability of your behavior that is going to dictate whether she is able to develop that trust and confidence in you that I know you want her to have. [*The last clause conveys preemptive empathy.*] But it's up to you to make it possible for her to develop that trust. [*Dave responded that he understood that.*]
>
> There's one other thing. I realize that you're not keen on the idea of transferring your job to another location [*preemptive empathy*],

and I'm not saying you have to do that. On the other hand, put yourself in Vicky's shoes. Where you are now is the place where you started your affair, and there are all these other females there, and that just makes Vicky feel really vulnerable and scared that it could happen all over again.

Dave chimed in that his changing locations "wouldn't really change anything" because there would be females at any of the other locations where he could work. I acknowledged his point, and continued:

In the end you may not need to change jobs or location, but I would suggest that you not close the door to the possibility. Also, your point only reinforces my earlier points in that it will be your nondefensive patience with Vicky's needs and questions and your absolutely impeccable behavior with other females by you maintaining solid boundaries with them that will make it possible, if anything will, for Vicky to be OK with you not changing locations. But I'd like to remind you of something I suggested last week, namely, that there are times when we do something for the good of the marriage that might go against our own personal preferences. I think the jury is out on this one.

Dave did not say anything, but looked at me with a look that conveyed that he understood what I was saying even if he did not agree. I had no illusions that I had convinced Dave of anything on the question of changing job locations. But I had at least managed to put the issue on the table and planted a seed for further reflection, and I was able to do so in a manner that was clear but left Dave feeling respected and not pressured. Moreover, even if Dave were never to change job locations, my hope was that a larger framework had been created to further reinforce for Dave the importance of his maintaining impeccable boundaries with other females.

This concluded my orientation session with Dave as to how I would like him to understand the issues that were before him and Vicky and what I believed would be necessary for him to do in order for the therapy, and the marriage, to have a successful outcome. The content of what I shared with Dave was rooted in a combination of what the literature reveals about some of the common themes that almost inevitably come up in the treatment of infidelity, and my own clinical experience in helping couples recover from the emotional trauma that follows in the wake of an affair. More to the point, however, this vignette illustrates how the therapist can take the initiative to proactively address some of those common themes, or the particular concerns pertaining to each unique couple, with a view to simultaneously building the therapeutic alliance with each member of the couple and helping to lay the foundation for a more effective therapy process. It also points to the flexibility inherent in the RE therapy model whereby the therapist is permitted to bring to bear to the clinical encounter whatever therapeutic tools or educational resources may be relevant to the therapy in order to facilitate a successful outcome.

Clinical Vignette 6: Using Individual Sessions in Conjunction With Joint Sessions When Treating an Affair

This final clinical vignette accomplishes two things. First, it recounts in summary form the thematic unfolding of a couples therapy process over its first 9 months to enable the reader to get a sense of the texture of an actual therapy case on a more extended basis. Second, this vignette illustrates how individual therapy sessions can be used to complement and reinforce the work of the couples therapy sessions while still maintaining the primacy of the couples sessions that are at the heart of the treatment of an affair in the RE therapy model. One of the defining characteristics of couples therapy is that the couple is the focal point of intervention. This is reinforced, both symbolically and practically, by beginning the therapy process by meeting with the couple together whenever a revealed affair is the main presenting issue for the therapy. This sends its own message that the therapist regards the couple and their relationship as the focal point of intervention, and I never miss an opportunity during a first meeting with a couple to reinforce that point explicitly by commenting on the fact that I have three clients present and that from one point of view the couple's relationship is my primary client. On the other hand, individual sessions with each member of a couple have their own utility, even in the context of couples therapy, and that utility is not limited to the individual time the therapist spends with each person as part of the clinical intake process. Subsequent individual therapy sessions can serve a number of valuable adjunctive purposes to the conjoint sessions. What is important, in such cases, is that the therapist have a clear objective in mind for having individual sessions. In addition, under most circumstances the therapist will schedule an individual session with each member of the couple in order to keep things balanced and in order to gain the perspective of both parties on the status or progress of the therapy.

Elaine and Lewis were a high-powered couple in rather public professions. They had been married approximately 10 years; this was Elaine's second and Lewis's first marriage. Elaine had an adolescent child from her previous marriage and they had one school-aged child together. They sought me out 1 month after Lewis's 2-year affair with a female coworker had been discovered by Elaine. It had many of the hallmarks of work-based affairs described so effectively by Glass (2003). Elaine was devastated. In the initial couple's session, Lewis stated that he wanted the marriage to work better and wanted them to have a fresh beginning. He acknowledged that he had a tendency to shut down emotionally and go into a "bunker." His typical mode was to avoid conflict by disengaging himself (in part because of Elaine's "temper"), but he would remain angry and nothing would get resolved between them. My empathy took the form of reading between the lines by saying that he was committed to rebuilding his marriage following the affair and that he recognized that his typical mode of avoiding conflict was no longer tenable if they were to have a chance to have a healthy relationship and save their marriage. He agreed.

Elaine said she needed to understand what had happened and to find a way to be able to trust again. Following my first empathic acknowledgment of her feelings, in which I used the word *deception* to characterize part of what it was that troubled her so much about the affair, Elaine indicated that she was indeed especially unsettled by the deception involved in her husband's 2-year affair. This illustrates how reading between the lines, in terms of what the therapist is aware that almost anyone in a client's circumstances would feel, enables the therapist to help clients get in touch with another piece of their experience. Elaine finished by stating, "I want to find out why we're together." I empathized with Elaine (once again reading between the lines) that she wanted to understand what made their relationship meaningful, and therefore worth continuing, and that she also needed to understand how Lewis could allow himself to make the choice to have an affair and to engage in deception the way he did, and in the process compromise what she thought they had together. This illustrates how the therapist, in the process of genuinely empathizing with a deeper level of one partner's experience, can simultaneously send an indirect message to the other partner designed to prompt reflection on something the therapist wishes that person to think about. In effect, the process of empathizing provides the therapist, through the careful choice of language and thematic emphasis, an opportunity to teach and educate clients without doing so in a direct manner.

Lewis picked up on the theme of deception and said that he wasn't comfortable with it himself, that, in effect, it was out of character for him. (Elaine concurred.) He then described how the affair "started small" but then grew and "it got beyond me." Initially, for him, it was "just about the sex," but then he got more emotionally involved, somewhat to his own surprise. He referred to the emotional distance in the marriage as part of the backdrop to the affair, but how he wasn't really comfortable with the affair because it would be on again/off again: "I didn't feel good about it while it was happening." After empathizing several times with Lewis, and having previously introduced the notion of deception, I decided to introduce the notion of self-deception as a framework to assist Lewis in thinking further about his own experience with the affair so that he could begin to address for himself how it was that he allowed himself to make the decision to have an affair. (I characterized self-deception as a person allowing his or her moral sensibilities to go on vacation through an extended process of denial and rationalization.) This illustrates the therapist choosing, under the rubric of Therapist Troubleshooting, to engage in teaching or educating a client in a more direct manner in order, in this case, to facilitate the husband's coming to terms with his own choices and behavior.

Both Elaine and Lewis took to the RE dialogue process quite readily, and used it effectively to explore the difficult emotional issues revolving around the affair and their marriage. On the basis of my assessment of all the issues the couple had listed on their Relationship Questionnaires, I proposed that their first dialogue focus on Elaine's concern about Lewis's tendency to "burrow in" in the face of difficult issues and the resulting anger and resentment that he would carry. I selected this particular issue because I thought it had the potential to ease the couple into experiencing the dialogue process while also opening up an area that almost certainly would have significant interplay with the dominant issue of the affair. My selecting and proposing this issue illustrates the therapist's responsibility for administering the RE therapy process in a manner that he or she hopes will increase its benefit to the couple. I was prepared for the couple to propose an alternative issue for their first dialogue (reflecting my desire for a collaborative approach even to the selection of the issue to be dialogued about), but it nonetheless is the therapist's responsibility to have a vision of how the therapy might usefully proceed.

Elaine and Lewis agreed to my proposal, and Elaine proceeded to talk about being frustrated at times with Lewis's tendency to burrow in and avoid issues while at other times she loved his ability to go deep in discussing issues with her, though she did wish he would initiate more of their conversations. For his part, Lewis expressed how much he appreciated his ability to talk with her about things he had never talked about with anyone before. On the other hand, he at times felt that she was not as open to his questions or interests (implying a lack of reciprocity). He also admitted his tendency to "shut down" and his desire to avoid conflict. She closed by indicating how important it was to her that they be able to talk about the affair, and that she needed him to initiate opening a space between them for that to happen.

At the next session, Elaine picked up on Lewis's childhood story (from two sessions prior during their Empathic skill practice) about his father's death when Lewis was a teenager, and his statement that as the oldest male in the household he "had to be the man" and hold everything together for everyone else in the family. Lewis had surmised that this may have left him in a double bind of needing to talk about his father's death but not being able to, and that this may have contributed to his burrowing in tendency. Elaine then observed:

> It seems that my mission in our relationship has been to draw you out of your burrowing in, and you seemed to love that. But you also seemed somewhat confused by that, and not quite comfortable with it. And, yet, you'd also complain about not feeling supported by me. That's confusing to me. I wonder whether your relationship with your mother over your dad's death may have played out in our marriage.

Lewis had been listening intently, and after empathizing responded by saying:

> I need to process all this. [*After a brief pause, he continued:*] I'm fascinated by your observations. My having to empathize slows down my [own] response [to what you said]. I'm intrigued [by what you said].

Lewis's initial response points to one of the important benefits of the dialogue process: that the obligation to first empathize before responding expressively enforces a slowing down of the listener's potential reactivity in a manner that permits a deeper taking-in of what the partner is communicating. This in turn encourages a more reflective response to what had been shared. Lewis went on to say that he never realized the potential long-term impact of his shutting down and his burrowing in around his father's death might have. He also stated that he now recognized for the first time a tension inside himself between his liking being drawn out by Elaine and it going "against the grain," leading him to pull back from her. He then stated that with the affair having happened, he was now wanting to go deeper with Elaine even though it did in some respects feel uncomfortable.

Elaine expressed her pleasure at hearing that, and her fear that once the "crisis" of the affair was over, that he would revert to old patterns. She needed to know that this would not be temporary, but that they would build a new kind of relationship. She stated that for the first time she saw the possibility that Lewis could become her "soul mate," the one thing that she felt had been missing from what otherwise felt to her like a strong relationship. But this prospect also scared her. Lewis empathized, and I modeled for him additional empathy to the effect that the stakes would now be even higher for her emotionally in that there would be even more to lose, because she feared that if he were to have another affair she would be absolutely and irretrievably devastated. Elaine confirmed my reading between the lines. As an Expresser, Lewis indicated that he understood that, he was learning a lot about both of them from this dialogue, and he was intrigued with her thoughts about their becoming soul mates. The session closed with Elaine putting out that she needed to talk about the honesty issue, which led me to remark that we would turn explicitly to the affair next time. These two sessions gave me reason to believe that a good foundation had been laid to enable this couple to begin to tackle the much more difficult and emotionally charged issue of the affair. I felt they had begun to experience both a sense of emotional safety fostered through the RE dialogue process as well as how the process of intimate dialoging could help bring them to a deeper level of engagement and emotional connection.

Over the next 7 months, Elaine and Lewis engaged in intensive (and virtually weekly) sessions devoted to exploring various dimensions of the affair and their marriage. Elaine, for example, talked about her emotional vulnerabilities following the affair and her fear that it could happen again, the latter despite her believing that Lewis was committed to being faithful and to working at rebuilding the marriage. Lewis explored his emotional vulnerabilities, rationalizations, and lack of discipline that allowed him to take the step of entering into an affair. He also talked about his sense of shame for having had the affair, his guilt over the pain it caused Elaine, and his own sense of punishment relative both to the pain he caused her and the uncertainty of the future between them. Elaine talked about her struggle over the part of her that has feelings of wanting him "to pay for his transgression" versus the spiritually inclined part of her that "is trying to ask what do we create positively from this?" They talked about the relationship dynamic of Elaine needing certain things from Lewis emotionally; his either not knowing what she needs because she is not clear about it or feeling overwhelmed by what he experiences as the magnitude of her needs; and, conversely, her feeling as though he is shut down emotionally and not receptive to her needs, specifically, her needing him to make her and their relationship a priority and to take more initiative in that regard.

We worked at helping Elaine feel OK about asking for what she needs and at helping Lewis to not become defensive in response to her expressing her needs (by his not taking them as demands or criticisms) and to be available to her when negative feelings around the affair surface. Elaine communicated her need for reassurance and peace of mind and her need for Lewis to make her a top priority in his life, both emotionally and in terms of day-to-day contact and attending to practical details in their life together. We worked at helping Elaine deal with her own negative feelings when they surfaced, especially when Lewis was not emotionally available and she was feeling all alone with her feelings. Elaine came to see the connection between Lewis's silence (sometimes a function of his introverted nature, sometimes a function of his attempt to protect the relationship by not engaging with Elaine when she was really angry) and her experience as a child of not being able to penetrate her father's "punishing" silence. Together they talked about sex, what it meant to each of them individually, and what it meant to the two of them together as a married couple, including their mutual need to feel wanted and desired by the other person.

My assessment after 6 months was that the couple had fully embraced and were making good use of the RE dialogue process and that, despite some emotional ups and downs, they were making good progress on their issues and with their marriage. Lewis embraced his sole responsibility for the choice to have an affair and the pain that caused Elaine, while Elaine willingly engaged in discussion of other issues in the marriage that constituted the backdrop to the affair, even though at times she found that to be quite difficult emotionally. I had come to have every confidence that this couple was going to make it, despite recognizing that difficult work still lay ahead. Of all the couples I have worked with for whom the main issue was the discovery and trauma of an affair, this couple had, more than any other, taken the opportunity of the affair and the safety engendered by the RE dialogue process to explore deeply both the meaning of the affair and the issues in their marriage with a view to building a new kind of relationship.

Yet, despite their progress, and my confidence, Elaine and Lewis came in one day with Elaine quite despondent and questioning whether they could or should remain married. The warning signs of some potential emotional stuckness in their process had emerged a few sessions earlier (about 6.5 months into the therapy, at the 21st session, and immediately following two sessions focused on sex and emotional intimacy), when Elaine in particular was feeling down and frustrated about the relationship: "I don't know how to deal with the [emotional] aftermath of the affair. You want to move on, but I need you to understand my feelings."

She went on to speak of how unfair everything felt to her and what a "lonely process" it was for her to have to deal with the emotional turmoil of the affair when she wasn't the one who had the affair. So when she heard

Lewis talk of his need to sometimes withdraw in the face of her emotions, she said, "It leaves me feeling abandoned.... When you go behind your wall, I can't reach you. You don't hear me. My pain seems not to get through to you."

After empathizing, Lewis acknowledged that he wished that things could be "more natural" between them, but he insisted, "I am open to your emotional needs with regard to the affair. But I can't know when you're [feeling bad] if you don't tell me."

I observed at the end of that session that we perhaps needed to revisit the issue of Elaine not asking for what she needs. Mentally, I made a note that there may be a need for individual sessions, though I also wanted to see how things would unfold before making such a decision since the general preference would be to work things out through the couple's dialogues if at all possible.

The next session appeared to represent a significant emotional breakthrough. Elaine expressed appreciation to Lewis for his having asked her between sessions how she was feeling about the affair. She went on to observe, however, that when she started to talk about the affair, she could "see the wall go up." She then exclaimed that, "It's exhausting for me to do most of the emotional lifting for both of us." Elaine then explicitly asked Lewis to make the effort to reach inside himself when the wall goes up and for him to tell her that he loves her when he sees that she's feeling down. In making this request, Elaine was taking the important step (for her) of clearly expressing one of her desires. For his part, Lewis acknowledged that what Elaine said made sense, but that there were times when she brought up the affair and he didn't want to talk about it, especially when Elaine would talk about "her" (the other woman), but, Lewis said, "you would aim your comments at me." This led Elaine to an impassioned statement:

> She tried to take my husband and I don't respect that. She threatened my life with a sustained campaign to steal my husband. So she's not a golden person, nor do I want you to see her that way. Your protectiveness toward her leaves me feeling uneasy.

Reading between the lines, I used Becoming to represent Elaine in the following way: "Your protectiveness toward her feels like a continuing subtle betrayal of our relationship."

Lewis took that line and empathized on his own by saying, "You need me to validate your anger toward her and that it makes sense to me."

To which Elaine responded, "Yes, because otherwise it feels to me like you're still in love with her, or with the image of her."

As Expresser, Lewis stated that Elaine's points were valid and that he hadn't grasped things the way they were expressed that day: "It was not my intention to 'protect' her. You're right. I can't justify what she did, and it should be condemned. I understand what you're saying, and I support it."

Elaine expressed her appreciation to Lewis for saying that, and that it helped her feel that they could move forward. I could not have been happier with this session because Elaine and Lewis were able to touch a very deep part of the trauma of the affair for Elaine, and she experienced some level of healing as a result. This session illustrates one of the common emotional needs of the hurt/betrayed partner, namely, to feel confident that the involved partner no longer is carrying positive feelings of fondness about the affair partner or feelings of longing for the affair.

Scheduling difficulties due to respective vacations resulted in a 1-month gap before the next session took place. Elaine expressed her appreciation for the last session, and commented to Lewis that she could now see that, in having the affair, "you did it not just to me, but to yourself" as well. This had allowed her to begin to think in terms of the possibility of forgiveness, but, she asked, "What does forgiveness look like [in this context]?" Lewis expressed his appreciation at hearing that, but how he still experienced the affair as a burden on his own shoulders:

> The affair is not something I can live down. It's part of the "record" now. It hovers over me, and it informs our relationship. I'm cognizant of it, and it feels like a permanent stain. Also, I'm not someone who wants to hurt anybody. But I hurt you. I feel bad about that. So I don't know what forgiveness looks like either, since current events get experienced through the lens of what transpired [with the affair].

I chose to make two observations. First, that forgiveness does not mean that feelings about the affair won't ever happen again. Second, that forgiveness is not a momentary decision, but an unfolding process. Elaine then expressed that she had "two enemies": first, the affair and her feelings about it, and second, her fear about his resentments toward her. She then spoke of their different "love languages," and how hers involved the receiving of appreciations and his involved physical contact. She also made an insightful observation about the danger they both faced of falling into a pattern of withholding from each other because one or both of them feels deprived. Lewis went on to describe how his love language also involved feeling supported, especially on his special project. Elaine immediately reacted defensively, saying, "I feel I have supported you in ways you don't see," and continued by saying that it felt to her as though there are all kinds of demands that are placed on her and that she is made to feel as though she fails to meet them. We were out of time at this point, so I observed that it would be important next time for us to explore her feelings of defensiveness around Lewis's expression of how he would feel loved by her, and her feelings of inadequacy around that.

At the next session (the 24th), Elaine and Lewis came in with despondent, withdrawn looks on their faces. After they shared partner appreciations, I asked them where they needed to focus today (suspending my normal procedure of picking up from the previous session, out of the recognition that something had happened that they were going to need to have an opportunity to process). Elaine began:

> Our conversation last night was very difficult and leaves me feeling like preparing for things to end between us. It feels like I can't get through to you. There's a wall there. I'm confused. I really need to hear those appreciations from you, and I wonder whether I'd ever hear things like that if we didn't come here. I was in pain after last night.

I decided to model empathy for Lewis, picking up on a theme from previous sessions: "She wishes you had seen her pain and reached out to her sooner."

After empathizing, Lewis stated, "I wish I had, too." He explained how he gets frustrated when their conversations go "down hill" and he can't get her to understand him: "It feels unequal to me sometimes because I'm the one who had the affair. Last night I wanted out of the dialogue, but you wouldn't let me."

I made a mental note that she needed connection and he needed a break from the intensity. I decided to model empathy for Elaine to give to Lewis: "You wish that I wouldn't take your inability to give me what I want in the moment as having larger negative implications for the relationship."

After she gave that piece of empathy, I modeled additional empathy for her (by implicitly following Expressive skill guideline 7):

> You feel it's unfair that I attribute a negative motivation to you in terms of a lack of commitment to being there for me when in the moment you are simply unable to engage in a deep interaction. It makes it harder for me to reach you when I react to you like that.

After empathizing (unenthusiastically), Elaine stated (not altogether skillfully):

I do question your motivation because all I hear are the negatives. You expressed resentment about my going away for 2 weeks after telling me to go. I never hear anything positive about our relationship. I don't get any warmth from you, so I do question your love for me.

Lewis empathized: "You don't feel loved by me when I have nothing positive to say in difficult moments."

I decided to steer Lewis in his role as Expresser in a direction that I believed would be helpful and posed this question as a prompt: "Given what you've heard about Elaine's experience and feelings about you, what do you think you can do to break this negative cycle between the two of you?"

Lewis responded, speaking to Elaine, "I need to take a pause and rise above my defenses and hear your needs."

As we were approaching the end of the session, I decided to make several observations to help clarify things for both of them. I first observed that Elaine was experiencing two levels of pain: Her first level of pain had to do with the affair, and everything that gets stirred up for her emotionally in terms of feeling vulnerable and unsafe, and her second level of pain had to do with her feeling that her pain over the affair was not being seen by Lewis, which then left her feeling alone, abandoned, and angry. I also pointed out that her second level of pain over Lewis not connecting with her pain was actually worse than the pain over the affair itself. I then made a second observation about a deep psychological paradox that was playing out between them: Lewis was wanting, out of a positive motivation of kindness and love, for Elaine to not experience pain over the affair (as evidenced by his not taking the initiative to ask her how she's feeling about it). But this positive motivation was getting in the way of his being able to see and connect with Elaine's pain about the affair, which in turn was preventing him from being with her in her pain, this being what she most needed from him, and what was causing her great despair over her not receiving that from him. The first observation constituted an empathic representation of Elaine's experience, while the second observation represented both an empathic representation and a cognitive reframing of each of their experiences in a way that, I hoped, would allow them to see the complex interaction and paradoxical interconnection of their respective experiences and to place them in as positive a light as possible. I then closed the session by observing that there are times in the couples therapy process where it can be helpful to have an individual session with each partner in order to check in with where he or she is with the process and that this could help give focus to how the couples therapy process might proceed. I then said that it felt to me that this was a useful time for us to do that. They both agreed.

By virtue of scheduling availability, my session with Lewis came first. I felt very confident about the strength of the therapeutic alliance that I had with each client individually as well as with the two of them as a couple. My agenda with Lewis was twofold: First, I genuinely wanted to hear where he was with the therapy process and his own internal work while, second, I also wanted to get his attention around how important it was for Elaine's healing and the healing of the marriage that he make the effort and find a way to connect and be with her in her pain over the affair. I also hoped that I had already set the stage for the latter with the observations that I had made at the close of the previous conjoint session. I began by simply asking him where he was with things. He stated that the last session had been emotionally draining, but that it had helped and had brought them back together some. He also bought Elaine flowers, which she appreciated. He then recounted how tense things had gotten for them the weekend prior when she asked to see his e-mail. Initially he said he was OK with it, but then was bothered by it, especially because it felt to him like it had come out of nowhere. He recognized on some level that she needed reassurance, but it felt like a test to him, so then he decided not to show her his e-mail. Elaine then said, according to Lewis, "Then we have to talk about ending it [the marriage]," and that he "just got angrier" in response. They argued, and eventually he let her see his e-mail. She said that she wondered whether he still loved her. He expressed his frustration over her tendency to "have another agenda behind what she asks," and how frustrating that is to him. "I feel like I'm under a microscope with her. She's suspicious, and there's a lack of trust." He also feared a "slippery slope" and wondered whether his cell phone would come under scrutiny next. I asked him what the big issues were in the marriage independent of the affair. He responded, sex, finances, yelling, their son, and in his opinion, Elaine not maximizing her potential and her feeling bad about that.

After empathizing with some of his feelings, I decided to begin my feedback to him by making observations about some of the things he had said so that, I hoped, he could see things from Elaine's point of view and in terms of the virtual inevitability of certain things happening relative to a process of recovery from an affair. I first explained that in terms of it feeling to him as though her suspiciousness came out of nowhere, that for her it still was as though the affair had happened and been discovered yesterday, and that this was not an unexpected thing to happen for someone recovering from the trauma of an affair. (This aimed to normalize the situation for Lewis.) I continued by observing that this meant that he needed to be prepared for such surges of insecure feelings and that his job was to not react defensively, but to respond in a manner that allowed her to regain a sense of security and confidence, because that would make it easier in the long run for both of them. I then explained that her wondering whether he still loves her was a reflection of her not feeling loved or perhaps even feeling unlovable, and that the challenge for him was again to not react defensively but instead simply to offer her the reassurance she needed.

As for his feeling frustrated over her having another agenda behind the questions she would ask, I explained that this is a common pattern for someone who is feeling distraught because that person is not at all clear about their feelings and what is driving their emotions. I suggested that his job was to place himself in the role of the Empathizer and to read between the lines to decipher what her need in the moment might be. I then asked Lewis to identify with her experience for a moment and to imagine what her core feeling or need might be. He responded, "She needs to feel safe." I said, "Right." I then reiterated an earlier observation by noting that the reservoir of pain is timeless, ever present, and deep, and that it can come out at any time. "It's neither rational, nor irrational," I observed, "but emotional." I continued by noting that what she needed from him was for him to surrender his ego and his pride, to embrace and hold her pain non-defensively, and to accept, through a self-surrender of his ego, that for the sake of her healing and the healing of their marriage, that he would need, metaphorically speaking, "to lay yourself prostrate before her and be willing to be there with her in her pain." I felt I could dare to use such potentially provocative imagery because of the strength of our therapeutic relationship and out of the conviction that powerful images in the long run will have a deeper impact than any string of convincing words will have. Lewis looked at me for a moment in silence, and then responded, "OK, I get it." At that moment I felt that I had accomplished my educational mission with Lewis, and I brought the session to a close. But I also had learned some valuable information from Lewis that would help me in my individual session with Elaine, namely, to talk with her about her feeling unsafe and insecure and her continued feelings of having difficulty trusting Lewis because of the trauma of the affair.

I began my session with Elaine with a simple, "Where are you at emotionally?" Her immediate response was that there had been a significant change in Lewis's behavior since my session with him. "He got your message. He needed to hear it from another male, especially your acknowledgment of his strength, and how it could get in the way." She was referring to my statement in the last couples session when I attributed a positive motivation to Lewis of wanting to protect Elaine from experiencing pain over the affair that effectively left him in a position of not being able to connect with her pain, a statement that Elaine indicated was helpful to her as well. Elaine also reported that Lewis told her about my comment about his needing to lay himself prostrate before her ("I liked that image!" she said in a light-hearted way) so that he could be with her in her pain, and that Lewis indicated that he finally got it in terms of what he needed to do and how he needed to be with her through her healing process. Elaine indicated that they were able to have a meaningful conversation about the big change for him when he got married for the first time in his thirties, and that he talked about his feelings of resentment melting away.

> He's been able to reach out to me several times since his session with you, and he's volunteered that he's sorry for the pain he's caused me. That means a lot to me, that he can say that. He really got the message that his not wanting to hurt me meant that he wasn't able to touch my pain.

I inquired about her asking to see Lewis's e-mail. Elaine responded that she asked to see them because she had experienced Lewis becoming disengaged again, and that reminded her all too much of his disconnection from her while he had been having the affair. "So I needed to make certain that nothing was happening. I couldn't deal with his being emotionally distant."

I acknowledged that made sense to me, and made a mental note to work that into a future couples session for Lewis's edification. I then brought my session with Elaine to a close and expressed my hope and conviction that they would be able to move forward in a positive way from here. Indeed, I truly could not have imagined a better outcome from these two individual sessions, or, from another point of view, from my single session with Lewis. I once again felt confident that this couple "was going to make it."

The couples therapy sessions resumed the following week, and Elaine opened with the following partner appreciation for Lewis:

> This person you are becoming feels different to me. It feels like a shift; there's more openness, more compassion. It feels safer to me, and gives me more of a sense of hope for us. I feel like you're engaged.

His appreciation to her was for her nurturing their relationship, which she appreciated hearing from him. I invited them to dialogue about the shift that had taken place. Elaine began by expressing how "frightening" the shift was for her:

> I'm accustomed to steeling myself for the worst, and then splitting. I need to put that away. But the fear is I'll be even more vulnerable. When I see your wall go up, I go, "Oh, that's familiar," and then I get scared. I want to trust, but it's also scary. But that's a fear that's good to have because it means we're moving to a different place.

After empathizing, Lewis stated that he understood her fear and her "tentativeness":

> My challenge is to not put up the wall when you raise questions about our progress or the affair, and to recognize that's just part of the process. In the past I've responded to your questions with frustration over feeling like it's never good enough.

After inviting Lewis to go deeper into that experience of it often not feeling that what he does is good enough, I turned back to Elaine and invited her to talk more about her fear since her trusting Lewis again was also making her feel vulnerable. Elaine said:

> It's a testimony to how good I feel that I feel so scared. I don't want you to feel that I use the affair as a cudgel, but I need you to know that the affair really hurt. I don't know how not to feel vulnerable. The shift for me is experiencing you being open to experiencing me, and that's really important to me.

During the following session Elaine picked up with the same theme of vulnerability. She related how she had been feeling safer in general, until Lewis went out of town for a week. She told him that on the phone, but they postponed talking about it. When he didn't bring it up, she got upset over feeling that, "It's all on my shoulders to bring things up," especially when Lewis knows what she's feeling. Elaine went on to explain, "When I experience you as 'cool' and silent, it feels really toxic because of my experience with my father. When you do that, it feels like an attack."

Lewis empathized, reading between the lines: "My silence also reminds you of when I had the affair." I modeled additional empathy for Lewis: "It stirs up your worst memories and your deepest fears."

Lewis went on to say how he had been aware that they had not talked and that he intended to when he suggested they go to the movies, but then she beat him to the punch, at which point her negative emotion affected their whole interaction. Lewis went on to make a plea to Elaine:

> My silence, when it happens, is not a weapon to drive you crazy. I'm thinking and processing. Also, I'm not your father. And I'm scared of your temper. Then I want to stop so things don't escalate. I just want to get away because I'm feeling self-protective.

After Elaine empathized, I modeled additional empathy: "You wish I could separate my experience of your silence from my memories of my father's silence."

Then I told Elaine that I would like to represent her for a moment by Becoming her:

> Part of my anger about your silence, Lewis, and you not reaching out to me, is that the burden of holding the feelings myself is so great that I'm desperately wanting you to reach out to me. When you withdraw to protect yourself and to prevent escalation, I'm left feeling that I'm holding the bag emotionally. So when you don't reach out to me, I feel abandoned emotionally, and then I get angry with you.

Elaine then picked up for herself:

> It's exhausting. When you withdraw now, it reminds me not of my father but of the period of your affair when you didn't talk to me. I don't know if you can connect with how awful it's been for me, and how awful it continues to be. It's going to take time for me to heal. You've done so much, but I still have needs, and I still need to heal. So I do want things from you, and wish you wouldn't see it as a denial of what you have done.

Lewis empathized:

> You need me to be patient with your needs, and you need me to reach out to you to help you heal the pain. When I don't, it just deepens the pain terribly.

In the next session (the last we will look at because it brings the current thematic focus to semiclosure), I briefly summarized the key themes of the last two sessions, concluding with a statement about Elaine needing Lewis to understand how deep the pain was for her. Lewis took the role of Expresser: "I understand your pain, because when I experience it they're like minidaggers to me, too, and I absorb the pain as well."

I prompted Lewis with a question: "What do you wish for Elaine, and for the two of you? What do you wish she could see and feel about you?"

Lewis said, "I'd like to be seen as complex, and as flawed, and as wonderful; and that some days will be great, and others not so great."

I further prompted him (in the form of a statement, but effectively as a piece of empathy): "And I wager you want Elaine to have faith in you and your feelings for her."

Lewis responded, "Yes, but it's hard for me to ask for that. Given the affair, it almost feels inappropriate. I want you to come to it on your own. I want you to be inspired to have faith in me by how I am with you."

I added, both as a form of empathy and as a prompt, "But you hope for that."

Lewis said, "Yes. I hope to inspire that confidence in me."

Elaine empathized and then as Expresser stated:

It's ironic. I understand. I would *love* for you to ask for my faith in you. That makes someone vulnerable, to ask for something like that. I *want* your vulnerability. You're right. It does have to be earned. But I like to be asked for it, as well. The simple fact that you want my faith in you can inspire it.

Lewis asked Elaine to say more. Elaine continued:

I've been feeling better lately. The first anniversary [of my discovering the affair] is coming up. I want the second year to be about more than just surviving the affair. I want it to be about looking at the good stuff in our relationship. When I think back on all the effort I put into the relationship while you were having the affair, it makes me crazy. So I need your vulnerability. I would like to know the pain you are experiencing. I wish you would move out of your comfort zone.

I added, by way of Becoming Elaine, "You're self-protectiveness actually scares me, Lewis, because I don't understand what's behind it. And that reminds me of the time of the affair." Lewis picked up the empathy with:

That's why you need me to be vulnerable with you, because if I were to do that it would say to you that I understand your experience and your pain, and that would give you more confidence that I will do what it takes for me to be with you.

Lewis again asked Elaine to say more about what that would look like for her. Elaine responded:

I've always been scared of your wall. I see your wall and I get scared that you're not seeing me. After all, I was shut out by you while you were having the affair. So when I see it now, I want to run. It's unbearable to me because I fear what's going on behind the wall. But it's not just the wall. It's also you not being vulnerable [that scares me]; you being self-protective; you staying in your comfort zone.

I prompted Lewis with a lead-in clause for his empathy: "My being vulnerable is so important to you because…"
Lewis continued, "Because … you want to feel safe with me."
Then Lewis continued as Expresser:

What I said to you about my feeling as though you having faith in me is something that I have to earn and inspire, is being more vulnerable for me than asking you to have faith in me. The reason is that I don't feel I have yet earned or inspired your trust, and saying *that* is even *more* vulnerable for me [than asking you to have trust in me].

Elaine closed the session by saying, "I appreciate you saying that. It helps me feel closer to you. I need to hear more like that from you."

My work with this couple continues at the time of the writing of this clinical vignette, but there no longer is any doubt about their future together, which is now secure. In addition to following in detail the thematic unfolding of this couple's work to recover from the trauma of an affair and in the process rebuild their relationship on a new foundation, this vignette illustrates how individual sessions can be used strategically to support the couples therapy sessions. I would not necessarily say that the individual sessions with Lewis and Elaine were the turning point in the therapy, but I do see them as having come at a critical juncture and as having helped deepen and extend the work of the couples therapy sessions. At the same time, this vignette also illustrates how much of the work of healing from the trauma of an affair can (and ideally is) done through the couple dialoguing directly with one another under the facilitation of the therapist. That is where the real work of healing the relationship from the trauma of infidelity takes place. From that point of view, RE therapy provides an ideal framework for the treatment of affairs.

Concluding Postscript

Couples' intimate dialogues are at the heart of the RE therapy process, and the success of RE therapy in any given instance stands or falls with the success of those dialogues. The skill of the therapist will naturally play an essential role in the success or failure of those dialogues. The therapist cannot manufacture feelings that the partners do not have, or do not desire to have. The therapist can, however, either succeed or fail at helping to uncover the depth of positive feelings that are present, even if they are deeply buried and (initially) outside the couple's awareness. An effective therapist therefore can make all the difference in the world to the outcome of the couples therapy process. And the model of therapy used can make all the difference in the world in terms of the therapist's ability to conduct effective couples therapy. As I hope this book has made clear, and as I hope readers will discover for themselves, Relationship Enhancement therapy provides an ideal model that empowers the therapist to conduct highly effective couples therapy.

Appendix A
Relationship Questionnaire

Date _____ Name _____

This questionnaire will encourage you to think about your relationship. Think about how you get along with each other and what improvements you would like to see. We want you to respond to each item as openly and honestly as possible; therefore, we ask that you do not show this to anyone, including each other.

Put A, B, or C in front of each item you list:
A = You would feel **comfortable** talking about it in the sessions now;
B = It would be **difficult**, but not impossible, to talk about it in the sessions now;
C = You **could not** talk about it in the sessions now.

1. **Positive Issues or Partner Appreciations.** List three important things about your relationship or partner that pleases you or that you admire, despite any problems you may have in your relationship. Do *not* choose things you wish would change significantly today. If it helps, think back to what first attracted you to your partner.

   a.

   b.

   c.

2. **Enhancement Issues.** List three ideas that would enrich your relationship. These ideas would make your relationship better or more enjoyable. They should add positives rather than eliminate negatives. They should be ideas that you believe your partner in principle is open to.

   The ideas should not be specific yet. For example, *do not* suggest, "I'd like to go for long walks together regularly." Give general ideas. For example, "I'd like for us to spend quality time together regularly."

   Avoid one-shot or temporary suggestions. For example, *do not* suggest, "I'd like for the two of us to get away for a weekend or two before our child is born." Suggestions should be enduring. For example, "I'd like for us to get away alone together at least one night a week."

   a.

   b.

   c.

3. **Minor Conflicts/Problems.** List three things you would like to change to improve your relationship(s). These may be troublesome issues to work through but not the "heaviest" or most difficult problems or conflicts.

   a.

   b.

   c.

4. **Major Problems.** List your major relationship conflicts or problems.

   a.

   b.

   c.

5. **Life Goals.** List your dreams for the future and individual and shared life goals.

   a.

   b.

   c.

Source: Guerney & Scuka (2005), *Relationship Enhancement Client Manual.* Reprinted with permission.

Appendix B
Relationship Enhancement Phrase Finder

Incite ...	Insight ...
You make me...	When you act that way, I get... When you talk that way, I feel...
You should...	I would like you to... I think it would be best if you...
Most men think... Most women feel... Most men do...	I wish you would... I would like it if you... I would like you to...
The right thing to do...	I would like you to... I wish you would... I would like it if you... [if talking about self] I would respect myself more if I...
The correct thing to do...	I would like it if you... [if talking about self] I would respect myself more if I...
A mature (nice, considerate, healthy, sociable, normal, moral, etc.) person would...	I would like you to... I wish you would... I would like it if you... [if talking about self] I would respect myself more if I...
A good father would... A good wife would... A good provider would...	I would like you to... I wish you would... I would like it if you...
You said you would...	As I remember it, you said you would...
We (you) (they) agreed that...	As I remember it, we (you) (they) agreed...
You're driving too fast!	I'm very nervous about this speed. It would be a big help to me if you slowed down some. I'd really appreciate that.

315

The following "incite" statement is subjective ("I think") but it requires a change. The revised statement gets rid of the generalization about character. It also includes a meaningful feeling statement.

I don't think (believe) you are a very caring (considerate, warm, thoughtful, energetic, sensitive) person.	When you act (talk) the way I've described, I don't feel cared for (loved, thought-about, understood, as though I can count on you to do things that need to be done around here, etc.).

Predictive statements are usually threatening and stimulate arguments. Putting "I think" in front is not much help. Try to make them more subjective and provide a "feeling" base.

When the time comes, you will...	Based on the way I thought you acted in the past [example may help], I'm *afraid* that when the time comes, you *may*...
The way you react to those situations is...	Based on my memory of our past reactions [examples?], I find myself being *nervous* because I think that you *might*...
When I "X," then you "Y."	I'm very uncomfortable when I think about doing "X" because, in my mind, there's a pattern. When I "X," I *expect* that you will "Y."

FEELINGS

Incite ...	Insight ...
I feel that (it) (they) (he) (she)...	I *think* that... "Feel" should not be followed by "that" but by an emotion (sad, upset, etc.). If you use the term "that" or "that you," you are not talking about a feeling. You are talking about a thought. If the reason you are using "feel" instead of "think" is to show tentativeness, say: I think perhaps... Perhaps... Maybe...

SPECIFYING RATHER THAN GENERALIZING

Incite ...	Insight ...
As I see it, you *always*...	As I see it, you frequently... It seems to me you often... I think that many times you...
As I see it, you *never*...	As I see it, you seldom... I don't think it's very often that you... I don't think it's very frequent that you...
I think you are an inconsiderate person...	I don't feel cared-about when you... I don't think our daughter feels cared for enough because... I doubt that your associates feel looked after when you don't...
As I see you, you're not one for hard work. You're lazy...	I'm distressed to see that you have failed several times this month... [followed by specific incidents] I am upset that you don't do more around the house... My understanding was that we agreed that you would...
My perception is that you're a slob...	To me, it still looks like a mess... I would like to talk to you about the way you keep your desk. The way it looks bothers me... I prefer this room to look more orderly than it does right now...
I feel you drive too fast...	I feel nervous and scared when we go at some of the speeds you often drive. Today was an example...

Note: In the examples above, making a statement subjective ("I feel," "I think," "As I see it," "My perception is") does not remove the problem of over-generalization ("too fast," "inconsiderate person," "lazy," "a slob"). This over-generalization must be corrected.

UNDERLYING POSITIVES

Incite ...	Insight ...
I get angry when you play golf on Saturdays...	I miss you when you're gone. I get frustrated and then angry at you when you play golf on Saturday. Saturday seems like one of the few times we can spend time together...
or	or
Most men stay with their families on weekends...	
or	*I enjoy your company* when you're here. I really look forward to our having time together on the weekends. It *lifts my spirits to be with you.* I think the *kids also like to be with you.* So, it's very disappointing to me—and I think to them—when we don't have the opportunity to be with you. I know how much golf means to you, but, I would really appreciate...
If you really cared about me and the kids, you'd spend more time at home...	
I would like you to take more responsibility for doing things around the house...	*I appreciate the things that you do around the house,* such as [give examples]. I also know that *your other responsibilities* don't give you much time for relaxation. However, I'm really feeling burdened, and I do think you care about that. I could really use some help and would like you to take more responsibility around the house...
(Father to teenager): I think it's very important for your future that you get into college. To assure that, I believe you need to get your grades up. So, I'd really feel less anxious if I saw you working harder to accomplish that...	I regard you as being *very bright.* I have also seen that *you are able to do very well in your schoolwork* when you set your mind to it. I really believe *you are capable of doing very well* in school. I think it's very important for your future that you get into college. To do that, I believe you need to get your grades up. I'd really feel less anxious if I saw you doing more to accomplish that...

Source: Guerney & Scuka (2005), *Relationship Enhancement Client Manual.* Reprinted with permission.

References

* Indicates items that may be ordered from the National Institute of Relationship Enhancement at www.nire.org.
** Indicates items that are most relevant to learning about or conducting RE therapy. For information about training, supervision, and certification in RE therapy, including a video-based home study program that includes three hours of telephone supervision, visit www.nire.org.

Accordino, M. P., & Guerney, B. G., Jr. (1993). Effects of the Relationship Enhancement program on community residential rehabilitation staff and clients. *Psychosocial Rehabilitation Journal, 17,* 131–144.

Accordino, M. P., & Guerney, B. G., Jr. (1998). An evaluation of the Relationship Enhancement program with prisoners and their wives. *International Journal of Offender Therapy and Comparative Criminology, 42,* 5–15.

Accordino, M. P., & Guerney, B. G., Jr. (2002). The empirical validation of Relationship Enhancement couple and family therapies. In D. J. Cain & J. Seeman (Eds.), *Humanistic psychotherapies: Handbook of research and practice* (pp. 403–442). Washington, DC: American Psychological Association.

Accordino, M. P., & Herbert, J. T. (1997). Relationship Enhancement as an intervention to facilitate rehabilitation of persons with severe mental illness. *Journal of Applied Rehabilitation Counseling, 28,* 47–52.

Ackerman, N. (1966). *Treating the troubled family.* New York: Basic Books.

Almeida, R. V., & Durkin, T. (1999). The cultural context model: Therapy for couples with domestic violence. *Journal of Marital and Family Therapy, 25,* 313–324.

Avery, A. W., & Thiessen, J. D. (1982). Communication skills training for divorcees. *Journal of Counseling Psychology, 29,* 203–205.

Axline, V. (1947). *Play therapy.* New York: Ballantine.

Bandura, A., & Walters, R. H. (1963). *Social learning and personality development.* New York: Holt, Rinehart & Winston.

Barrett-Lennard, G. T. (1993). The phases and focus of empathy. *British Journal of Medical Psychology, 66,* 3–14.

Boegner, I., & Zielenback-Coenen, H. (1984). On maintaining change in behavioral marital therapy. In K. Hahlweg & N. S. Jacobsen (Eds.), *Marital interaction: Analysis and modification* (pp. 27–35). New York: Guilford.

Bograd, M., & Mederos, F. (1999). Battering and couples therapy: Universal screening and selection of treatment modality. *Journal of Marital and Family Therapy, 25,* 291–312.

Bowen, M. (1978). On the differentiation of self. In M. Bowen (Ed.), *Family therapy in clinical practice* (pp. 467–528). New York: Jason Aronson.

Brazier, D. (1995). *Zen therapy: Transcending the sorrows of the human mind.* New York: Wiley.

Brock, G. W. (1974). *A follow-up study of an intensive conjugal Relationship Enhancement program.* Unpublished master's thesis, Pennsylvania State University, University Park, PA.

Brock, G. W., & Joanning, H. (1983). A comparison of the Relationship Enhancement Program and the Minnesota Couple Communication Program. *Journal of Marital and Family Therapy, 9*, 413–421.

Bronowski, J. (1973). *The ascent of man.* Boston: Little, Brown.

Brooks, L. W. (1997). *An investigation of Relationship Enhancement therapy in a group format with rural, southern couples.* Unpublished doctoral dissertation, Florida State University School of Social Work, Tallahassee, FL.

Brown, E. M. (1991). *Patterns of infidelity and their treatment.* New York: Brunner/Mazel.

Cadigan, J. D. (1980). *RETEACH program and project: Relationship Enhancement in a therapeutic environment as clients head out.* Unpublished doctoral dissertation, Pennsylvania State University, University Park, PA.

Cavedo, L. C., & Guerney, B. G., Jr. (1999). Relationship Enhancement (RE) enrichment/problem-prevention programs: Therapy-derived, powerful, versatile. In R. Berger & M. T. Hannah (Eds.), *Preventive approaches in couples therapy* (pp. 73–105). New York: Brunner/Mazel.

Christensen, A., & Jacobson, N. S. (2000) *Reconcilable differences.* New York: Guilford.

Davis, M., McKay, M., & Eshelman, E.R. (2000). *Relaxation and stress reduction workbook.* Oakland, CA: New Harbinger.

Doherty, W. (2002). Bad couples therapy: Getting past the myth of therapist neutrality. *Psychotherapy Networker, 26* (6), 26–33.

Giblin, P., Sprenkle, D. H., & Sheehan, R. (1985). Enrichment outcome research: A meta-analysis of premarital, marital and family interventions. *Journal of Marital and Family Therapy, 11*, 257–271.

Ginsberg, B. G. (1997). *Relationship enhancement family therapy.* New York: Wiley.

Ginsberg, B. G. (2000). Relationship Enhancement couples therapy. In F. M. Dattilio & L. J. Bevilacqua (Eds.), *Comparative treatments for relationship dysfunction* (pp. 273–300). New York: Springer.

Ginsberg, B., & Vogelsong, E. L. (1977). Premarital relationship improvement by maximizing empathy and self-disclosure: The PRIMES Program. In B. G. Guerney, Jr. *Relationship Enhancement: Skill-training programs for therapy, problem prevention, and enrichment* (pp. 268–288). San Francisco: Jossey-Bass.

Glass, S. P. (2000, January). *Infidelity* (Clinical Update Number 1052). Washington, DC: American Association of Marriage and Family Therapy.

Glass, S. P. (2002). Couple therapy after the trauma of infidelity. In A. S. Gurman & N. S. Jacobson (Eds.), *Clinical handbook of couple therapy* (3rd ed.) (pp. 488–507). New York, Guilford.

Glass, S. P. (2003). *Not "just friends": Protect your relationship from infidelity and heal the trauma of betrayal.* New York: Free Press.

Goldner, V. (1999). Morality and multiplicity: Perspectives on the treatment of violence in intimate life. *Journal of Marital and Family Therapy, 25* (3), 325–336.

Goleman, D. (1995). *Emotional intelligence.* New York: Bantam.

Gottman, J. M. (1994). *Why marriages succeed or fail.* New York: Simon & Schuster.

Gottman, J. M. (1999). *The marriage clinic: A scientifically-based marital therapy.* New York: Norton.

Gottman, J. M., Coan, J., Carrere, S., & Swanson, C. (1998). Predicting marital happiness and stability from newlywed interactions. *Journal of Marriage and the Family, 60* (1), 5–22.

Gottman, J. M., Coan, J., Carrere, S., & Swanson, C. (2000). Reply to "From basic research to intervention." *Journal of Marriage and the Family, 62* (1), 265–273.

Greenberg, L. S., & Johnson, S. M. (1986). Emotionally focused couples treatment: An integrated affective systemic approach. In N. S. Jacobson & A. S. Gurman, (Eds.), *Clinical handbook of marital therapy.* New York: Guilford.

Greenberg, L. S., & Johnson, S. M. (1998). *Emotionally focused therapy for couples.* New York: Guilford.

Greene, K., & Bogo, M. (2002). The different faces of intimate violence: Implications for assessment and treatment. *Journal of Marital and Family Therapy, 28*, 455–466.

Griffin, J. M., Jr., & Apostal, R. A. (1983). The influence of Relationship Enhancement training on differentiation of self. *Journal of Marital and Family Therapy, 19*, 267–272.

**Griffin, J. M., Jr., & Guerney, B. G., Jr. (2001). *Relationship Enhancement couple group therapy: Leader's manual.* Bethesda, MD: IDEALS.

Guerney, B. G., Jr. (1969). Filial therapy: Description and rationale. In B. G. Guerney, Jr. (Ed.), *Psychotherapeutic agents: New roles for nonprofessionals, parents, and teachers* (pp. 450–460). New York: Holt, Rinehart & Winston. (Original work published 1964.)

Guerney, B. G., Jr. (1977). *Relationship Enhancement: Skill-training programs for therapy, problem prevention, and enrichment.* San Francisco: Jossey-Bass.

Guerney, B. G., Jr. (1985). The medical vs. the educational model as a base for family therapy research. In L. F. Andreozzi & R. F. Levant (Eds.), *Integrating research and clinical practice* (pp. 71–79). Rockville, MD: Aspen Systems.

Guerney, B. G., Jr. (1990). Creating therapeutic and growth-inducing family systems: Personal moorings, landmarks and guiding stars. In F. Kaslow (Ed.), *Voices in family psychology* (pp. 114–138). Beverly Hills, CA: Sage.

Guerney, B. G., Jr. (1994a). The role of emotion in Relationship Enhancement marital/family therapy. In S. M. Johnson & L. S. Greenberg (Eds.), *The heart of the matter: Perspectives on emotion in marital therapy* (pp. 124–147). New York: Brunner/Mazel.

**Guerney, B. G., Jr. (1994b). *Relationship Enhancement audio program* [Audiotape]. Bethesda, MD: IDEALS.

Guerney, B. G., Jr. (1997a). *Relationship Enhancement program: Participants' manual* (2nd ed.). Bethesda, MD: IDEALS.

Guerney, B. G., Jr. (1997b). *Relationship Enhancement program: Auxiliary manual* (2nd ed.). Bethesda, MD: IDEALS.

**Guerney, B. G., Jr. (1999a). *Relationship Enhancement family therapy: The experiential format (P-family)* [VHS videotapes]. Bethesda, MD: IDEALS.

Guerney, B. G., Jr. (1999b). *The Relationship Enhancement (RE) program* [Audiotape]. Retrieved April 22, 2003 from The Resource Link: http://www.the-resource-link.com.

Guerney, B. G., Jr. (2003). *Relationship Enhancement client manual.* Bethesda, MD: IDEALS.

**Guerney, B. G., Jr. (2005). *Relationship Enhancement couple/marital/family therapist's manual* (4th ed.). Bethesda, MD: IDEALS.

Guerney, B. G., Jr., Coufal, J., & Vogelsong, E. (1981). Relationship Enhancement versus a traditional approach to therapeutic/preventative/enrichment parent–adolescent program. *Journal of Consulting and Clinical Psychology, 49,* 927–939.

Guerney, B. G., Jr., Guerney, L., & Andronico, M. (1966). Filial therapy: Historical introduction. *Yale Scientific Magazine, 40,* 6–14.

Guerney, B. G., Jr., Guerney, L., & Stollak, G. (1971–1972). The potential advantages of changing from a medical to an educational model in practicing psychology. *Interpersonal Development, 2* (4), 238–245.

**Guerney, B. G., Jr., Jungkuntz, D., & Scuka, M. (1999). *Demonstration of coaching and troubleshooting in Relationship Enhancement therapy* [VHS videotape]. Bethesda, MD: IDEALS.

Guerney, B. G., Jr., & Maxson, P. (1990). Marital and family enrichment research: A decade review and look ahead. *Journal of Marriage and the Family, 52,* 1127–1135.

**Guerney, B. G., Jr., Nordling, W., & Scuka, R. (2000). *How to conduct Relationship Enhancement therapy with couples and families* [VHS videotapes and home study program]. Bethesda, MD: IDEALS.

*Guerney, B. G., Jr., & Scuka, R. (2004a). *Relationship Enhancement program: Participants' manual* (3rd ed.). Bethesda, MD: IDEALS.

*Guerney, B. G., Jr., & Scuka, R. F. (2004b). *Relationship Enhancement program: Auxiliary manual* (3rd ed.). Bethesda, MD: IDEALS.

**Guerney, B. G., Jr., & Scuka, R. F. (2005). *Relationship Enhancement client manual* (4th ed.). Bethesda, MD: IDEALS.

*Guerney, B. G., Jr., Scuka, R., & Scuka, M. (1999). *How to conduct a couples Relationship Enhancement program* [VHS videotapes and home study program]. Bethesda, MD: IDEALS.

Guerney, B. G., Jr., Stollak, G., & Guerney, L. (1971). The practicing psychologist as educator—An alternative to the medical practitioner model. *Professional Psychology, 2* (3), 276–282.

**Guerney, B. G., Jr., & Vogelsong, E. (1981a). *Relationship Enhancement demonstration tapes: Solving marital problems.* Bethesda, MD: IDEALS. ✓

**Guerney, B. G., Jr., & Vogelsong, E. (1981b). *Relationship Enhancement program: Leader demonstration tape.* Bethesda, MD: IDEALS.

Guerney, B. G., Jr., Vogelsong, E., & Coufal, J. (1983). Relationship Enhancement versus a traditional treatment: Follow-up and booster effects. In D. Olson & B. Miller (Eds.), *Family studies review yearbook* (Vol. 1, pp. 738–756). Beverly Hills, CA: Sage.

Guerney, B. G., Jr., Waldo, M., & Firestone, L. (1987). Wife battering: A theoretical construct and case report. *The American Journal of Family Therapy, 15,* 34–43.

*Guerney, L. (1995). *Parenting: A skills training manual* (5th ed.). Silver Spring, MD: Relationship Press.

Hahlweg, K., & Markman, H. J. (1988). Effectiveness of behavioral marital therapy: Empirical status of behavioral techniques in preventing and alleviating marital distress. *Journal of Counseling and Clinical Psychology, 56,* 440–447.

Hahlweg, K., Schindler, L., Revenstorf, D., & Brengelmann, J. C. (1984). The Munich marital therapy study. In K. Hahlweg & N. S. Jacobsen (Eds.), *Marital interaction: Analysis and modification* (pp. 3–26). New York: Guilford.

Hanh, T. N. (2003). *Creating true peace: Ending violence in yourself, your family, your community and the world.* New York: Free Press.

Harman, M. J., Waldo, M., & Johnson, J. A. (1994). Relationship Enhancement therapy: A case study for treatment of vaginismus. *The Family Journal: Counseling and Therapy for Couples and Families, 2,* 122–128.

Holtzworth-Munroe, A., Meehan, J. C., Rehman, U., & Marshall, A. D. (2002). Intimate partner violence: An introduction for couple therapists. In A. S. Gurman & N. S. Jacobson (Eds.), *Clinical handbook of couple therapy* (3rd ed., pp. 441–465). New York: Guilford.

Ibrahim, F. A., & Schroeder, D. G. (1990). Cross-cultural couples counseling: A developmental, psychoeducational intervention. *Journal of Comparative Family Studies, 21,* 193–205.

Jacobson, N. S., & Addis, M. E. (1993). Research on couples and couple therapy: What do we know? Where are we going? *Journal of Consulting and Clinical Psychology, 61* (1), 85–93.

Jacobson, N. S., & Christiansen, A. (1996). *Integrative couples therapy: Promoting acceptance and change.* New York: Norton.

Jessee, R., & Guerney, B. G., Jr. (1981). A comparison of Gestalt and Relationship Enhancement treatments with married couples. *American Journal of Family Therapy, 9,* 31–41.

Johnson, S. (1996). *The practice of emotionally focused marital therapy: Creating connection.* New York: Brunner/Mazel.

Johnson, S., & Denton, W. (2002). Emotionally focused couples therapy: Creating secure connections. In A. S. Gurman & N. S. Jacobson (Eds.), *Clinical handbook of couples therapy* (3rd ed., pp. 221–250). New York: Guilford.

Johnson, S., & Lebow, J. (2000). The "coming of age" of couple therapy: A decade review. *Journal of Marital and Family Therapy, 26* (1), 23–38.

Keil, W. (1996). Hermeneutic empathy in client-centered therapy. In U. Esser, H. Pabst, & G. Speirer (Eds.), *The power of the person-centered approach: New challenges, perspectives and answers.* Koln, Germany: GwG.

Kiesler, D. J. (1996). *Contemporary interpersonal theory and research.* New York: Wiley.

Kohut, H. (1977). *The restoration of the self.* New York: International Universities Press.

Kohut, H. (1984). *How does analysis cure?* (A. Goldberg, Ed.). Chicago: University of Chicago Press.

Leary, T. (1957). *Interpersonal diagnosis of personality.* New York: Ronald Press.

Matter, M., McAllister, W., & Guerney, B. G., Jr. (1984). Relationship Enhancement for the recovering couple: Working with the intangible. *Focus on Family and Chemical Dependency, 7* (5), 21–23, 40.

Maugh, T. H. (1998, February 21). Study's advice to husbands: Accept wife's influence in marriage: Data showing compliance is best cast doubt on "active listening," a common counseling approach. *Los Angeles Times,* p. A1.

McCarthy, B., & McCarthy, E. (2003). *Rekindling desire: A step-by-step program to help low-sex and no-sex marriages.* New York: Brunner-Routledge.

McCrady, B., Stout, R., Noel, N., Abrams, D., & Nelson, H. (1991). Comparative effectiveness of three types of spouse-involved alcohol treatment: Outcomes 18 months after treatment. *British Journal of Addiction, 86,* 1415–1424.

McKay, M., & Rogers, P. (2000). *The anger control workbook*. Oakland, CA: New Harbinger.

Mitchell, S. (1988). *Relational concepts in psychoanalysis: An integration*. Cambridge, MA: Harvard University Press.

Moore, C. D., & Fletcher, B. J. (n.d.). *Relationship Enhancement family therapy: A culturally sensitive approach with African Americans*. Unpublished manuscript.

Moreno, J. L. (1985). *Psychodrama* (Vol. 1). Ambler, PA: Beacon House.

Nordling, W. (Ed.). (1993). *To love and to cherish*. Washington, DC: Archdiocese of Washington, DC.

*Nordling, W., & Guerney, B. G., Jr. (1992). *Family Relationship Enhancement program: Leader's manual*. Bethesda, MD: IDEALS.

Nordling, W., Scuka, R., & Guerney, B. G., Jr. (1998). *Couples' Relationship Enhancement program: Leader's manual* (2nd ed.). Bethesda, MD: IDEALS.

O'Farrell, T. J., & Rotunda, R. J. (1997). Couples interventions and alcohol abuse. In W. K. Halford & H. J. Markman (Eds.), *Clinical handbook of marriage and couples interventions* (pp. 555–588). New York: Wiley.

*Ortwein, M. (in press-a). *Love's cradle: The Relationship Enhancement program to build strong families*. Bethesda, MD: IDEALS.

*Ortwein, M. (in press-b). *ER: Emotional regulation in the RE tradition*. Bethesda, MD: IDEALS.

Pittman, F. (1989). *Private lies: Infidelity and the betrayal of intimacy*. New York: Norton.

Pittman, F. (1995). Crises of infidelity. In N. S. Jacobson & A. S. Gurman, (Eds.), *Clinical handbook of couple therapy* (pp. 259–316). New York: Guilford.

Rappaport, A. F. (1971). *The effects of an intensive conjugal relationship modification program*. Unpublished doctoral dissertation, Pennsylvania State University, University Park, PA.

Rappaport, A. F. (1976). Conjugal Relationship Enhancement program. In D. H. Olson (Ed.), *Treating relationships* (pp. 41–66). Lake Mills, IA: Graphic.

Rogers, C. (1951). *Client-centered therapy*. Boston: Houghton-Mifflin.

Rogers, C. (1962). The interpersonal relationship: The core of guidance. *Harvard Educational Review, 3* (2/4), 416–429.

Rosen, K. H., Matheson, J. L., Stith, S. M., McCollum, E. E., & Locke, L. D. (2003). Negotiated time-out: A de-escalation tool for couples. *Journal of Marital and Family Therapy, 29*, 291–298.

Ross, E. R., Baker, S. B., & Guerney, B. G., Jr. (1985). Effectiveness of Relationship Enhancement therapy versus therapist's preferred therapy. *The American Journal of Family Therapy, 13*, 11–21.

Sams, W. P. (1983). *Marriage preparation: An experimental comparison of the Premarital Relationship Enhancement (PRE) and the Engaged Encounter (EE) Programs*. Unpublished doctoral dissertation, Pennsylvania State University, University Park, PA.

*Santhouse, R. (2003). *The use of Relationship Enhancement therapy in the treatment of anorexia nervosa and bulimia nervosa* [Audiotape]. Bethesda, MD: IDEALS.

Schwartz, R. (1995). *Internal family systems*. New York: Guilford.

**Scuka, R. F. (2003). *Demonstration of identification mode of empathy within the Relationship Enhancement model* [Videotape]. Bethesda, MD: IDEALS.

**Scuka, R. F., Nordling, W., & Guerney, B. G., Jr. (2004). *Couples' Relationship Enhancement program: Leader's manual* (3rd ed.). Bethesda, MD: IDEALS.

*Scuka, R. F., & Scuka, M. (1998). *Relationship Enhancement skills demonstration conducted by two leaders* [Videotape]. Bethesda, MD: IDEALS.

Snyder, M. (1992a). Gender-informed model of couple and family therapy: Relationship Enhancement therapy. *Contemporary Family Therapy, 14*, 15–31.

Snyder, M. (1992b). The meaning of empathy: Comments on Hans Strupp's case of Helen R. *Psychotherapy, 29* (2), 318–322.

Snyder, M. (1994a). Couple therapy with narcissistically vulnerable clients: Using the Relationship Enhancement model. *The Family Journal, 2*, 27–35.

Snyder, M. (1994b). The development of intelligence in psychotherapy: Empathic and dialogic processes. *Journal of Humanistic Psychology, 34*, 84–108.

Snyder, M. (1995). "Becoming": A method for expanding systemic thinking and deepening empathic accuracy. *Family Process, 34*, 241–253.

**Snyder, M. (1996). *Demonstrations of becoming and laundering in Relationship Enhancement couple therapy* [Videotape]. Bethesda: IDEALS.

Snyder, M. (2000). The loss and recovery of erotic intimacy in primary relationships: Narrative therapy and Relationship Enhancement therapy. *The Family Journal: Counseling and Therapy for Couples and Families, 8,* 37–46.

Snyder, M., & Guerney, B. G., Jr. (1993). Brief Relationship Enhancement marital therapy. In R. A. Wells & V. J. Giannetti (Eds.), *Casebook of the brief psychotherapies* (pp. 221–234). New York: Plenum.

Snyder, M., & Guerney, B. G., Jr. (1999). The power of shared subjectivity: Revitalizing intimacy through Relationship Enhancement couples therapy. In J. Carlson & L. Sperry (Eds.), *The intimate couple* (pp. 359–380). New York: Brunner/Mazel.

Spanier, G. B. (1976). Measuring dyadic adjustment: New scales for assessing quality of marriage and similar dyads. *Journal of Marriage and the Family, 38,* 15–28.

Spring, J. A. (1996). *After the affair: Healing the pain and rebuilding trust when a partner has been unfaithful.* New York: HarperCollins/Perennial.

Spring, J. A. (2004). *How can I forgive you? The courage to forgive, the freedom not to.* New York: HarperCollins.

Stanley, S. M., Blumberg, S. L., & Markman, H. J. (1999). Helping couples fight *for* their marriages: The PREP approach. In R. Berger & M. Hannah (Eds.), *Handbook of preventive approaches in couples therapy* (pp. 279–303). New York: Brunner/Mazel.

Stanley, S. M., Bradbury, T. M., & Markman, H. J. (2000). Structural flaws in the bridge from basic research on marriage to interventions for couples. *Journal of Marriage and the Family, 62,* 256–264.

Steinweg, C. K. M. (1990). *A comparison of the effectiveness of Relationship Enhancement and strategic marital therapy using the strength of the therapeutic alliance to predict statistically significant and clinically meaningful outcome.* Unpublished doctoral dissertation, Purdue University, Lafayette, IN.

Stith, S. M., Rosen, K. H., & McCollum, E. E. (2003). Effectiveness of couples treatment for spouse abuse. *Journal of Marital and Family Therapy, 29,* 407–426.

Stolorow, R., Brandchaft, G., & Atwood, G. (1987). *Psychoanalytic treatment: An intersubjective approach.* Hillsdale, NJ: Analytic Press.

Stosny, S. (1995). *Treating attachment abuse: A compassionate approach.* New York: Springer.

Stosny, S. (2003). *The powerful self: A workbook of therapeutic self-empowerment.* New York: Booksurge.

Strean, J. S. (2000). *The extramarital affair.* Northvale, NJ: Jason Aronson.

Streng, F. J. (1967). *Emptiness: A study in religious meaning.* Nashville, TN: Abingdon Press.

Sullivan, H. S. (1953). *The interpersonal theory of psychiatry.* New York: Norton.

Thiessen, J., Avery, A. W., & Joanning, H. (1980). Facilitating post-divorce adjustment in females through communication skills training. *Journal of Divorce, 4,* 35–44.

Vaughn, P. (1998). *The monogamy myth: A personal handbook for recovering from affairs.* New York: Newmarket Press.

Vogelsong, E., Guerney B. G., Jr., & Guerney L. (1983). Relationship Enhancement therapy with inpatients and their families. In R. Luber & C. Anderson (Eds.), *Family intervention with psychiatric inpatients* (pp. 48–68). New York: Human Sciences Press.

von Bertalanffy, L. (1956). General systems theory. *General Systems Yearbook, 1,* 1–10.

Waldo, M. (1986). Group counseling for military personnel who battered their wives. *Journal for Specialists in Group Work, 2,* 132–138.

Waldo, M. (1988). Relationship Enhancement counseling groups for wife abusers. *Journal of Mental Health Counseling, 10,* 37–45.

Waldo, M., & Guerney, B. G., Jr. (1983). Marital Relationship Enhancement therapy in the treatment of alcoholism. *Journal of Marital and Family Therapy, 9* (3), 321–323.

Waldo, M., & Harman, M. J. (1993). Relationship Enhancement therapy with borderline personality. *The Family Journal, 1,* 25–30.

Watson, J. C. (2002). Re-visioning empathy. In D.J. Cain & J. Seeman (Eds.), *Humanistic psychotherapies: Handbook of research and practice* (pp. 445–471). Washington, DC: American Psychological Association.

Watzlawick, P., Beavin, J., & Jackson, D. (1967). *Pragmatics of human communication.* New York: Norton.

Whisman, M. A., Dixon, A. E., & Johnson, B. (1997). Therapists' perspectives of couple problems and treatment issues in couple therapy. *Journal of Family Psychology, 11,* 361–366.

Wieman, R. J. (1973). *Conjugal relationship modification and reciprocal reinforcement: A comparison of treatments for marital discord*. Unpublished doctoral dissertation, Pennsylvania State University, University Park, PA.

Yalom, I. D. (1980). *Existential psychotherapy*. New York: Basic.

Zahniser, J. H., & Falk, D. R. (1993). Relationship Enhancement marital therapy with a schizophrenic couple: A case study. *The Family Journal, 1*, 136–143.

Zander, R. S., & Zander, B. (2000). *The art of possibility: Transforming professional and personal life*. Boston: Harvard University Business School.

Index

A

Abreaction, catharsis, distinguished, 6
Acceptance, nonjudgmental, as value
  embodied in Relationship Enhancement
  model, 21
Accordino and Guerney research studies, 25
Administering for Relationship Enhancement
  therapy process, 16
Affairs, 34, 263–274, 292–309
  assumption of responsibility by party to,
    265–274
  Becoming technique, 272
  betrayal in, 266
  blocking, 270
  communication skills, 273–274
  compassion, 274
  Conflict Management skill, 272
  core relationship skills, 273
  Crisis Intervention, 272
  deep empathy, 273
  dialogue process, 273
  difficulty in treatment of, 263
  Doublebecoming technique, 272
  emotionally safe environment, 272
  empathy, 265–266, 276–285
  Expressive skill, 272–273
  forgiveness, 270–271
  healing process, 268
  Identification Mode of empathy, 273
  implicit moralizing, 264
  individual issues, within context of couples
    sessions, 271–272
  individual sessions, within context of
    couples sessions, 271, 292–309

joint sessions, maintaining primary of,
    271–272
  Laundering technique, 272
  literature on treatment of, 264
  moral righteousness in use of terms, 264
  parties to, 264
  preoccupation with, overcoming, 267
  primary reference point, experience of
    hurt partner, 267
  problems in marriage, impact of, 263
  psychological perspective, moral
    perspective, ideological division between,
    265
  relationship as entity transcending each
    individual, 273
  Relationship Enhancement therapy,
    272–274
    clinical examples, 275–318
  responsibility for, acceptance of, 267–268
  revelation of, 85
    as trauma, 266
  scapegoating hurt partner, avoiding, 268
  terminological considerations, 264–265
  thematic considerations, 265–271
  Therapist Troubleshooting technique, 272,
    285–292
  undisclosed, ongoing, 72–75
    complicity issues, on part of therapist, 73
    duty to warn, when unprotected sex is
      issue, 73
    not conducting conjoint sessions with, 74
  unhappiness in marriage, assumption
    regarding, 263
  utilizing literature, 264